P9-DVU-325

fushigi yûgi™

The Mysterious Play
VOL. 3: DISCIPLE

Story & Art By
YÛ WATASE

FUSHIGI YÛGI
THE MYSTERIOUS PLAY
VOL. 3: DISCIPLE
SHÔJO EDITION

This volume contains the FUSHIGI YÛGI installments from Animerica Extra Vol. 2, No. 11, through Vol. 3, No. 4, in their entirety.

STORY AND ART BY YÛ WATASE

English Adaptation/Yuji Oniki
Translation Assist/Kaori Kawakubo Inoue
Touch-up & Lettering/Andy Ristaino
Design/Hidemi Sahara
First Edition Editor/William Flanagan
Shôjo Edition Editor/Elizabeth Kawasaki

Managing Editor/Annette Roman
Editor-in-Chief/Alvin Lu
Production Manager/Noboru Watanabe
Sr. Director of Licensing & Acquisitions/Rika Inouye
V.P. of Marketing/Liza Coppola
Executive Vice President/Hyoe Narita
Publisher/Seiji Horibuchi

© 1992 Yuu Watase/Shogakukan, Inc. First published by Shogakukan, Inc. in Japan as "Fushigi Yugi." New and adapted artwork and text © 2004 VIZ, LLC. The Fushigi Yûgi logo is a trademark of VIZ, LLC. All rights reserved.

The stories, characters and incidents mentioned in this publication are entirely fictional. No portion of this book may be reproduced or transmitted in any form or by any means without written permission from the copyright holders.

Printed in Canada

Published by VIZ, LLC
P.O. Box 77010
San Francisco, CA 94107

Shôjo Edition
10 9 8 7 6 5 4 3 2 1
First printing, June 2004
1st English edition published August 2000

www.viz.com

store.viz.com

STORY THUS FAR

Chipper junior high school girl Miaka is trying as hard as she can to get into Jonan High School like her mother wants her to. During a study session in the library, Miaka and her best friend, Yui, are physically drawn into the world of a strange book—THE UNIVERSE OF THE FOUR GODS. The handsome-but-greedy Tamahome rescues them before they are returned to the real world.

Following an argument with her mother, Miaka returns alone to the world of the book, and is offered the role of the lead character, the Priestess of Suzaku. After a few months of adventures, Miaka returns to the modern world once more, aided by Yui, but this time it's Yui who has disappeared! During her short time back home, Miaka realizes how much she has come to love Tamahome.

Returning a third time to ancient China, this time to find Yui, Miaka is told that in order to avert a war between Hong-Nan and its neighboring country, Qu-Dong, she must gather all seven celestial warriors of Suzaku. She knows about the handsome Tamahome, regal Hotohori and super-strong, cross-dressing Nuriko, but four of her warriors still remain undiscovered. Miaka sets out with Nuriko to find Tamahome again, but as soon as she is reunited with him, Miaka is abducted by a mysterious man in the shadows!

THE UNIVERSE OF THE FOUR GODS is based on ancient Chinese legend, but Japanese pronunciation of Chinese names differs slightly from their Chinese equivalents. Here is a short glossary of the Japanese pronunciation of the Chinese names in this graphic novel:

CHINESE	JAPANESE	PERSON OR PLACE	MEANING
Hong-Nan	Konan	Southern Kingdom	Crimson South
Qu-Dong	Kutô	Eastern Kingdom	Gathered East
Zhong-Rong	Chûei	Second son	Loyalty & Honor
Chun-Jing	Shunkei	Third son	Spring & Respect
Yu-Lun	Gyokuran	Eldest daughter	Jewel & Orchid
Jie-Lian	Yuire	Youngest daughter	Connection & Lotus
Tai Yi-Jun	Tai Itsukun	An Oracle	Preeminent Person
Daichi-San	Daikyokuzan	A Mountain	Greatest Mountain
Lai Lai	Nyan Nyan	A Servant	Nanny

CONTENTS

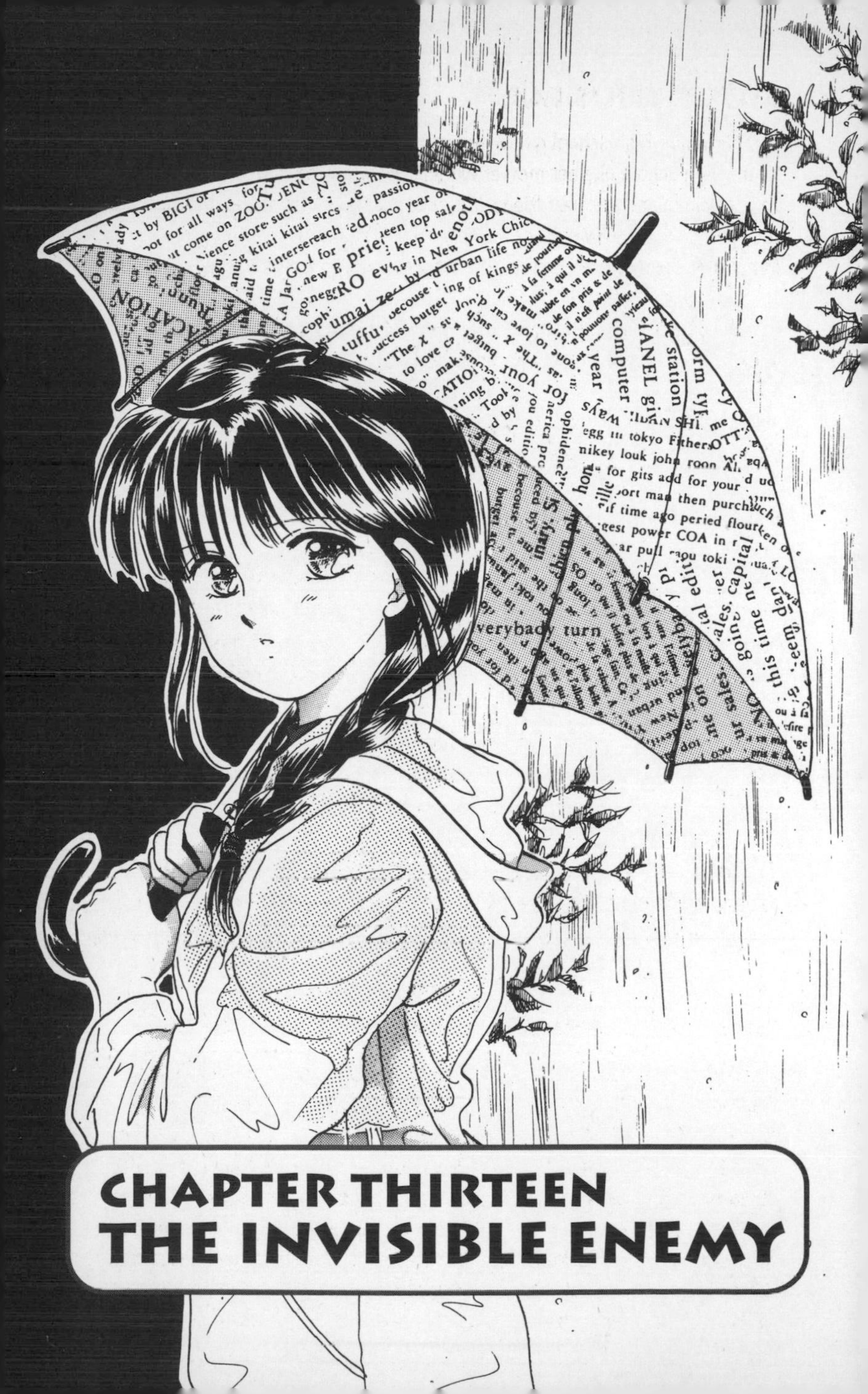

CHAPTER THIRTEEN
THE INVISIBLE ENEMY

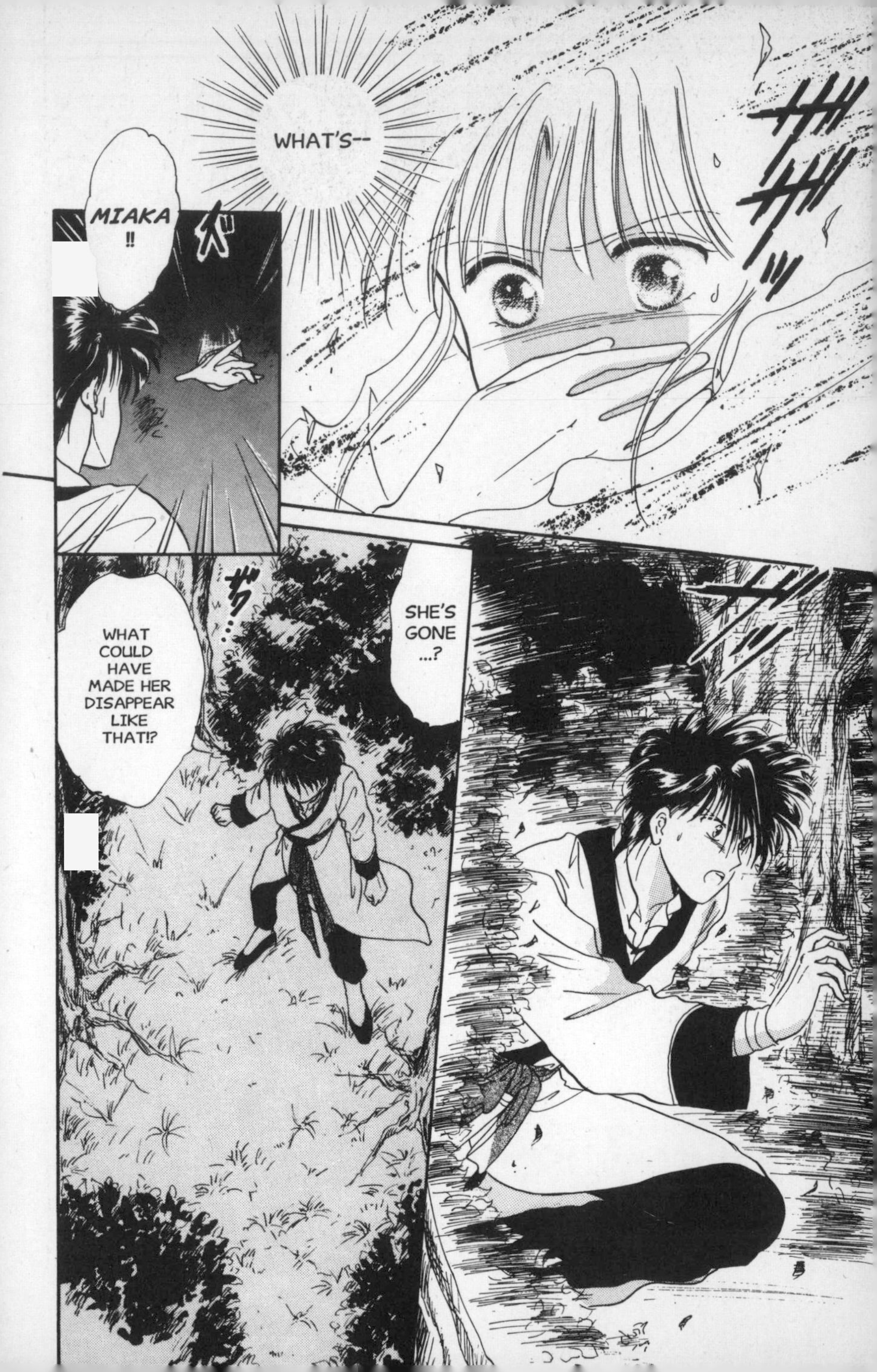
WHAT'S--
MIAKA !!
SHE'S GONE ...?
WHAT COULD HAVE MADE HER DISAPPEAR LIKE THAT!?

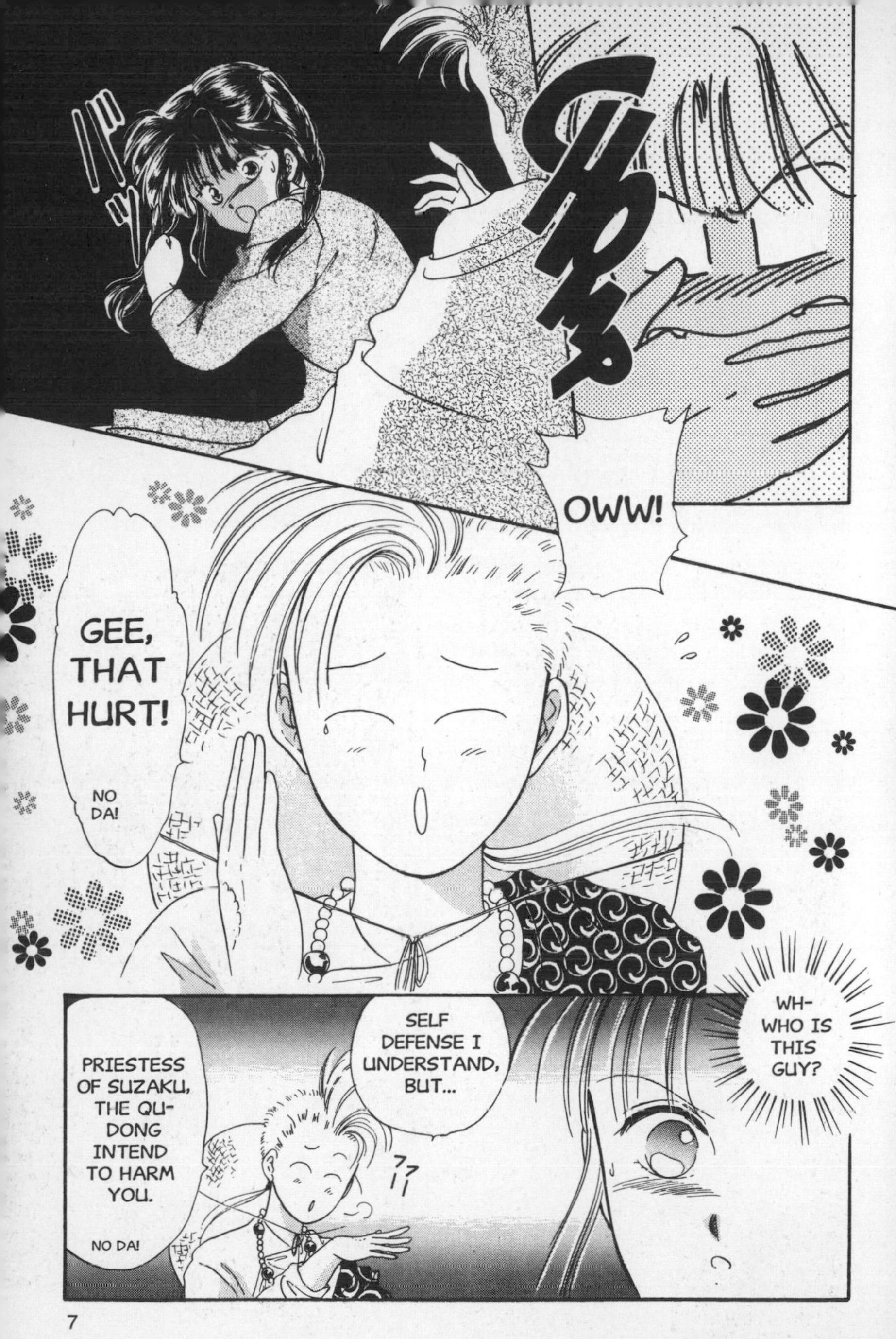
CHOMP
OWW!
GEE, THAT HURT!
NO DA!
WH- WHO IS THIS GUY?
SELF DEFENSE I UNDERSTAND, BUT...
PRIESTESS OF SUZAKU, THE QU-DONG INTEND TO HARM YOU.
NO DA!

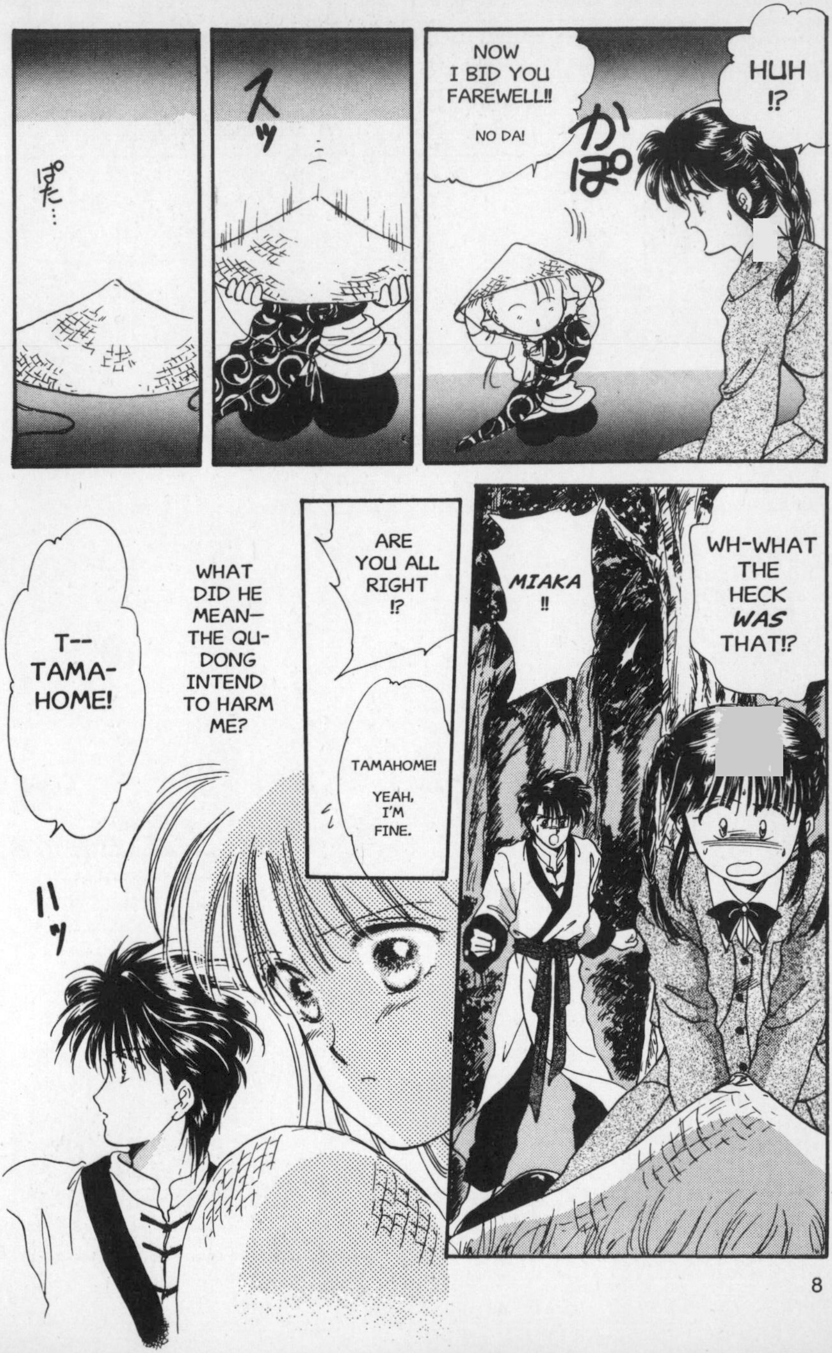
HUH !?
NOW I BID YOU FAREWELL!!
NO DA!
かぽ
スッ
ぱた…
WH-WHAT THE HECK *WAS* THAT!?
MIAKA !!
ARE YOU ALL RIGHT !?
TAMAHOME!
YEAH, I'M FINE.
WHAT DID HE MEAN— THE QU-DONG INTEND TO HARM ME?
T-- TAMA-HOME!
ハッ

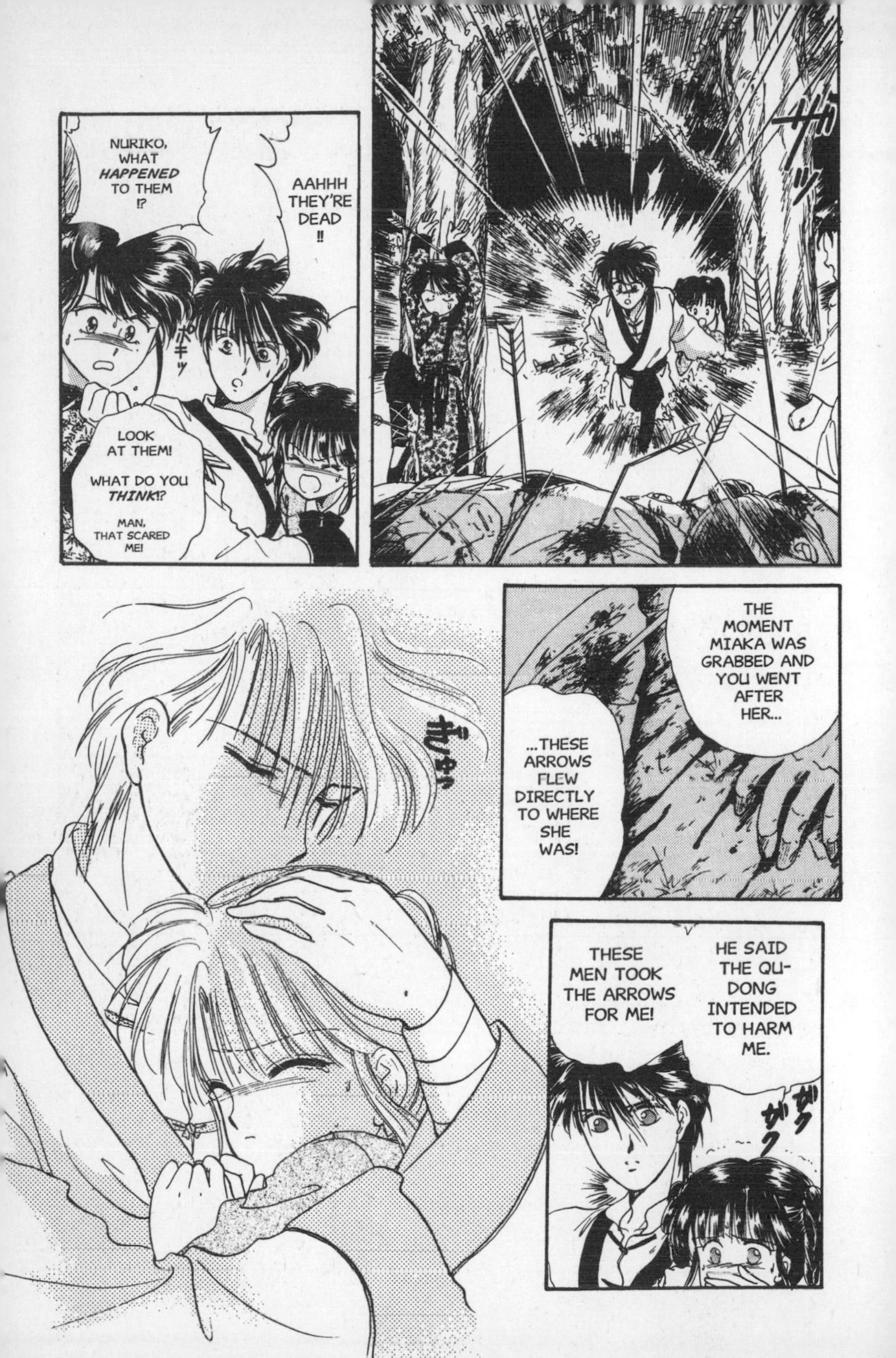

ザクッ
AAHHH THEY'RE DEAD!!
NURIKO, WHAT *HAPPENED* TO THEM!?
ポキッ
LOOK AT THEM!
WHAT DO YOU *THINK*!?
MAN, THAT SCARED ME!
THE MOMENT MIAKA WAS GRABBED AND YOU WENT AFTER HER...
...THESE ARROWS FLEW DIRECTLY TO WHERE SHE WAS!
HE SAID THE QU-DONG INTENDED TO HARM ME.
THESE MEN TOOK THE ARROWS FOR ME!
がくがく
ぎゅっ

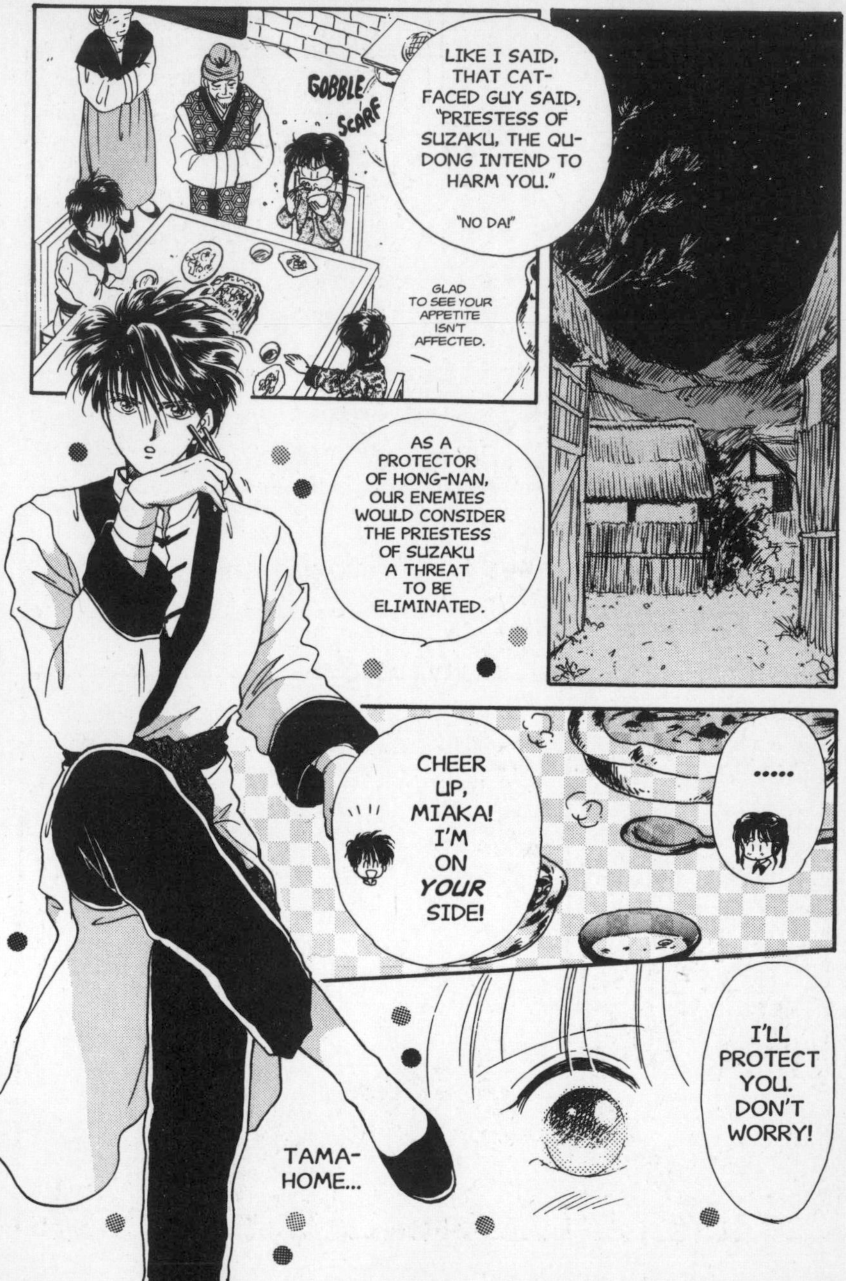
LIKE I SAID, THAT CAT-FACED GUY SAID, "PRIESTESS OF SUZAKU, THE QU-DONG INTEND TO HARM YOU."
"NO DA!"
GOBBLE
SCARF
GLAD TO SEE YOUR APPETITE ISN'T AFFECTED.
AS A PROTECTOR OF HONG-NAN, OUR ENEMIES WOULD CONSIDER THE PRIESTESS OF SUZAKU A THREAT TO BE ELIMINATED.
.....
CHEER UP, MIAKA! I'M ON *YOUR* SIDE!
I'LL PROTECT YOU. DON'T WORRY!
TAMA-HOME...

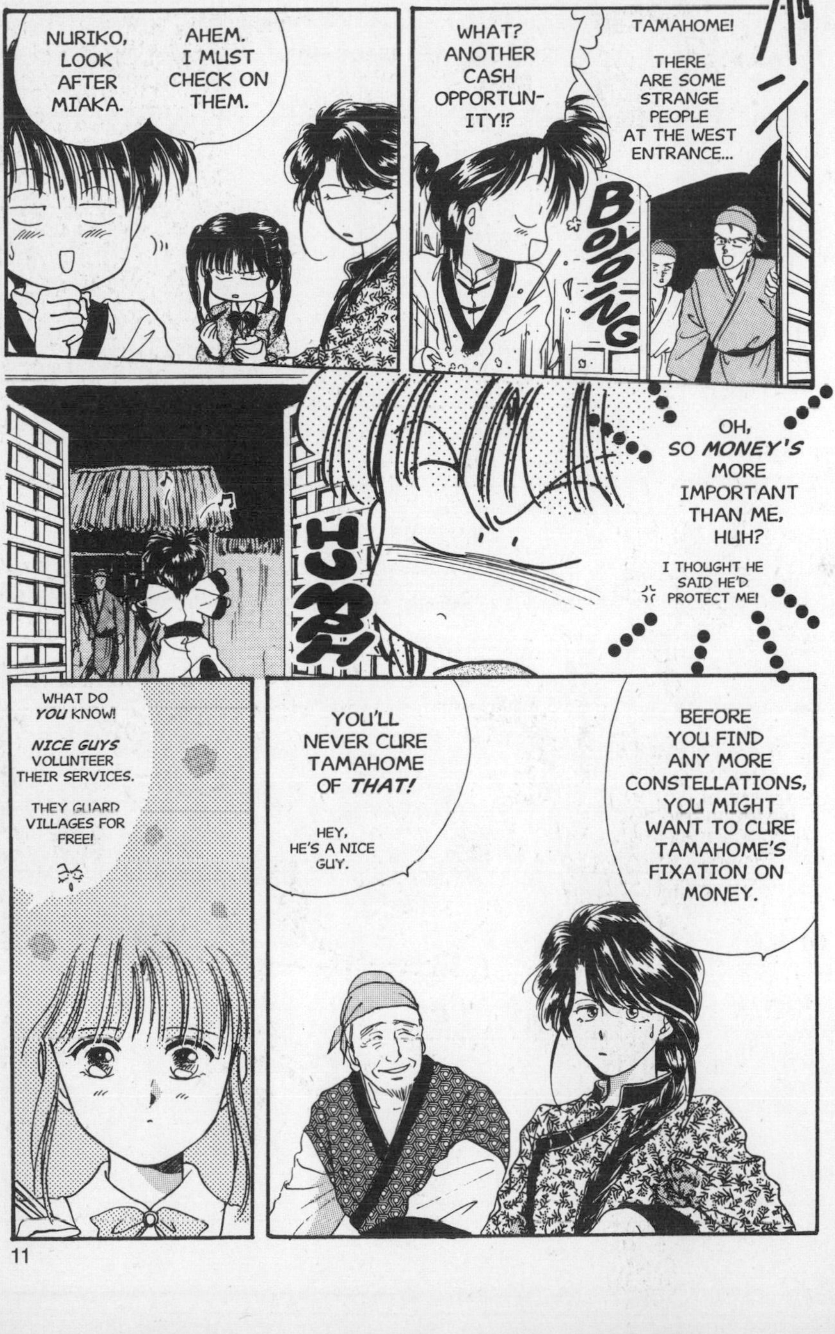
TAMAHOME!
THERE ARE SOME STRANGE PEOPLE AT THE WEST ENTRANCE...
WHAT? ANOTHER CASH OPPORTUN-ITY!?
BOYOING
AHEM. I MUST CHECK ON THEM.
NURIKO, LOOK AFTER MIAKA.
OH, SO MONEY'S MORE IMPORTANT THAN ME, HUH?
I THOUGHT HE SAID HE'D PROTECT ME!
HUMPH
BEFORE YOU FIND ANY MORE CONSTELLATIONS, YOU MIGHT WANT TO CURE TAMAHOME'S FIXATION ON MONEY.
YOU'LL NEVER CURE TAMAHOME OF THAT!
HEY, HE'S A NICE GUY.
WHAT DO YOU KNOW!
NICE GUYS VOLUNTEER THEIR SERVICES.
THEY GUARD VILLAGES FOR FREE!

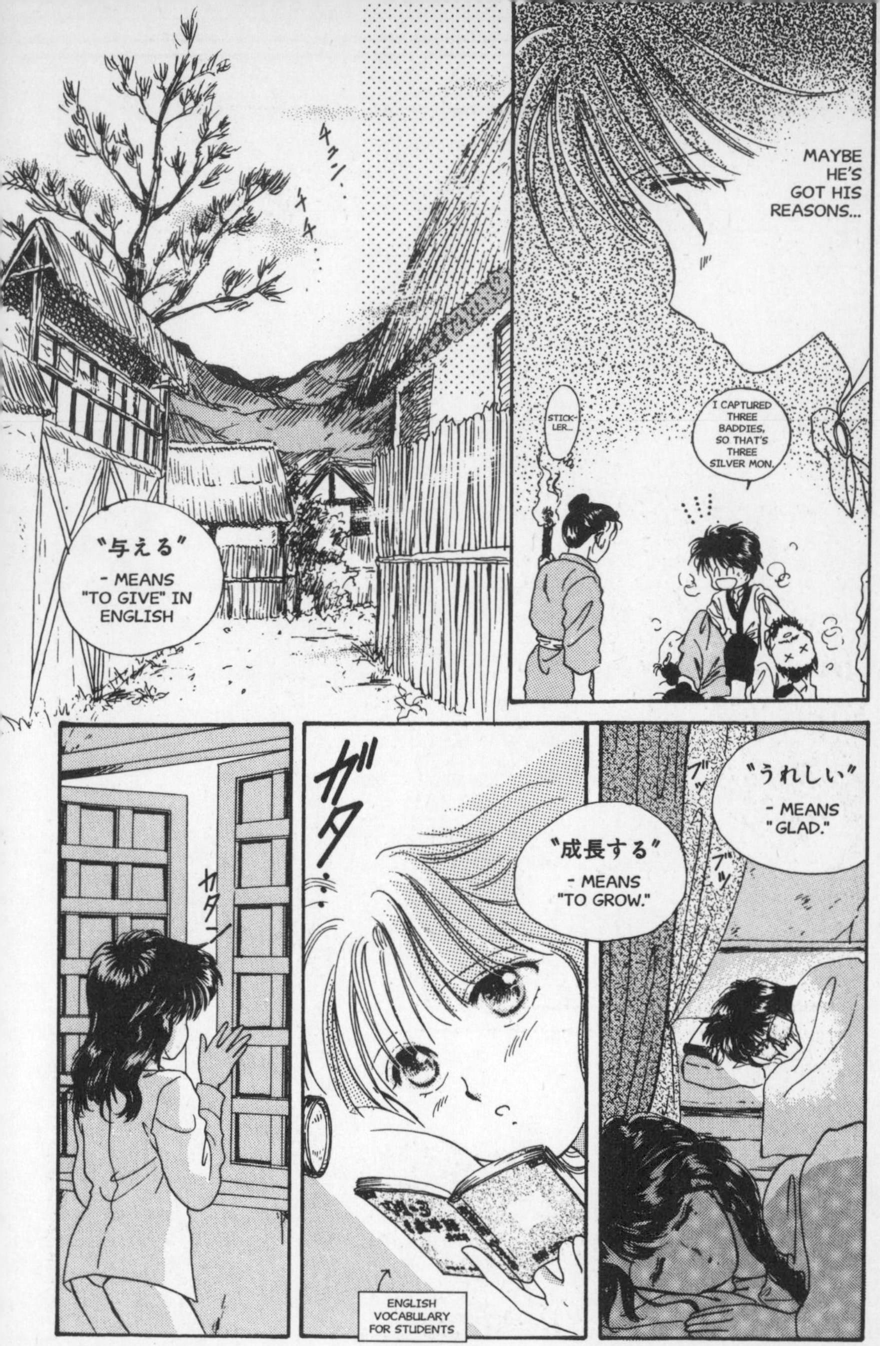
MAYBE HE'S GOT HIS REASONS...
I CAPTURED THREE BADDIES, SO THAT'S THREE SILVER MON.
STICK-LER...
チュン
チチ
"与える" - MEANS "TO GIVE" IN ENGLISH
ブッ
ブッ
"うれしい" - MEANS "GLAD."
ガタ
"成長する" - MEANS "TO GROW."
ENGLISH VOCABULARY FOR STUDENTS
カタン

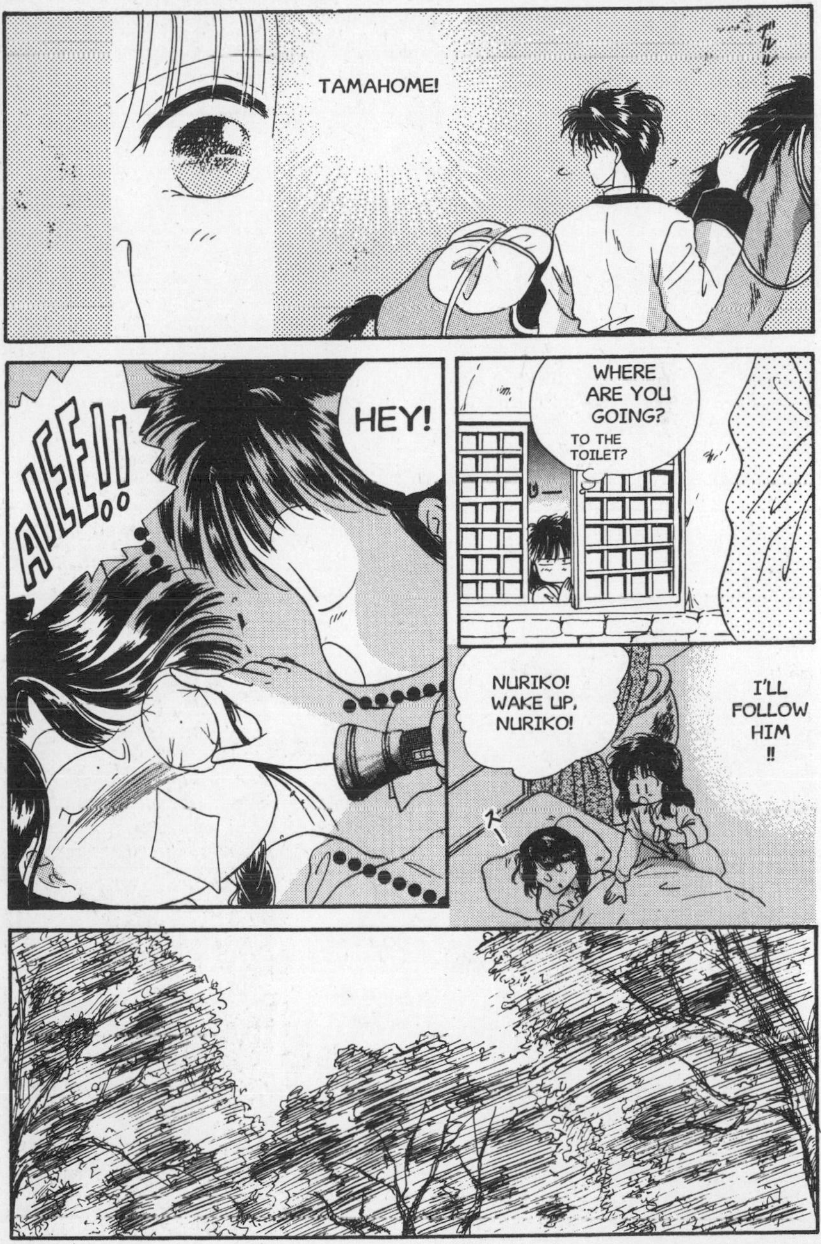
TAMAHOME!
WHERE ARE YOU GOING?
TO THE TOILET?
NURIKO! WAKE UP, NURIKO!
I'LL FOLLOW HIM!!
HEY!
AIEE!!

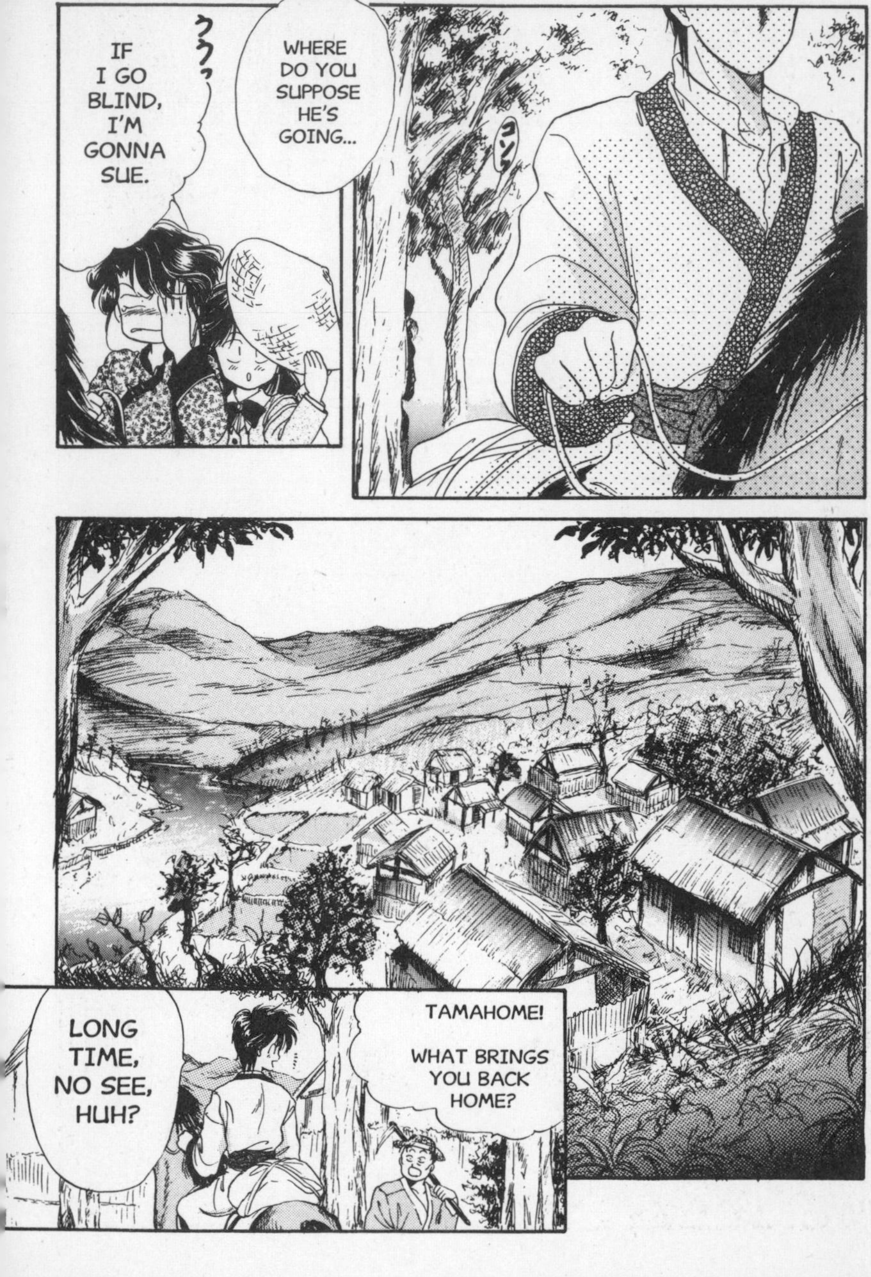
WHERE DO YOU SUPPOSE HE'S GOING...
IF I GO BLIND, I'M GONNA SUE.
TAMAHOME!
WHAT BRINGS YOU BACK HOME?
LONG TIME, NO SEE, HUH?

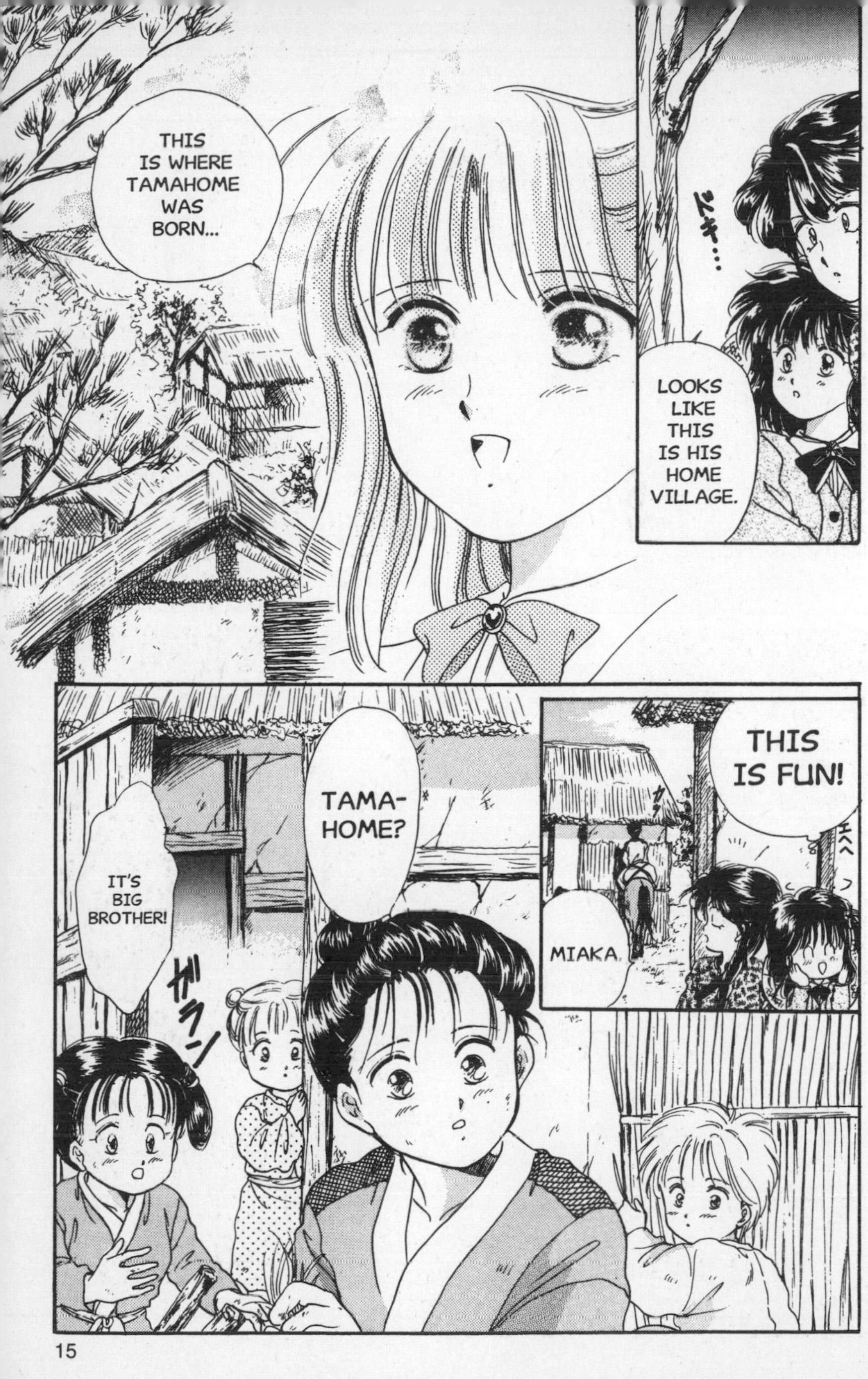
ドキ…
LOOKS LIKE THIS IS HIS HOME VILLAGE.
THIS IS WHERE TAMAHOME WAS BORN...
THIS IS FUN!
エヘヘ
MIAKA.
TAMA-HOME?
IT'S BIG BROTHER!
ガラン

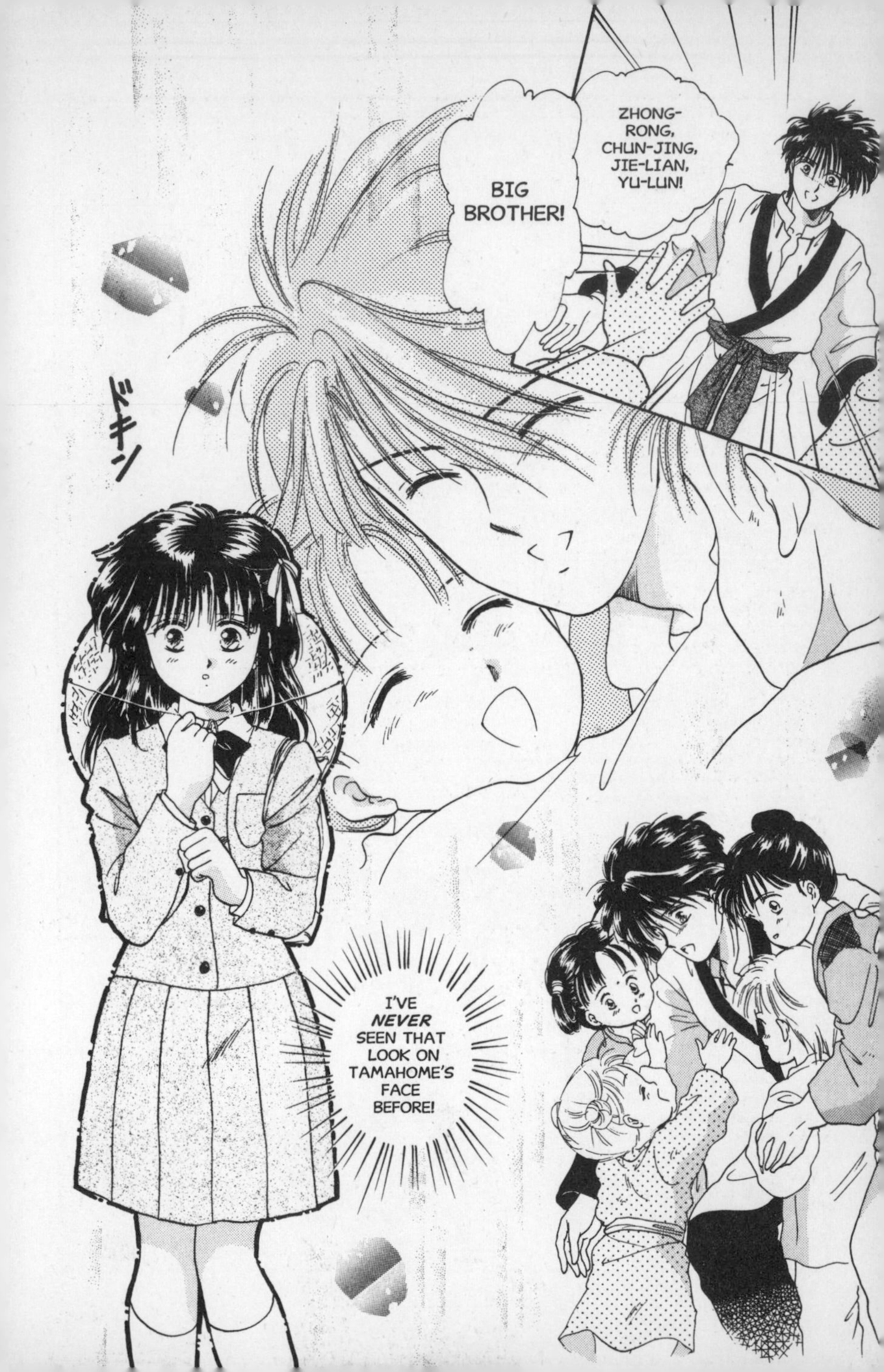
ZHONG-RONG, CHUN-JING, JIE-LIAN, YU-LUN!
BIG BROTHER!
ドキン
I'VE *NEVER* SEEN THAT LOOK ON TAMAHOME'S FACE BEFORE!

How are you all doing? This'll be the start of the third volume!! Time passes quickly. Right now, I'm drawing the last issue of the volume.
I thought at first, given this rapid pace, the story might be completed soon, but that ain't-a gonna happen. (Where'd the old-west sheriff come from?) If I don't watch myself, it could easily go into 10 volumes. That might not even be enough. Enjoy the ride!

I received many letters of encouragement after my whining in volume 2. I really wasn't begging for letters. Sorry to have worried you. I'm all right. I usually don't get depressed at all. Nobody could be depressed and still be a successful manga artist. Usually I draw with a grin on my face. But sometimes I frown when I concentrate.

I like my manga and my drawings! (You can't draw if you hate your own drawings!) When I said I couldn't face my own art, I was just exaggerating. When I see the first printing of my manga, I'm really happy, and I'm always asking for my editor to send me more copies. I was just complaining because my art hasn't fully matured. I'll keep on improving, waiting for that day when I'm perfect. Will it ever really come?
One thing I know for sure: more than anything else, I love drawing manga. Nobody could like drawing manga more than I do! But I'll bet other manga artists say the same thing.
Maybe my readership has gotten wider because I only hear, "I can't stand your manga," once in a very blue moon.

They can say it if they want. They're just criticizing my entire existence, that's all! I'm crushed!
Recently, several other manga-artist friends and I have come up with the proper response. "Then why don't you try drawing manga, huh!? You can't even draw, you loser!!" Actually this thought occurs to many a manga artist when his or her work is rejected by an editor. (Yeah!) And I've decided to say that to anyone with harsh criticism of my work!

Like I ever could! I'm just acting strong.

sniff

1: I said I like them--not that I'm any good at them! :)

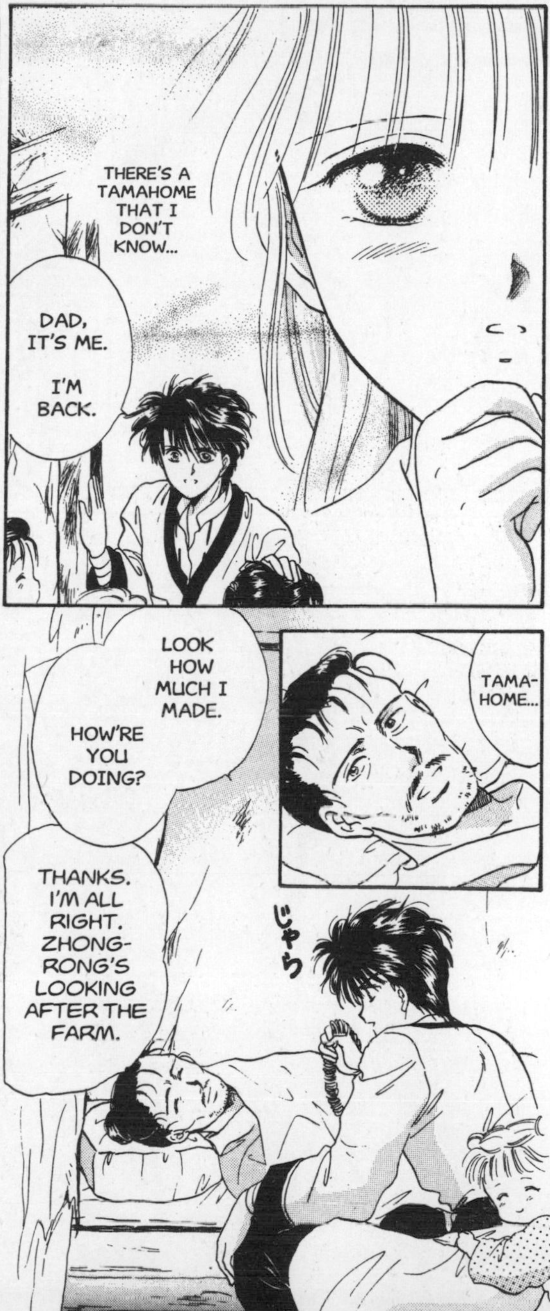
THERE'S A TAMAHOME THAT I DON'T KNOW...
DAD, IT'S ME. I'M BACK.
TAMA-HOME...
LOOK HOW MUCH I MADE.
HOW'RE YOU DOING?
じゃら
THANKS. I'M ALL RIGHT. ZHONG-RONG'S LOOKING AFTER THE FARM.

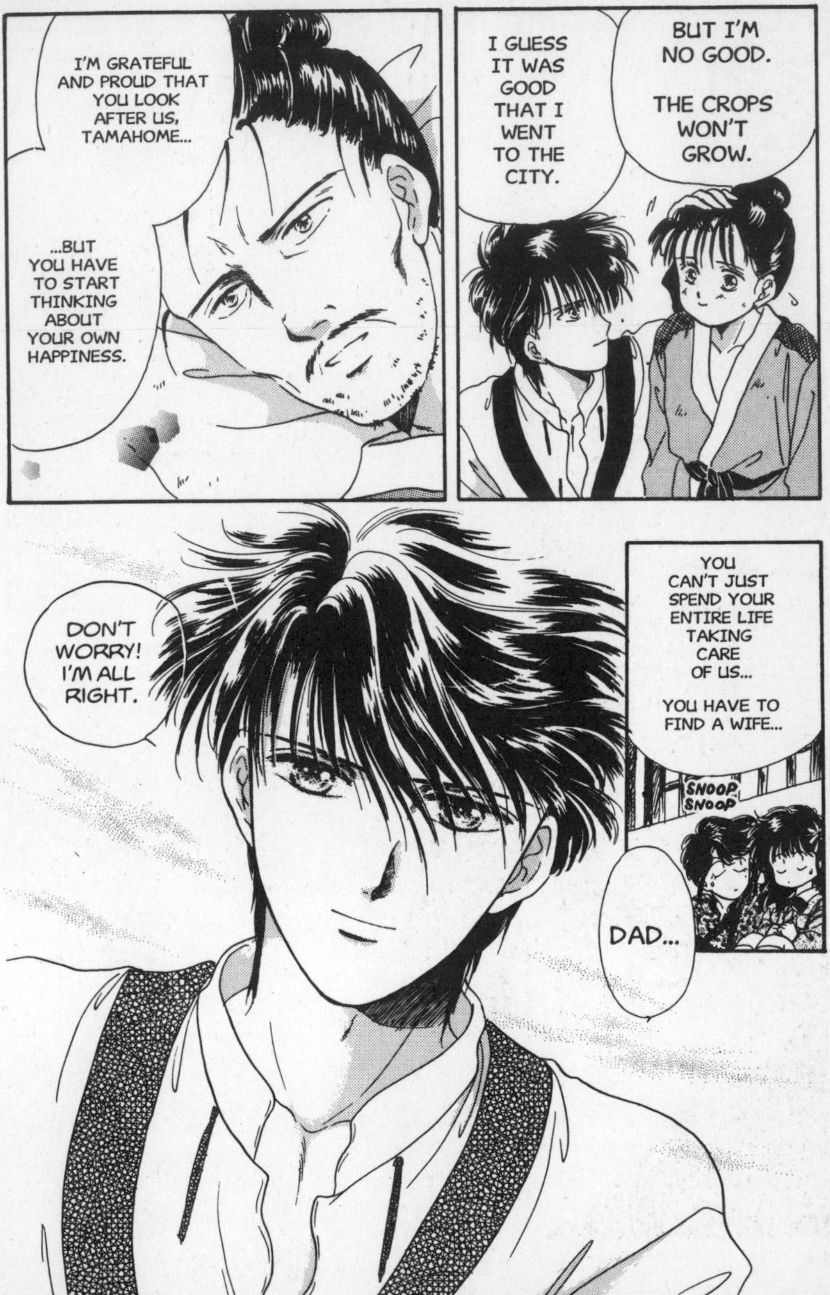
BUT I'M NO GOOD.
THE CROPS WON'T GROW.
I GUESS IT WAS GOOD THAT I WENT TO THE CITY.
I'M GRATEFUL AND PROUD THAT YOU LOOK AFTER US, TAMAHOME...
...BUT YOU HAVE TO START THINKING ABOUT YOUR OWN HAPPINESS.
YOU CAN'T JUST SPEND YOUR ENTIRE LIFE TAKING CARE OF US...
YOU HAVE TO FIND A WIFE...
SNOOP SNOOP
DAD...
DON'T WORRY! I'M ALL RIGHT.

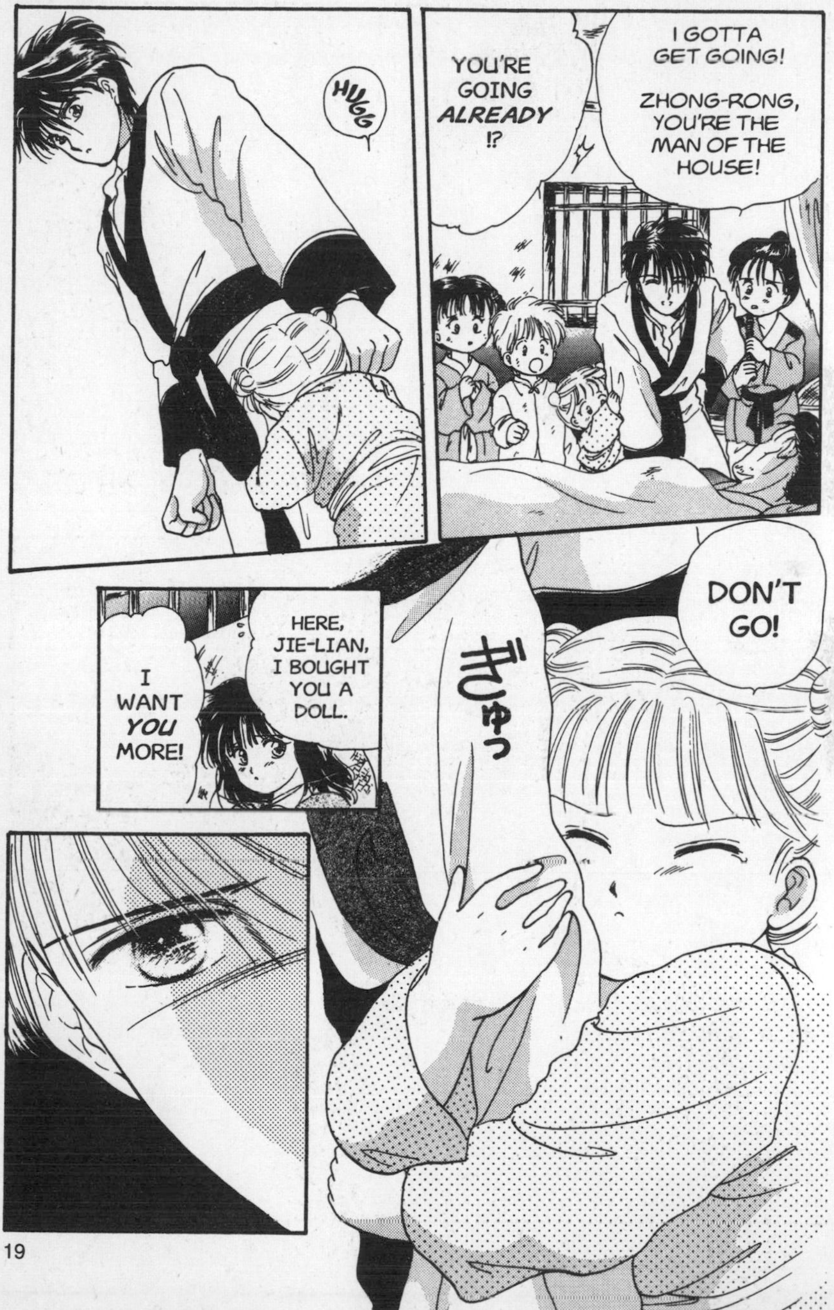
I GOTTA GET GOING! ZHONG-RONG, YOU'RE THE MAN OF THE HOUSE!
YOU'RE GOING *ALREADY* !?
HUGG
DON'T GO!
ぎゅっ
HERE, JIE-LIAN, I BOUGHT YOU A DOLL.
I WANT *YOU* MORE!

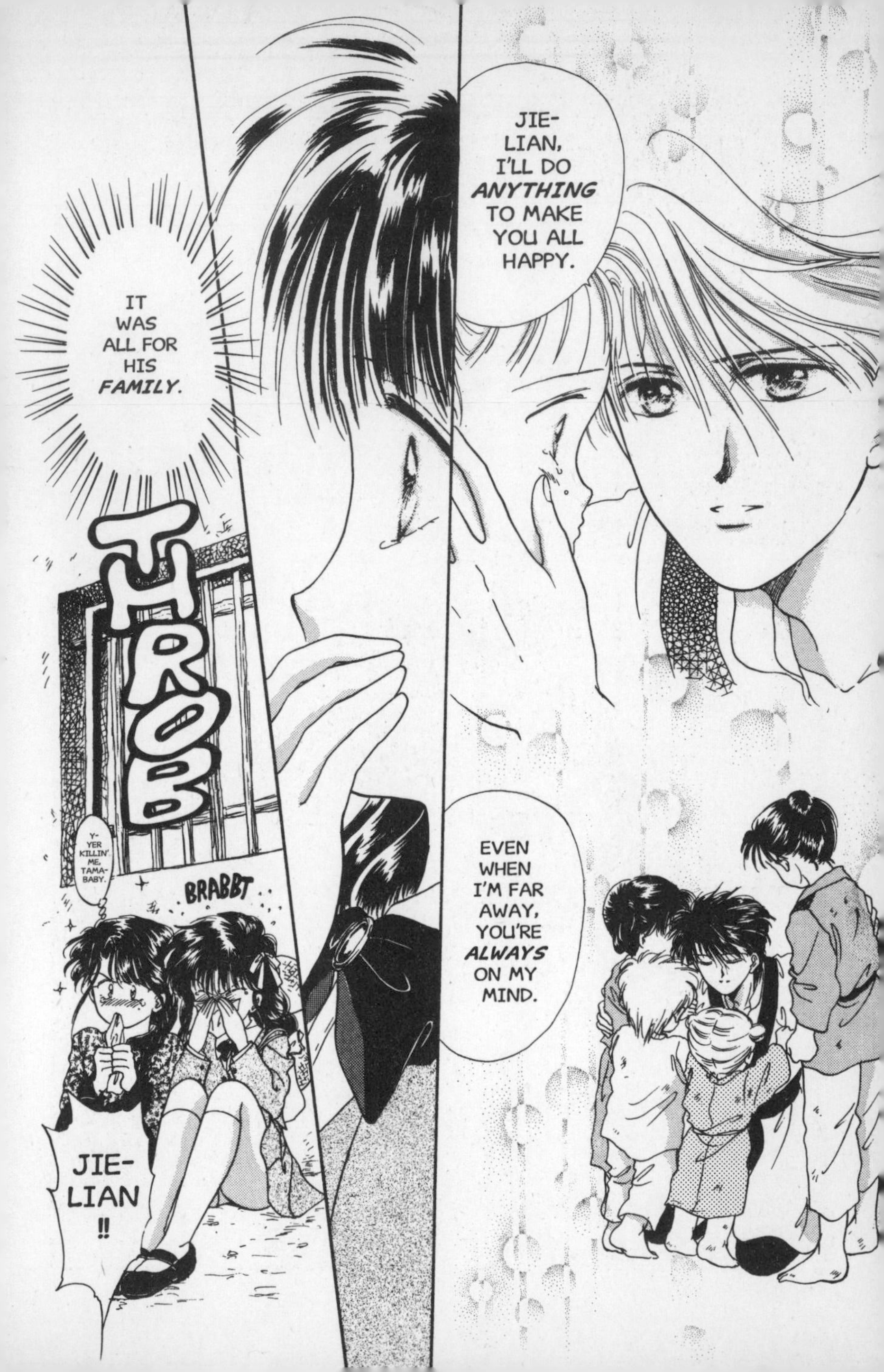
JIE-LIAN, I'LL DO *ANYTHING* TO MAKE YOU ALL HAPPY.
EVEN WHEN I'M FAR AWAY, YOU'RE *ALWAYS* ON MY MIND.
IT WAS ALL FOR HIS *FAMILY*.
THROB
Y-YER KILLIN' ME, TAMA-BABY.
BRABBT
JIE-LIAN!!

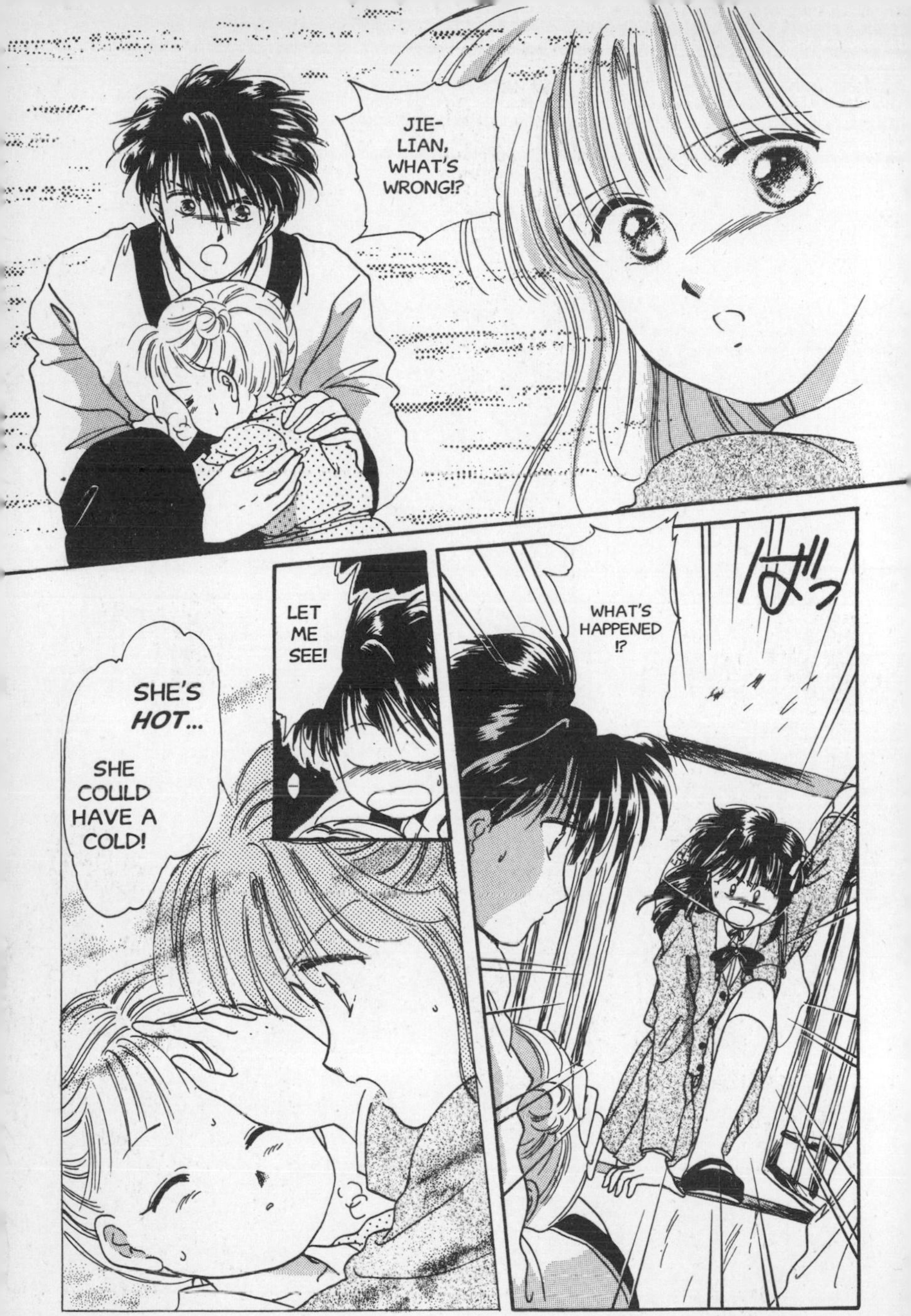
JIE-LIAN, WHAT'S WRONG!?
ぱっ
WHAT'S HAPPENED !?
LET ME SEE!
SHE'S *HOT*...
SHE COULD HAVE A COLD!

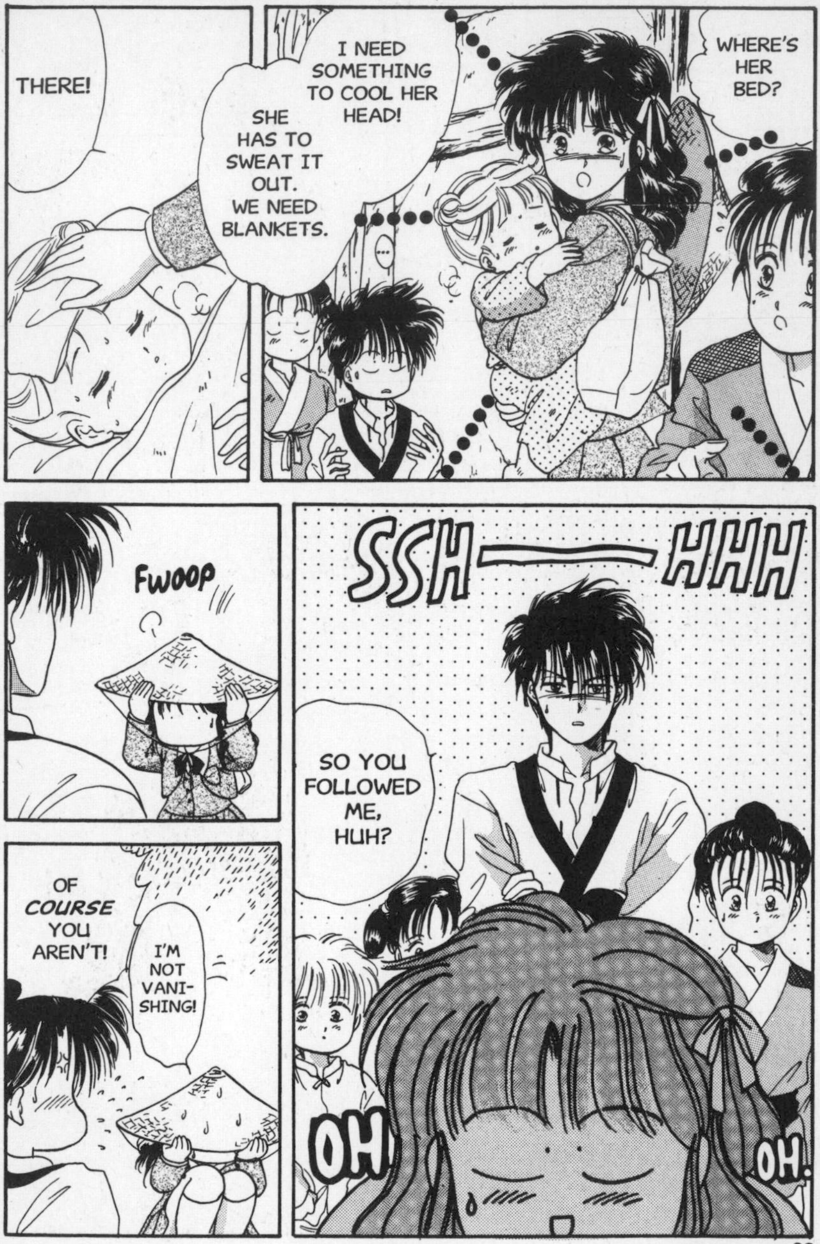
WHERE'S HER BED?
I NEED SOMETHING TO COOL HER HEAD!
SHE HAS TO SWEAT IT OUT. WE NEED BLANKETS.
...
THERE!
SSH——HHH
SO YOU FOLLOWED ME, HUH?
OH.
OH.
FWOOP
I'M NOT VANISHING!
OF *COURSE* YOU AREN'T!

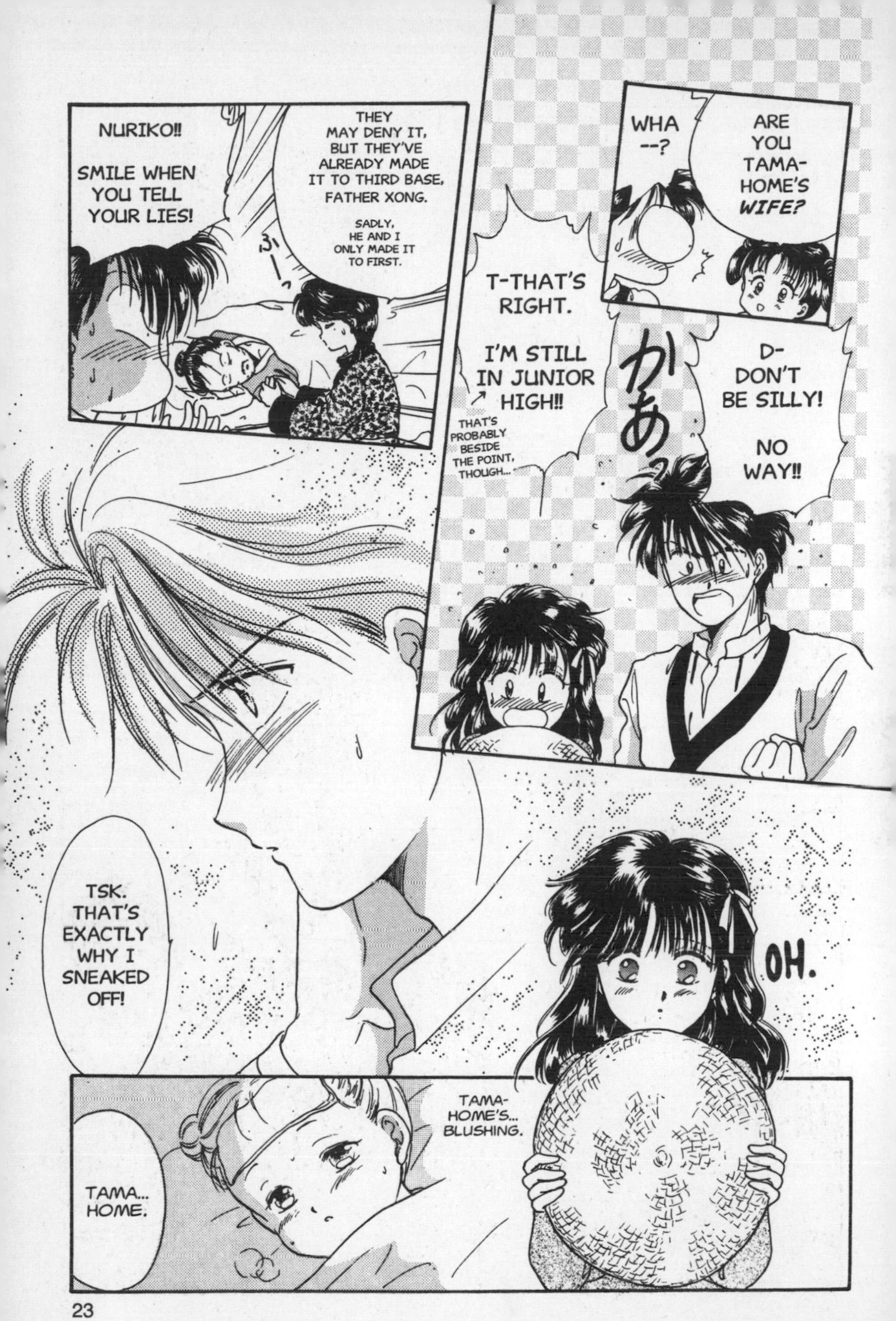
ARE YOU TAMA-HOME'S *WIFE?*
WHA --?
D- DON'T BE SILLY!
NO WAY!!
かあっ
T-THAT'S RIGHT.
I'M STILL IN JUNIOR HIGH!!
THAT'S PROBABLY BESIDE THE POINT, THOUGH...
THEY MAY DENY IT, BUT THEY'VE ALREADY MADE IT TO THIRD BASE, FATHER XONG.
SADLY, HE AND I ONLY MADE IT TO FIRST.
NURIKO!!
SMILE WHEN YOU TELL YOUR LIES!
OH.
TSK. THAT'S EXACTLY WHY I SNEAKED OFF!
TAMA-HOME'S... BLUSHING.
TAMA... HOME.

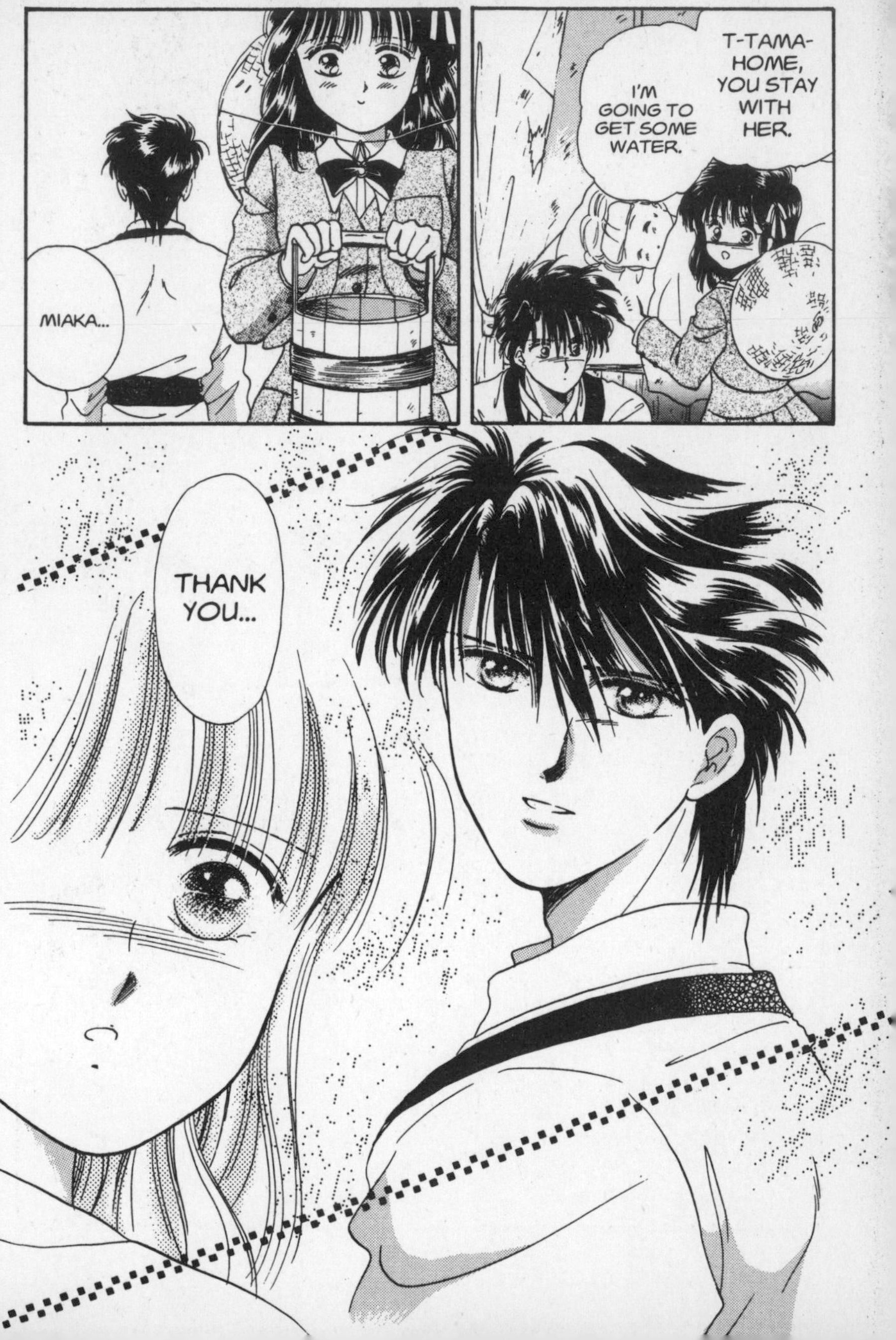
T-TAMA-HOME, YOU STAY WITH HER.
I'M GOING TO GET SOME WATER.
MIAKA...
THANK YOU...

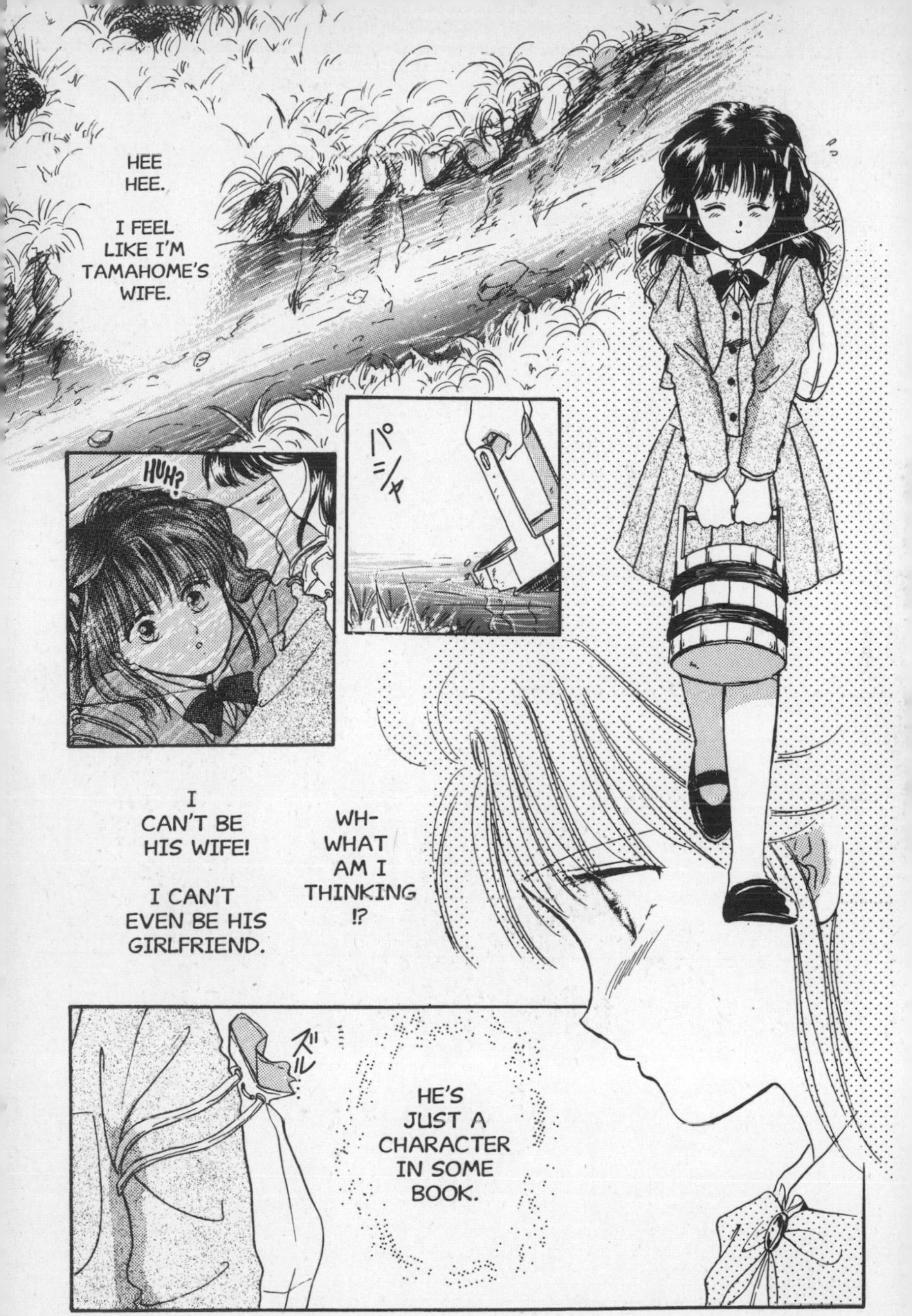
HEE HEE.
I FEEL LIKE I'M TAMAHOME'S WIFE.
パシャ
HUH?
WH- WHAT AM I THINKING!?
I CAN'T BE HIS WIFE!
I CAN'T EVEN BE HIS GIRLFRIEND.
ズル
HE'S JUST A CHARACTER IN SOME BOOK.

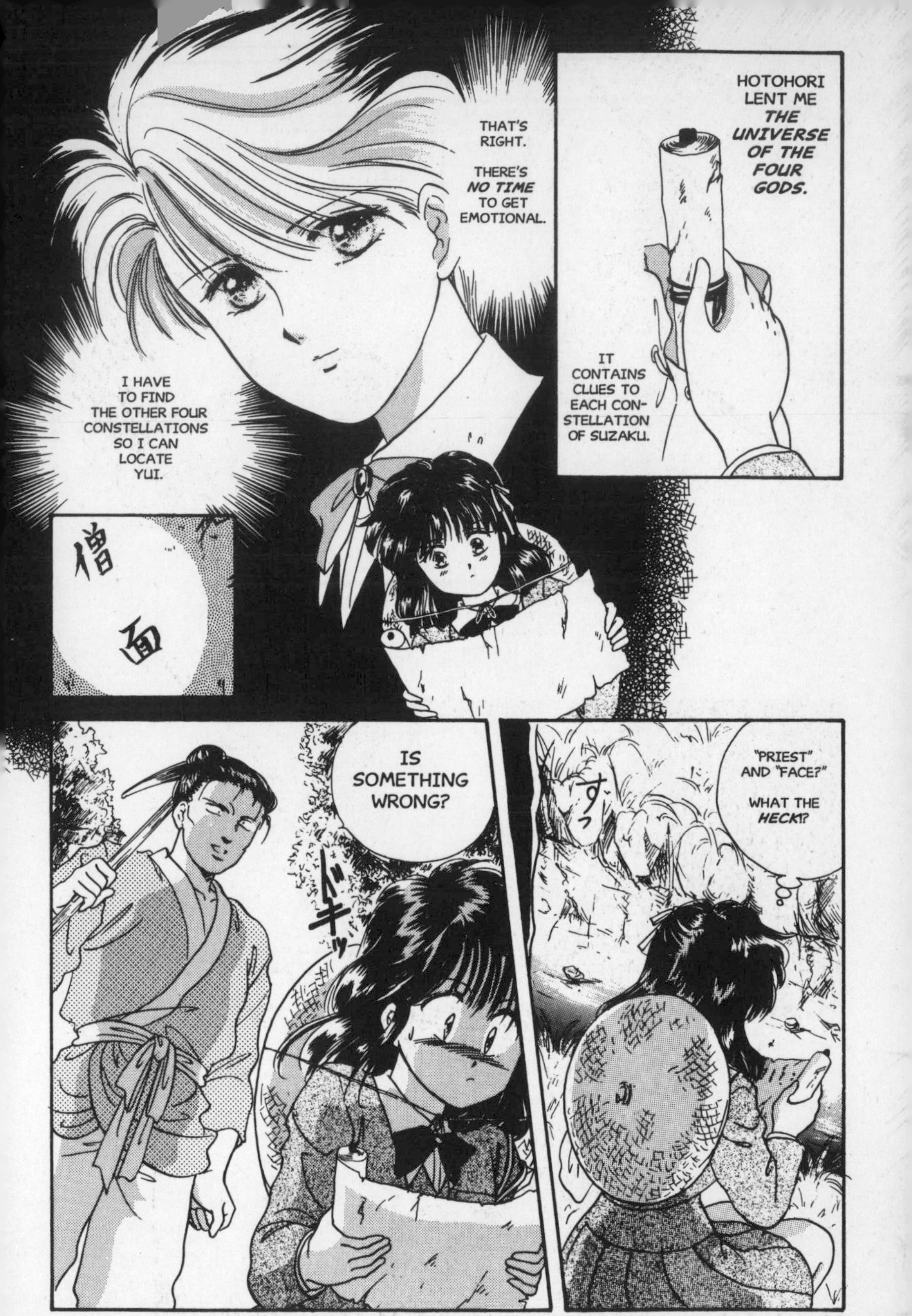
HOTOHORI LENT ME *THE UNIVERSE OF THE FOUR GODS.*
IT CONTAINS CLUES TO EACH CON-STELLATION OF SUZAKU.
THAT'S RIGHT.
THERE'S *NO TIME* TO GET EMOTIONAL.
I HAVE TO FIND THE OTHER FOUR CONSTELLATIONS SO I CAN LOCATE YUI.
僧
面
"PRIEST" AND "FACE?"
WHAT THE *HECK!?*
IS SOMETHING WRONG?

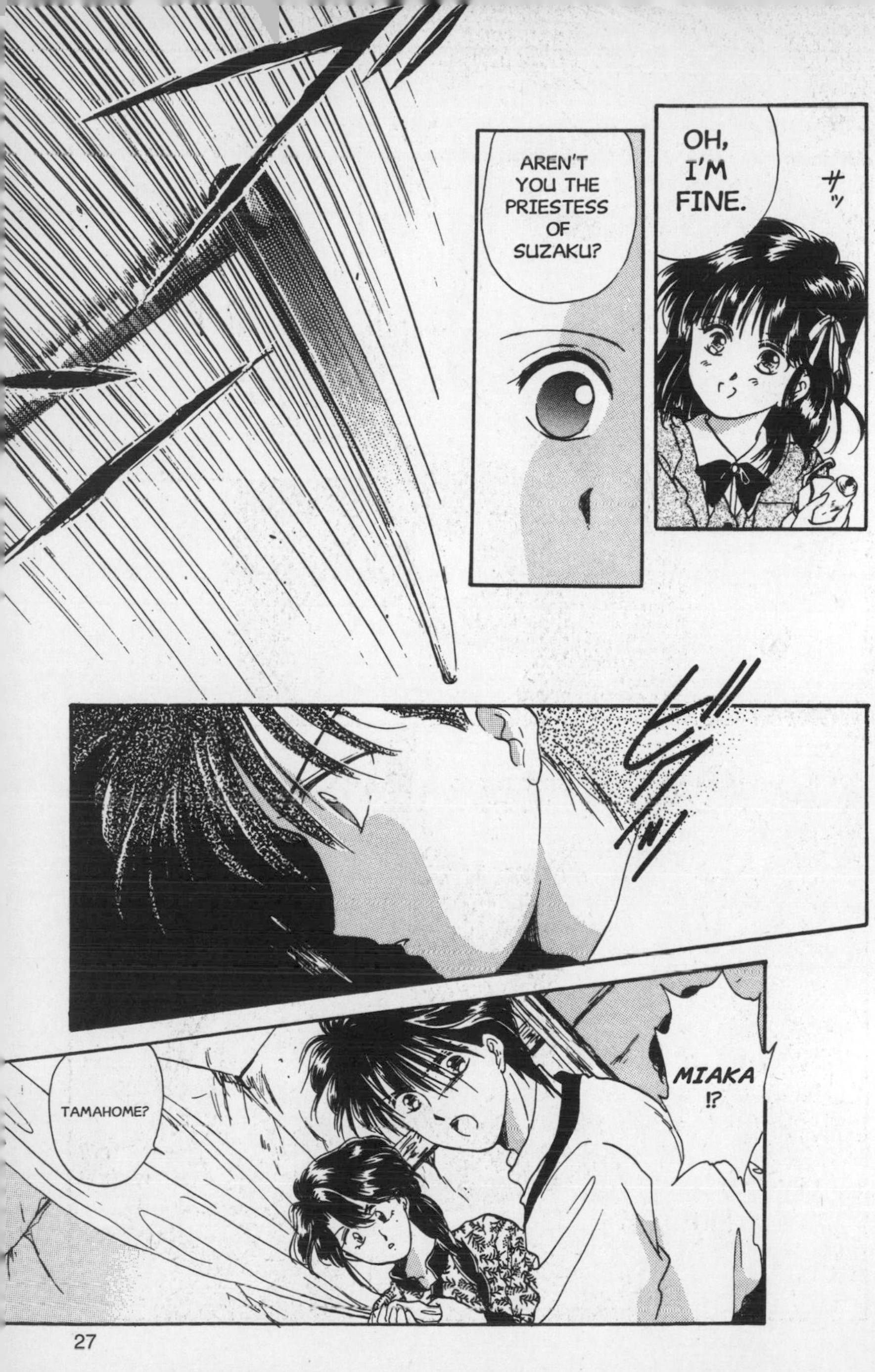
OH, I'M FINE.
サッ
AREN'T YOU THE PRIESTESS OF SUZAKU?
MIAKA !?
TAMAHOME?

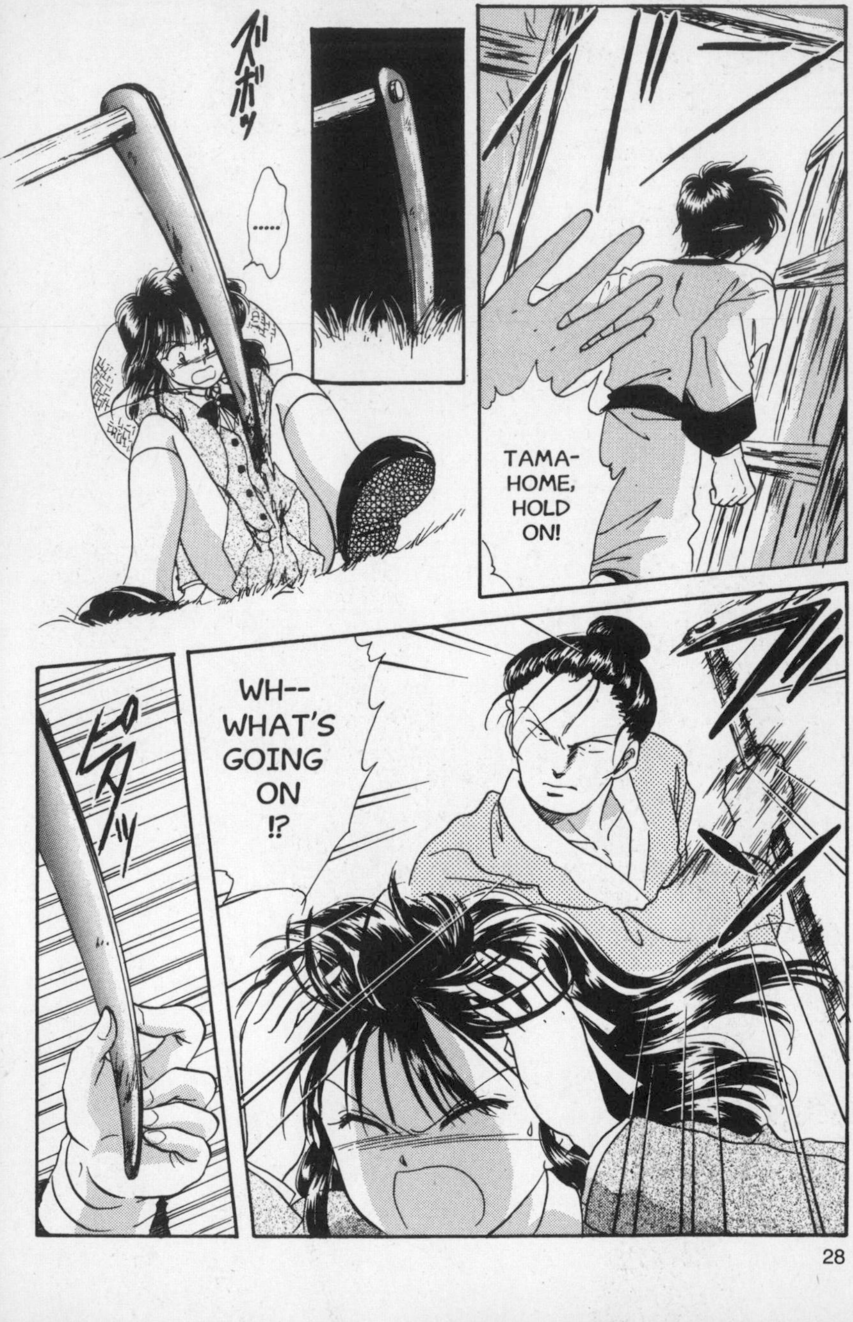
TAMA-
HOME,
HOLD
ON!
ズボッ
......
WH--
WHAT'S
GOING
ON
!?
ピタッ

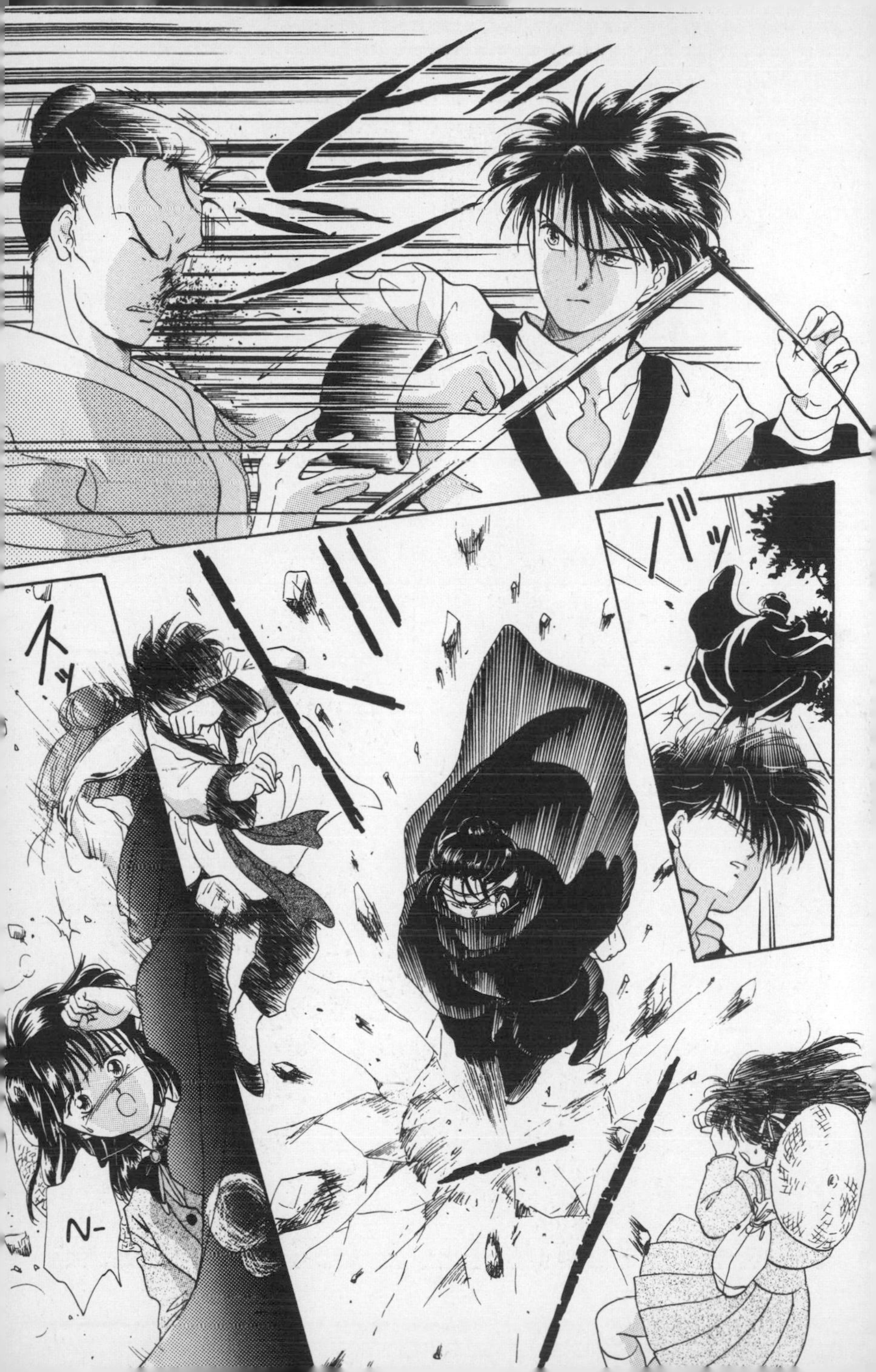
バッ
トッ
N-

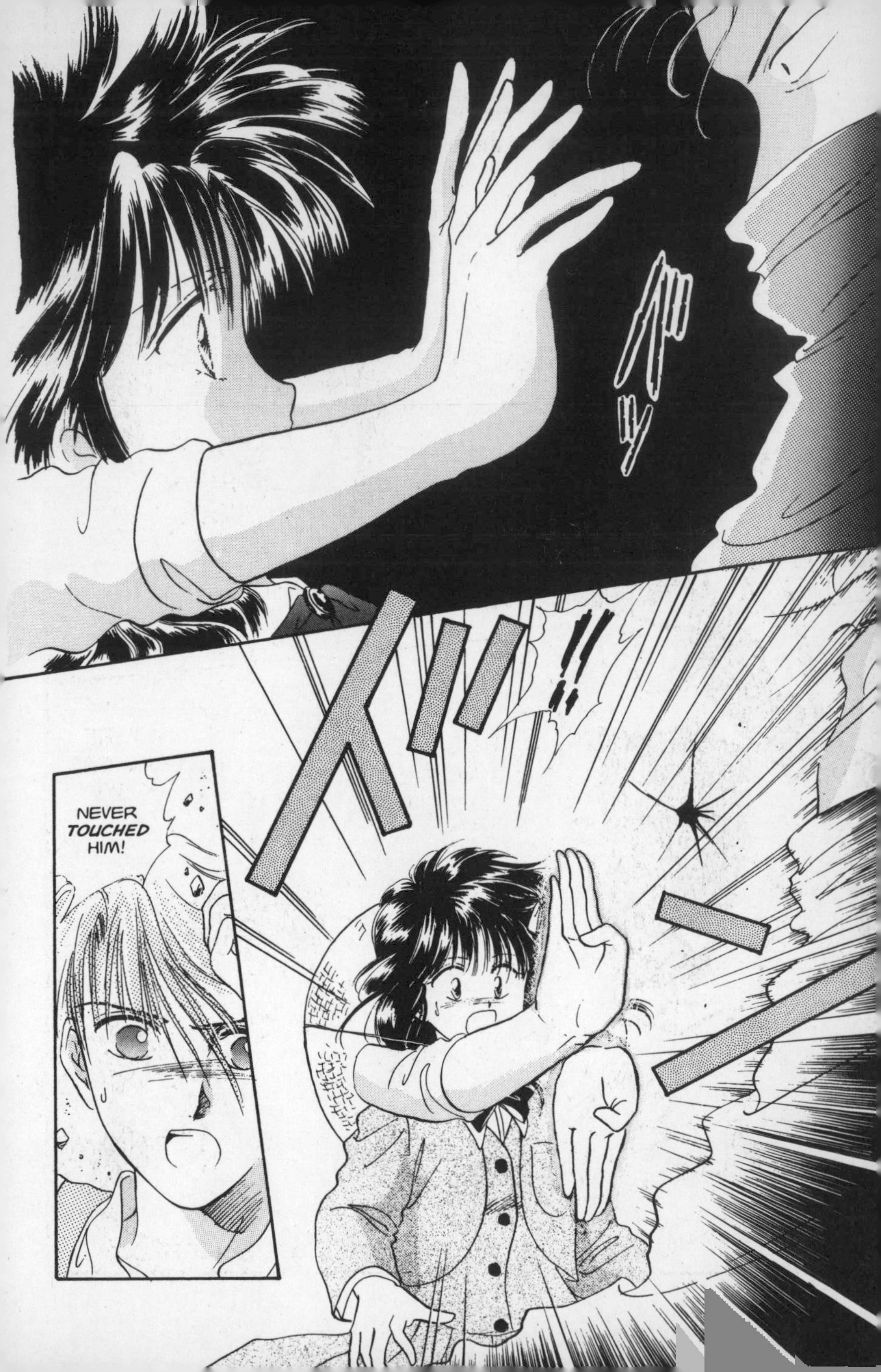
NEVER *TOUCHED* HIM!

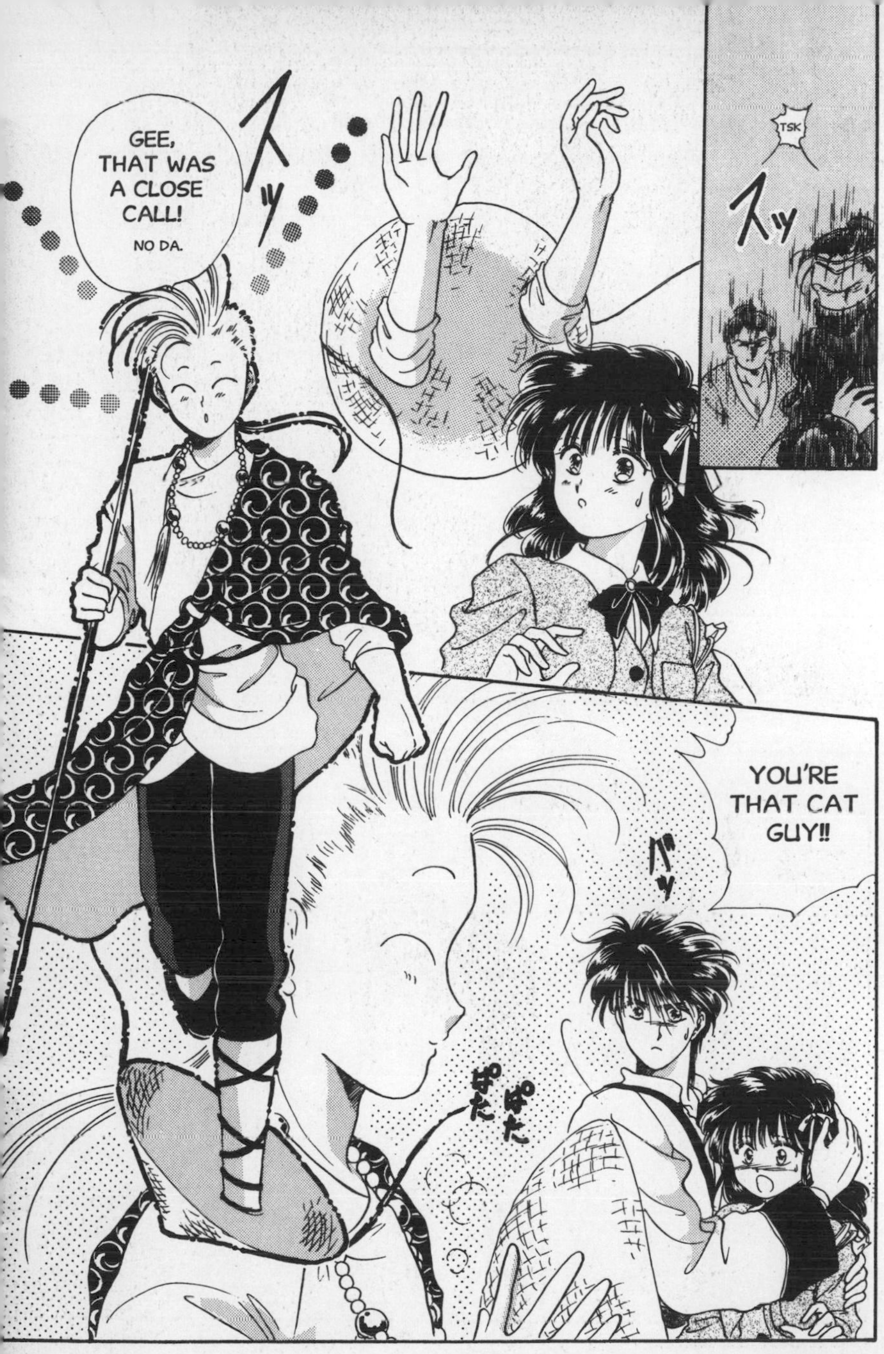
TSK
スッ
GEE, THAT WAS A CLOSE CALL!
NO DA.
スッ
YOU'RE THAT CAT GUY!!
バッ
ぱた ぱた

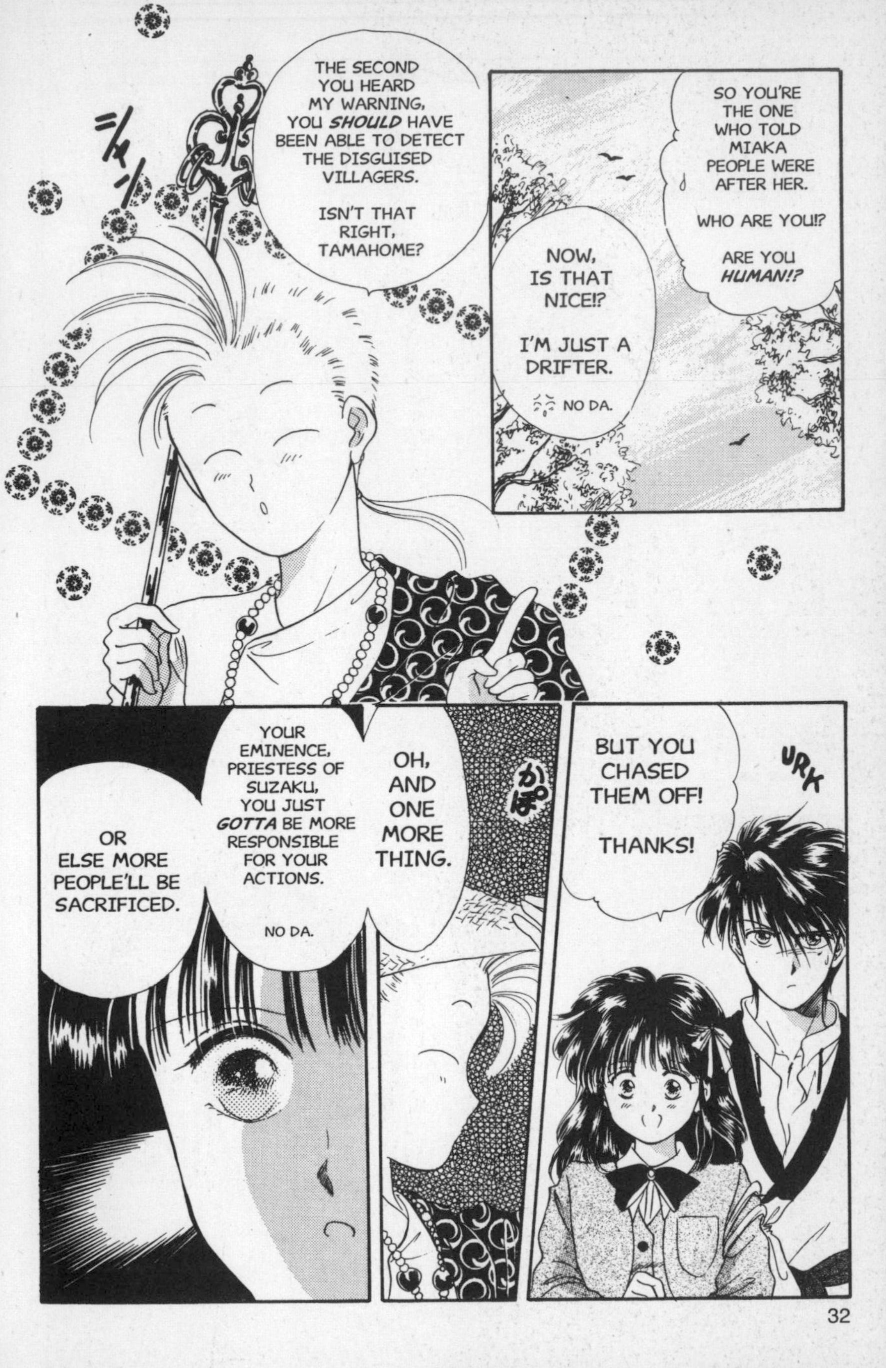
SO YOU'RE THE ONE WHO TOLD MIAKA PEOPLE WERE AFTER HER.
WHO ARE YOU!?
ARE YOU *HUMAN!?*
NOW, IS THAT NICE!?
I'M JUST A DRIFTER.
NO DA.
THE SECOND YOU HEARD MY WARNING, YOU *SHOULD* HAVE BEEN ABLE TO DETECT THE DISGUISED VILLAGERS.
ISN'T THAT RIGHT, TAMAHOME?
BUT YOU CHASED THEM OFF!
THANKS!
URK
OH, AND ONE MORE THING.
かぽ
YOUR EMINENCE, PRIESTESS OF SUZAKU, YOU JUST *GOTTA* BE MORE RESPONSIBLE FOR YOUR ACTIONS.
NO DA.
OR ELSE MORE PEOPLE'LL BE SACRIFICED.

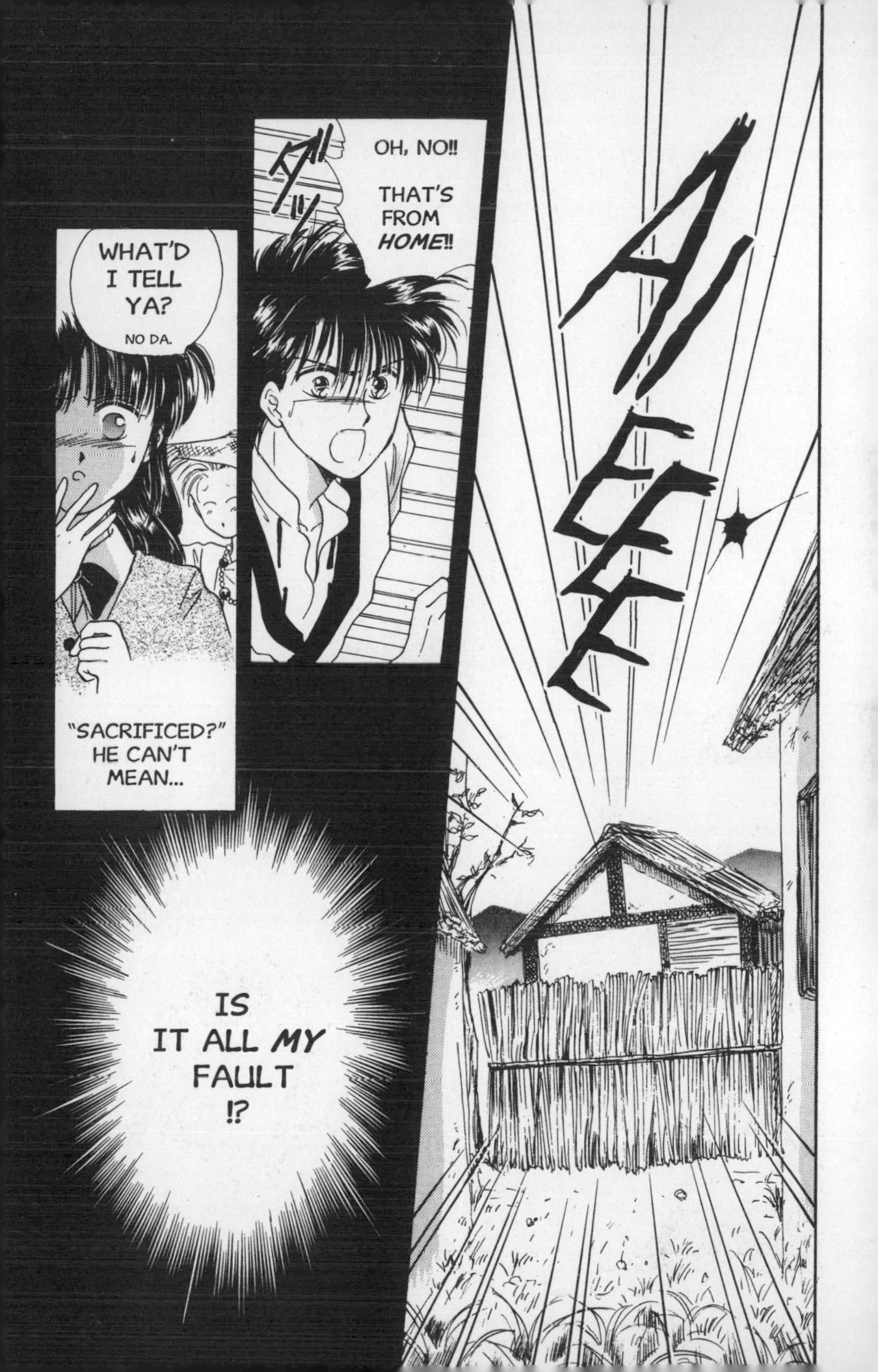
AIEEEE
OH, NO!!
THAT'S FROM *HOME*!!
WHAT'D I TELL YA?
NO DA.
"SACRIFICED?" HE CAN'T MEAN...
IS IT ALL *MY* FAULT !?

TELL ME MORE ABOUT "THE UNIVERSE OF THE FOUR GODS"

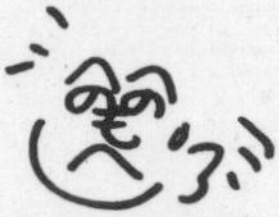

This is one of the questions I hear frequently. If you keep reading the story, you'll find out all about it. But for the impatient who still INSIST! I've decided to expose a few details.

I've never seen constellations attributed to the Four Gods, so I might be the first. (Usually they've been used as compass directions or for the identities of monsters. Other than that, their names have been used for invocations.) The anime OAV Maryū Senki used them as monsters. I think Suzaku was female, but this anime gets pretty heavily into erotic-grotesque so I can't recommend it... I'll describe the gods and their constellations. (That way you can find them in the night sky.)

We'll list the Four Gods according to ancient Chinese astrological names rather than geographical areas (which might appear later in the story) or compass directions.

EASTERN SEIRYU SEVEN CONSTELLATIONS (MAY-JULY) Suboshi (Virgo), Amiboshi (Virgo), Tomo (Libra), Soi (Scorpio), Nakago (Scorpio), Ashitare (Scorpio), Mi (Sagittarius)

WESTERN BYAKKO SEVEN CONSTELLATIONS (NOVEMBER-JANUARY) Tokaki (Andromeda), Tatara (Aries), Kokie (Aries), Subaru (Taurus), Amefuri (Taurus), Toroki (Orion), Karasuki (Orion)

SOUTHERN SUZAKU SEVEN CONSTELLATIONS (FEBRUARY-MAY) Chichiri (Gemini), Tamahome (Cancer), Nuriko (Hydra), Chiriko (Hydra), Tasuki (Crater), Mitsukake (Corvus)

NORTHERN GENBU SEVEN CONSTELLATIONS (AUGUST-NOVEMBER) Hikitsu (Sagittarius), Inami (Capricorn), Uruki (Aquarius), Urumiya (Aquarius), Hatsui (Pegasus), Namame (Pegasus)

Usually, when you see the character for Chichiri's name, you read it as "I," and when you see the character for Tamahome's name, you see it as "ki," etc. So most of the tables list the constellation names with the Chinese pronunciations for each of the characters. There are very few which list the Japanese phonetic reading such as "Tamahome," but in the Buddhist Philosophy Encyclopedia I have, the character was listed as "Tamahome." (You'll only find this book at a large bookstore. It costs a whopping ¥80,000!)
The rest I looked up in the constellation tables in the appendices of a Japanese/Chinese dictionary I used in high school. A star in "Hotohori" is second magnitude, and the brightest star is Suzaku (Alpha Hadrae, also known as Alphard or the Solitary One. – Ed.)

The names for the Four Gods were taken from these constellation listings. The Southern Seven Star Constellations look like they have short tails so the ancients called them a bird, the Western Seven Star Constellations resemble a tiger, and so on.

Between February and May, you can see the Suzaku constellations appear in the night sky. The brightest star in Cancer is Tamahome.

I love the cosmos, so I get a kick out of naming my characters after constellations.

I've also been told that "Nuriko" is "Meriko," but I think it can be named both ways (most of the time it's called Nuriko). Also, Mitsukake can be read both as Mitsukake and Mitsuuchi. Some said that Tamahome and crew were part of Byakko, but they're mistaken.

Genbu is pretty sad. Dragons like Seiryu are kind of cool, but the idea of a turtle and snake copulating!! Blech! I am not into that!!

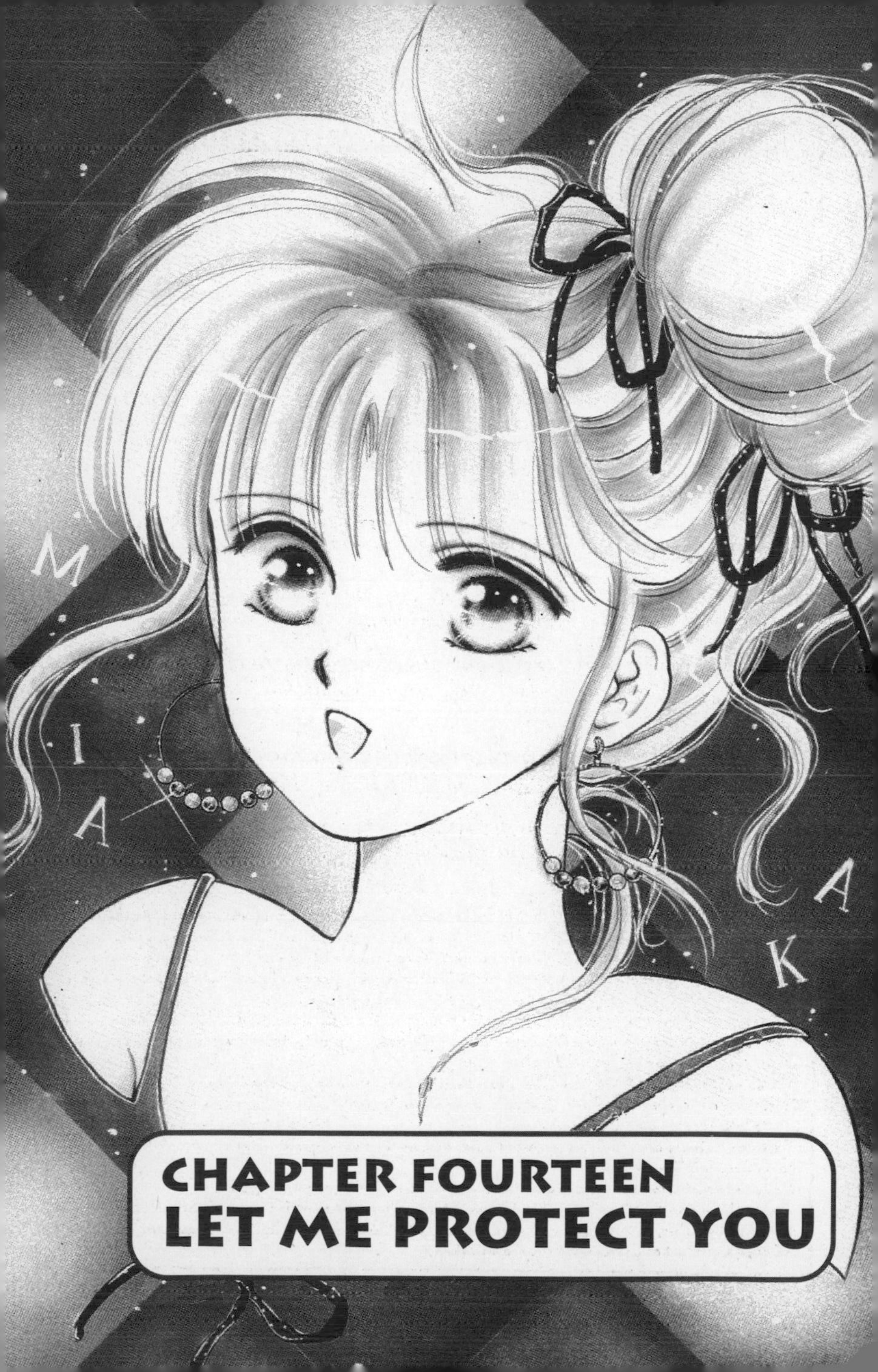
MIAKA
CHAPTER FOURTEEN
LET ME PROTECT YOU

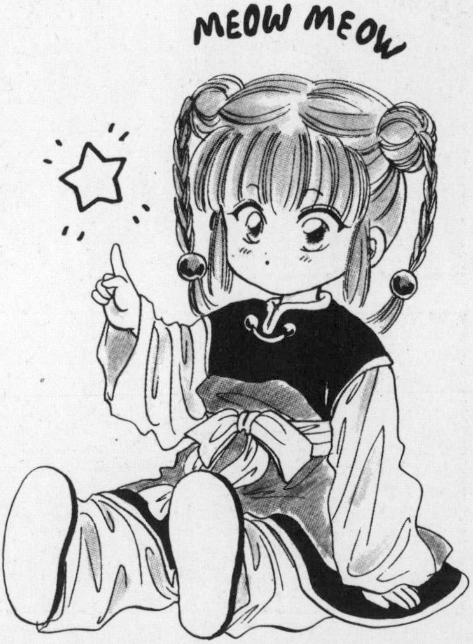
MEOW MEOW

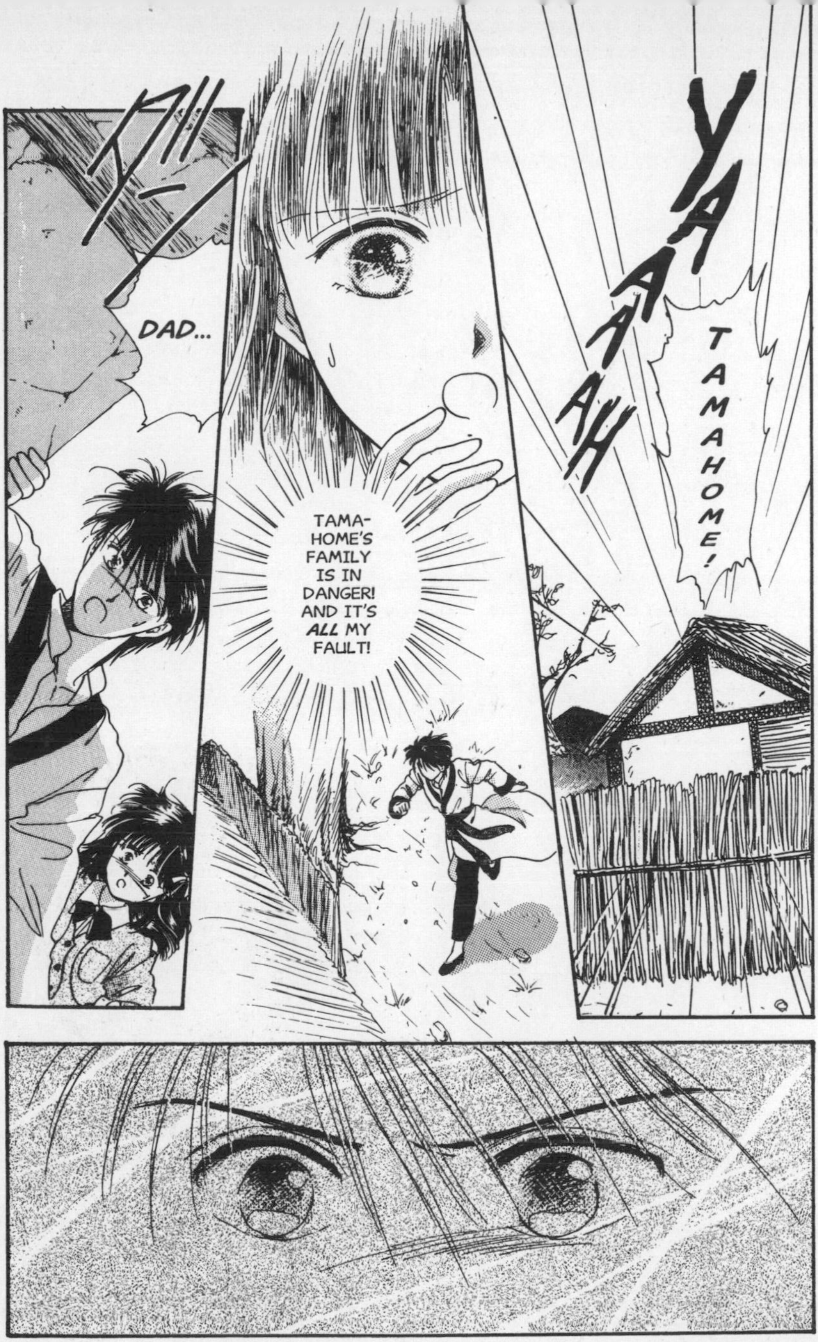
YAAAAH
TAMAHOME!
TAMA-HOME'S FAMILY IS IN DANGER! AND IT'S *ALL* MY FAULT!
DAD...

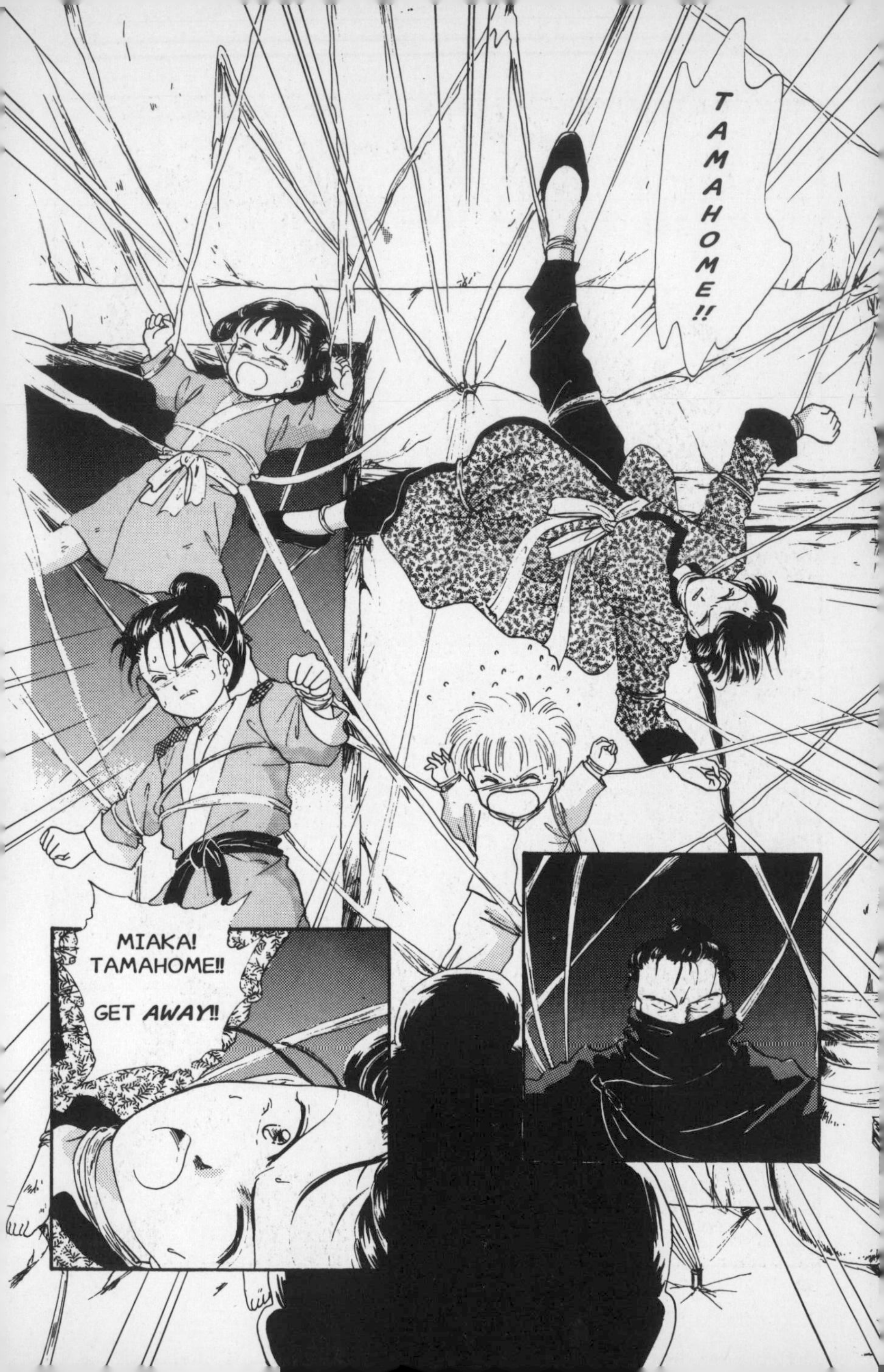
TAMAHOME!!
MIAKA! TAMAHOME!!
GET *AWAY*!!

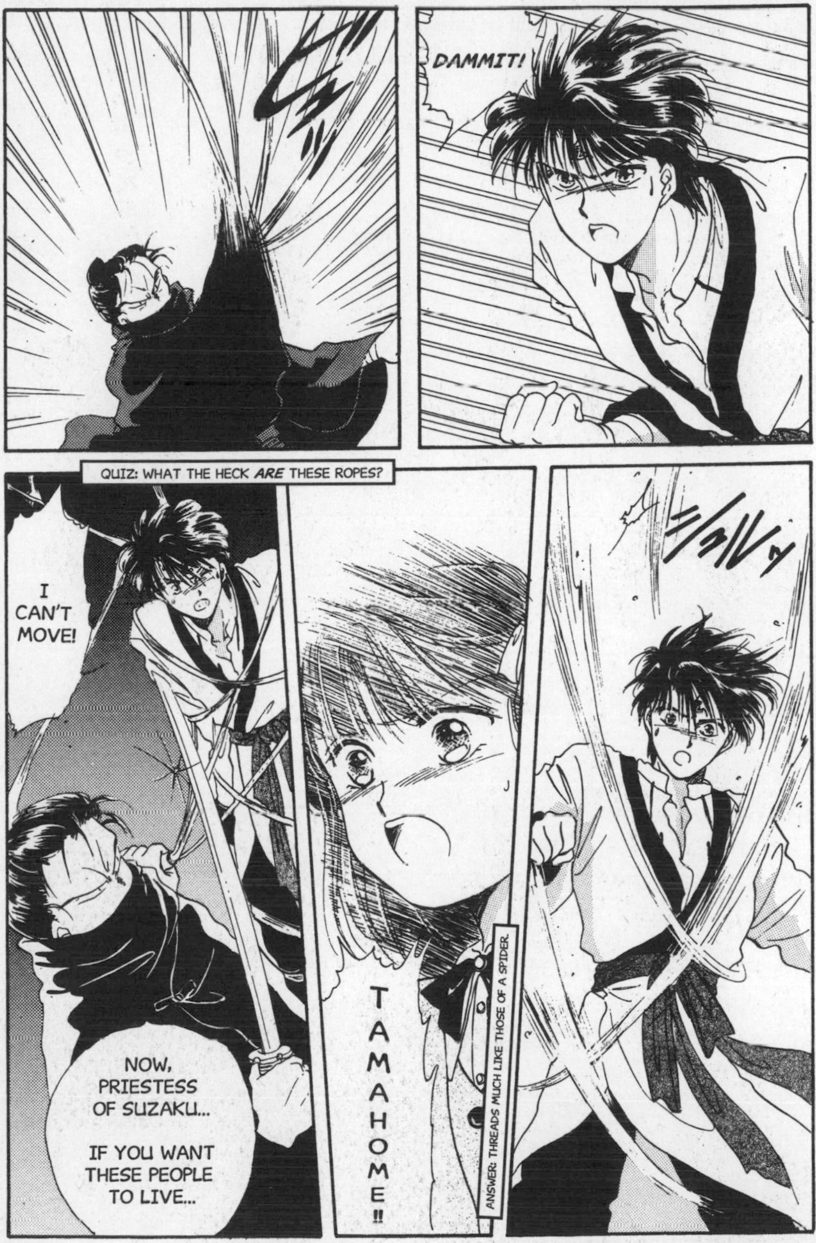
DAMMIT!
ANSWER: THREADS MUCH LIKE THOSE OF A SPIDER.
TAMAHOME!!
QUIZ: WHAT THE HECK *ARE* THESE ROPES?
I CAN'T MOVE!
NOW, PRIESTESS OF SUZAKU...
IF YOU WANT THESE PEOPLE TO LIVE...

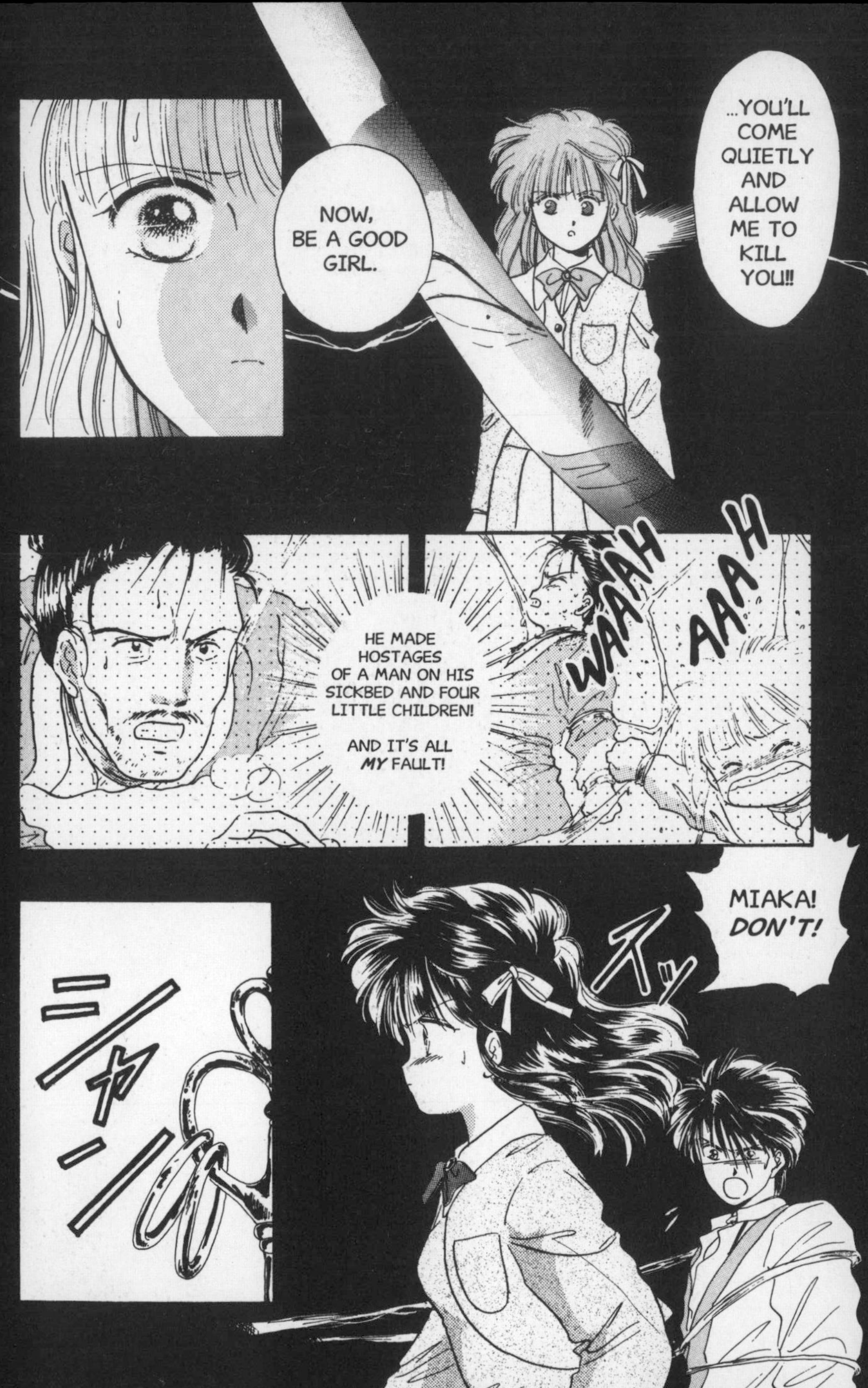
...YOU'LL COME QUIETLY AND ALLOW ME TO KILL YOU!!
NOW, BE A GOOD GIRL.
WAAAH
AAAAH
HE MADE HOSTAGES OF A MAN ON HIS SICKBED AND FOUR LITTLE CHILDREN!
AND IT'S ALL *MY* FAULT!
MIAKA! *DON'T!*

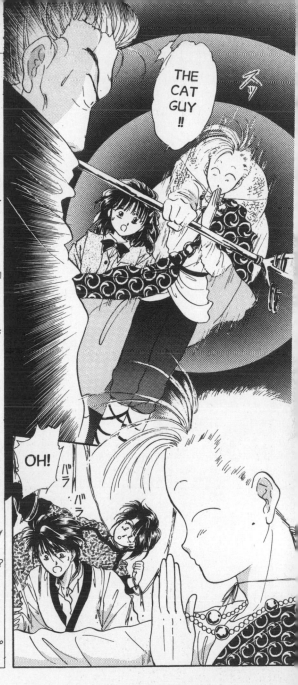

I mentioned before how I've been reading your fan mail, and I'm surprised at the huge number of questions. You're all so concerned about the remaining warriors in the constellations of Suzaku. Some of you have even sent me illustrations and suggestions for the rest of the warriors. But to tell the truth, I decided on all seven characters before I even started drawing the comic. So I'll introduce them one by one, the same way I envisioned them. I find it fascinating how all the characters get their own fans. The Tamahome fans don't like Hotohori, and the Hotohori fans look down on Tamahome. Nuriko's been gaining popularity. Keisuke, Miaka's brother, has a set of fans, too. Well, they're all cute so I don't mind. All of my assistants rate their favorites differently. Sometimes they play "Who'd be the best voice actor for each character?" and everyone gets all worked up. Fans have suggested some in their letters, but most of them don't seem right to me. (Sorry!). That's not to say my ideas are any better. We had a dramatic section in "Toy Box '93" so I was allowed to choose the actors for Miaka and Tamahome (but only them). I talked it over with my assistants then made my decision. Give it a listen and see what you think. I like voices that are mature and masculine (and a little erotic). What else? Oh, yes, I heard that all the merchandise at the Animate store sold out! ♡♡ And we got a lot of complaints! I never got any myself!! The least they could do is save a sample for me!! Did you hear there was a bonus poster with every ¥2,000 purchase!? Gimme!! Calendars are posted in bookstores without my knowledge. And I never knew it had been printed!! Speaking of calendars, I think you should know that I had to fight to get an original drawing into that calendar. It also took a lot of work to convince my editor that I should draw for the CD book, too.

There are really very few who like both!

Supposedly, they only display July and August

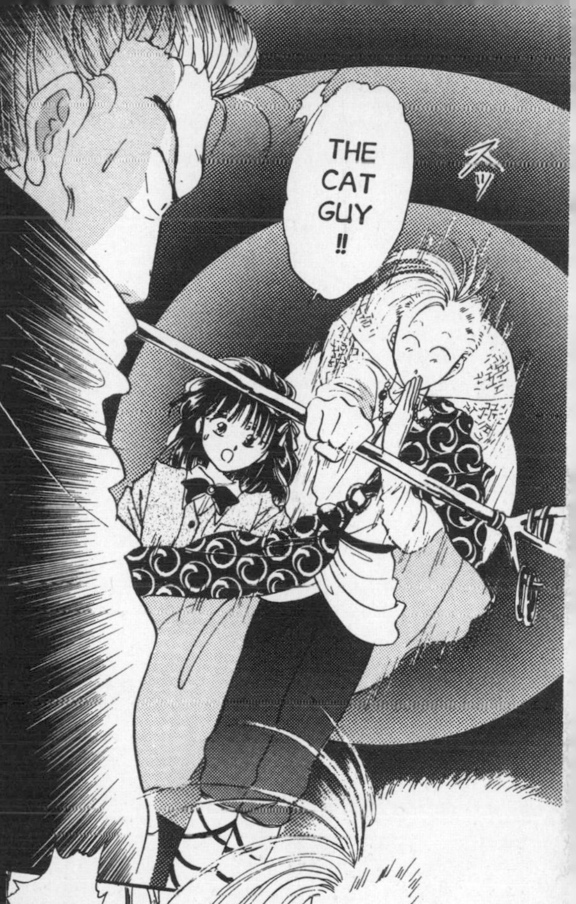
THE CAT GUY !!
スッ
OH!
バラ
バラ

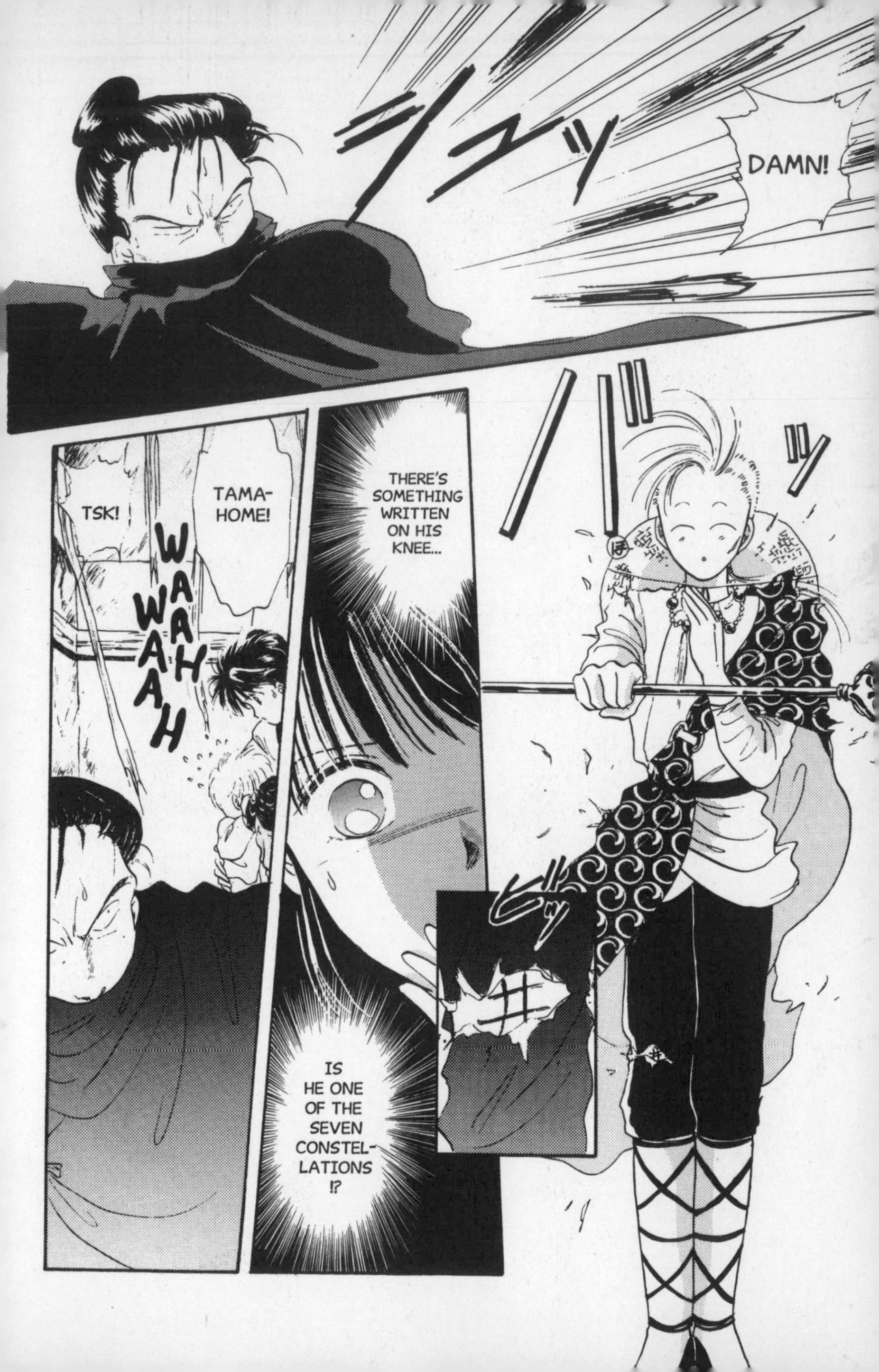
DAMN!
THERE'S SOMETHING WRITTEN ON HIS KNEE...
IS HE ONE OF THE SEVEN CONSTELLATIONS !?
TAMA-HOME!
TSK!
WAAH WAAH

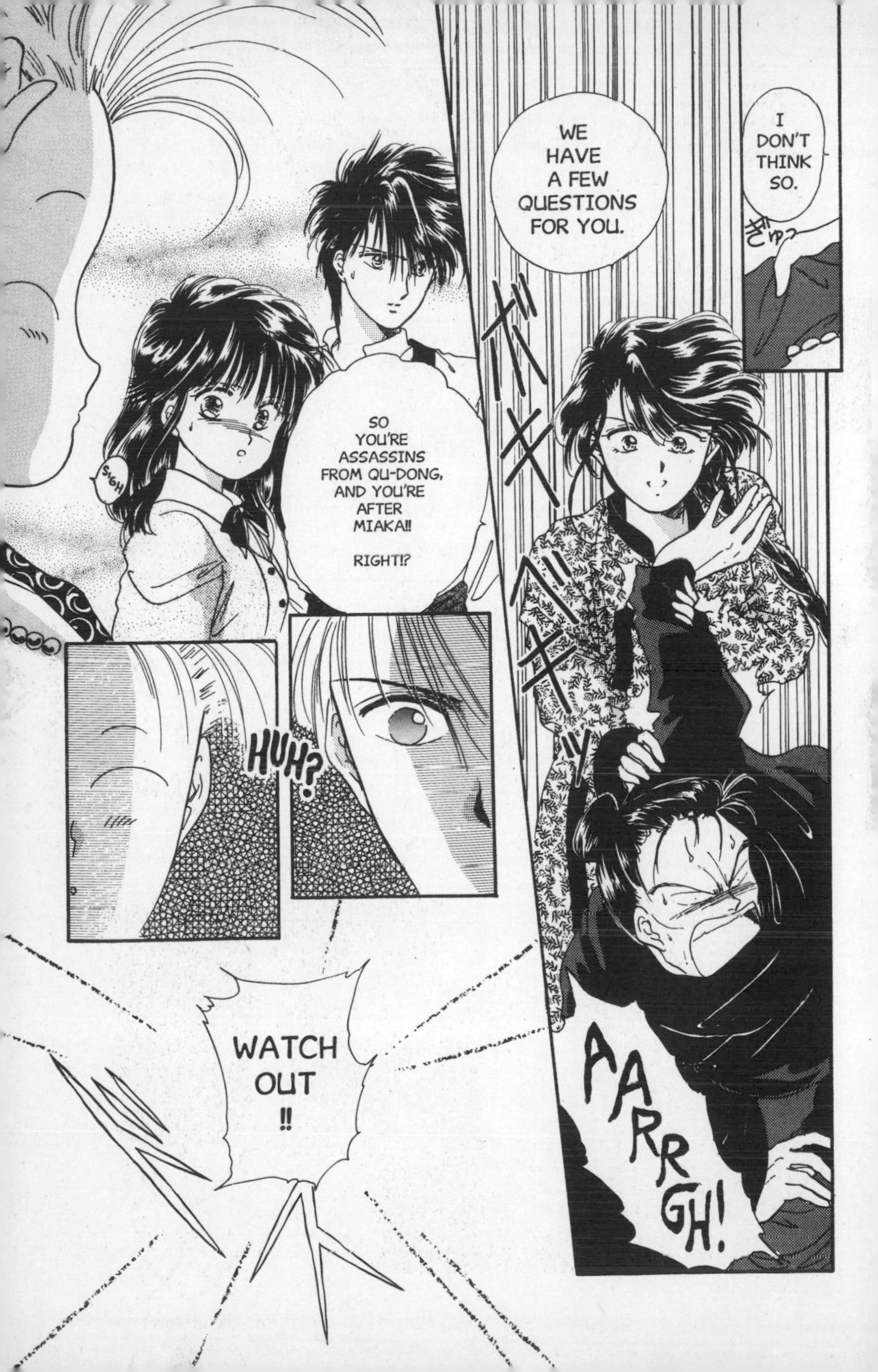
WE HAVE A FEW QUESTIONS FOR YOU.
I DON'T THINK SO.
ぎゅっ
ボキボキッ
AARRGH!
SIGH
SO YOU'RE ASSASSINS FROM QU-DONG, AND YOU'RE AFTER MIAKA!!
RIGHT!?
HUH?
WATCH OUT !!

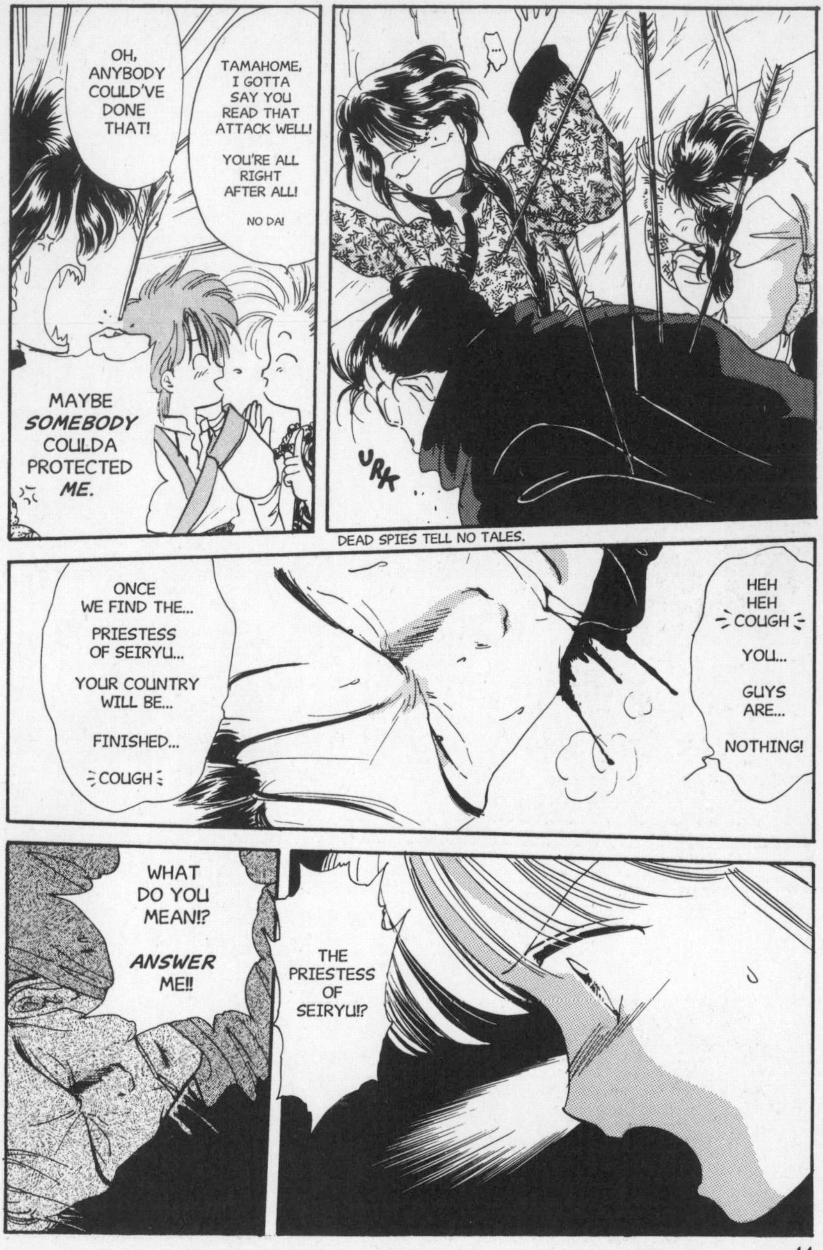
...
URK ...
TAMAHOME, I GOTTA SAY YOU READ THAT ATTACK WELL!
YOU'RE ALL RIGHT AFTER ALL!
NO DA!
OH, ANYBODY COULD'VE DONE THAT!
MAYBE SOMEBODY COULDA PROTECTED ME.
DEAD SPIES TELL NO TALES.
HEH HEH COUGH
YOU... GUYS ARE... NOTHING!
ONCE WE FIND THE... PRIESTESS OF SEIRYU...
YOUR COUNTRY WILL BE... FINISHED...
COUGH
THE PRIESTESS OF SEIRYU!?
WHAT DO YOU MEAN!?
ANSWER ME!!

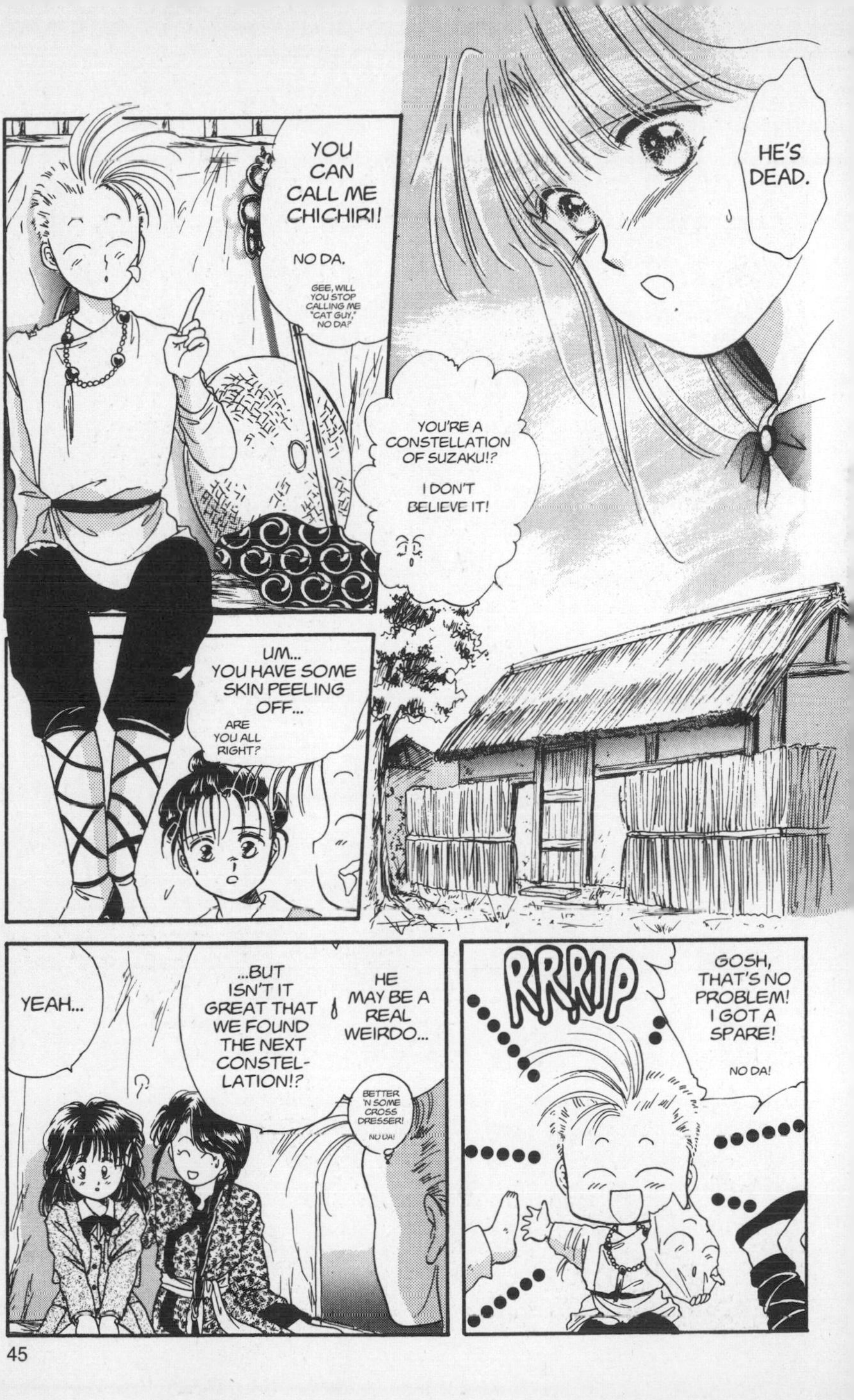
HE'S DEAD.
YOU'RE A CONSTELLATION OF SUZAKU!? I DON'T BELIEVE IT!
YOU CAN CALL ME CHICHIRI!
NO DA.
GEE, WILL YOU STOP CALLING ME "CAT GUY," NO DA?
UM... YOU HAVE SOME SKIN PEELING OFF...
ARE YOU ALL RIGHT?
RRRIP
GOSH, THAT'S NO PROBLEM! I GOT A SPARE!
NO DA!
HE MAY BE A REAL WEIRDO...
...BUT ISN'T IT GREAT THAT WE FOUND THE NEXT CONSTEL-LATION!?
BETTER 'N SOME CROSS DRESSER! NO DA!
YEAH...

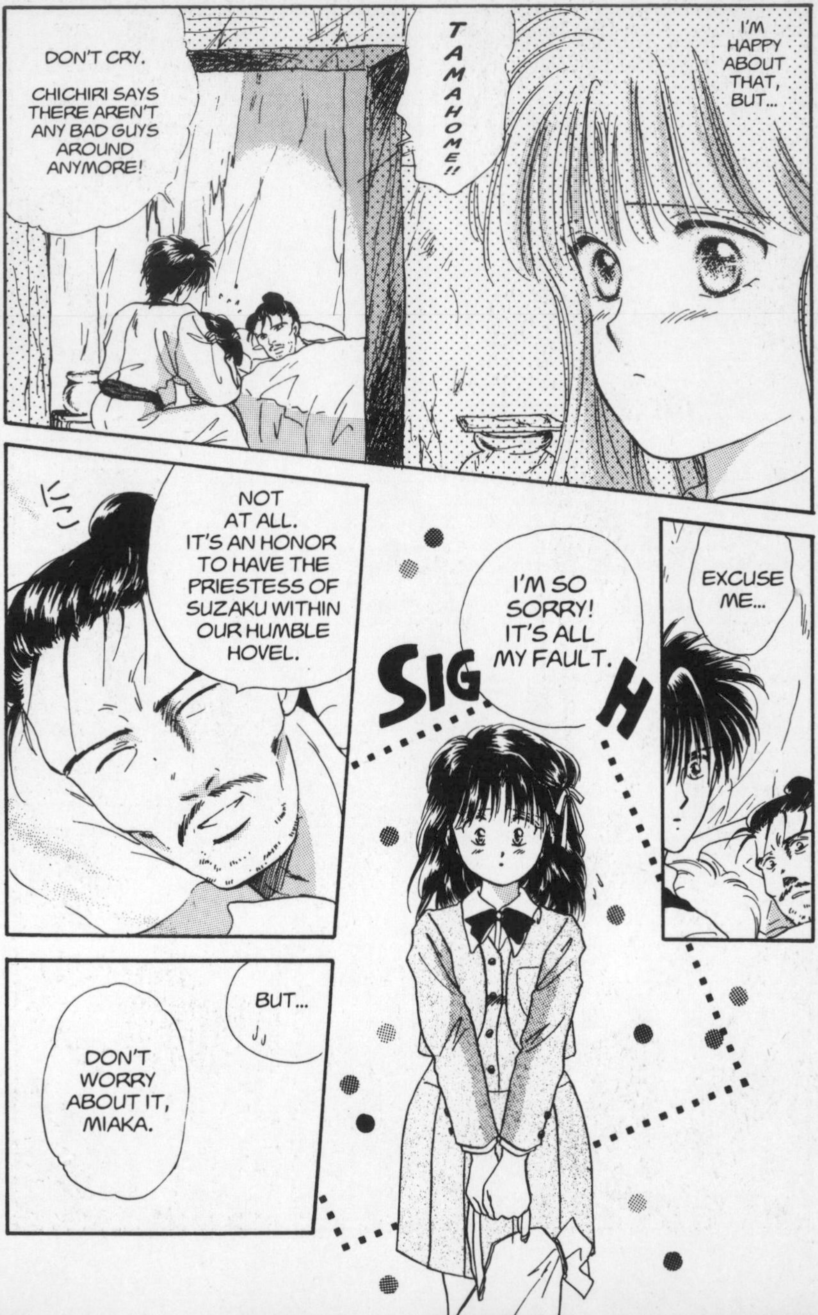
I'M HAPPY ABOUT THAT, BUT...
TAMAHOME!!
DON'T CRY.
CHICHIRI SAYS THERE AREN'T ANY BAD GUYS AROUND ANYMORE!
EXCUSE ME...
I'M SO SORRY! IT'S ALL MY FAULT.
SIGH
NOT AT ALL. IT'S AN HONOR TO HAVE THE PRIESTESS OF SUZAKU WITHIN OUR HUMBLE HOVEL.
BUT...
DON'T WORRY ABOUT IT, MIAKA.

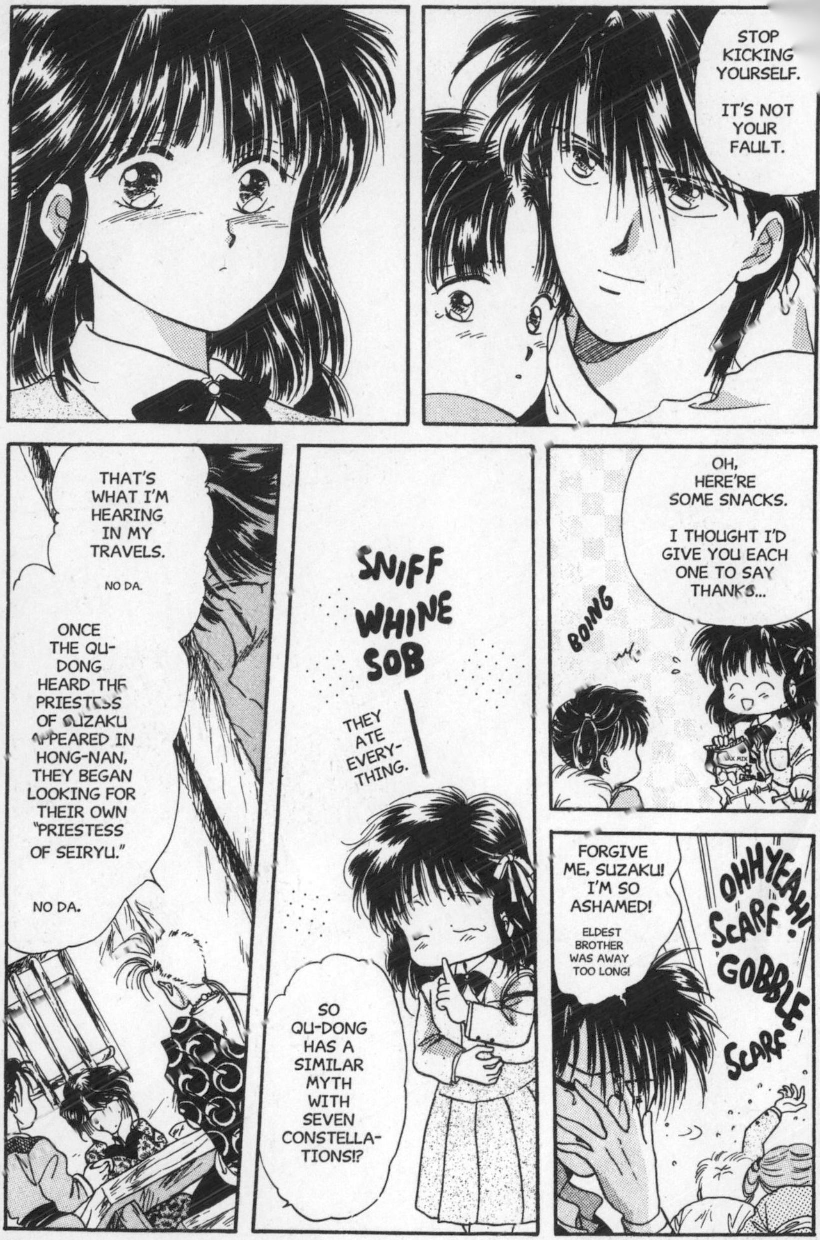
STOP KICKING YOURSELF.
IT'S NOT YOUR FAULT.
OH, HERE'RE SOME SNACKS.
I THOUGHT I'D GIVE YOU EACH ONE TO SAY THANKS...
BOING
FORGIVE ME, SUZAKU! I'M SO ASHAMED!
ELDEST BROTHER WAS AWAY TOO LONG!
OHHYEAH!
SCARF
GOBBLE
SCARF
SNIFF
WHINE
SOB
THEY ATE EVERY-THING.
SO QU-DONG HAS A SIMILAR MYTH WITH SEVEN CONSTELLA-TIONS!?
THAT'S WHAT I'M HEARING IN MY TRAVELS.
NO DA.
ONCE THE QU-DONG HEARD THE PRIESTESS OF SUZAKU APPEARED IN HONG-NAN, THEY BEGAN LOOKING FOR THEIR OWN "PRIESTESS OF SEIRYU."
NO DA.

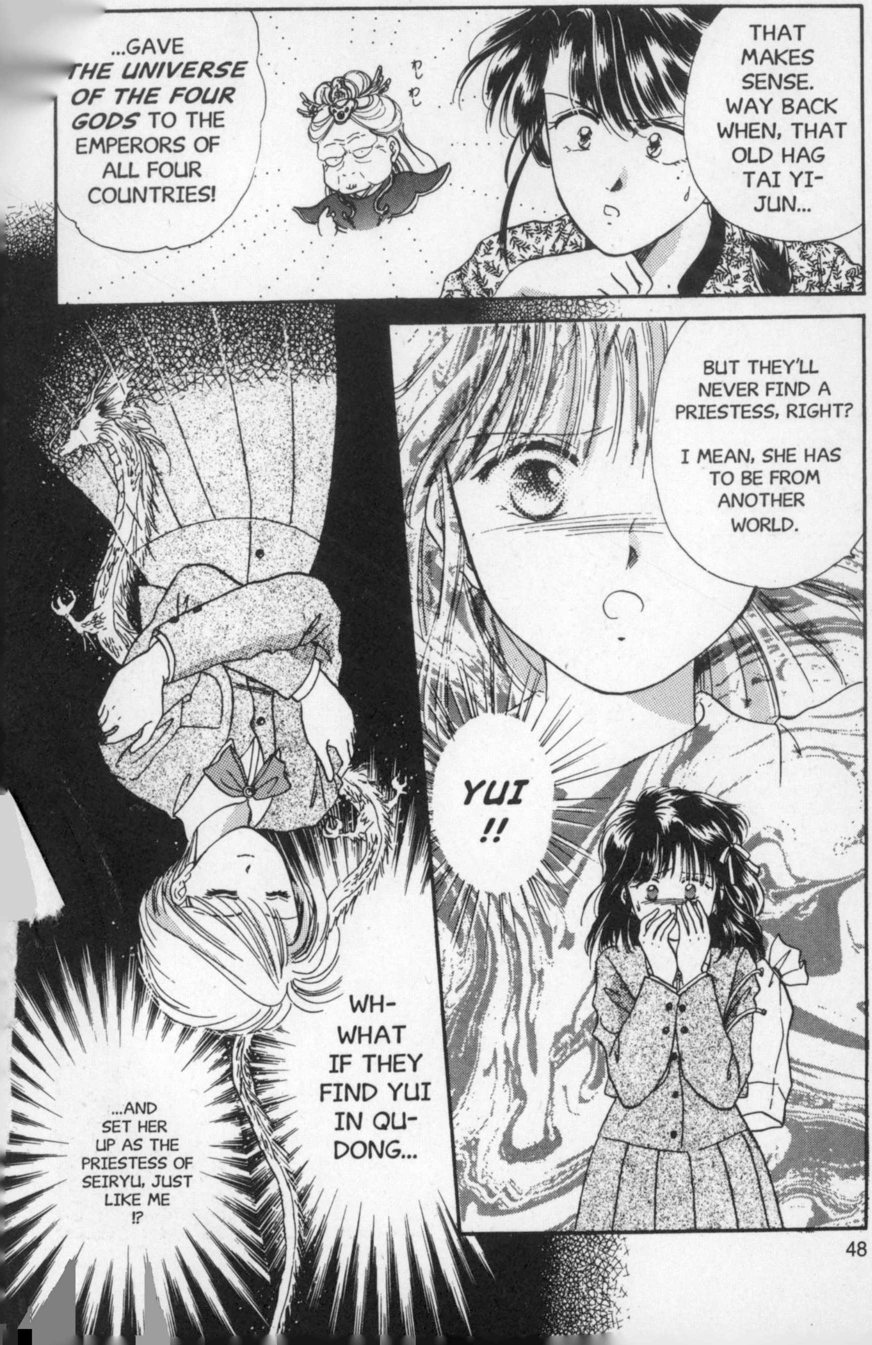
THAT MAKES SENSE. WAY BACK WHEN, THAT OLD HAG TAI YI-JUN...
...GAVE THE UNIVERSE OF THE FOUR GODS TO THE EMPERORS OF ALL FOUR COUNTRIES!
BUT THEY'LL NEVER FIND A PRIESTESS, RIGHT?
I MEAN, SHE HAS TO BE FROM ANOTHER WORLD.
YUI !!
WH- WHAT IF THEY FIND YUI IN QU-DONG...
...AND SET HER UP AS THE PRIESTESS OF SEIRYU, JUST LIKE ME !?

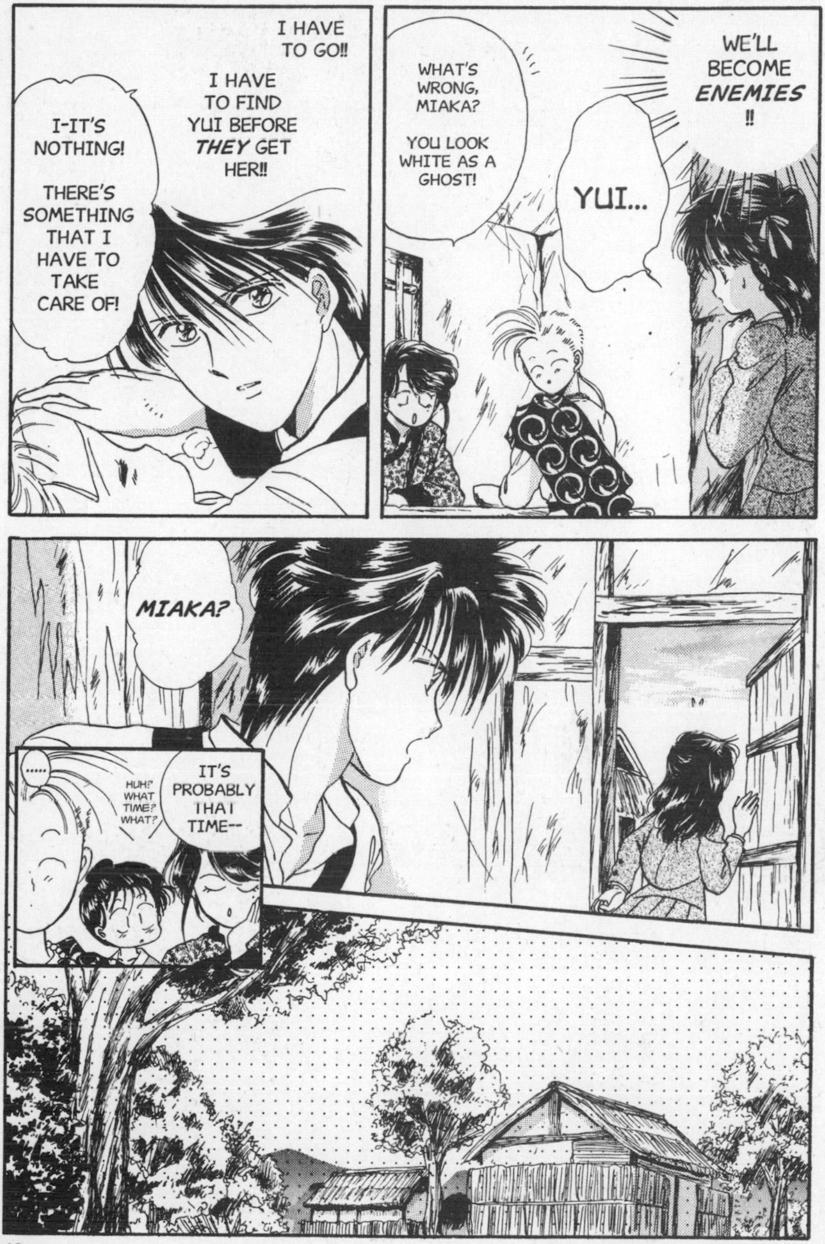
WE'LL BECOME ENEMIES!!
YUI...
WHAT'S WRONG, MIAKA?
YOU LOOK WHITE AS A GHOST!
I HAVE TO GO!!
I HAVE TO FIND YUI BEFORE THEY GET HER!!
I-IT'S NOTHING!
THERE'S SOMETHING THAT I HAVE TO TAKE CARE OF!
MIAKA?
IT'S PROBABLY THAT TIME--
HUH? WHAT TIME? WHAT?
......

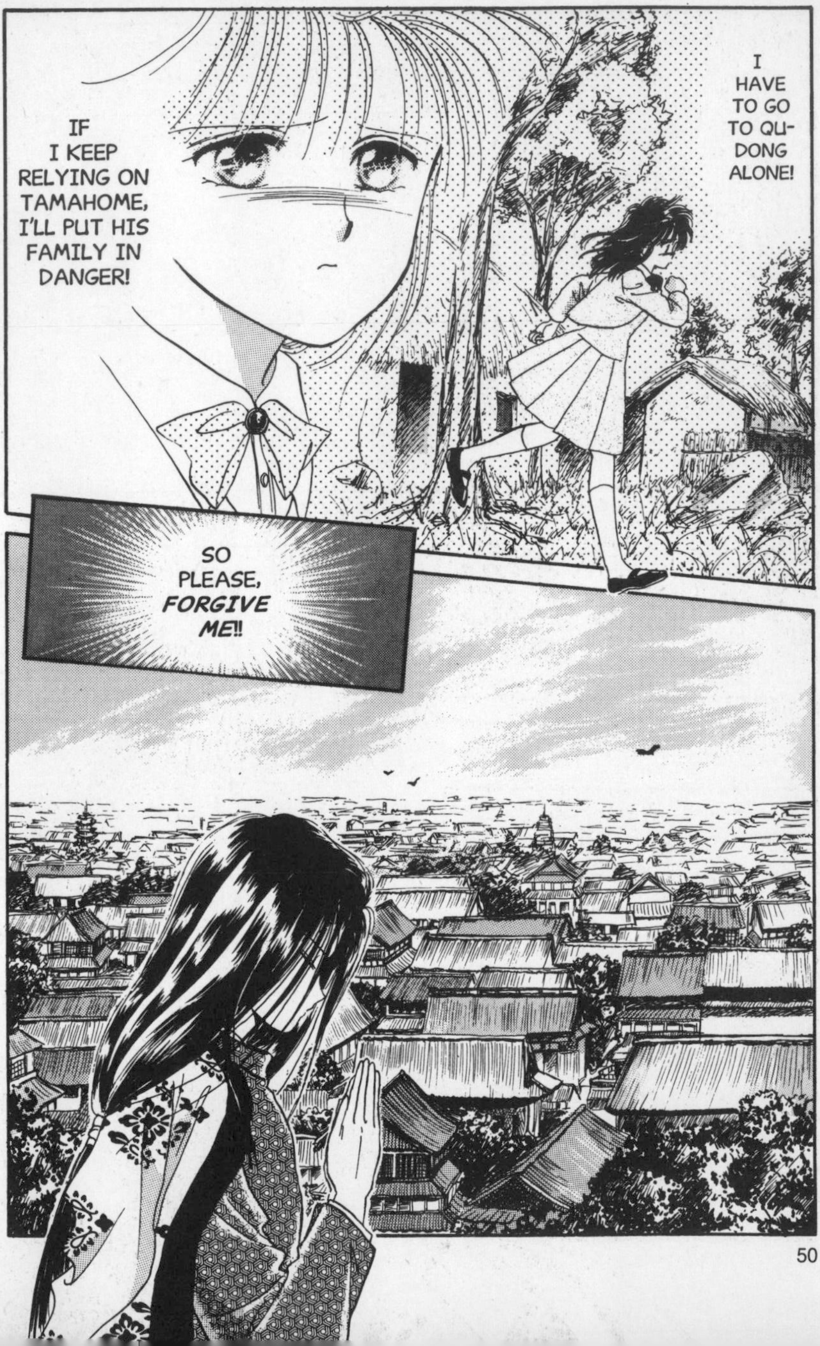
I HAVE TO GO TO QU-DONG ALONE!
IF I KEEP RELYING ON TAMAHOME, I'LL PUT HIS FAMILY IN DANGER!
SO PLEASE, *FORGIVE ME*!!

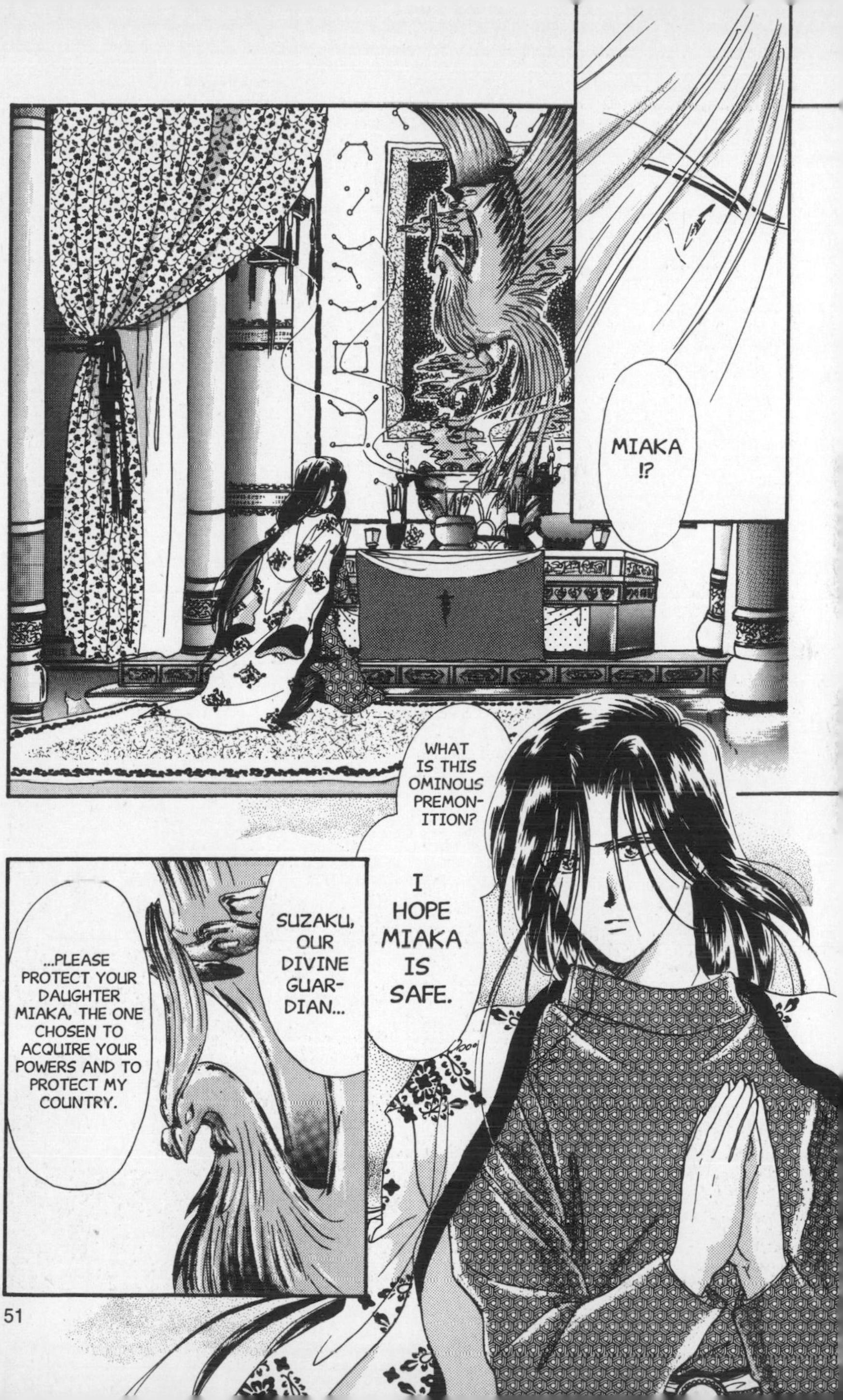
MIAKA !?
WHAT IS THIS OMINOUS PREMON-ITION?
I HOPE MIAKA IS SAFE.
SUZAKU, OUR DIVINE GUAR-DIAN...
...PLEASE PROTECT YOUR DAUGHTER MIAKA, THE ONE CHOSEN TO ACQUIRE YOUR POWERS AND TO PROTECT MY COUNTRY.

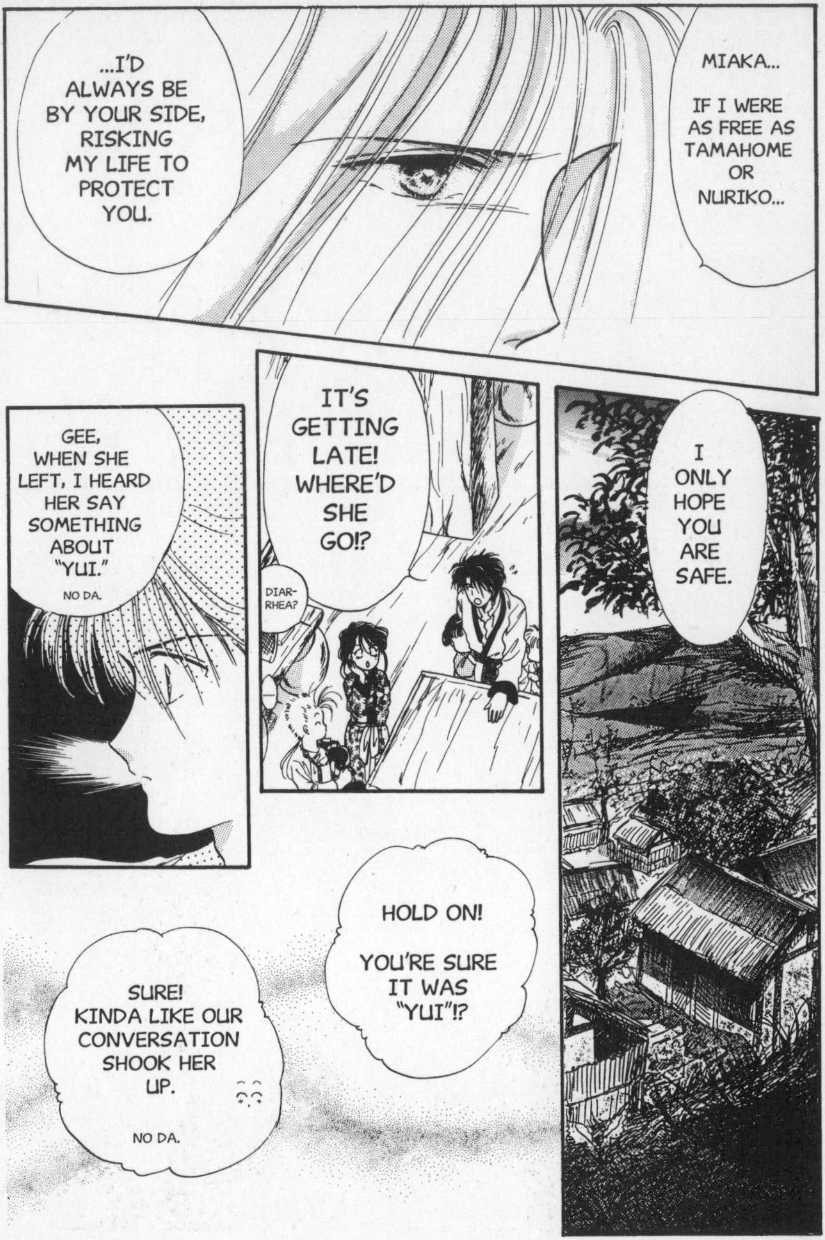
MIAKA... IF I WERE AS FREE AS TAMAHOME OR NURIKO...
...I'D ALWAYS BE BY YOUR SIDE, RISKING MY LIFE TO PROTECT YOU.
I ONLY HOPE YOU ARE SAFE.
IT'S GETTING LATE! WHERE'D SHE GO!?
DIARRHEA?
......
GEE, WHEN SHE LEFT, I HEARD HER SAY SOMETHING ABOUT "YUI."
NO DA.
HOLD ON! YOU'RE SURE IT WAS "YUI"!?
SURE! KINDA LIKE OUR CONVERSATION SHOOK HER UP.
NO DA.

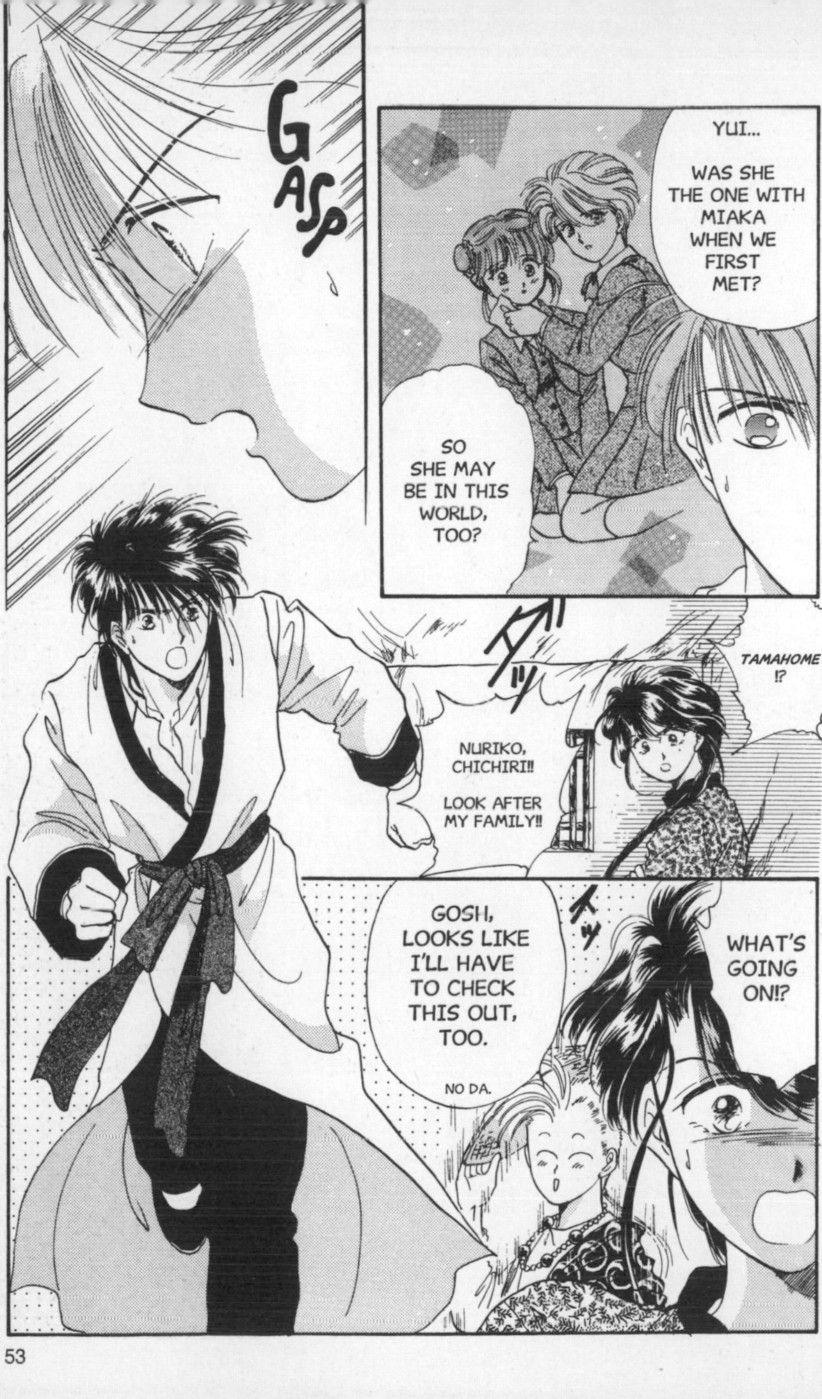
YUI...
WAS SHE THE ONE WITH MIAKA WHEN WE FIRST MET?
SO SHE MAY BE IN THIS WORLD, TOO?
GASP
NURIKO, CHICHIRI!!
LOOK AFTER MY FAMILY!!
TAMAHOME!?
WHAT'S GOING ON!?
GOSH, LOOKS LIKE I'LL HAVE TO CHECK THIS OUT, TOO.
NO DA.

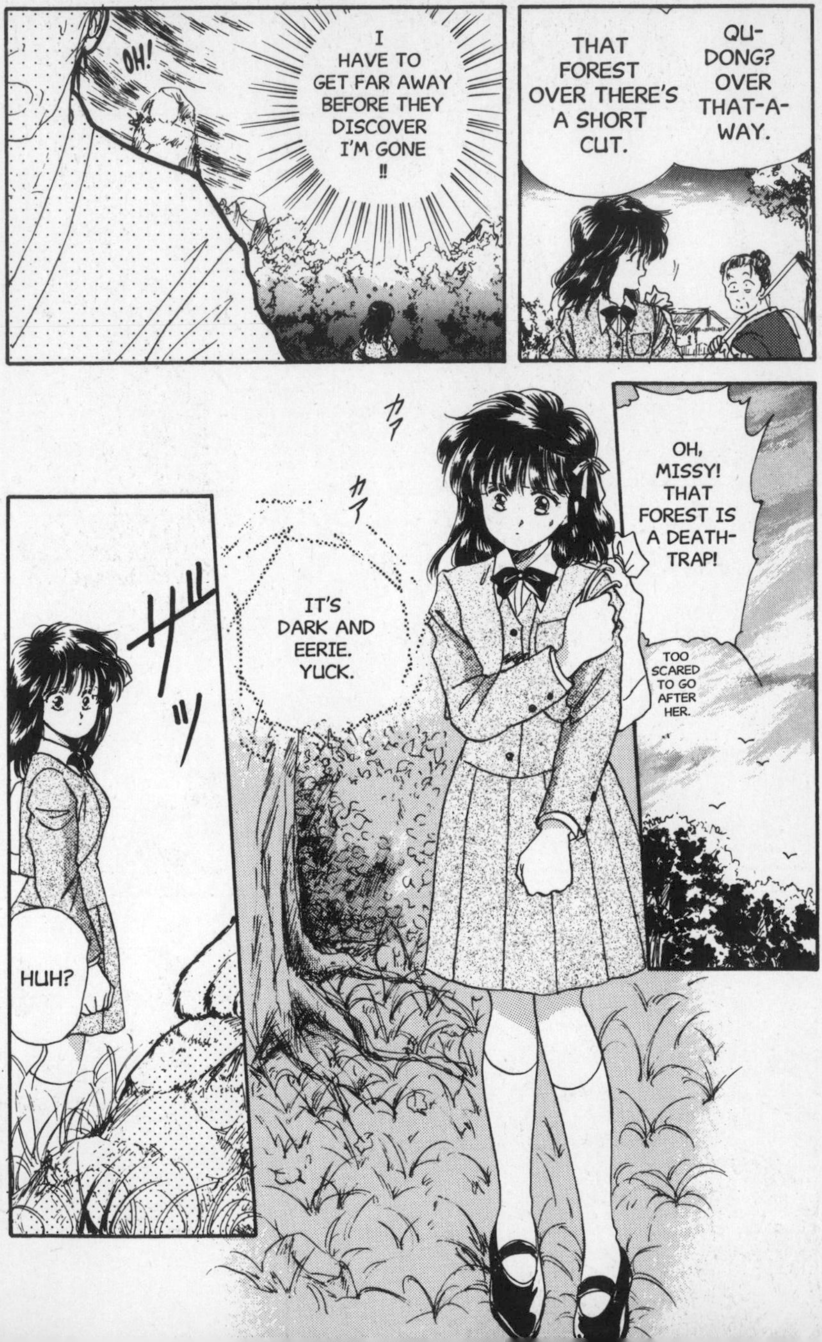
QU-DONG? OVER THAT-A-WAY.
THAT FOREST OVER THERE'S A SHORT CUT.
I HAVE TO GET FAR AWAY BEFORE THEY DISCOVER I'M GONE!!
OH!
OH, MISSY! THAT FOREST IS A DEATH-TRAP!
TOO SCARED TO GO AFTER HER.
カァ
カァ
IT'S DARK AND EERIE. YUCK.
ザッ
HUH?

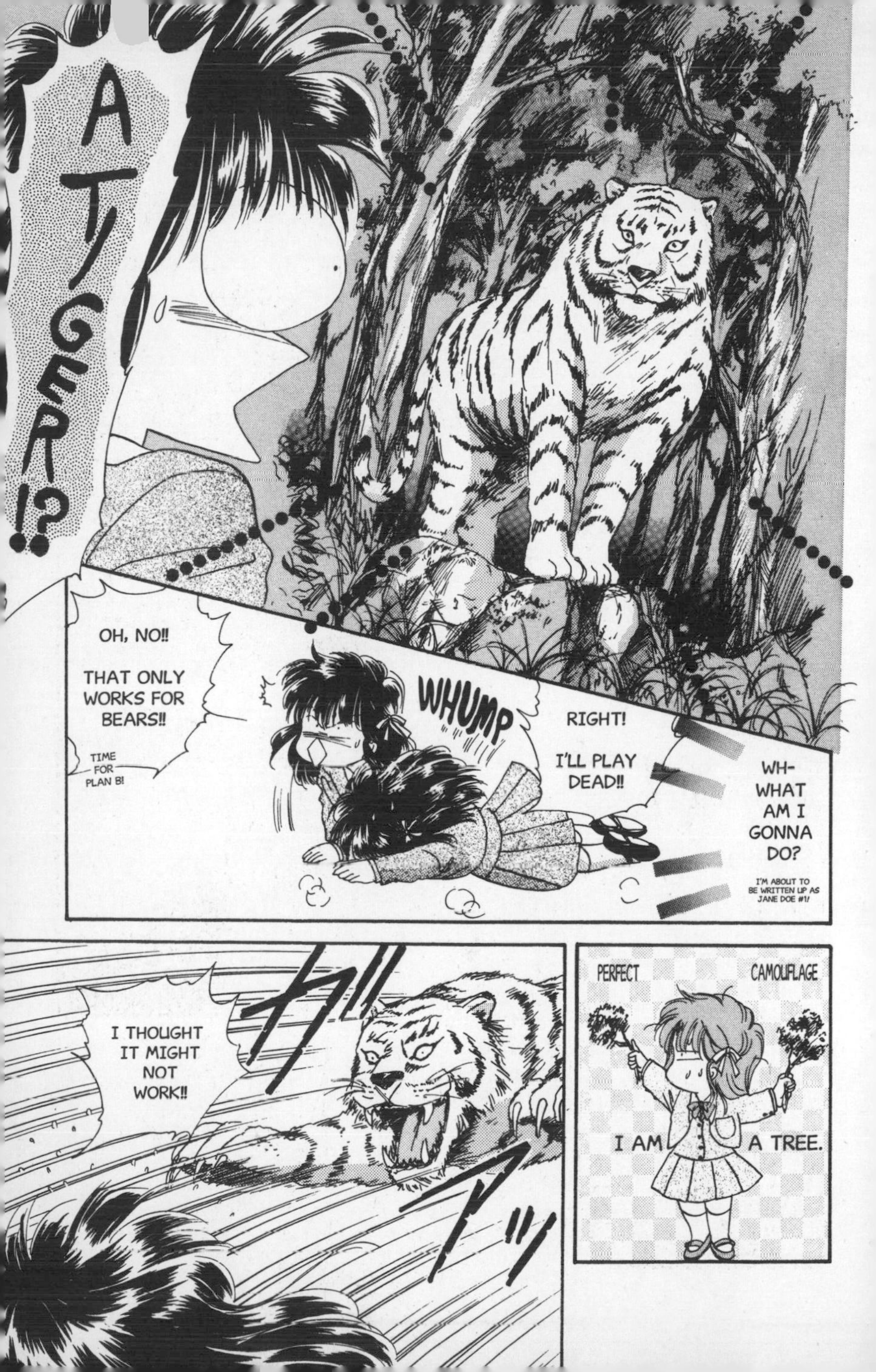
A TIGER!?
WH- WHAT AM I GONNA DO?
I'M ABOUT TO BE WRITTEN UP AS JANE DOE #1!
RIGHT! I'LL PLAY DEAD!!
WHUMP
OH, NO!! THAT ONLY WORKS FOR BEARS!!
TIME FOR PLAN B!
PERFECT CAMOUFLAGE
I AM A TREE.
I THOUGHT IT MIGHT NOT WORK!!

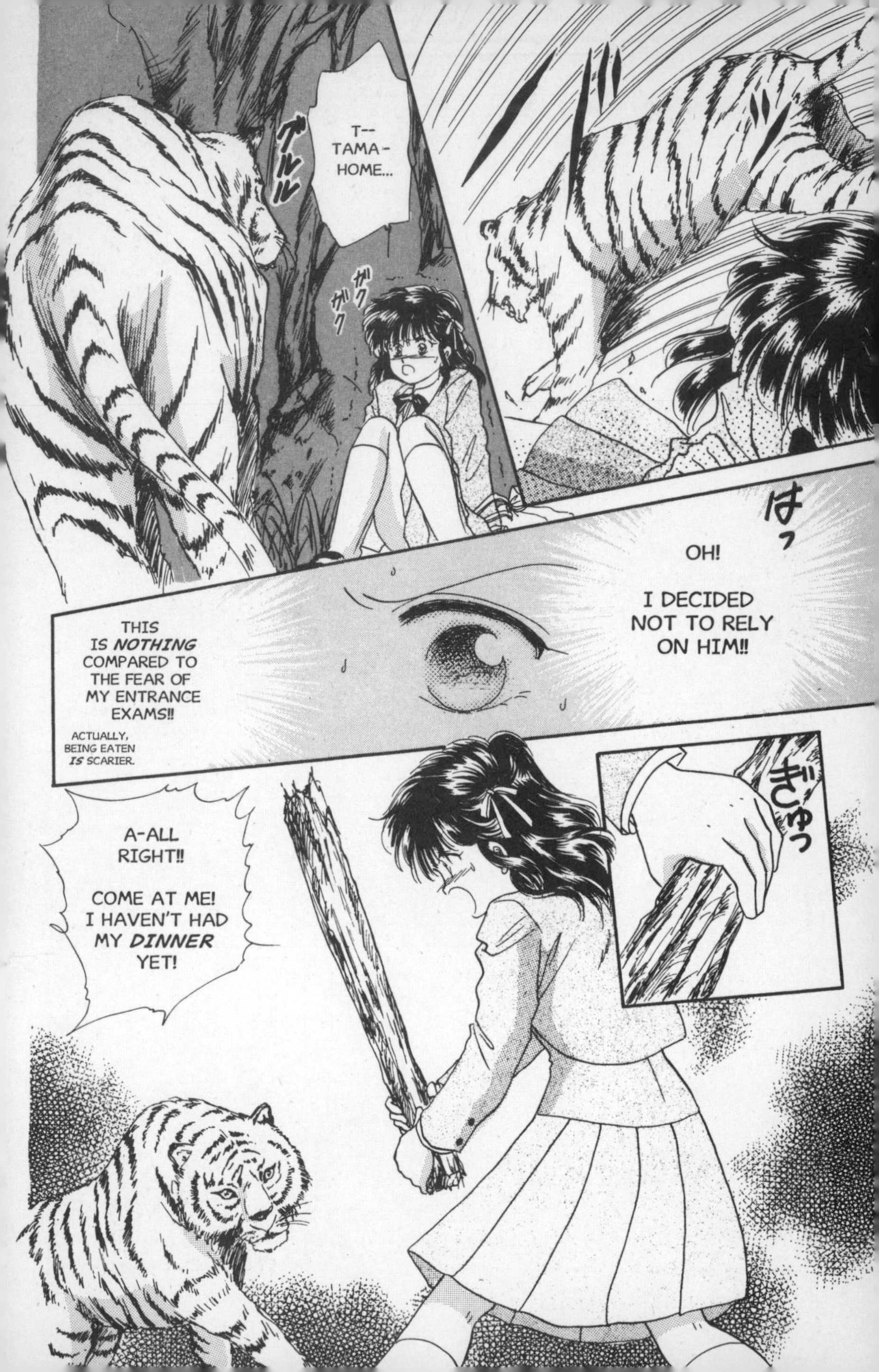

グルル
T-- TAMA-HOME...
ガクガク
はっ
OH!
I DECIDED NOT TO RELY ON HIM!!
THIS IS *NOTHING* COMPARED TO THE FEAR OF MY ENTRANCE EXAMS!!
ACTUALLY, BEING EATEN *IS* SCARIER.
ぎゅっ
A-ALL RIGHT!!
COME AT ME! I HAVEN'T HAD MY *DINNER* YET!

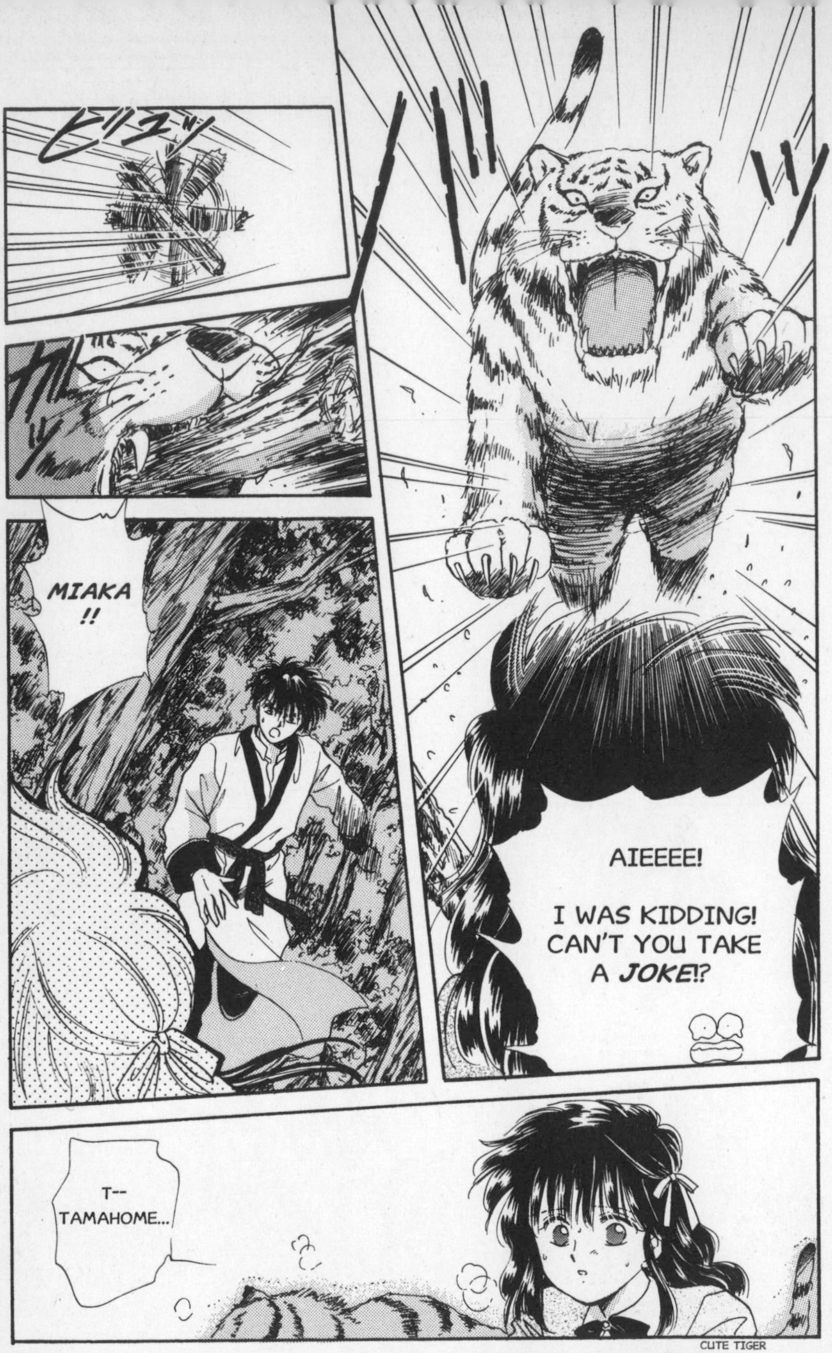
AIEEEE!
I WAS KIDDING! CAN'T YOU TAKE A ***JOKE***!?
MIAKA !!
T-- TAMAHOME...
CUTE TIGER

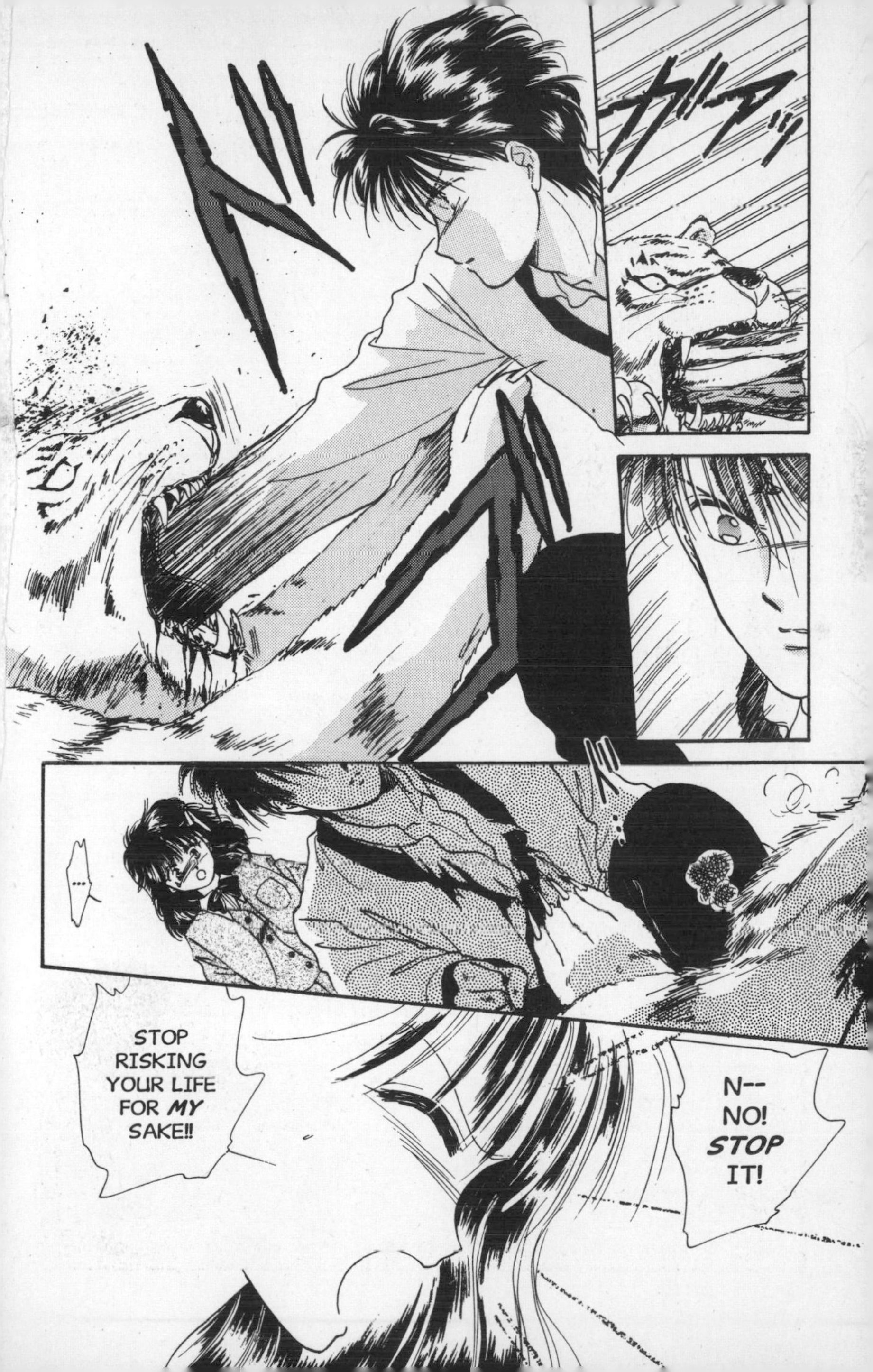
...
N-- NO! *STOP* IT!
STOP RISKING YOUR LIFE FOR *MY* SAKE!!

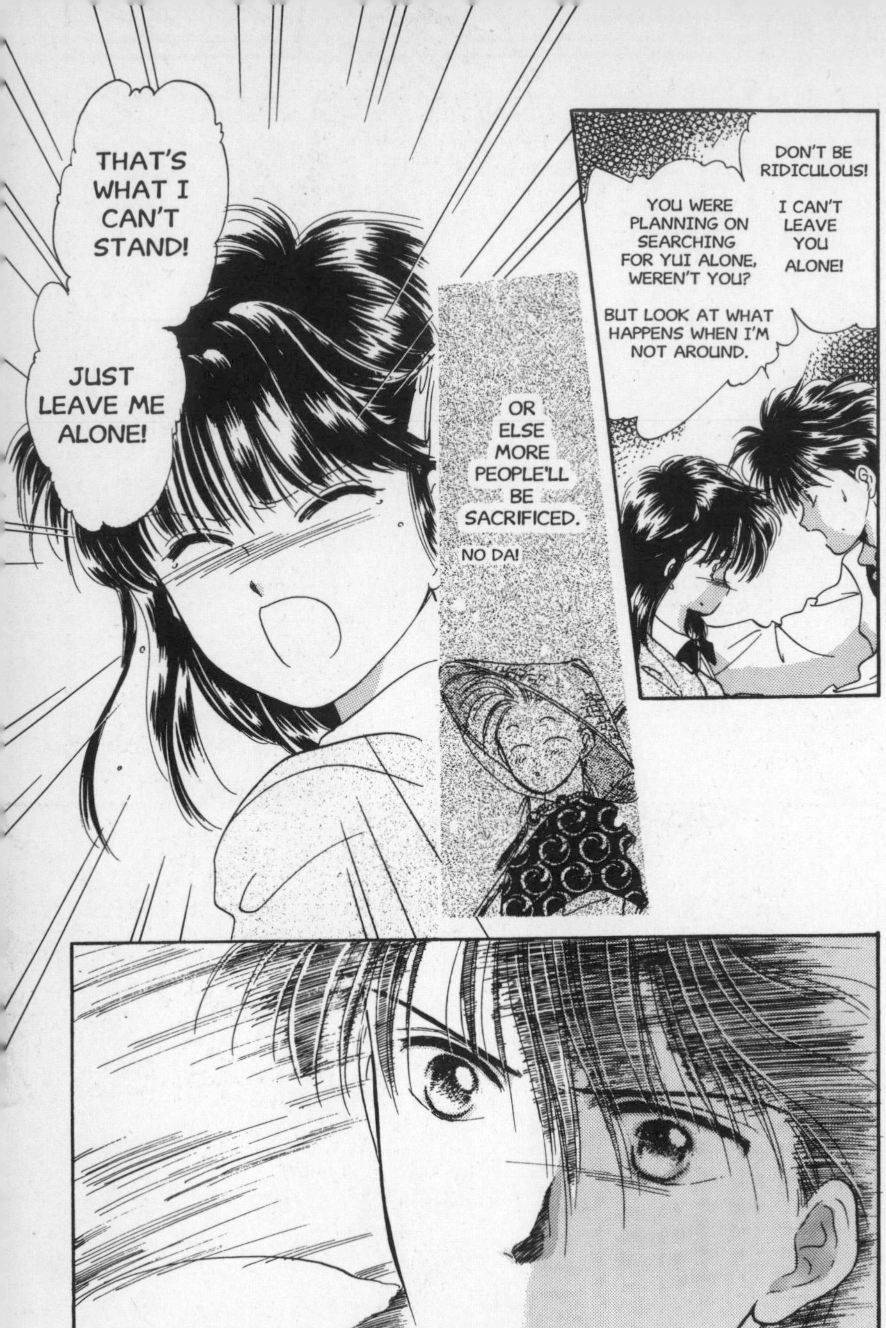
DON'T BE RIDICULOUS!
I CAN'T LEAVE YOU ALONE!
YOU WERE PLANNING ON SEARCHING FOR YUI ALONE, WEREN'T YOU?
BUT LOOK AT WHAT HAPPENS WHEN I'M NOT AROUND.
OR ELSE MORE PEOPLE'LL BE SACRIFICED.
NO DA!
THAT'S WHAT I CAN'T STAND!
JUST LEAVE ME ALONE!

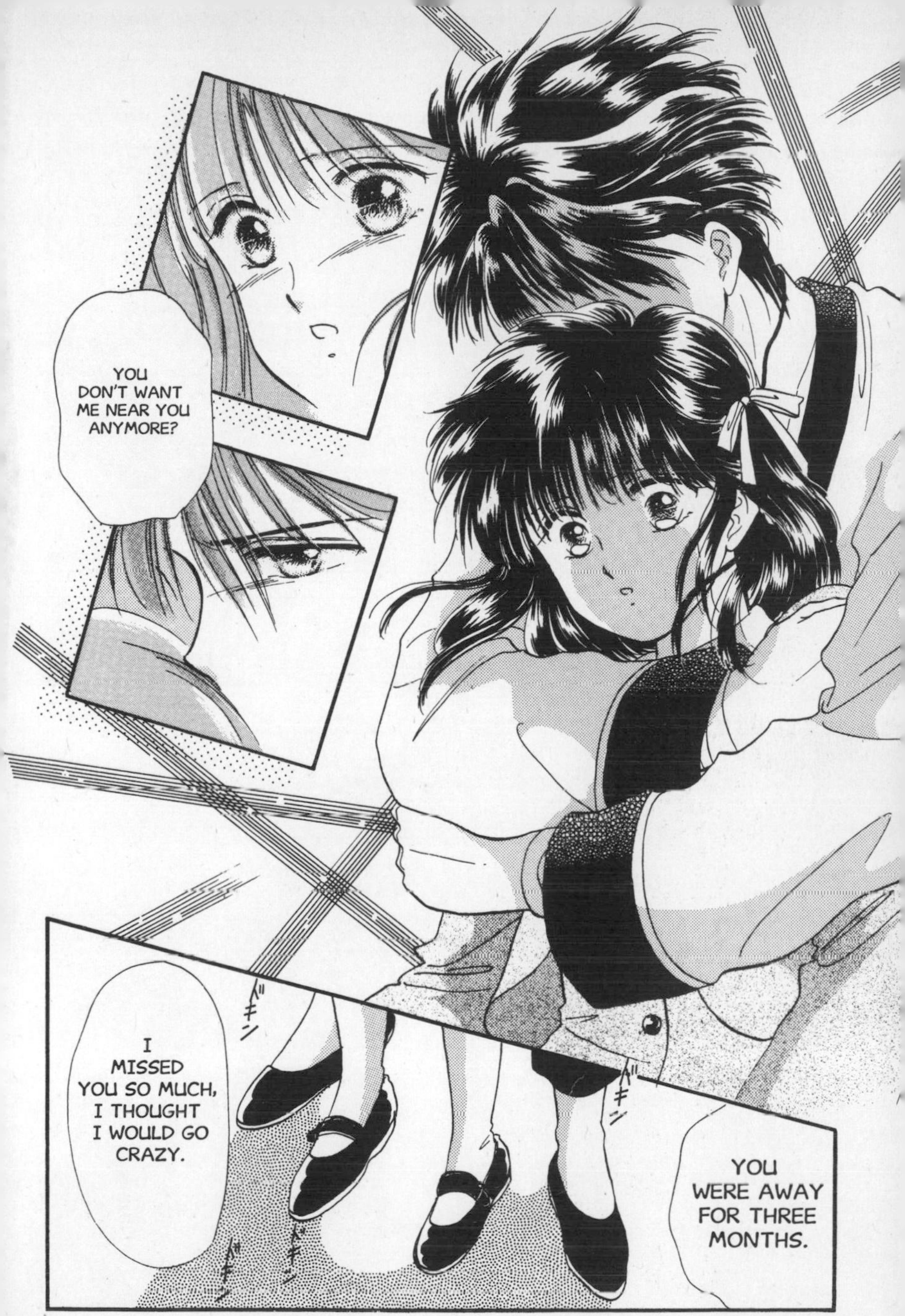
YOU DON'T WANT ME NEAR YOU ANYMORE?
YOU WERE AWAY FOR THREE MONTHS.
I MISSED YOU SO MUCH, I THOUGHT I WOULD GO CRAZY.

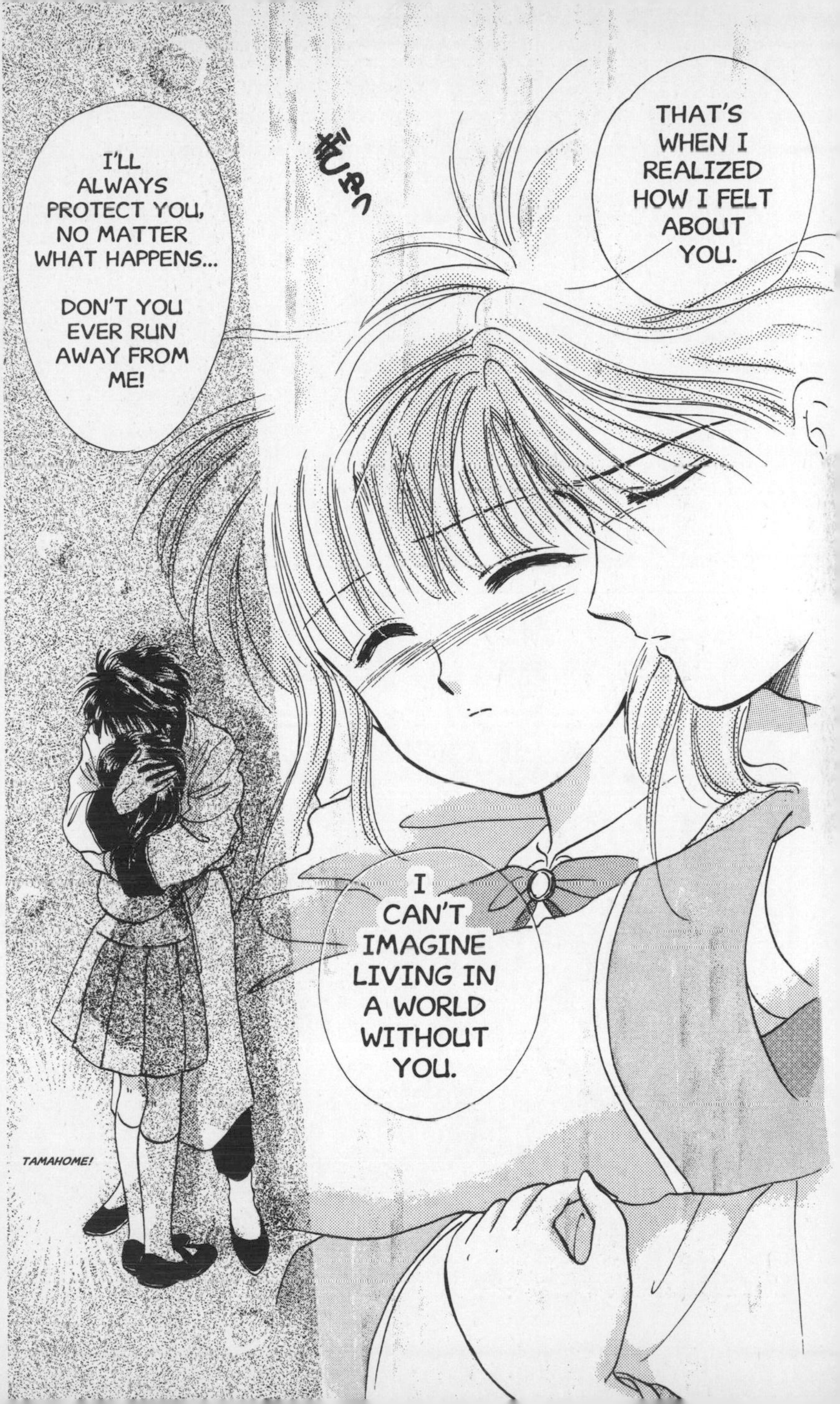
THAT'S WHEN I REALIZED HOW I FELT ABOUT YOU.
I CAN'T IMAGINE LIVING IN A WORLD WITHOUT YOU.
ぎゅっ
I'LL ALWAYS PROTECT YOU, NO MATTER WHAT HAPPENS... DON'T YOU EVER RUN AWAY FROM ME!
TAMAHOME!

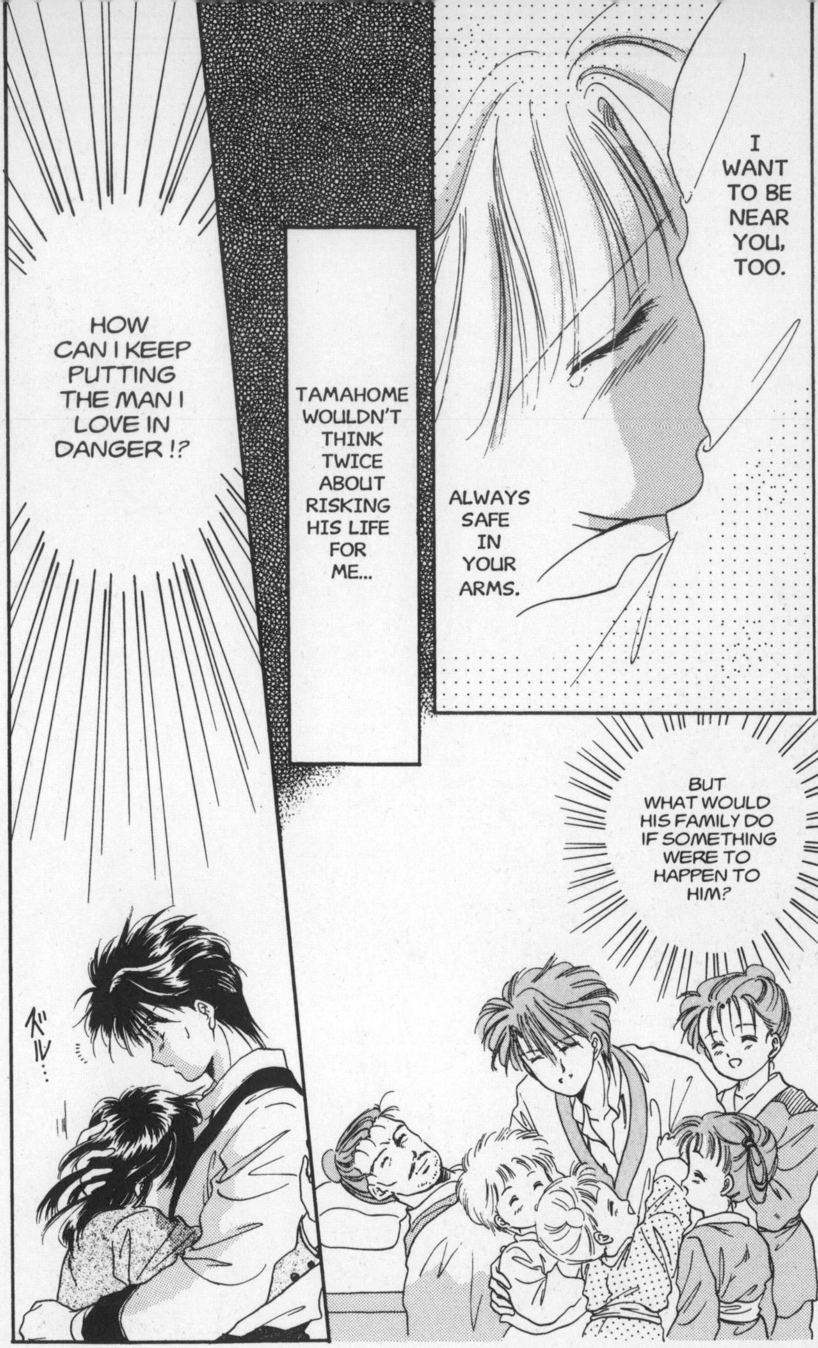
I WANT TO BE NEAR YOU, TOO.
ALWAYS SAFE IN YOUR ARMS.
TAMAHOME WOULDN'T THINK TWICE ABOUT RISKING HIS LIFE FOR ME...
BUT WHAT WOULD HIS FAMILY DO IF SOMETHING WERE TO HAPPEN TO HIM?
HOW CAN I KEEP PUTTING THE MAN I LOVE IN DANGER !?
ズル…

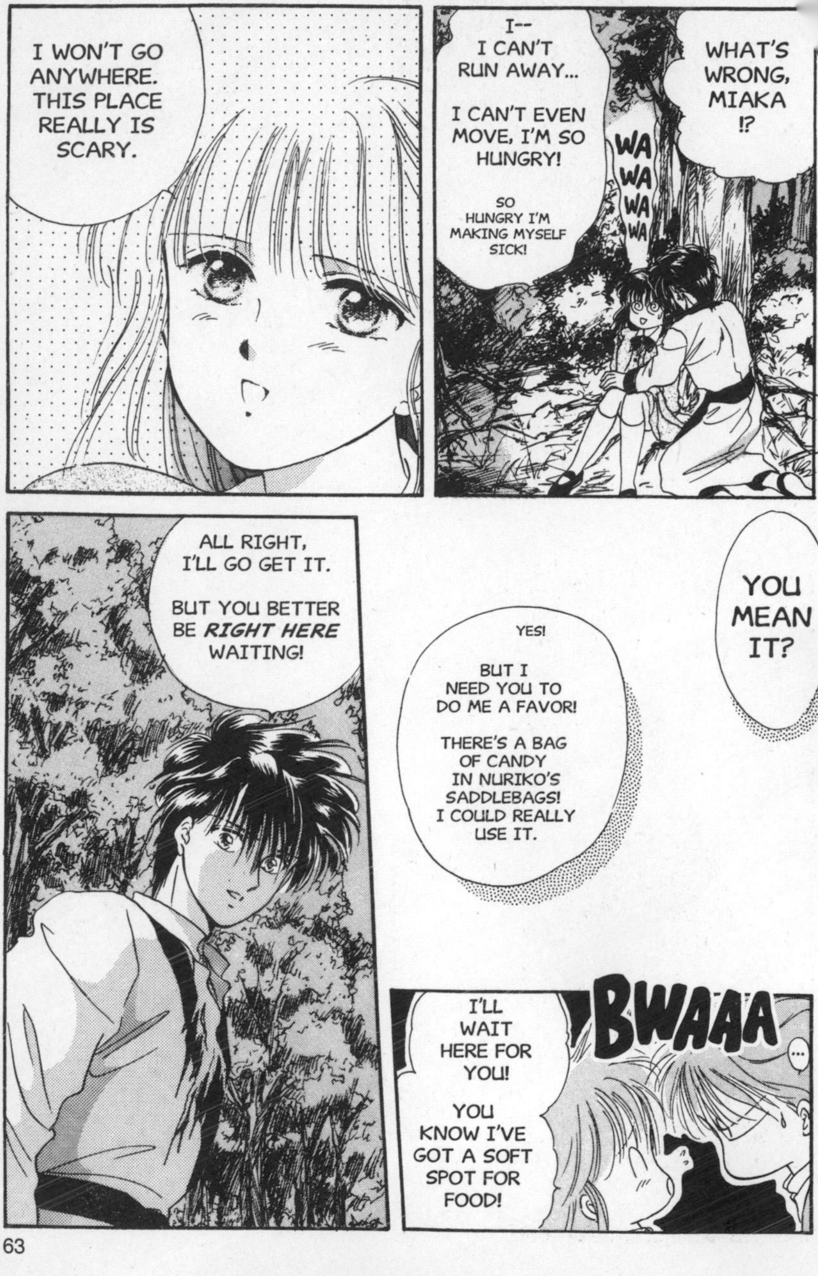
WHAT'S WRONG, MIAKA !?
I-- I CAN'T RUN AWAY...
I CAN'T EVEN MOVE, I'M SO HUNGRY!
WA WA WA WA
SO HUNGRY I'M MAKING MYSELF SICK!
I WON'T GO ANYWHERE. THIS PLACE REALLY IS SCARY.
YOU MEAN IT?
YES!
BUT I NEED YOU TO DO ME A FAVOR!
THERE'S A BAG OF CANDY IN NURIKO'S SADDLEBAGS! I COULD REALLY USE IT.
ALL RIGHT, I'LL GO GET IT.
BUT YOU BETTER BE *RIGHT HERE* WAITING!
BWAAA
...
I'LL WAIT HERE FOR YOU!
YOU KNOW I'VE GOT A SOFT SPOT FOR FOOD!

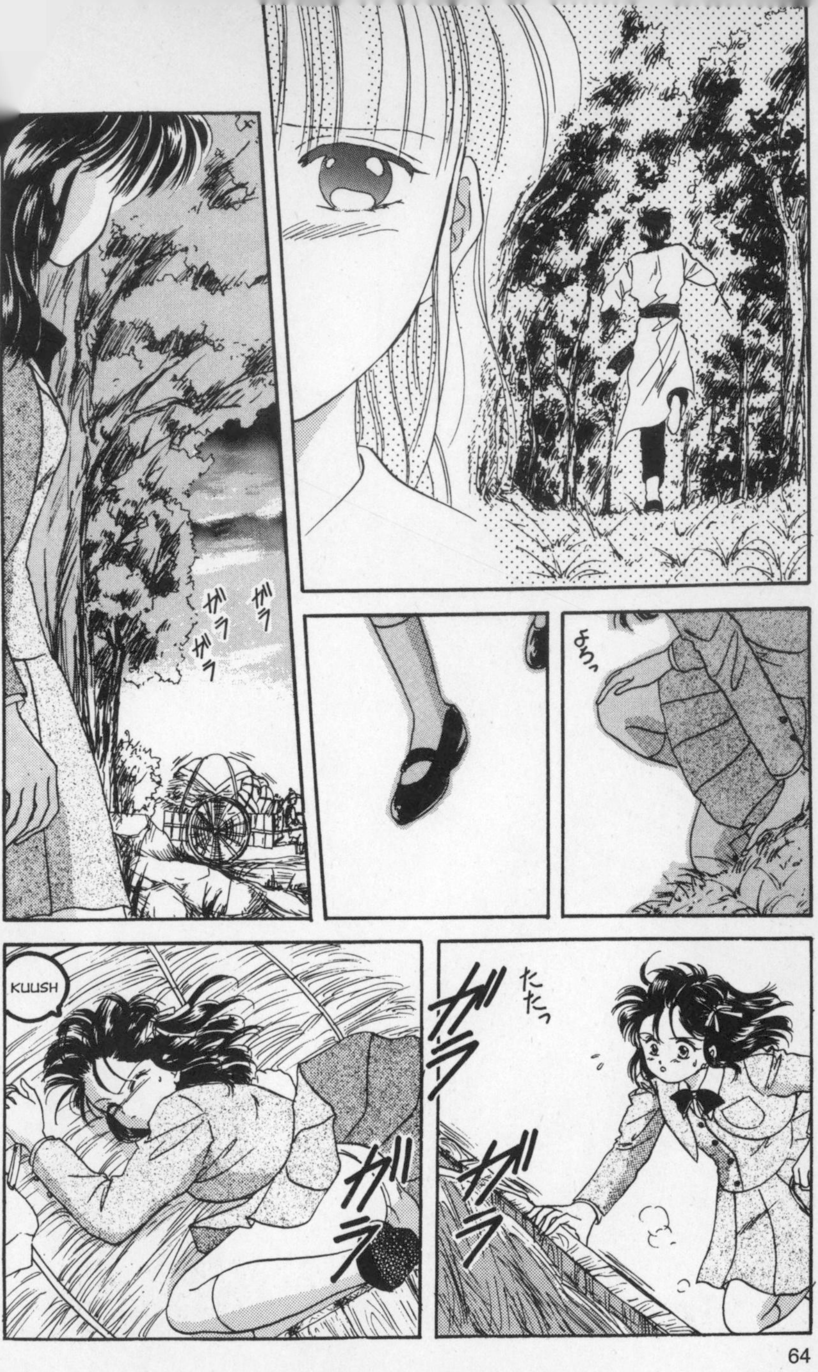
よろっ
ガラ
ガラ
ガラ
たたっ
ガラ
ガラ
KUUSH
ガラ

I'M SORRY, TAMAHOME.

I *HAVE* TO FIND YUI.

IT'S A MATTER OF FRIEND-SHIP.

Xong Gui Siu
琮 鬼 宿

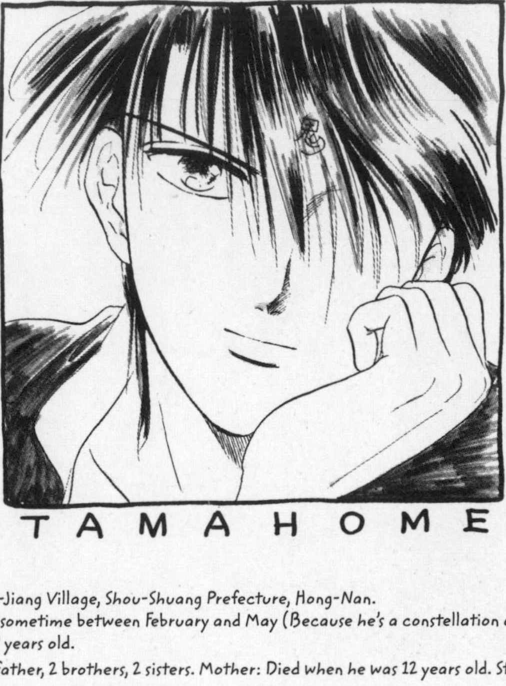

Cancer

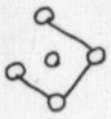

T A M A H O M E

- Born in Bai-Jiang Village, Shou-Shuang Prefecture, Hong-Nan.
  Birthday is sometime between February and May (Because he's a constellation of Suzaku).
  Presently 17 years old.
- Relations: father, 2 brothers, 2 sisters. Mother: Died when he was 12 years old. Strengths: Martial arts (A natural-born talent)
- Height: 5'9" Blood type: O Hobby: Making money
- Eldest son taking the place of his ill father to support his family. Whatta great big brother! He's very caring, but at the same time, he can cause a lot of trouble for others. But everyone cuts him a break. On the outside, he is very chipper, and that leads to some comic expressions. But he's tough on the inside (so he thinks). On the other hand, he is very shy. (He had to become stoic for his family's sake.) That's why he was hard on Miaka in the first issue. Sacrifices himself for the sake of others, and won't back down against an enemy.

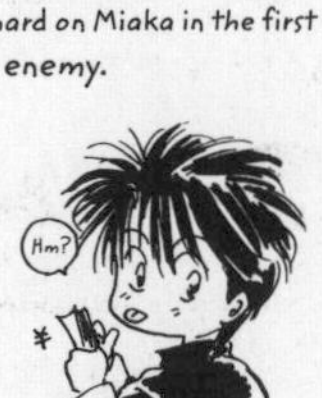
Hm?

It looks like you've all become accustomed to the Tamahome with short hair, but have you noticed how his hair's grown since graphic novel #2? My assistants and I complain about how none of the readers wrote in concerning it.

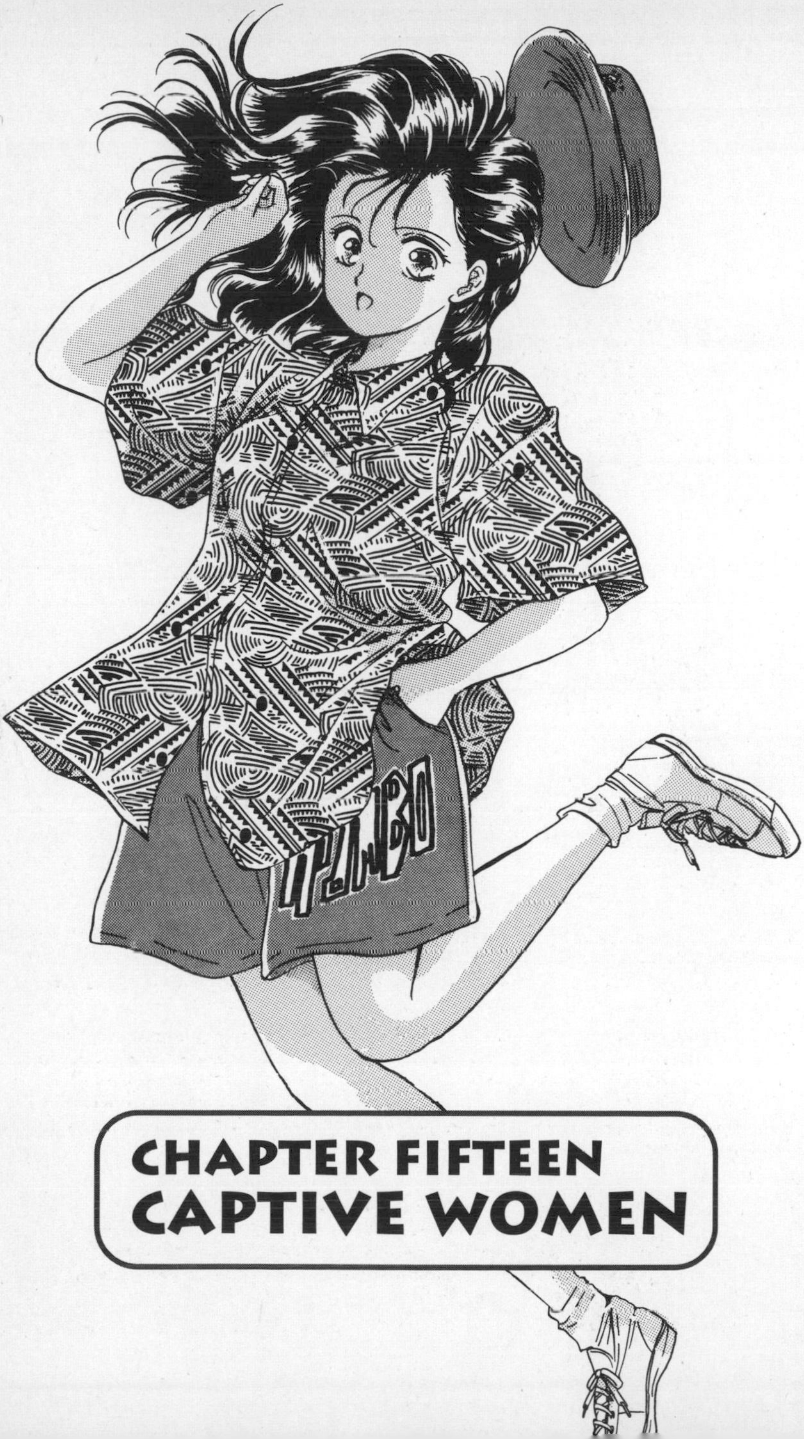

CHAPTER FIFTEEN
CAPTIVE WOMEN

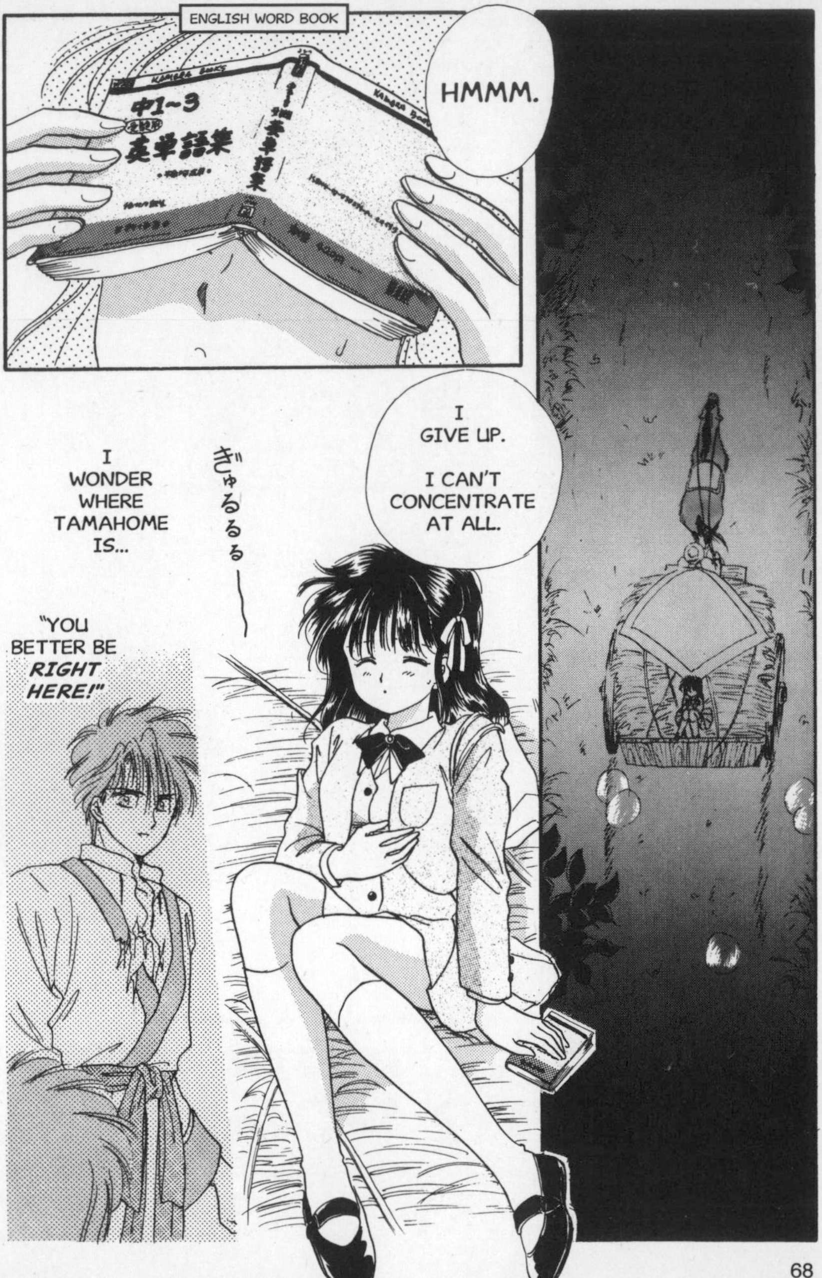
HMMM.
ENGLISH WORD BOOK
中1~3
英単語集
I GIVE UP.
I CAN'T CONCENTRATE AT ALL.
ぎゅるるる
I WONDER WHERE TAMAHOME IS...
"YOU BETTER BE *RIGHT HERE!*"

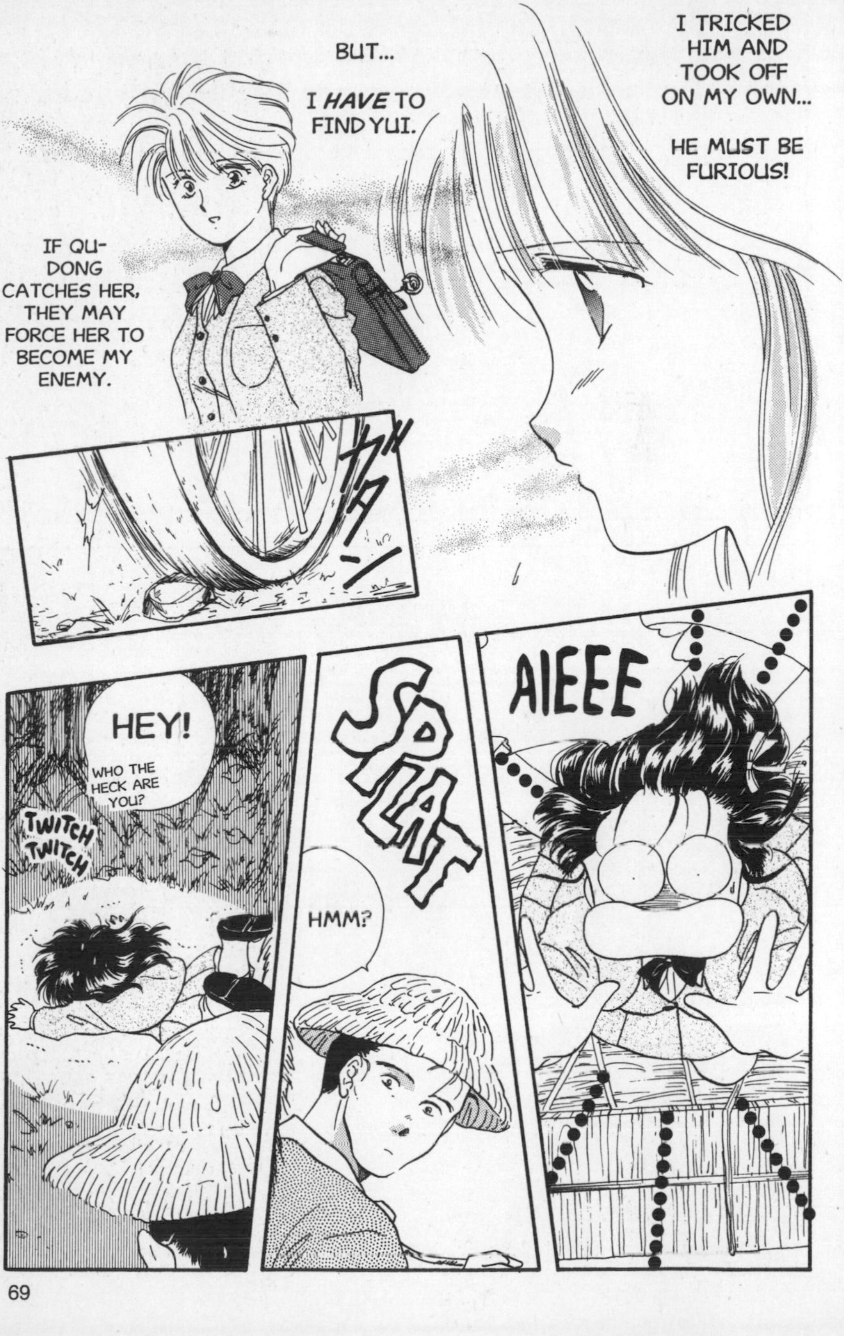
I TRICKED HIM AND TOOK OFF ON MY OWN...
HE MUST BE FURIOUS!
BUT...
I *HAVE* TO FIND YUI.
IF QU-DONG CATCHES HER, THEY MAY FORCE HER TO BECOME MY ENEMY.
AIEEE
SPLAT
HMM?
HEY!
WHO THE HECK ARE YOU?
TWITCH TWITCH

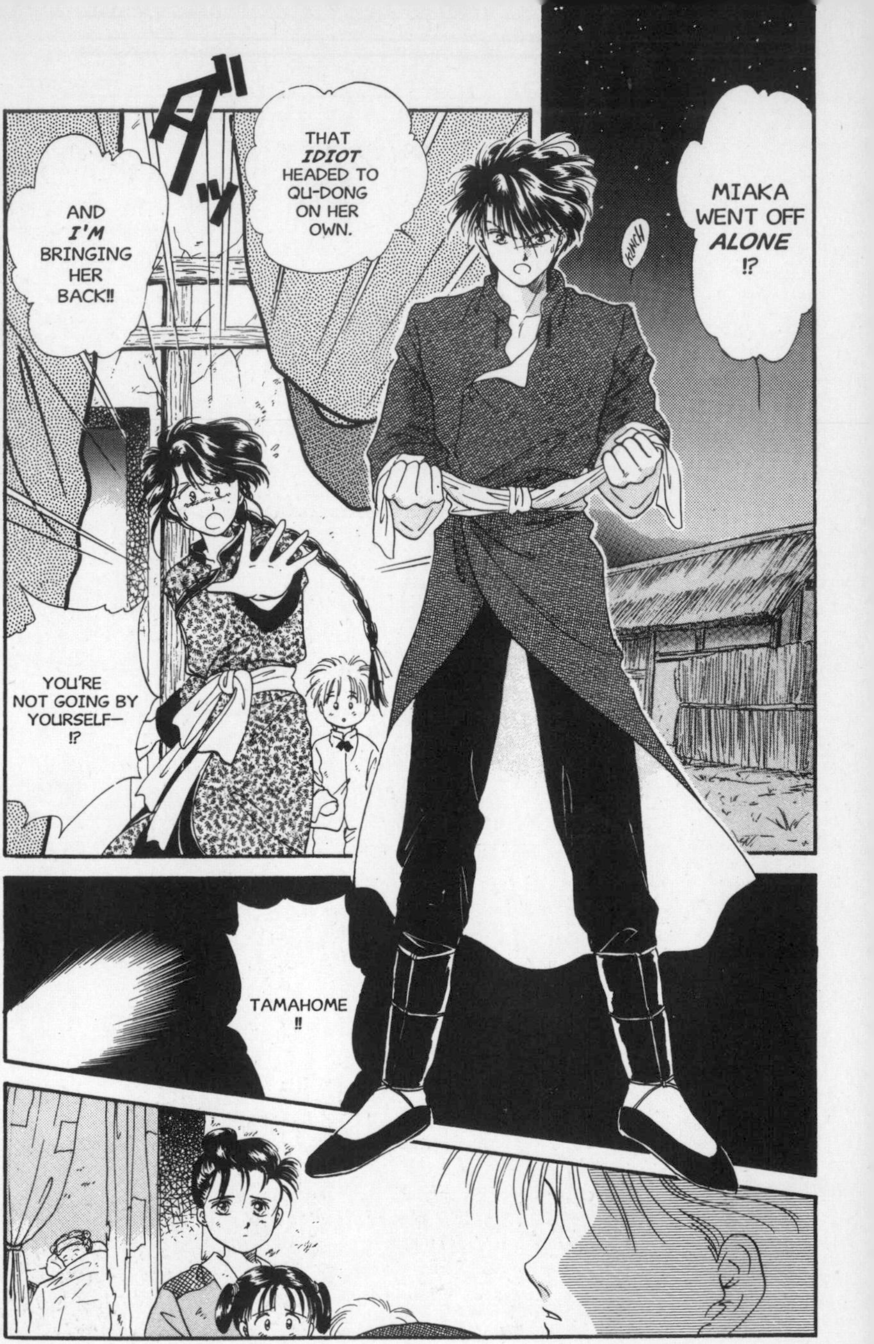
MIAKA WENT OFF *ALONE* !?
KINCH
THAT *IDIOT* HEADED TO QU-DONG ON HER OWN.
AND *I'M* BRINGING HER BACK!!
YOU'RE NOT GOING BY YOURSELF— !?
TAMAHOME !!

I was so busy this year, I wasn't able to go home for the annual festival. But much to my amazement, even though I was in Tokyo, the festivals were given a lot of coverage on TV!! I used to think my area was the middle of the boonies, but I guess it's becoming famous. But I couldn't look when one of the ceremonial wagons went crashing into a telephone pole, killing seven people! Things were out of control! What's going on Kishi---da!? (Must remain anonymous.)

If I'd gone home, I would've been both furious and terrified. But I have no problem watching it on TV.
Hmm. Maybe I should have promoted myself more when I lived there. (Promoted what!?) My little brother really wanted to go back, but my mom isn't too thrilled with the idea. (She's scared.)

My parents were born in Osaka so they're not actually from the town. But the minute I hear the sound of those taiko drums, it starts my blood flowing.

When I was a senior in high school, I always went to the festival wearing a happi coat, but I didn't pull the float. Now guys look pretty good in happi coats. The designs vary from town to town, but our town's design was simple (white lettering on black cloth). The whole town preferred that festival even to New Year's. Town natives who moved away to places over the country take vacations to come home for the festival. (I didn't. Sorry!) They even close down the grade schools for it. Amazing, really! The downtown district has its festival in September, and the uptown district has its in October. The uptown kids (like me) had vacation days for both.
The year after I moved to Tokyo when I came back for the festival, my cousin (♀) was pulling the float when she fell, but she held onto the rope for a couple dozen meters. Even though she was scraped and bleeding, she caught her feet and still helped out. If you let go of the rope, you get run over by the float, so you can't let go even if you fall. Of course, some of the older guys act as guardians to save you in case of an accident. It can be scary.
Anyway, a lot of famous people are from the area. Kiyohara of the Seibu Lions, the designers, the Koshinos (former neighbors of mine) and a few actors.... I'm the first manga artist to come from there (I think).

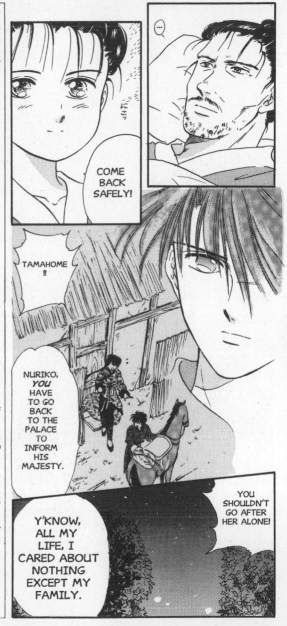

I'll go back next year!

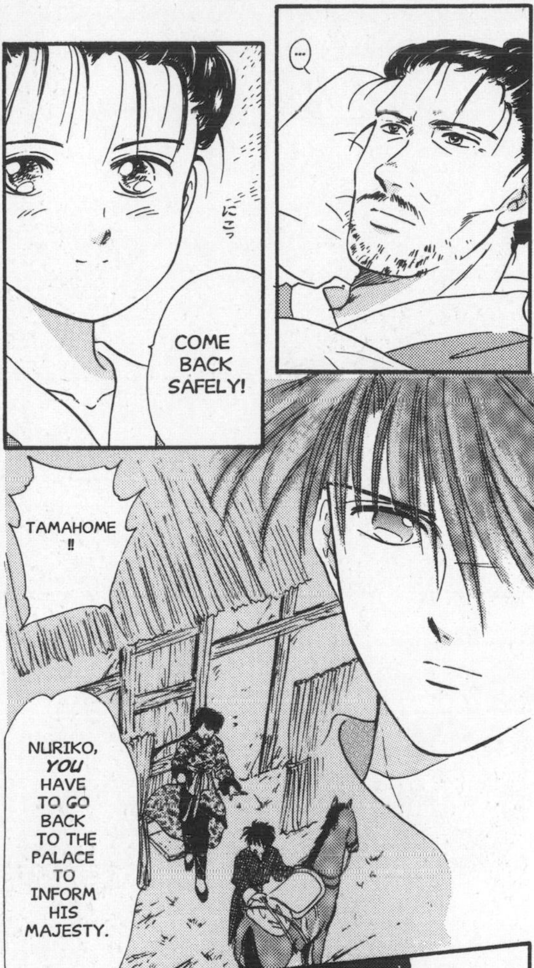
...
にこっ
COME BACK SAFELY!
TAMAHOME !!
NURIKO, *YOU* HAVE TO GO BACK TO THE PALACE TO INFORM HIS MAJESTY.
YOU SHOULDN'T GO AFTER HER ALONE!
Y'KNOW, ALL MY LIFE, I CARED ABOUT NOTHING EXCEPT MY FAMILY.

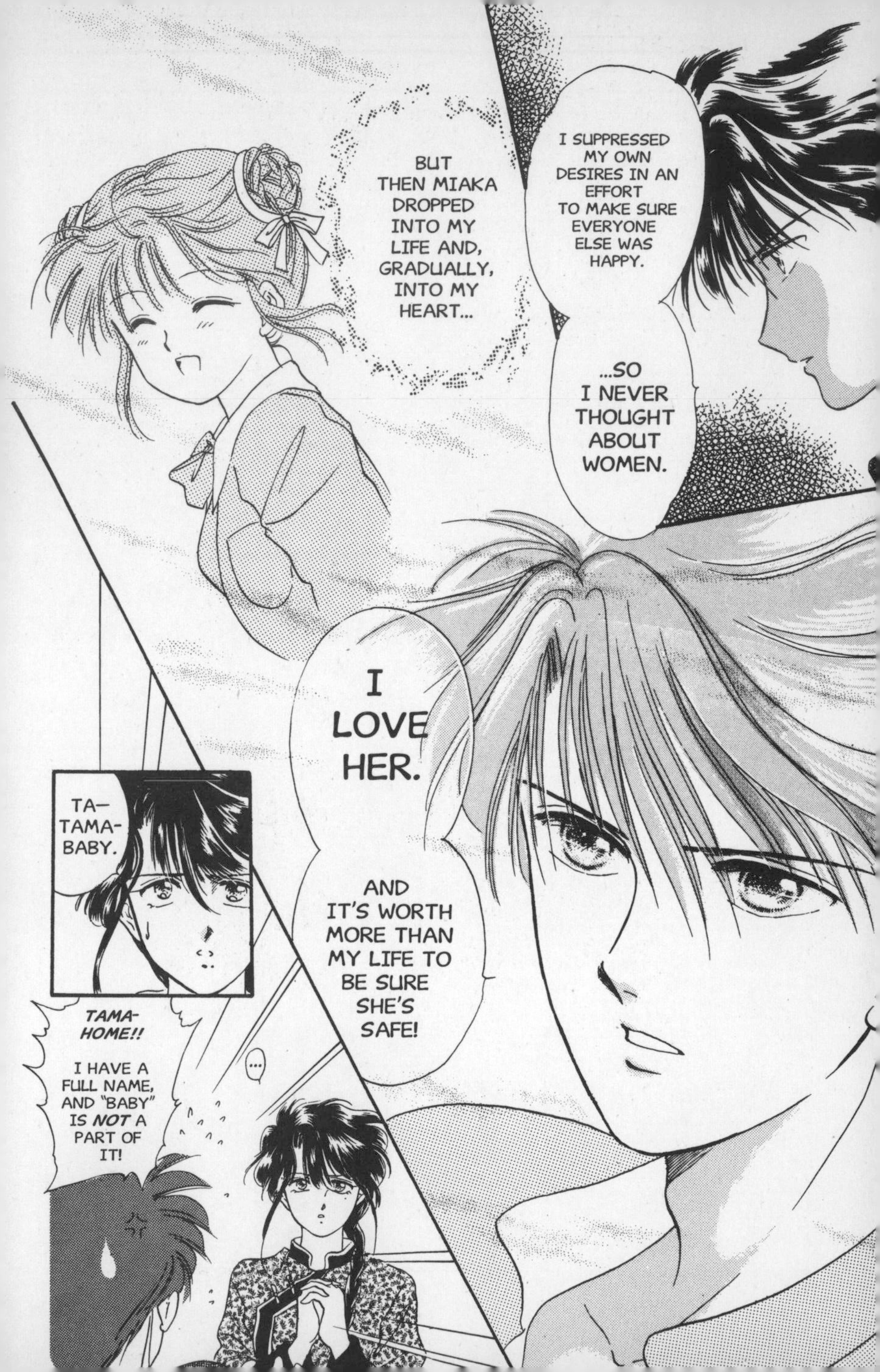
I SUPPRESSED MY OWN DESIRES IN AN EFFORT TO MAKE SURE EVERYONE ELSE WAS HAPPY.
...SO I NEVER THOUGHT ABOUT WOMEN.
BUT THEN MIAKA DROPPED INTO MY LIFE AND, GRADUALLY, INTO MY HEART...
I LOVE HER.
AND IT'S WORTH MORE THAN MY LIFE TO BE SURE SHE'S SAFE!
TA— TAMA-BABY.
TAMA-HOME!!
I HAVE A FULL NAME, AND "BABY" IS *NOT* A PART OF IT!
...

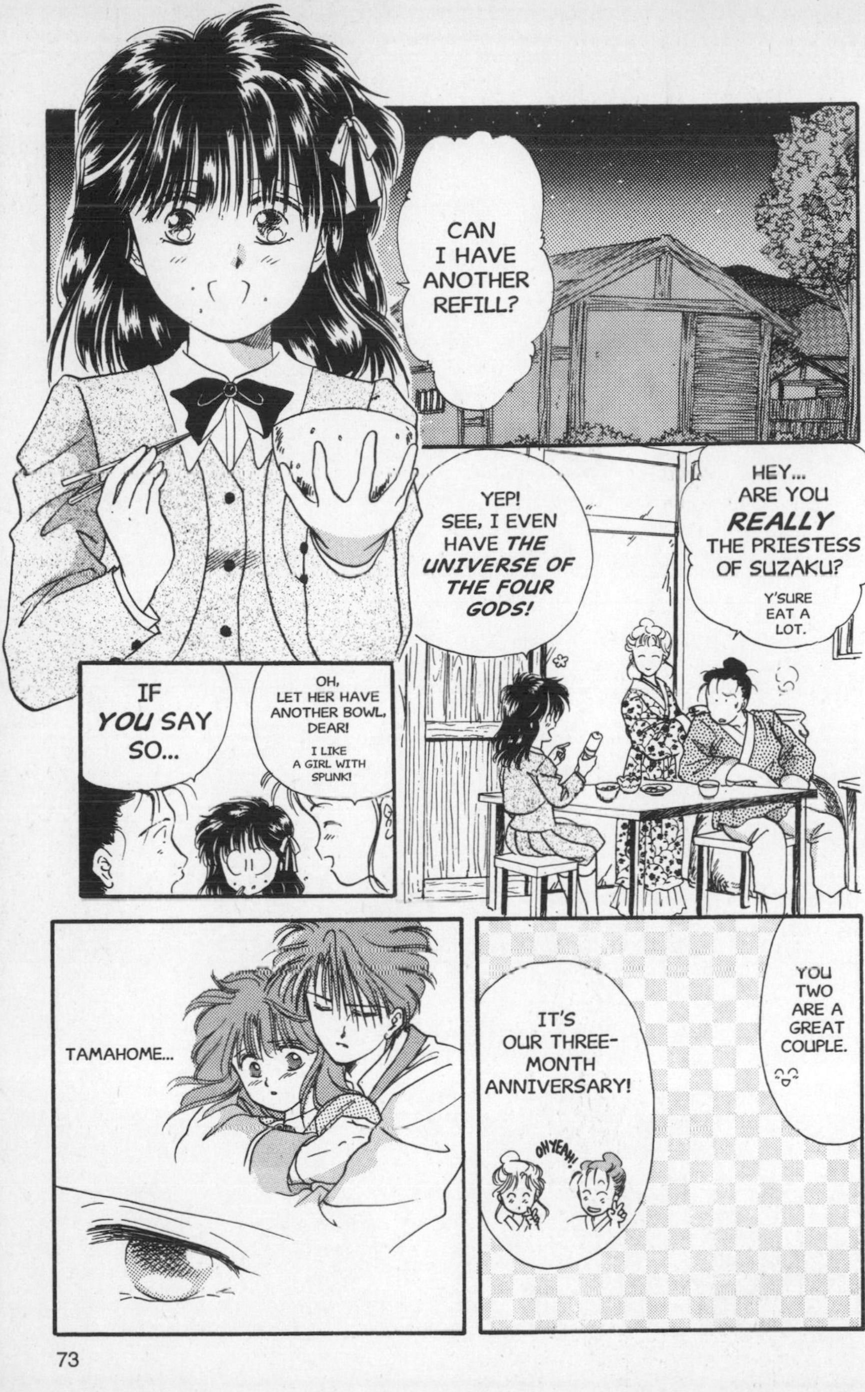
CAN I HAVE ANOTHER REFILL?
HEY... ARE YOU *REALLY* THE PRIESTESS OF SUZAKU?
Y'SURE EAT A LOT.
YEP! SEE, I EVEN HAVE *THE UNIVERSE OF THE FOUR GODS!*
OH, LET HER HAVE ANOTHER BOWL, DEAR!
I LIKE A GIRL WITH SPUNK!
IF *YOU* SAY SO...
YOU TWO ARE A GREAT COUPLE.
IT'S OUR THREE-MONTH ANNIVERSARY!
OH YEAH!
TAMAHOME...

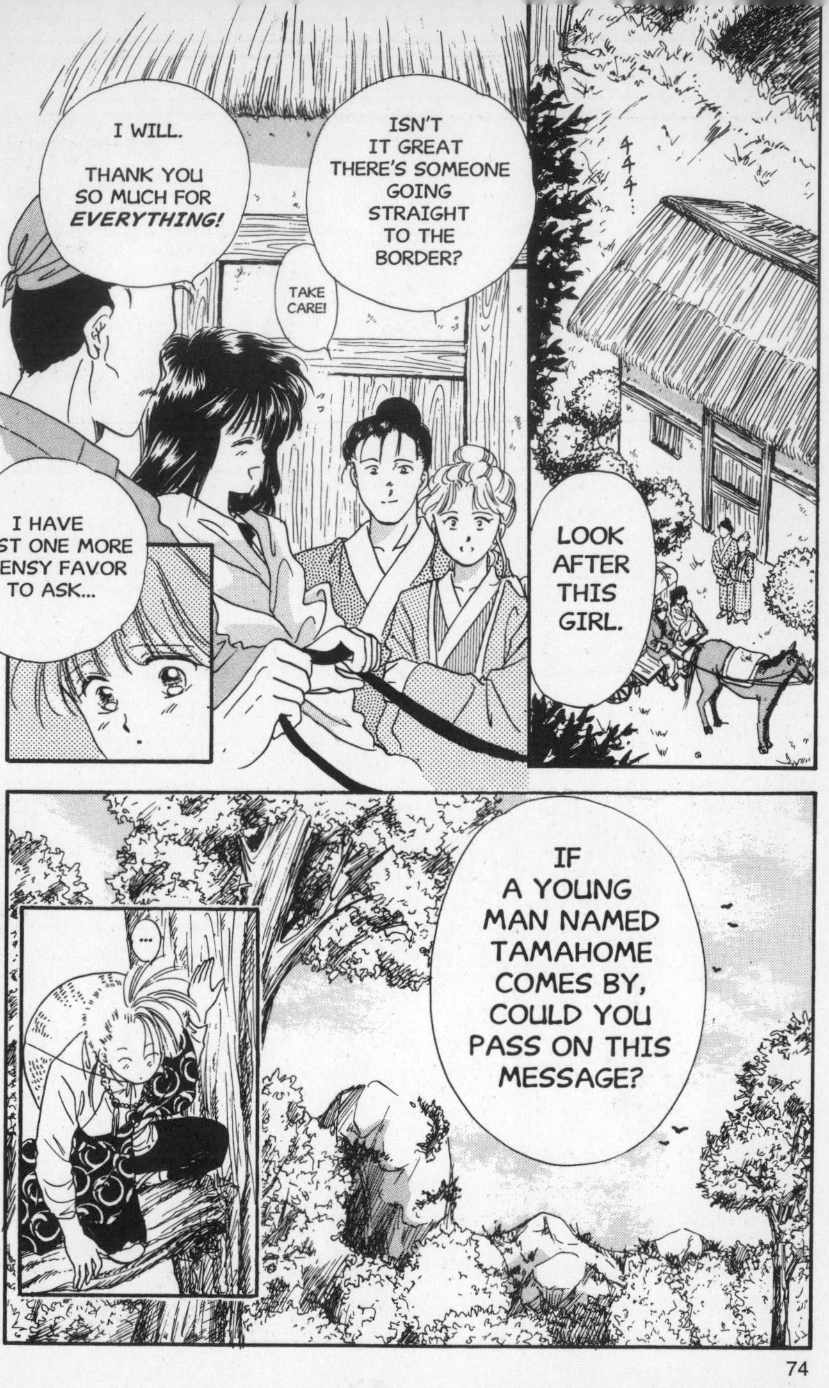
LOOK AFTER THIS GIRL.
ISN'T IT GREAT THERE'S SOMEONE GOING STRAIGHT TO THE BORDER?
TAKE CARE!
I WILL. THANK YOU SO MUCH FOR *EVERYTHING!*
I HAVE JUST ONE MORE TEENSY FAVOR TO ASK...
IF A YOUNG MAN NAMED TAMAHOME COMES BY, COULD YOU PASS ON THIS MESSAGE?
...

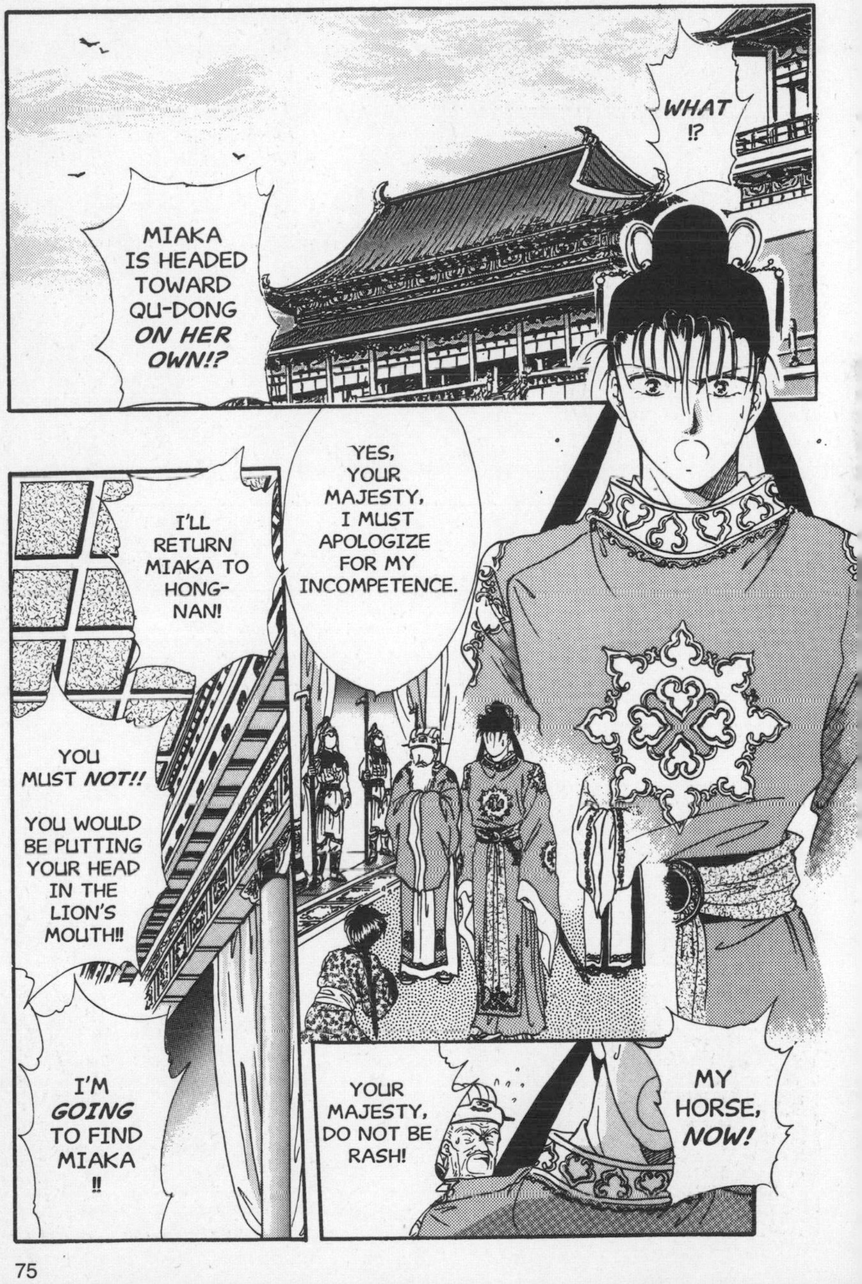
WHAT!?
MIAKA IS HEADED TOWARD QU-DONG ON HER OWN!?
YES, YOUR MAJESTY, I MUST APOLOGIZE FOR MY INCOMPETENCE.
I'LL RETURN MIAKA TO HONG-NAN!
YOU MUST NOT!!
YOU WOULD BE PUTTING YOUR HEAD IN THE LION'S MOUTH!!
I'M GOING TO FIND MIAKA!!
MY HORSE, NOW!
YOUR MAJESTY, DO NOT BE RASH!

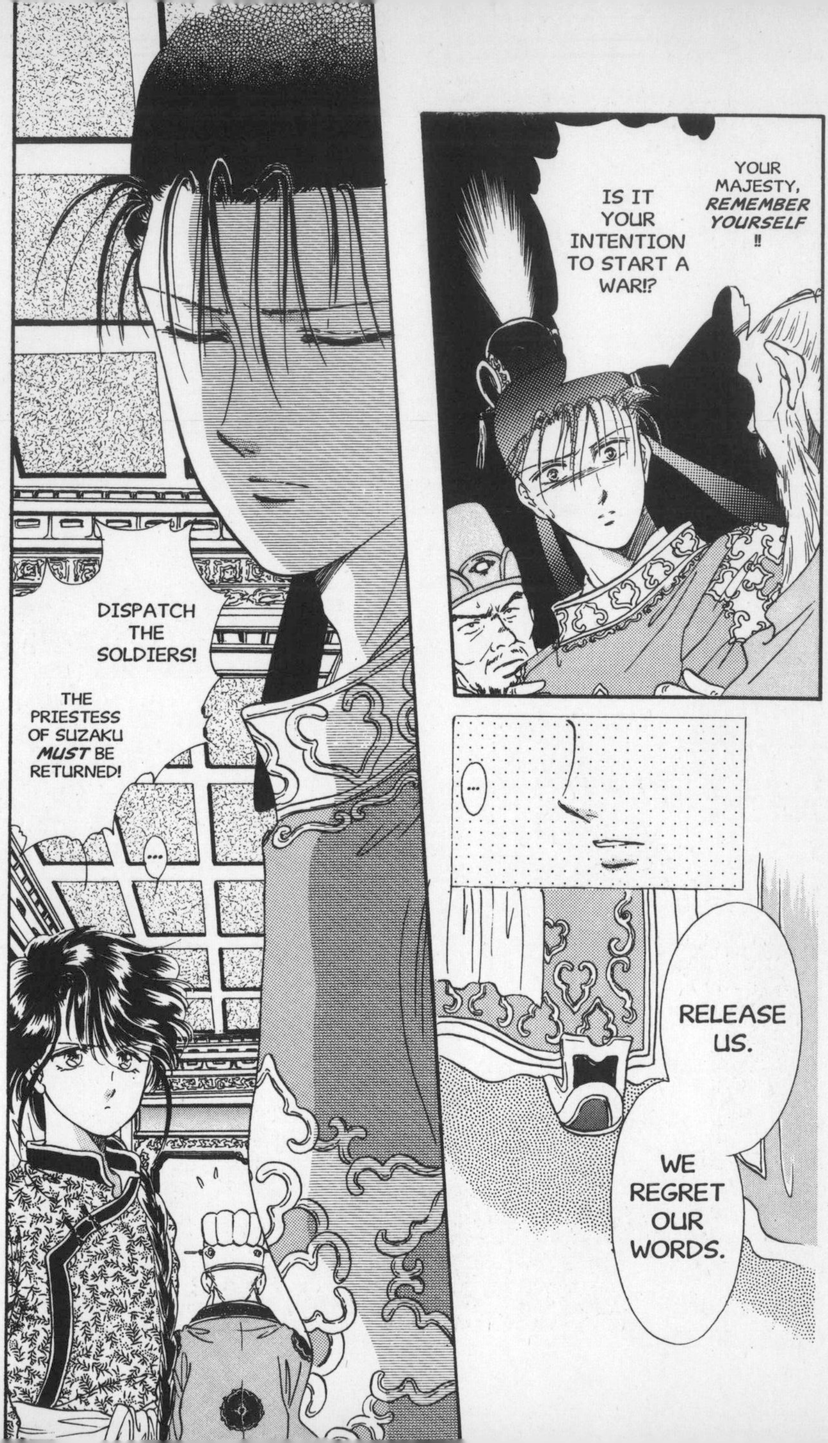
YOUR MAJESTY, *REMEMBER YOURSELF* !!
IS IT YOUR INTENTION TO START A WAR!?
...
RELEASE US.
WE REGRET OUR WORDS.
DISPATCH THE SOLDIERS!
THE PRIESTESS OF SUZAKU *MUST* BE RETURNED!
...

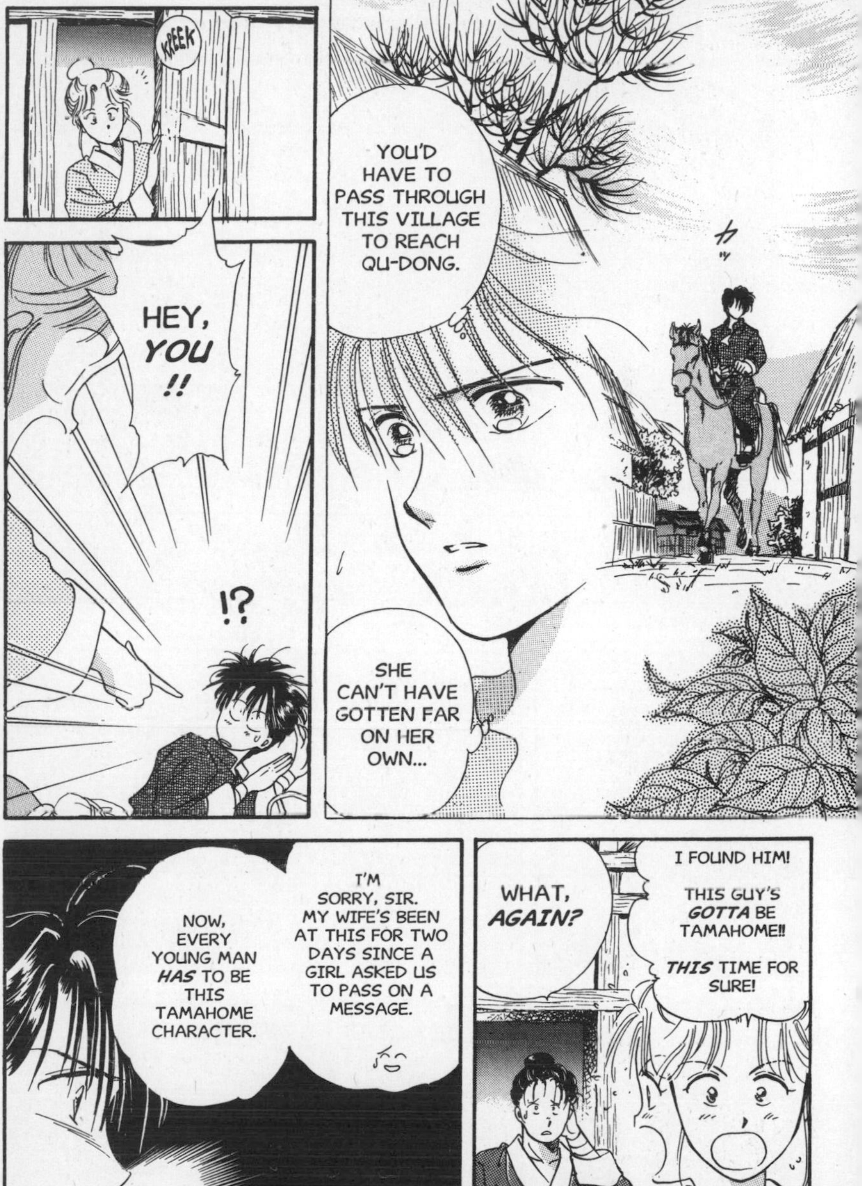
YOU'D HAVE TO PASS THROUGH THIS VILLAGE TO REACH QU-DONG.
カッ
SHE CAN'T HAVE GOTTEN FAR ON HER OWN...
KREEK
HEY, *YOU* !!
!?
I FOUND HIM!
THIS GUY'S *GOTTA* BE TAMAHOME!!
THIS TIME FOR SURE!
WHAT, *AGAIN?*
I'M SORRY, SIR. MY WIFE'S BEEN AT THIS FOR TWO DAYS SINCE A GIRL ASKED US TO PASS ON A MESSAGE.
NOW, EVERY YOUNG MAN *HAS* TO BE THIS TAMAHOME CHARACTER.

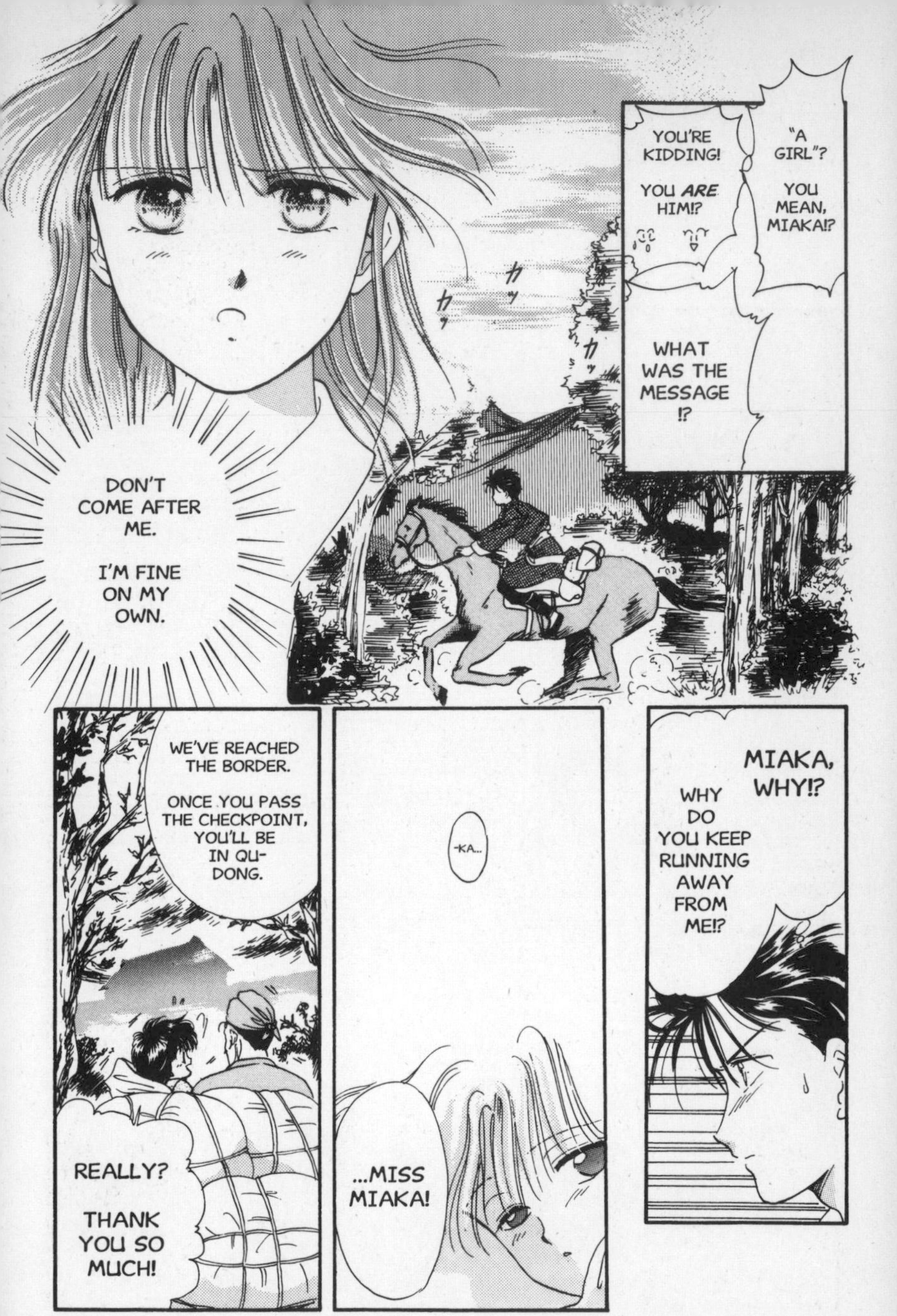
"A GIRL"? YOU MEAN, MIAKA!?
YOU'RE KIDDING! YOU *ARE* HIM!?
WHAT WAS THE MESSAGE !?
カッ
カッ
カッ
DON'T COME AFTER ME. I'M FINE ON MY OWN.
MIAKA, WHY!?
WHY DO YOU KEEP RUNNING AWAY FROM ME!?
-KA...
...MISS MIAKA!
WE'VE REACHED THE BORDER. ONCE YOU PASS THE CHECKPOINT, YOU'LL BE IN QU-DONG.
REALLY? THANK YOU SO MUCH!

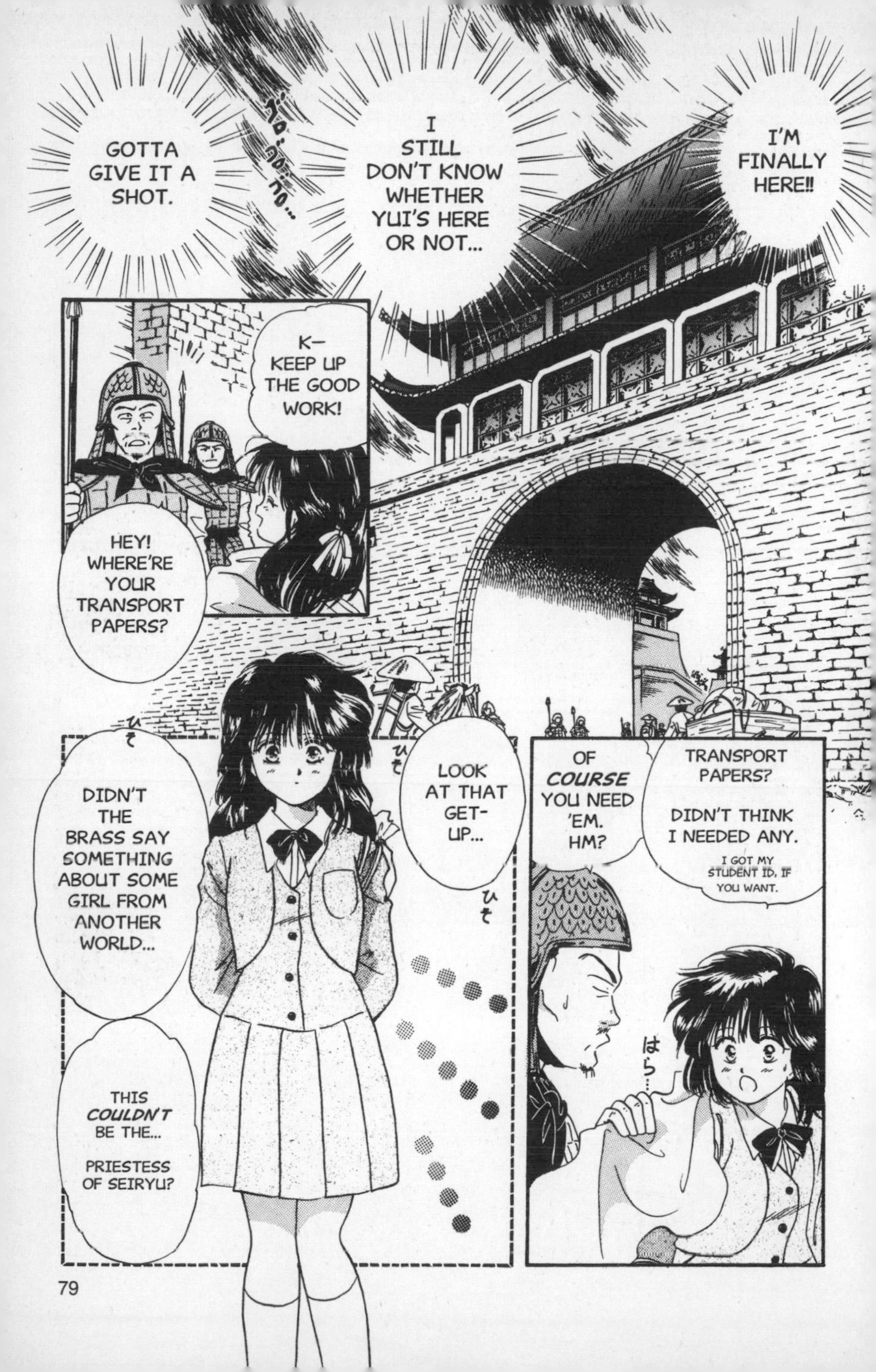
I'M FINALLY HERE!!
I STILL DON'T KNOW WHETHER YUI'S HERE OR NOT...
GOTTA GIVE IT A SHOT.
K— KEEP UP THE GOOD WORK!
HEY! WHERE'RE YOUR TRANSPORT PAPERS?
TRANSPORT PAPERS? DIDN'T THINK I NEEDED ANY.
I GOT MY STUDENT ID, IF YOU WANT.
OF *COURSE* YOU NEED 'EM. HM?
はら…
ひそ
ひそ
LOOK AT THAT GET-UP...
ひそ
DIDN'T THE BRASS SAY SOMETHING ABOUT SOME GIRL FROM ANOTHER WORLD...
THIS *COULDN'T* BE THE... PRIESTESS OF SEIRYU?

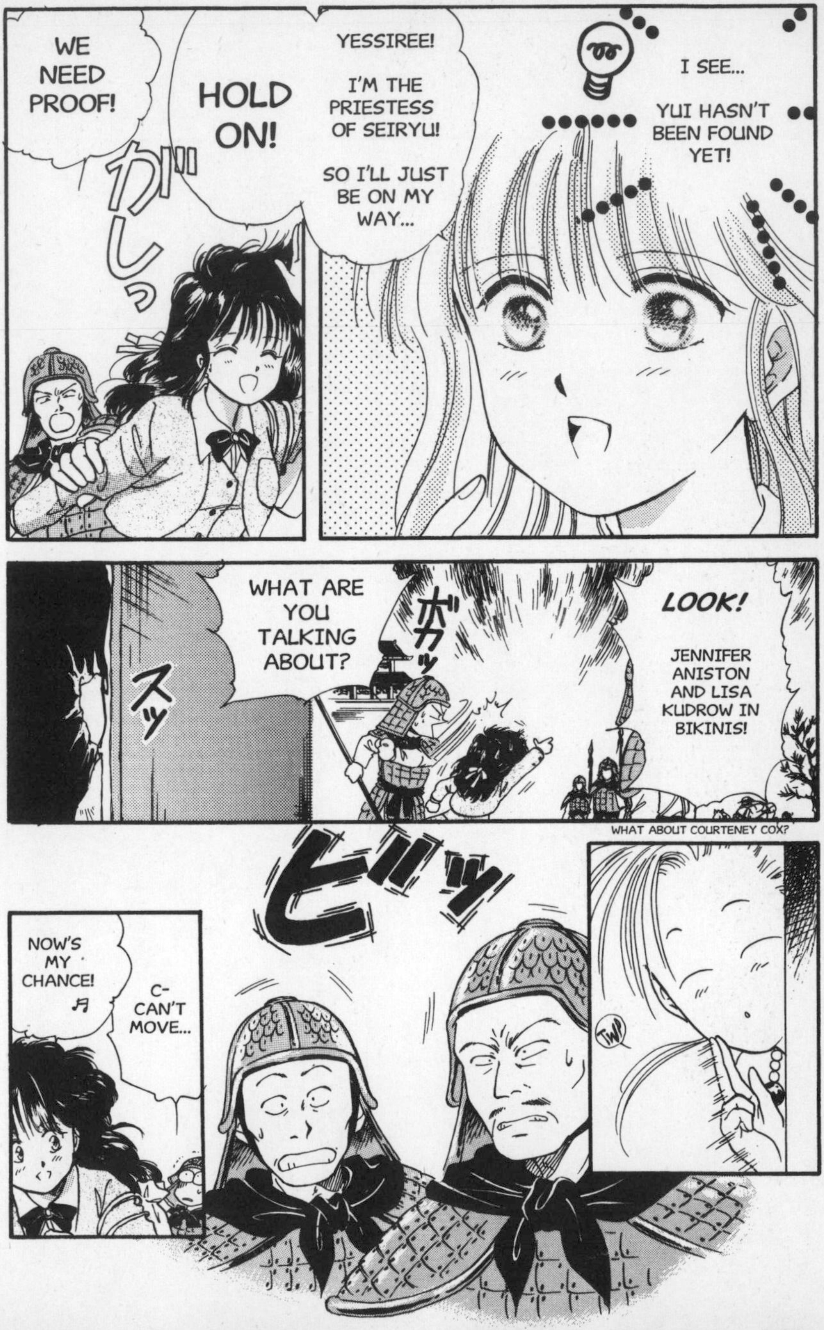
I SEE...
YUI HASN'T BEEN FOUND YET!
YESSIREE!
I'M THE PRIESTESS OF SEIRYU!
SO I'LL JUST BE ON MY WAY...
HOLD ON!
WE NEED PROOF!
がしっ
LOOK!
JENNIFER ANISTON AND LISA KUDROW IN BIKINIS!
WHAT ARE YOU TALKING ABOUT?
WHAT ABOUT COURTENEY COX?
C- CAN'T MOVE...
NOW'S MY CHANCE!

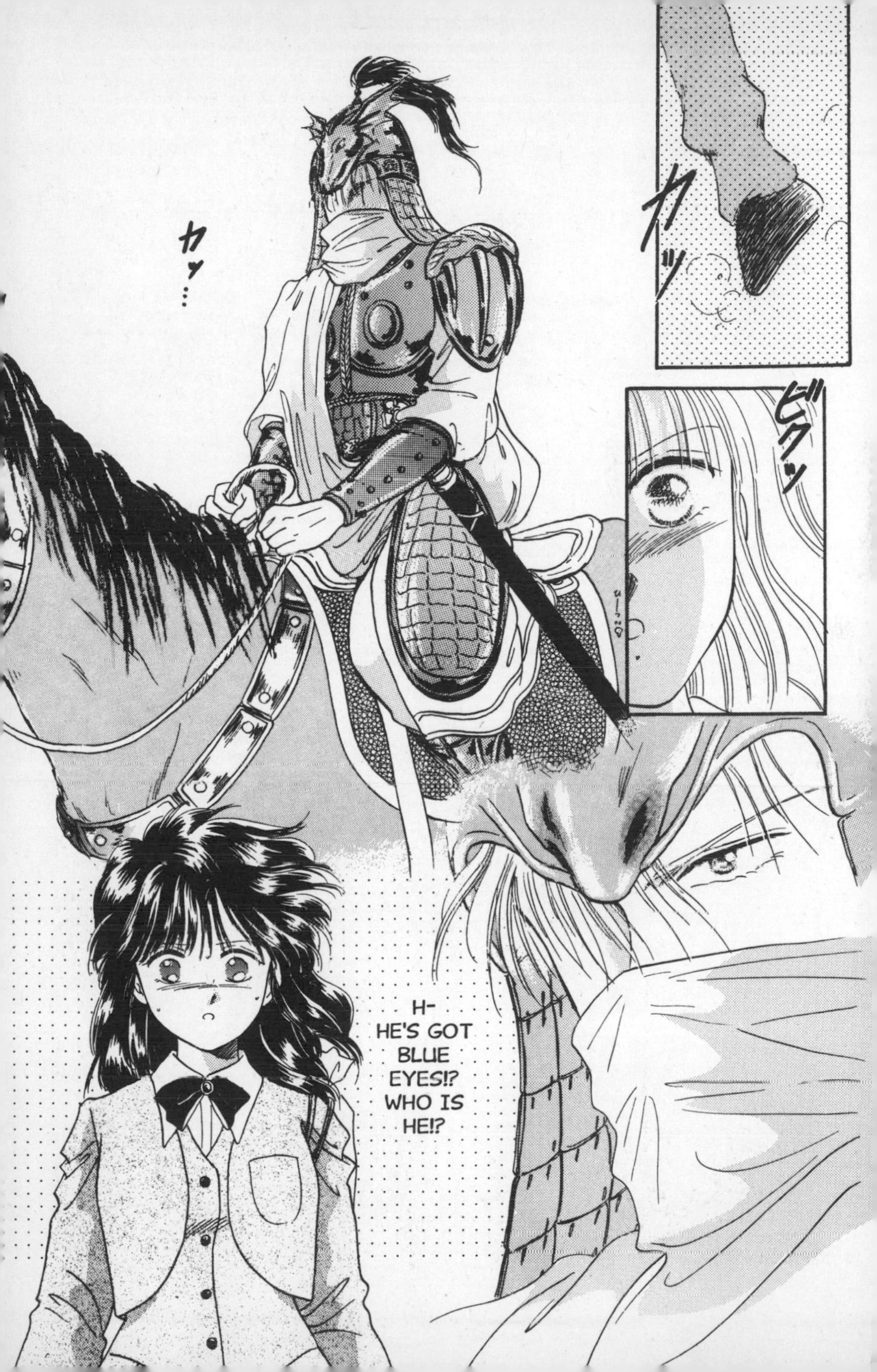
カッ
ビクッ
カッ…
H-
HE'S GOT
BLUE
EYES!?
WHO IS
HE!?

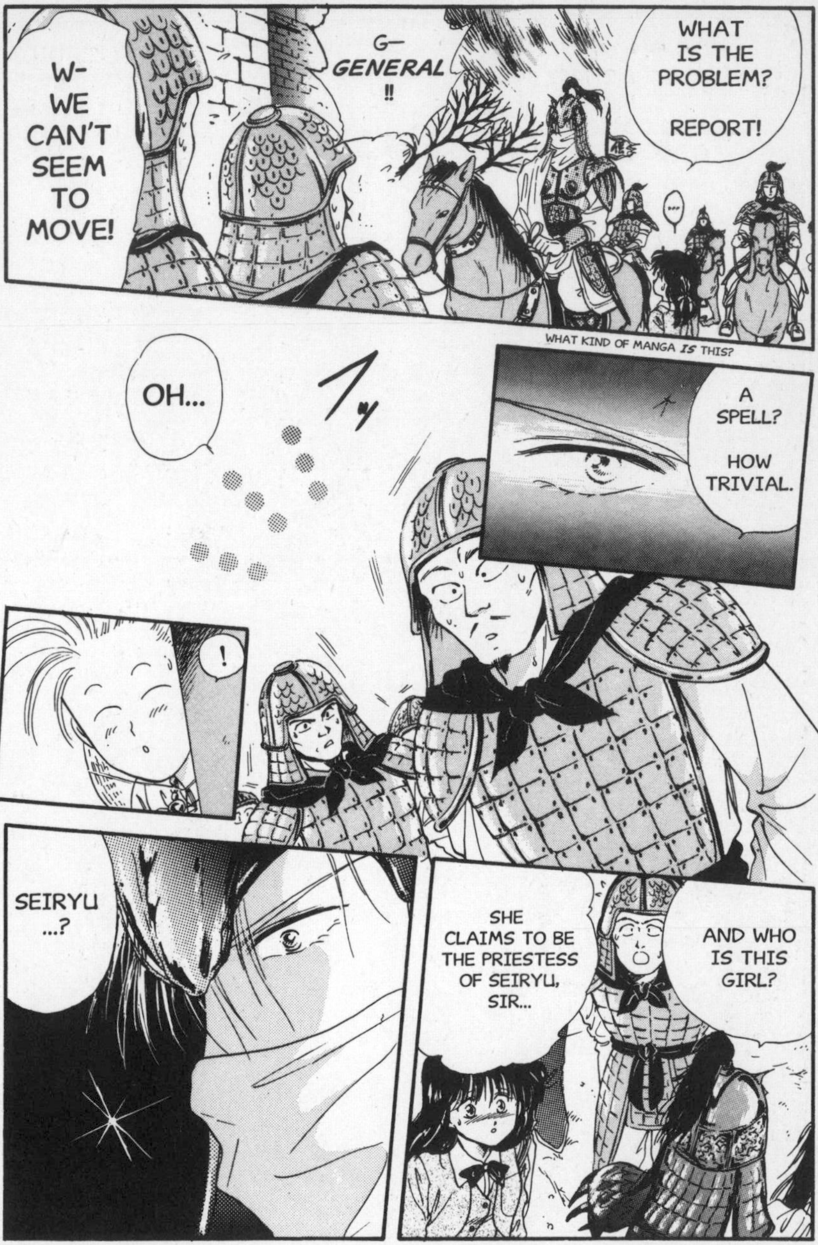
WHAT IS THE PROBLEM? REPORT!
...
G— GENERAL !!
W-WE CAN'T SEEM TO MOVE!
WHAT KIND OF MANGA IS THIS?
A SPELL? HOW TRIVIAL.
OH...
!
AND WHO IS THIS GIRL?
SHE CLAIMS TO BE THE PRIESTESS OF SEIRYU, SIR...
SEIRYU ...?

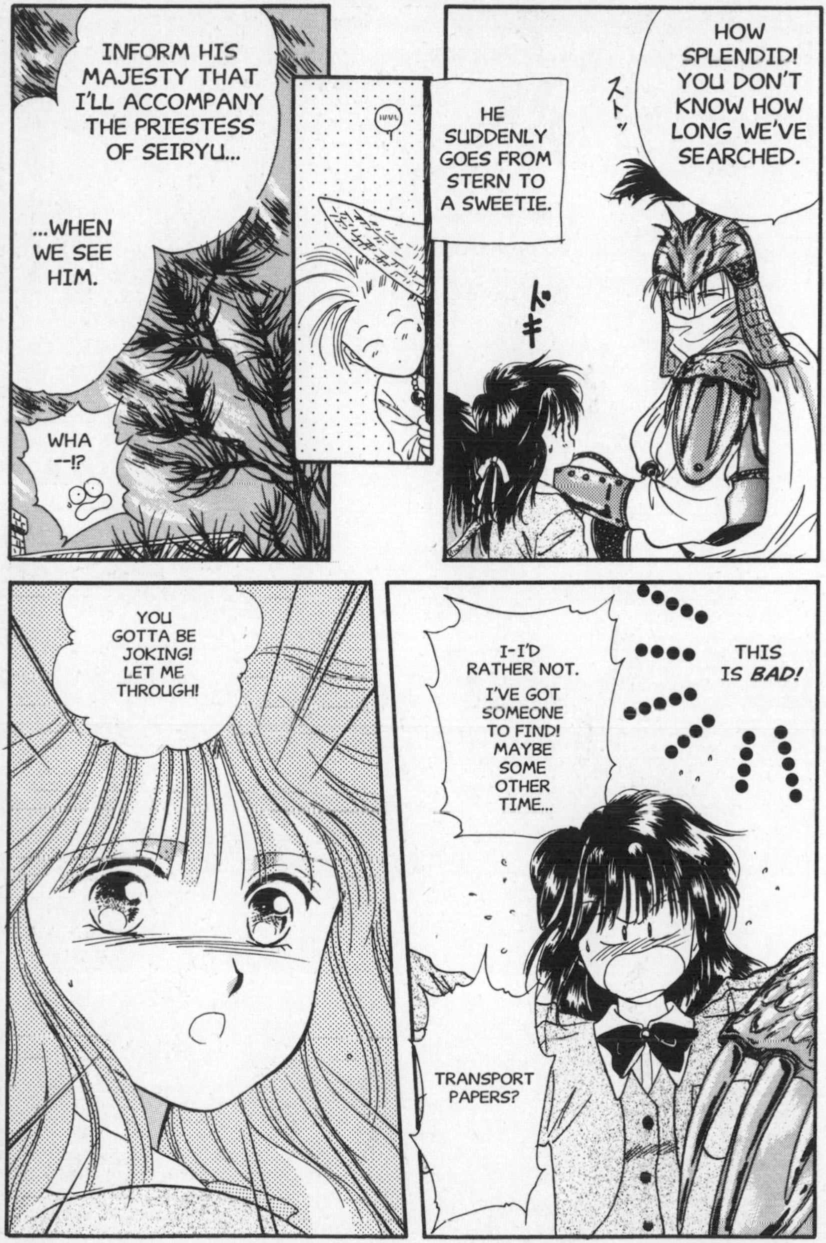
HOW SPLENDID! YOU DON'T KNOW HOW LONG WE'VE SEARCHED.
ストッ
ドキ
HE SUDDENLY GOES FROM STERN TO A SWEETIE.
INFORM HIS MAJESTY THAT I'LL ACCOMPANY THE PRIESTESS OF SEIRYU...
...WHEN WE SEE HIM.
WHA--!?
THIS IS BAD!
I-I'D RATHER NOT.
I'VE GOT SOMEONE TO FIND! MAYBE SOME OTHER TIME...
TRANSPORT PAPERS?
YOU GOTTA BE JOKING! LET ME THROUGH!

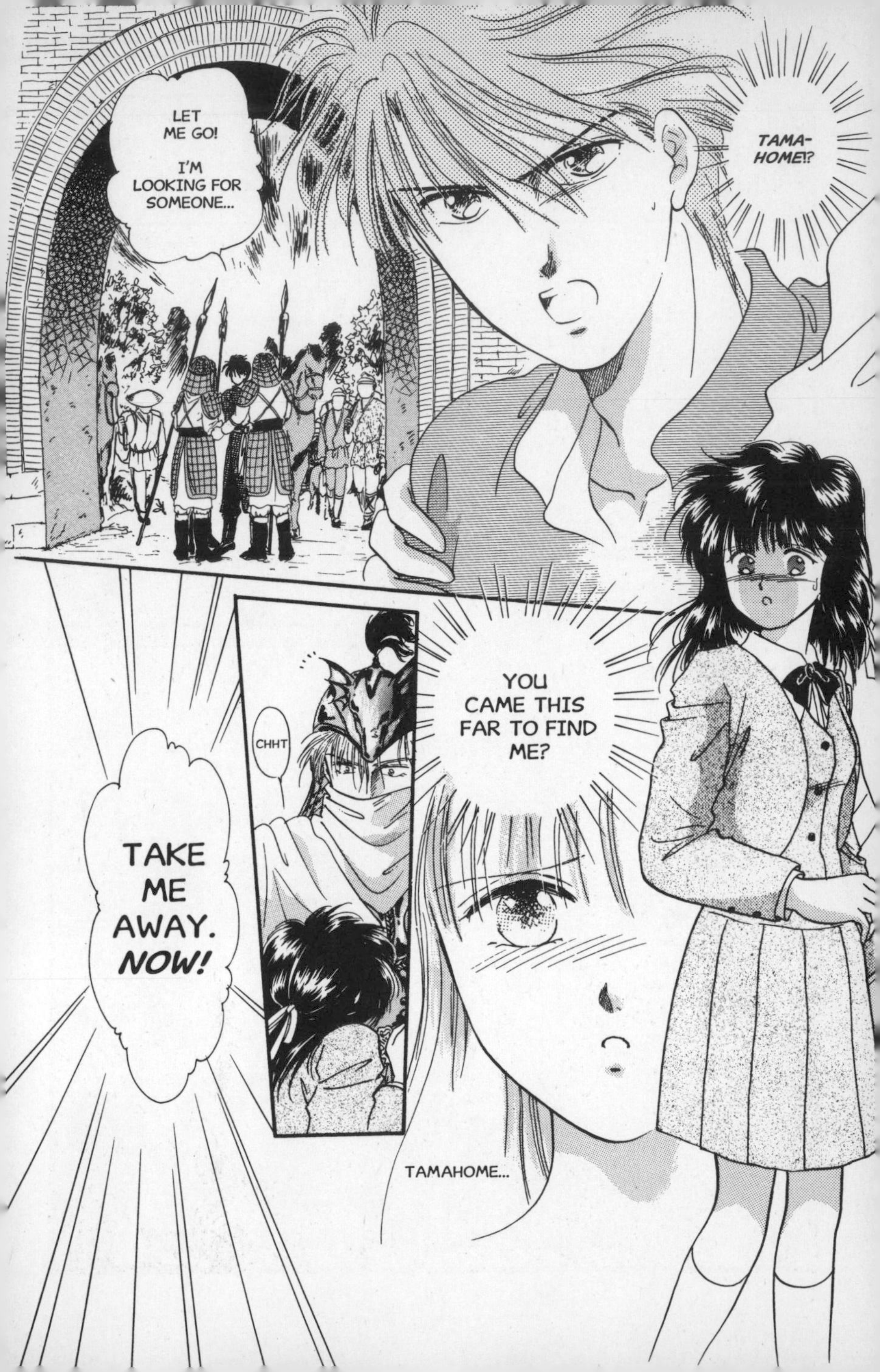
TAMA-HOME!?
LET ME GO! I'M LOOKING FOR SOMEONE...
YOU CAME THIS FAR TO FIND ME?
TAMAHOME...
CHHT
TAKE ME AWAY. NOW!

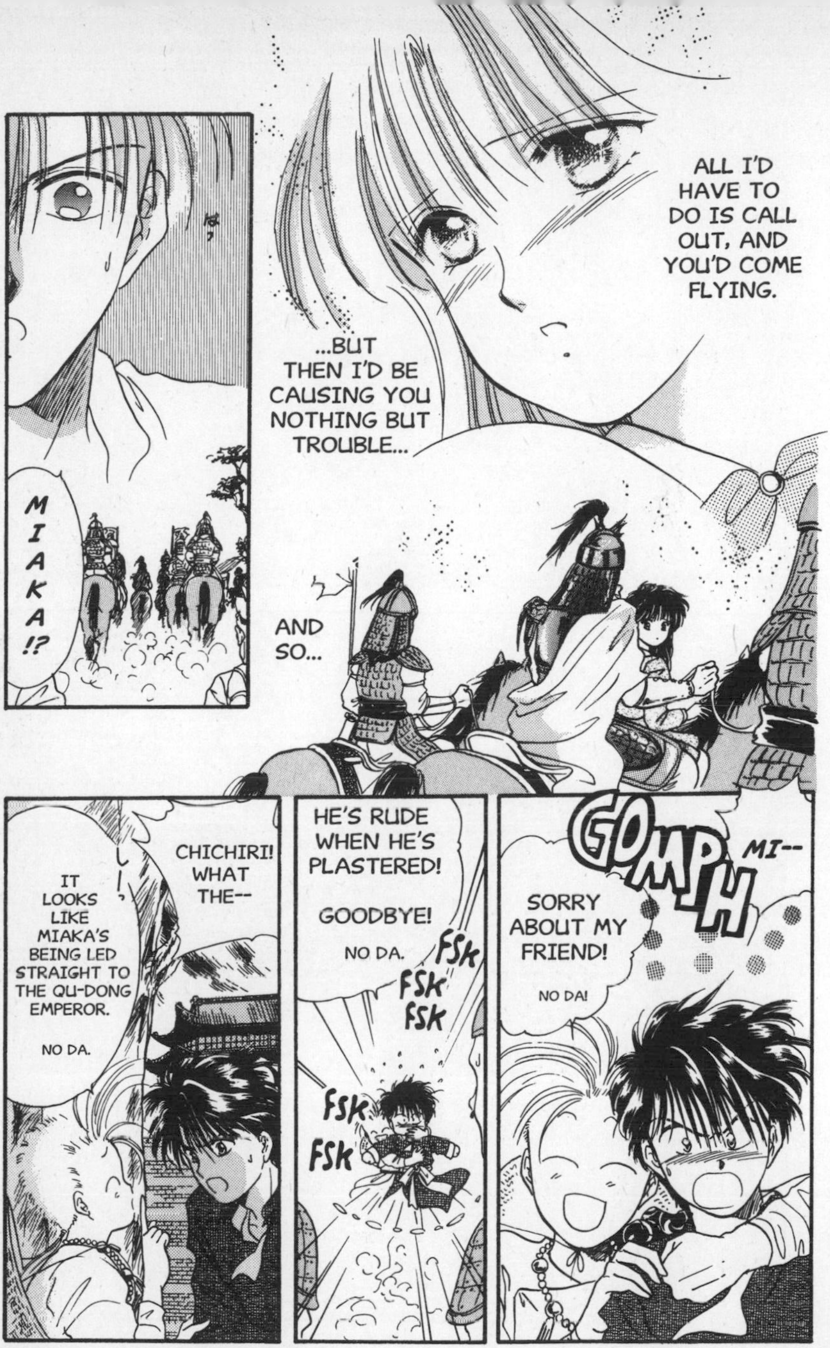
ALL I'D HAVE TO DO IS CALL OUT, AND YOU'D COME FLYING.
...BUT THEN I'D BE CAUSING YOU NOTHING BUT TROUBLE...
AND SO...
MIAKA!?
MI--
GOMPH
SORRY ABOUT MY FRIEND!
NO DA!
HE'S RUDE WHEN HE'S PLASTERED!
GOODBYE!
NO DA.
FSK FSK FSK
FSK FSK
CHICHIRI! WHAT THE--
IT LOOKS LIKE MIAKA'S BEING LED STRAIGHT TO THE QU-DONG EMPEROR.
NO DA.

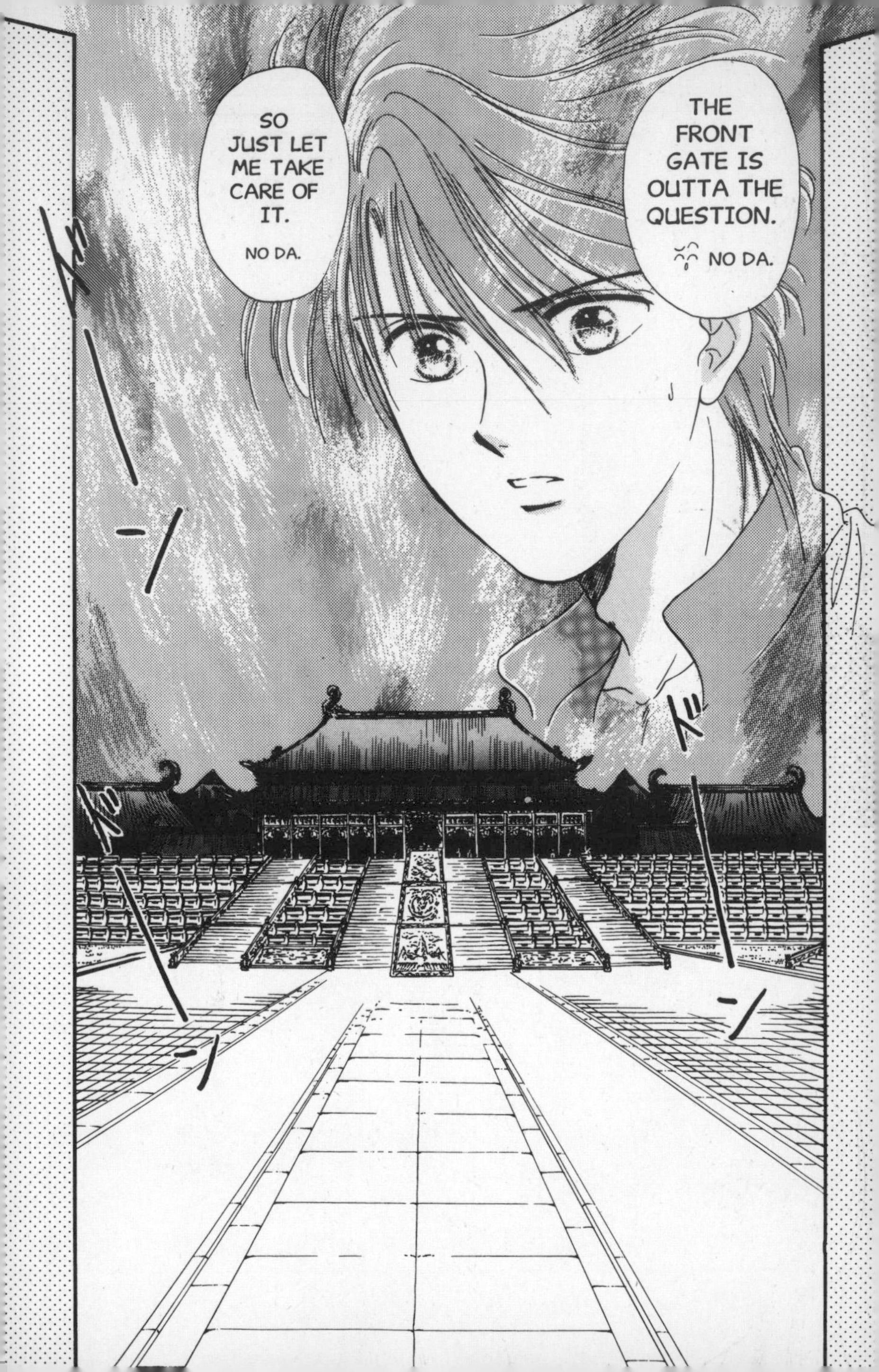
THE FRONT GATE IS OUTTA THE QUESTION.
NO DA.
SO JUST LET ME TAKE CARE OF IT.
NO DA.

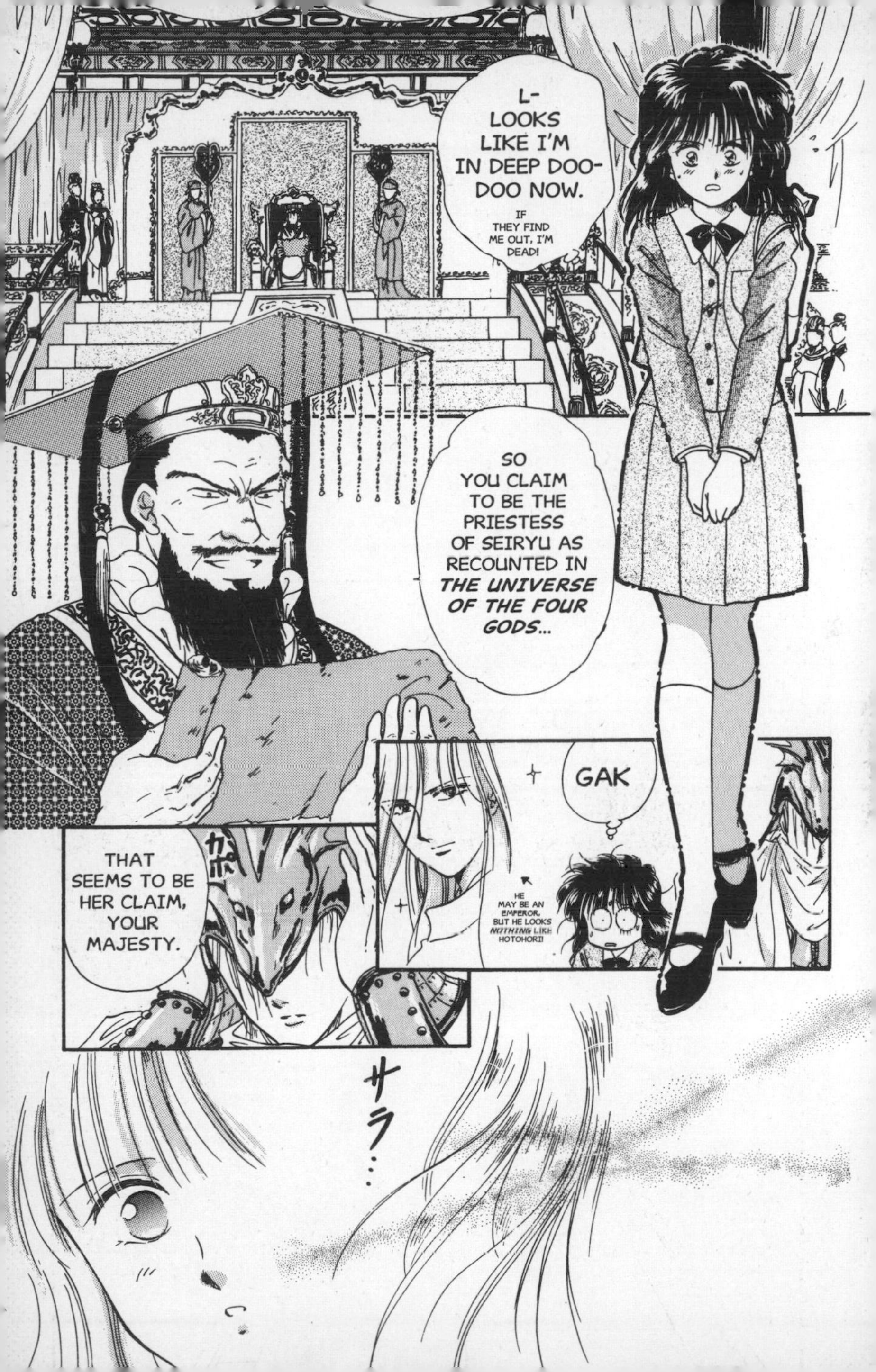
L- LOOKS LIKE I'M IN DEEP DOO-DOO NOW.
IF THEY FIND ME OUT, I'M DEAD!
SO YOU CLAIM TO BE THE PRIESTESS OF SEIRYU AS RECOUNTED IN *THE UNIVERSE OF THE FOUR GODS*...
GAK
HE MAY BE AN EMPEROR, BUT HE LOOKS *NOTHING* LIKE HOTOHORI!
THAT SEEMS TO BE HER CLAIM, YOUR MAJESTY.
カポ
サラ…

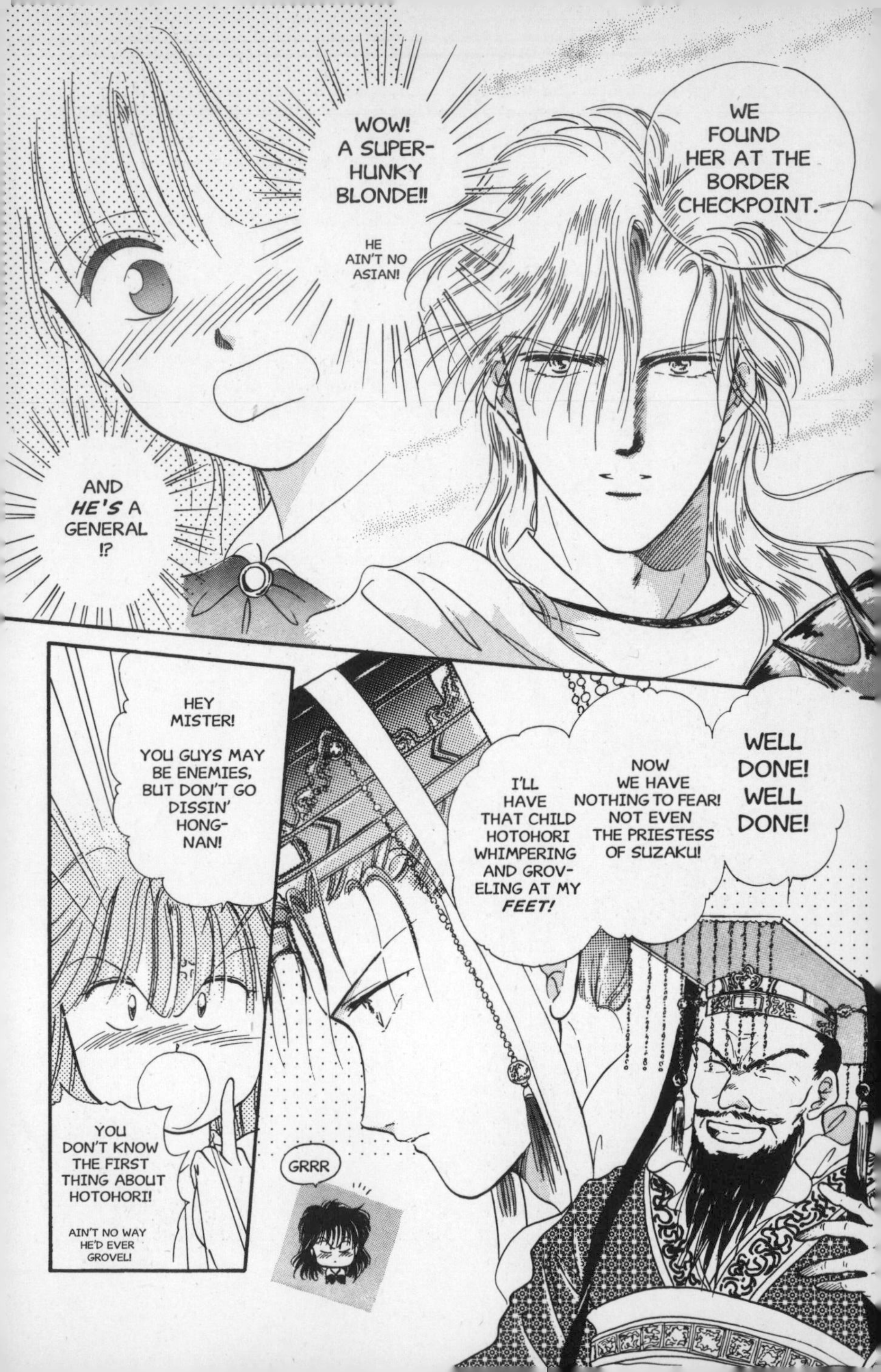
WE FOUND HER AT THE BORDER CHECKPOINT.
WOW! A SUPER-HUNKY BLONDE!!
HE AIN'T NO ASIAN!
AND *HE'S* A GENERAL !?
WELL DONE! WELL DONE!
NOW WE HAVE NOTHING TO FEAR! NOT EVEN THE PRIESTESS OF SUZAKU!
I'LL HAVE THAT CHILD HOTOHORI WHIMPERING AND GROVELING AT MY *FEET!*
HEY MISTER!
YOU GUYS MAY BE ENEMIES, BUT DON'T GO DISSIN' HONG-NAN!
YOU DON'T KNOW THE FIRST THING ABOUT HOTOHORI!
AIN'T NO WAY HE'D EVER GROVEL!
GRRR

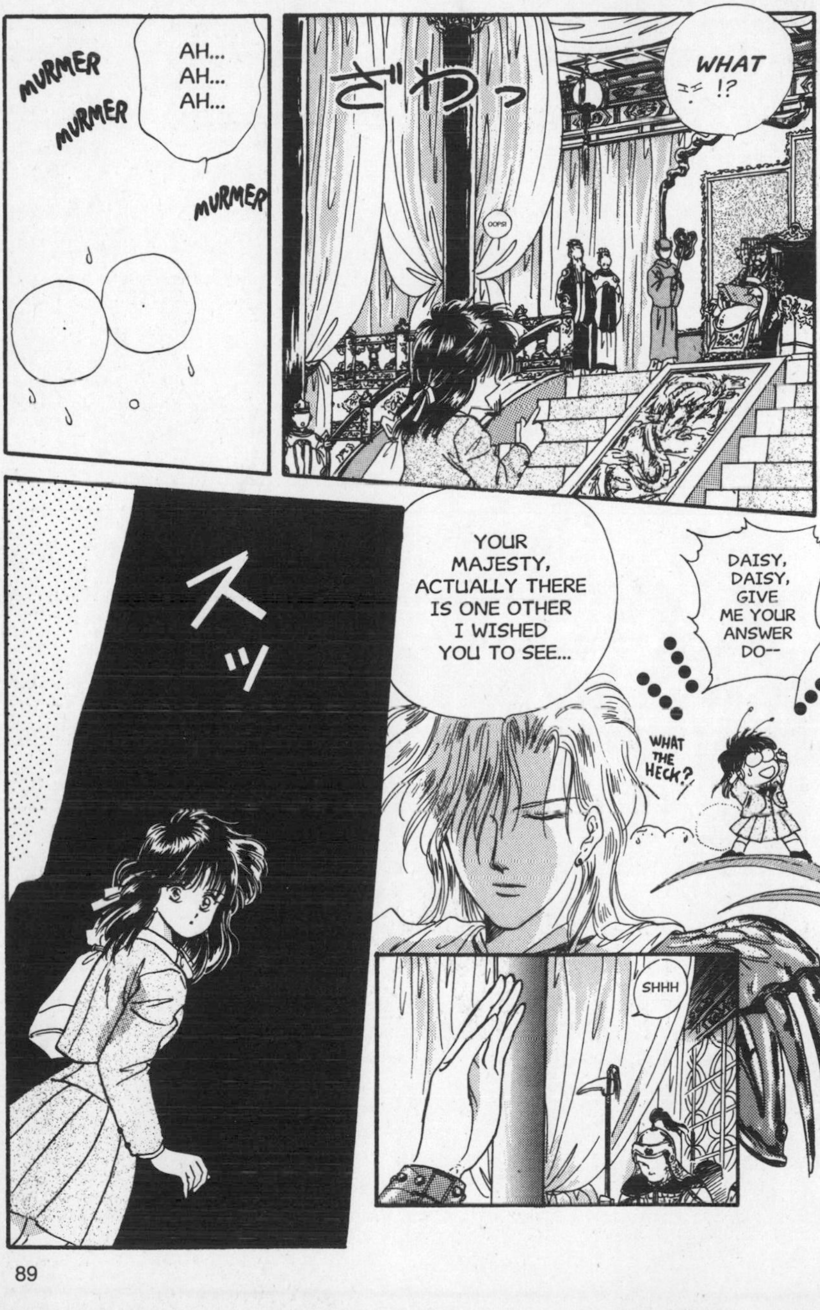
ざわっ
OOPS!
WHAT !?
MURMER
MURMER
MURMER
AH... AH... AH...
YOUR MAJESTY, ACTUALLY THERE IS ONE OTHER I WISHED YOU TO SEE...
DAISY, DAISY, GIVE ME YOUR ANSWER DO--
WHAT THE HECK?
SHHH
スッ

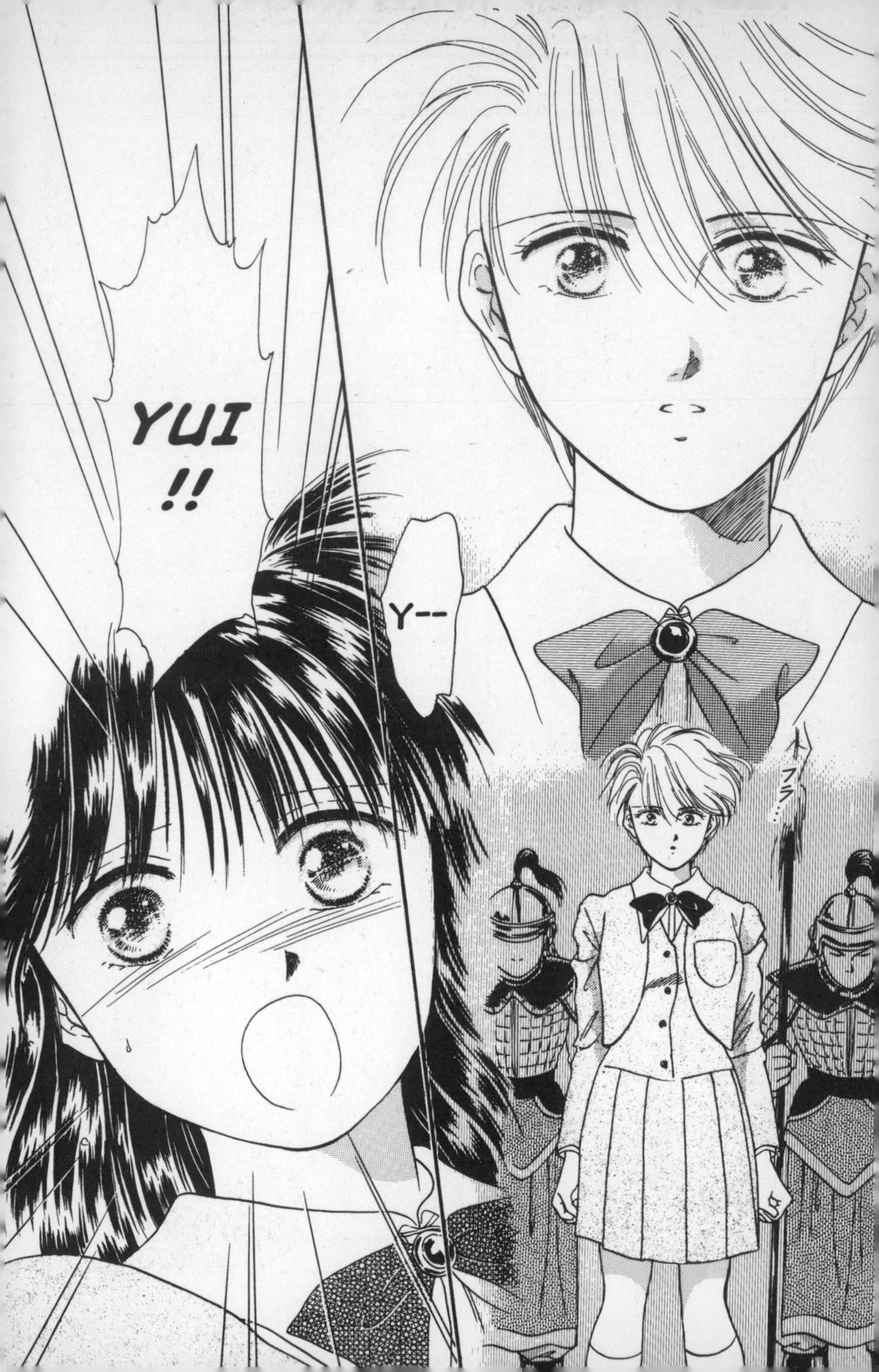
ホフラ…
Y--
YUI !!

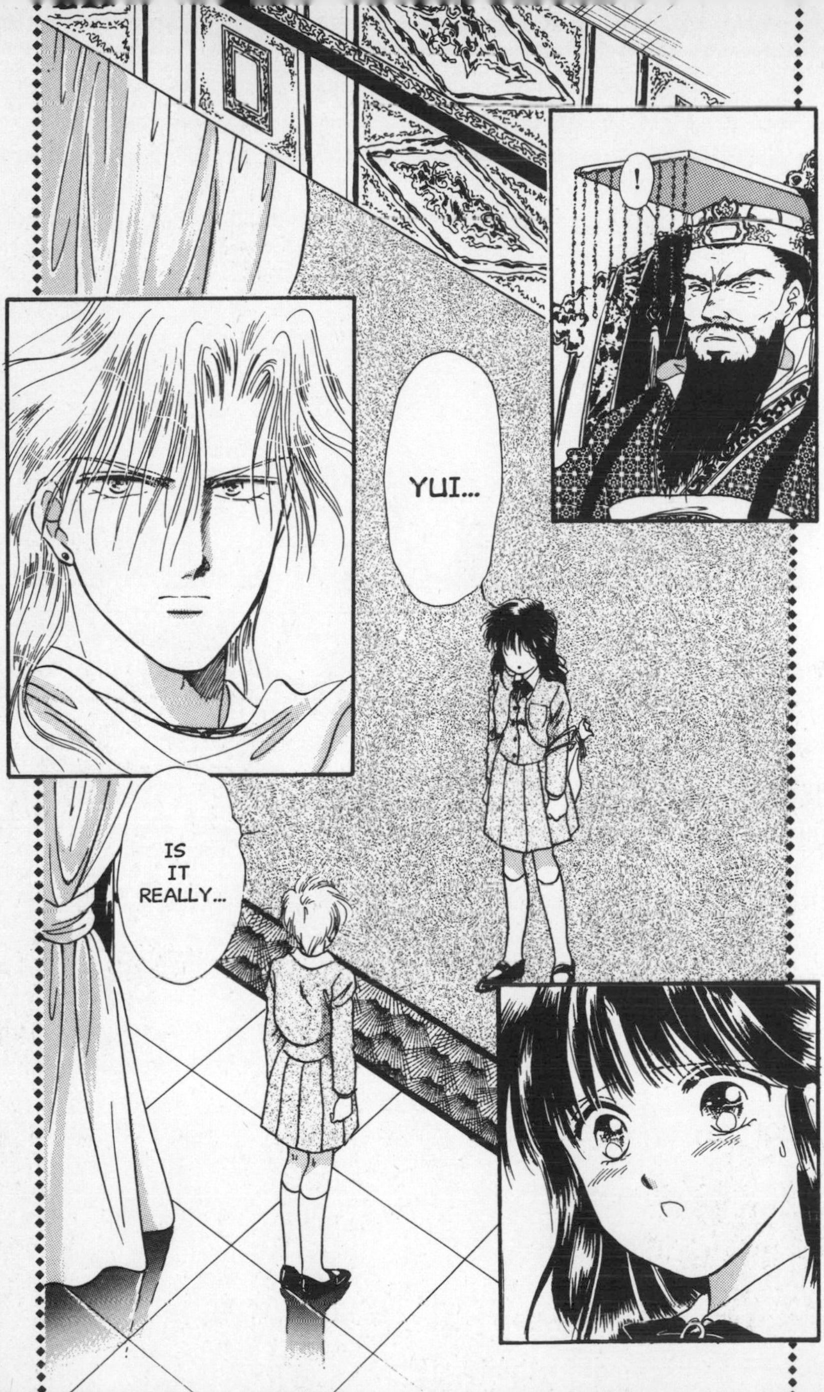
!
YUI...
IS IT REALLY...

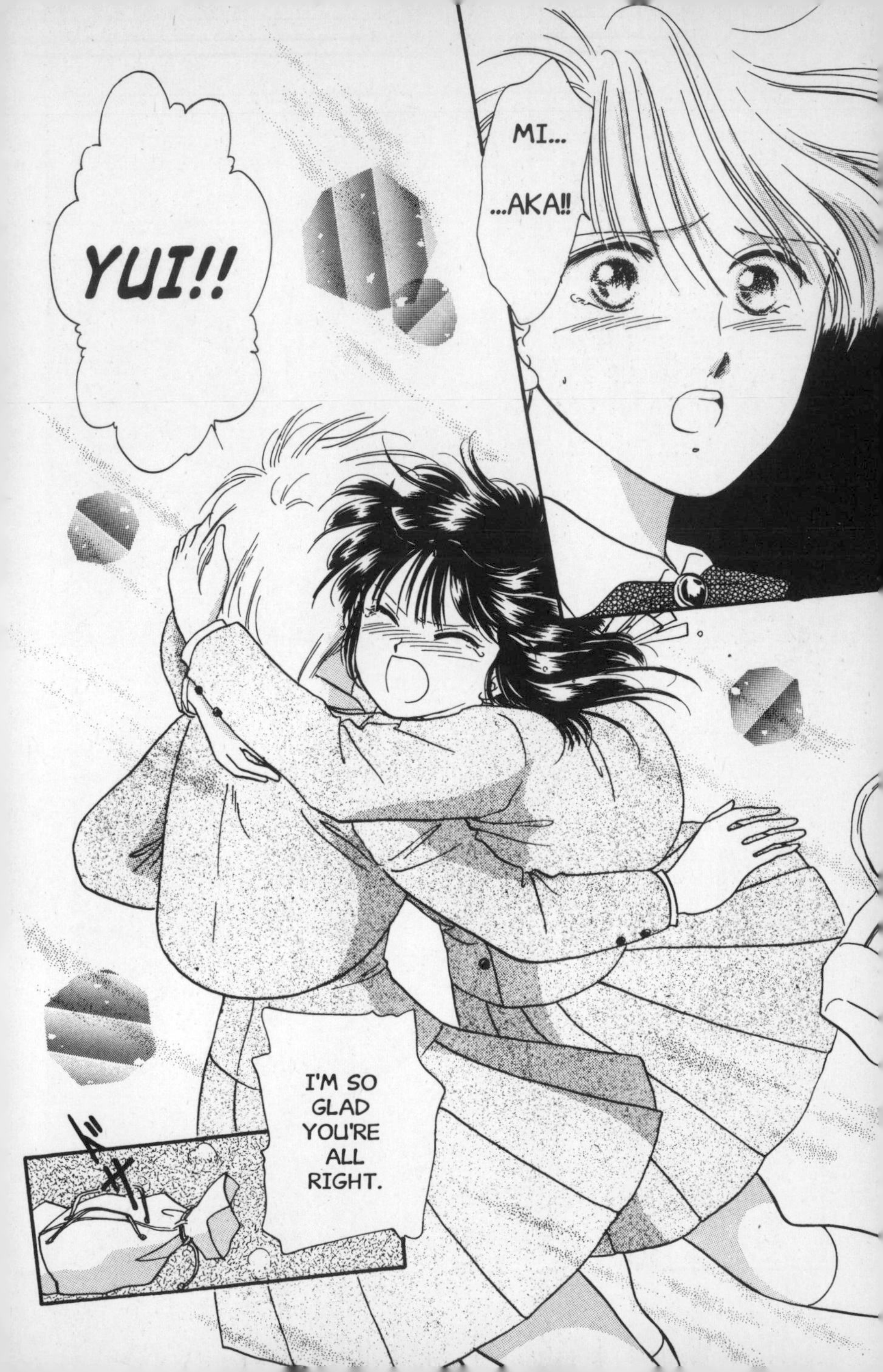
MI...
...AKA!!
YUI!!
I'M SO GLAD YOU'RE ALL RIGHT.
ドサ

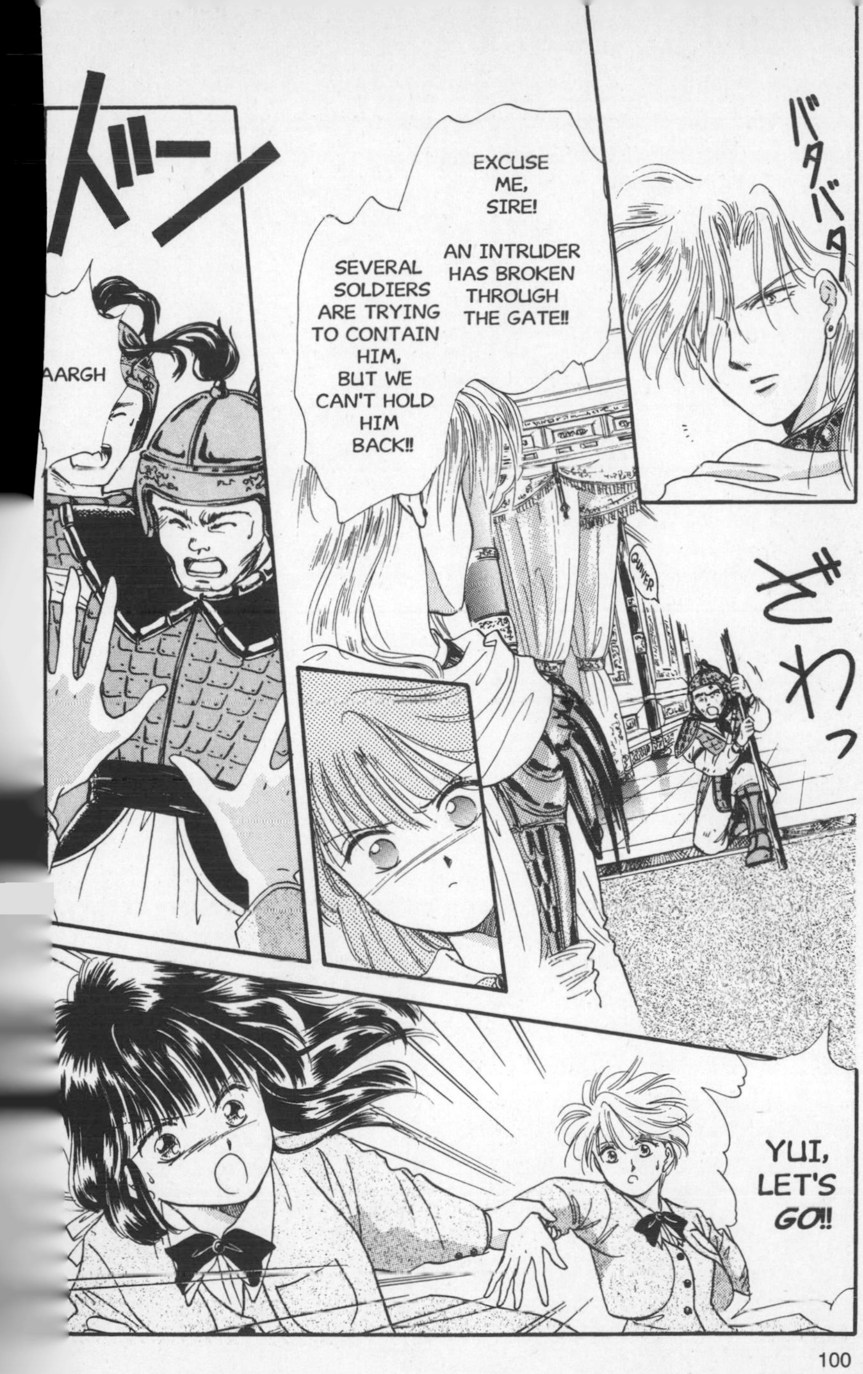
バタバタ
EXCUSE ME, SIRE!
AN INTRUDER HAS BROKEN THROUGH THE GATE!!
SEVERAL SOLDIERS ARE TRYING TO CONTAIN HIM, BUT WE CAN'T HOLD HIM BACK!!
ざわっ
QUIVER
ズドーン
AARGH
YUI, LET'S *GO*!!

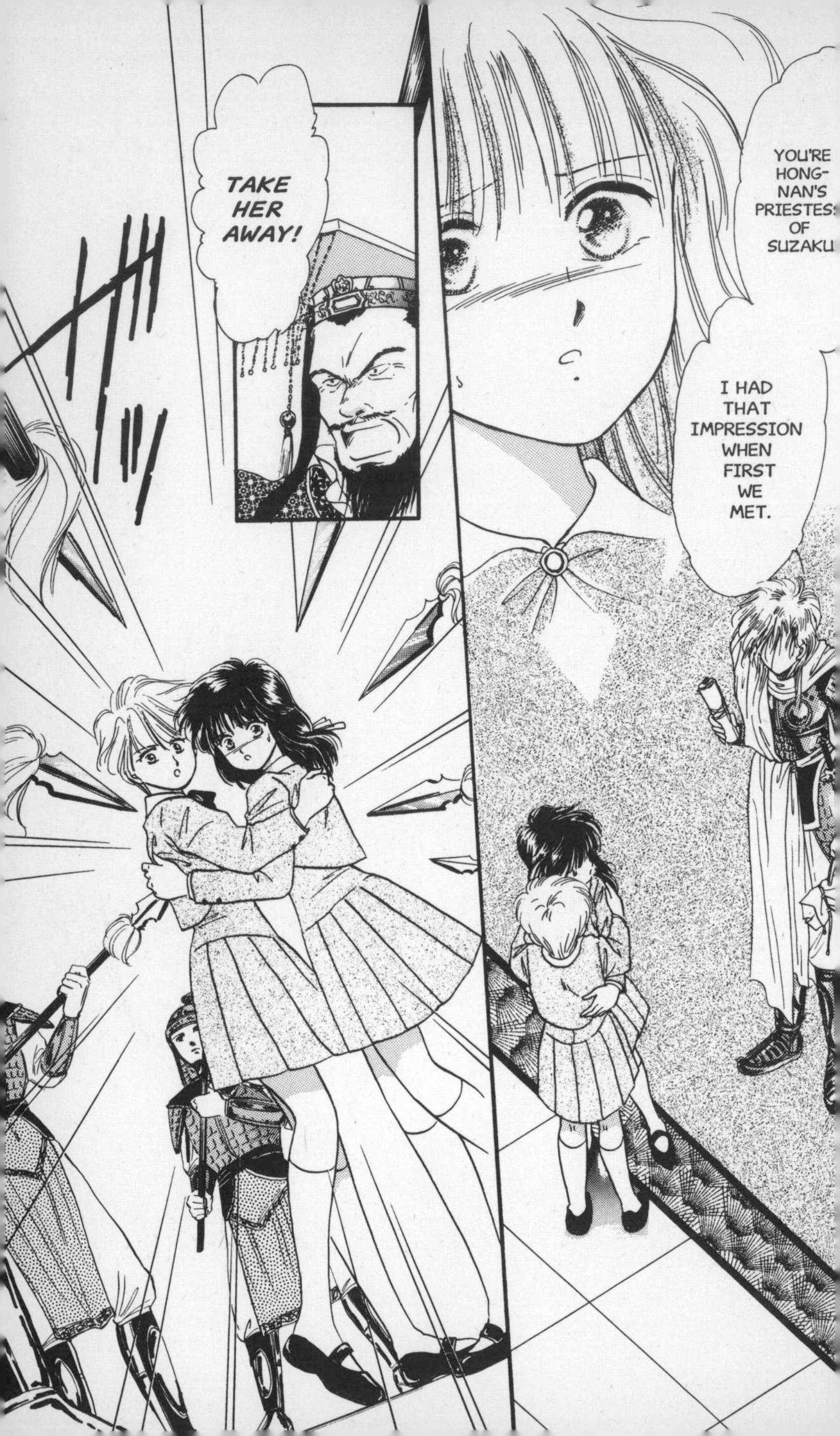
YOU'RE HONG-NAN'S PRIESTESS OF SUZAKU
I HAD THAT IMPRESSION WHEN FIRST WE MET.
TAKE HER AWAY!

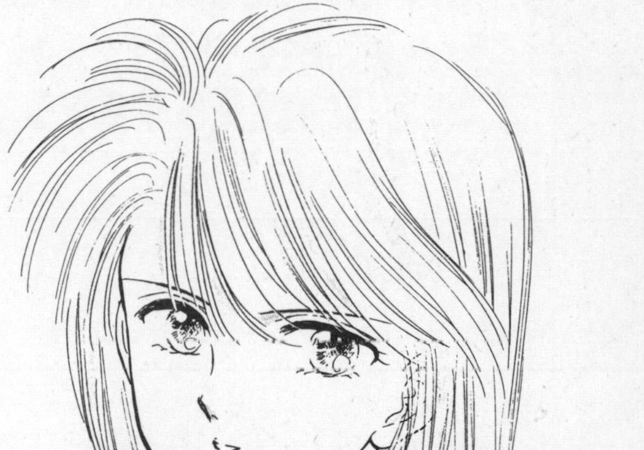

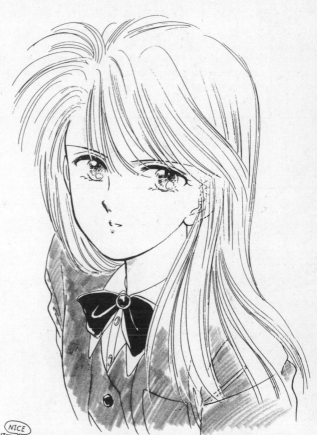

NICE

YUI WITH LONG HAIR.

SHE HAD IT LONG UNTIL THE 8TH GRADE. SHE CUT IT SHORT TO AVOID ALL THE ATTENTION SHE WAS GETTING FROM THE BOYS.

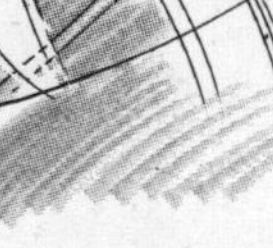
I'M SO PROUD SHE'S MY FRIEND!

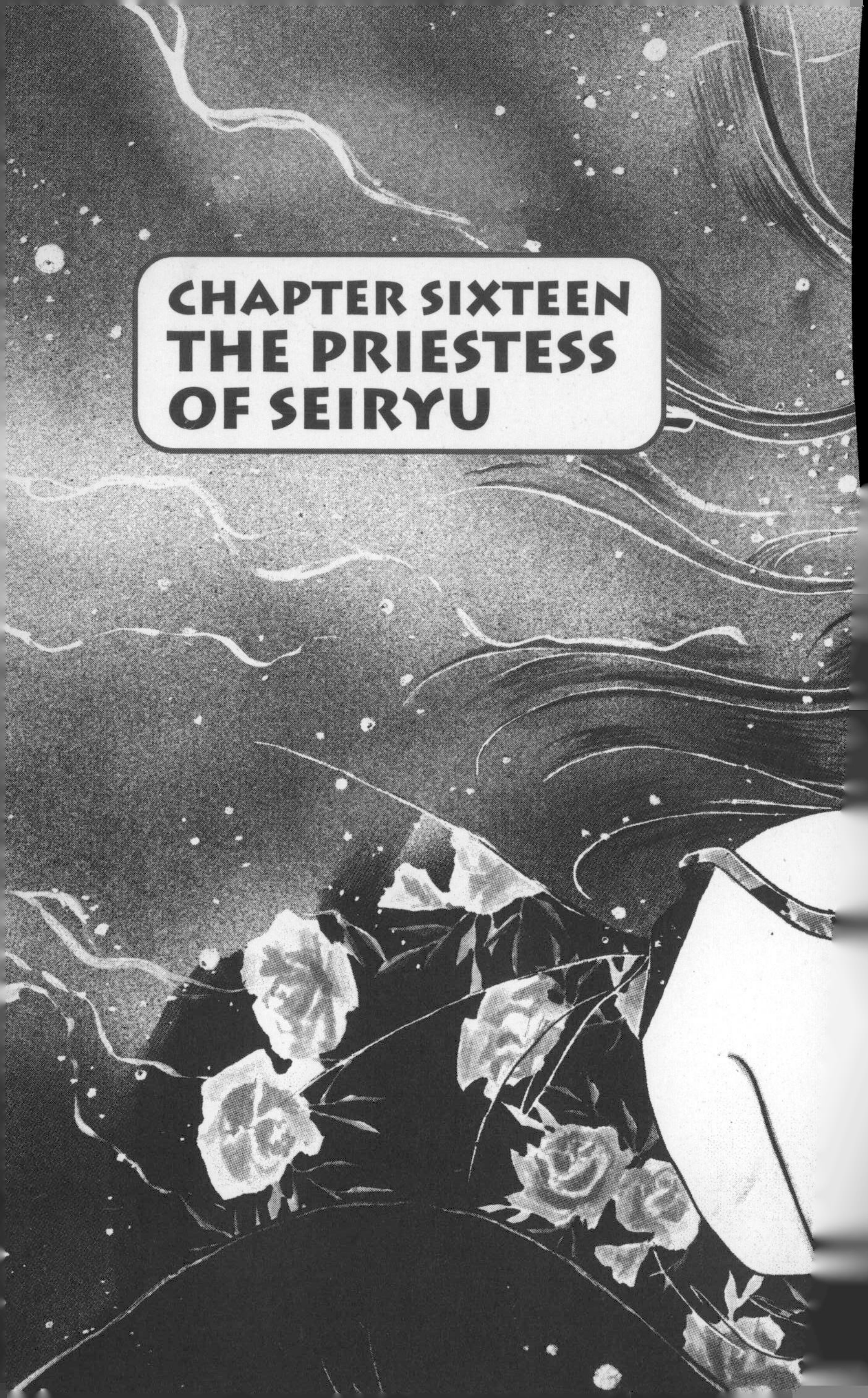
CHAPTER SIXTEEN
THE PRIESTESS OF SEIRYU

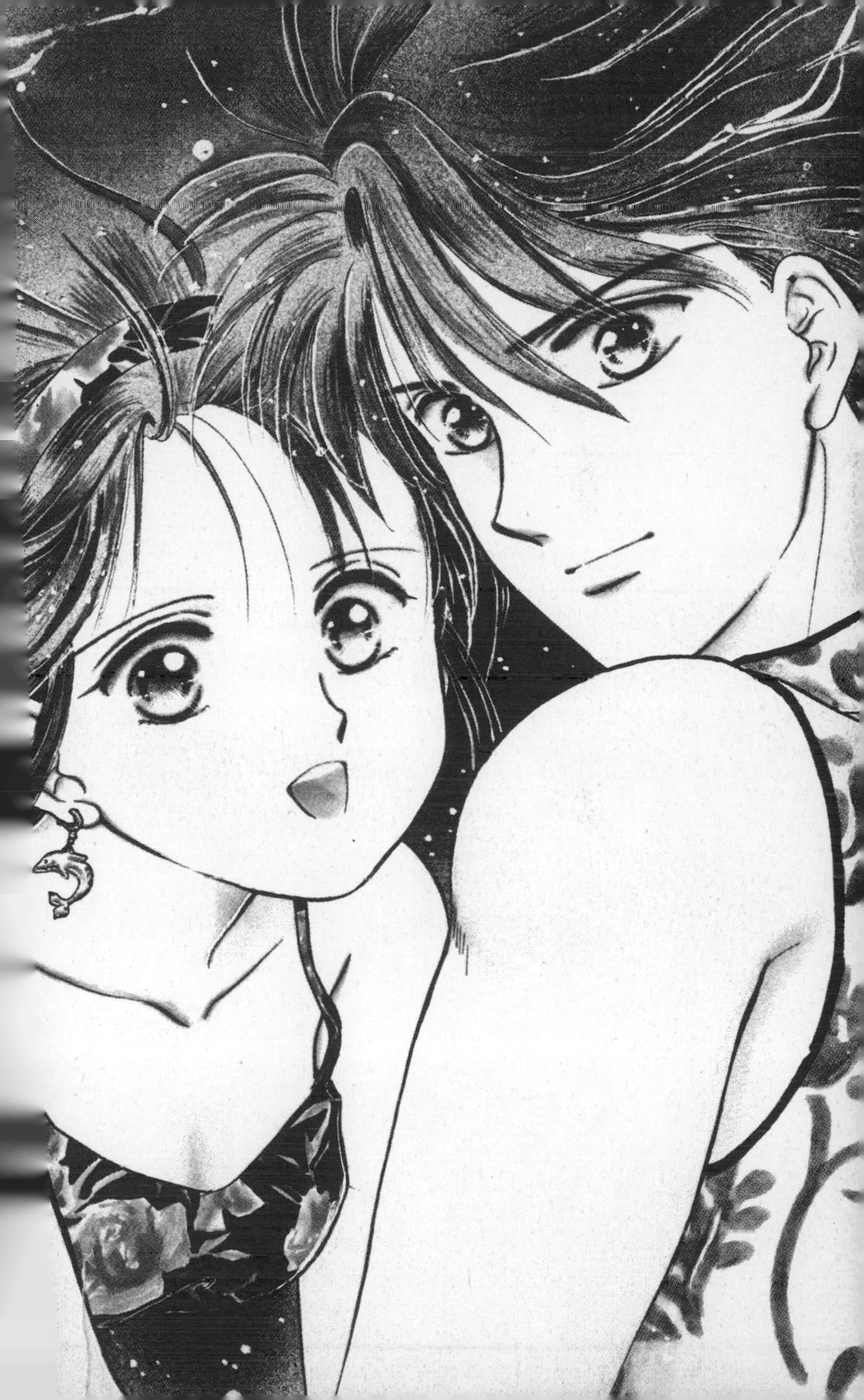

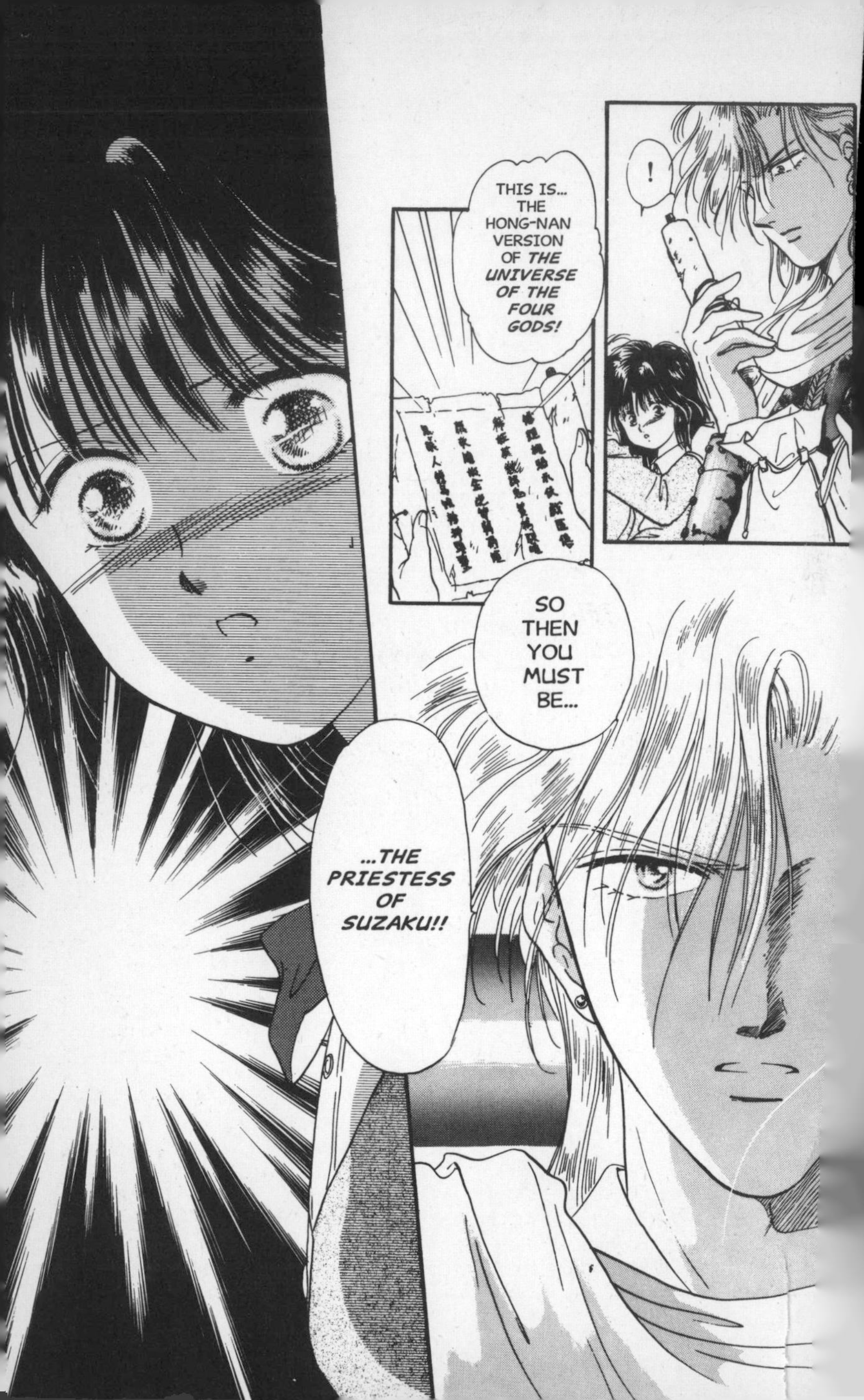
!
THIS IS... THE HONG-NAN VERSION OF *THE UNIVERSE OF THE FOUR GODS!*
SO THEN YOU MUST BE...
...THE PRIESTESS OF SUZAKU!!

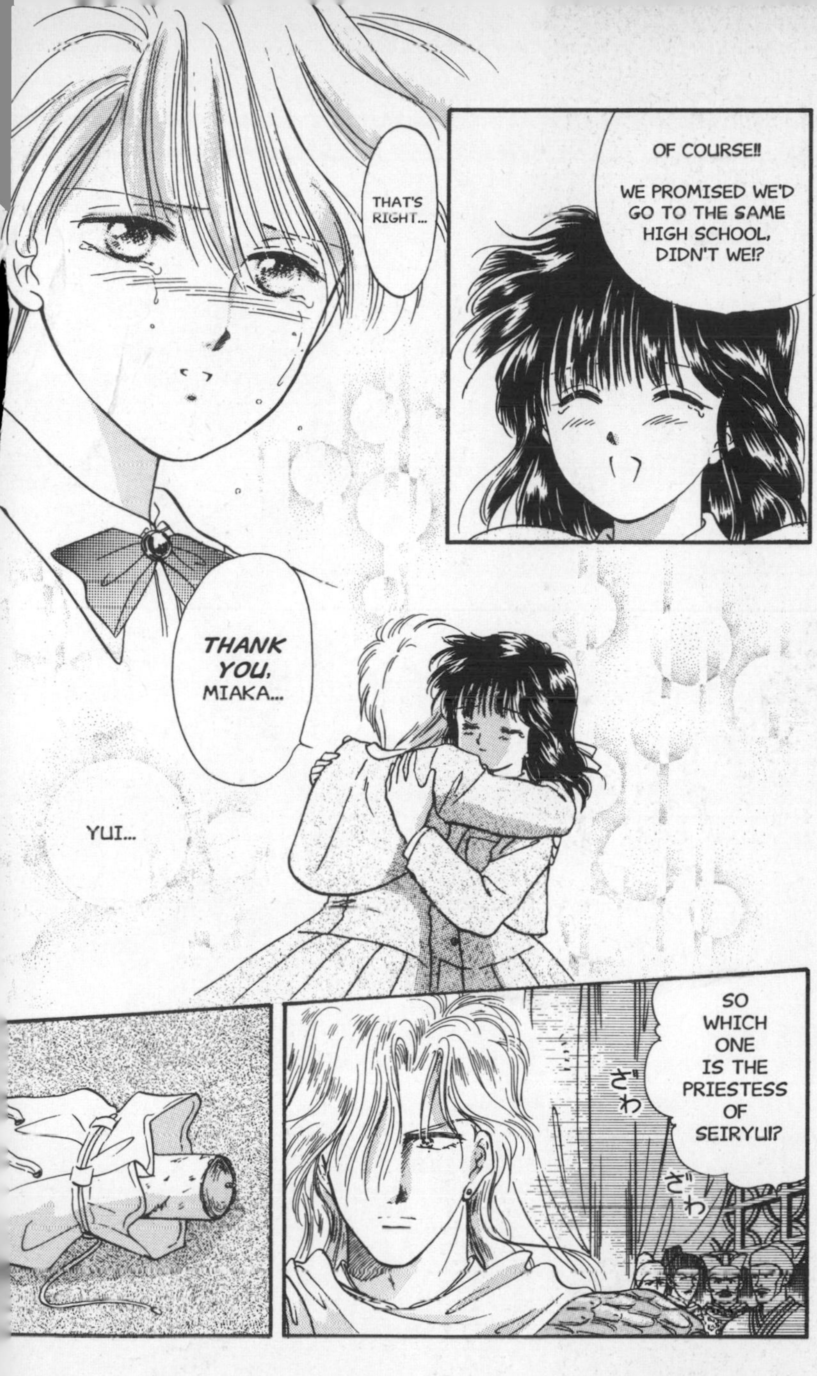
OF COURSE!!
WE PROMISED WE'D GO TO THE SAME HIGH SCHOOL, DIDN'T WE!?
THAT'S RIGHT...
THANK YOU, MIAKA...
YUI...
SO WHICH ONE IS THE PRIESTESS OF SEIRYU!?
ざわ
ざわ

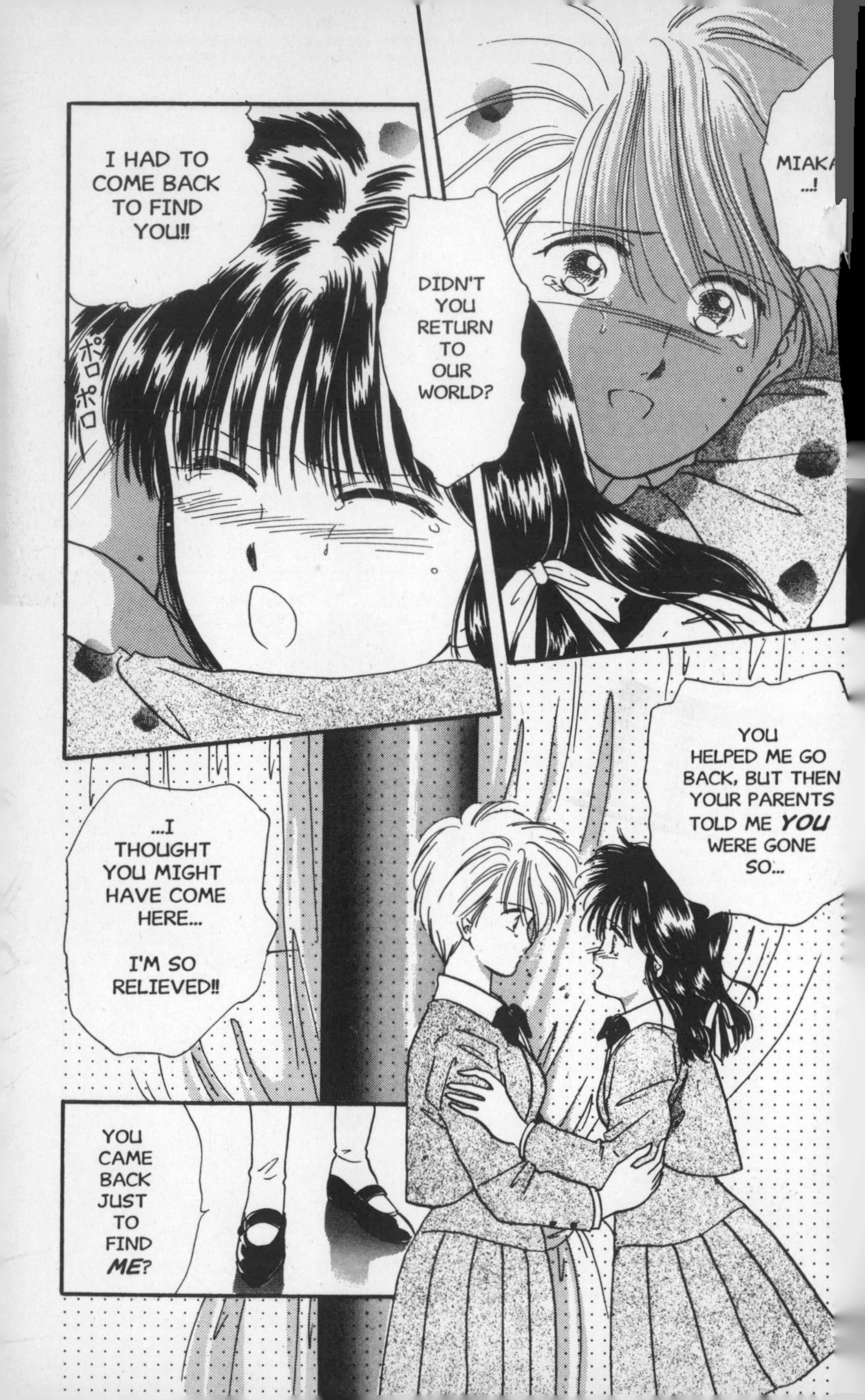
MIAKA ...!
DIDN'T YOU RETURN TO OUR WORLD?
I HAD TO COME BACK TO FIND YOU!!
ポロポロ
YOU HELPED ME GO BACK, BUT THEN YOUR PARENTS TOLD ME ***YOU*** WERE GONE SO...
...I THOUGHT YOU MIGHT HAVE COME HERE...
I'M SO RELIEVED!!
YOU CAME BACK JUST TO FIND ***ME***?

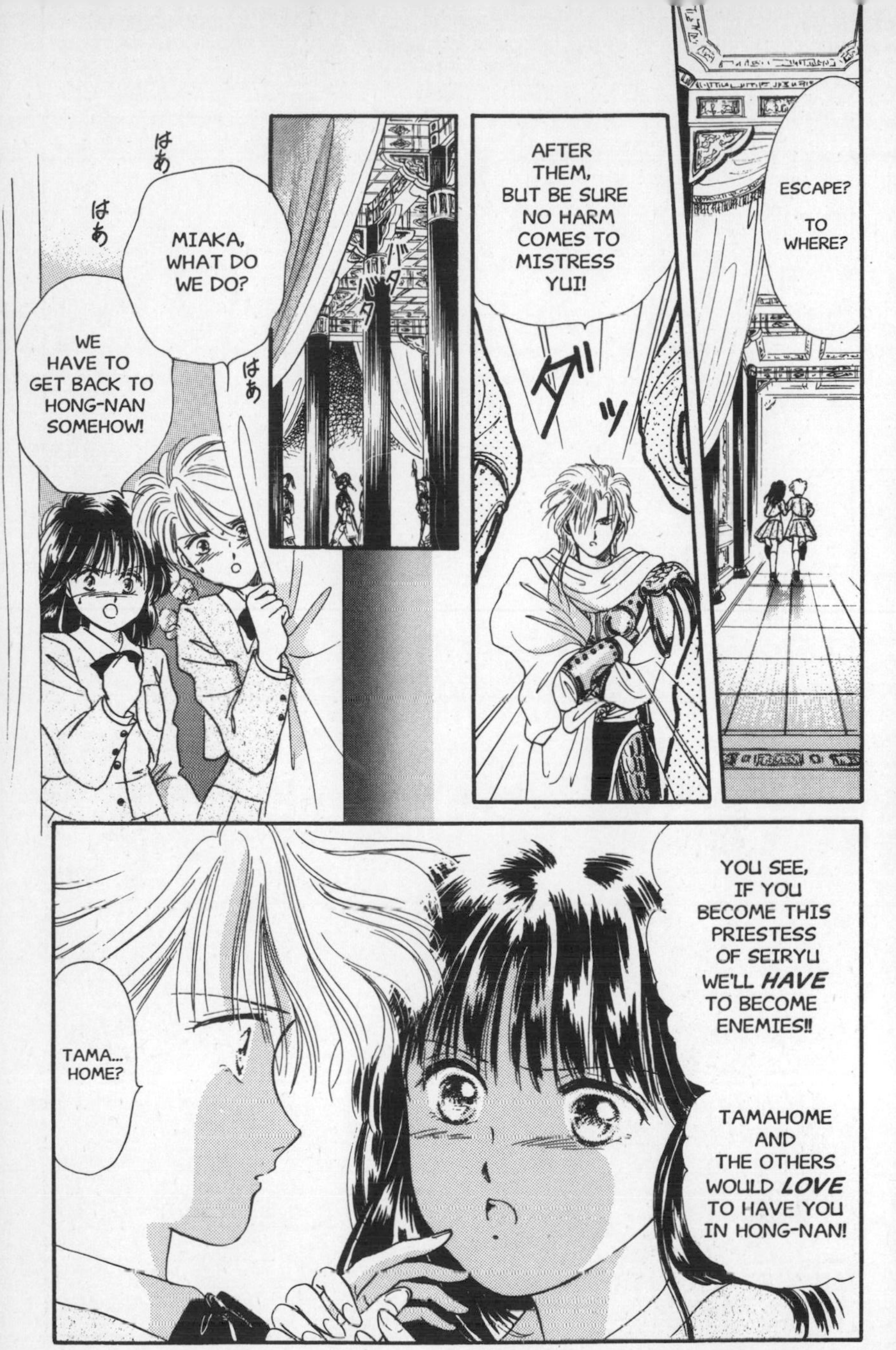
ESCAPE?
TO WHERE?
AFTER THEM, BUT BE SURE NO HARM COMES TO MISTRESS YUI!
ダッ
はあ
はあ
MIAKA, WHAT DO WE DO?
WE HAVE TO GET BACK TO HONG-NAN SOMEHOW!
はあ
YOU SEE, IF YOU BECOME THIS PRIESTESS OF SEIRYU WE'LL *HAVE* TO BECOME ENEMIES!!
TAMAHOME AND THE OTHERS WOULD *LOVE* TO HAVE YOU IN HONG-NAN!
TAMA... HOME?

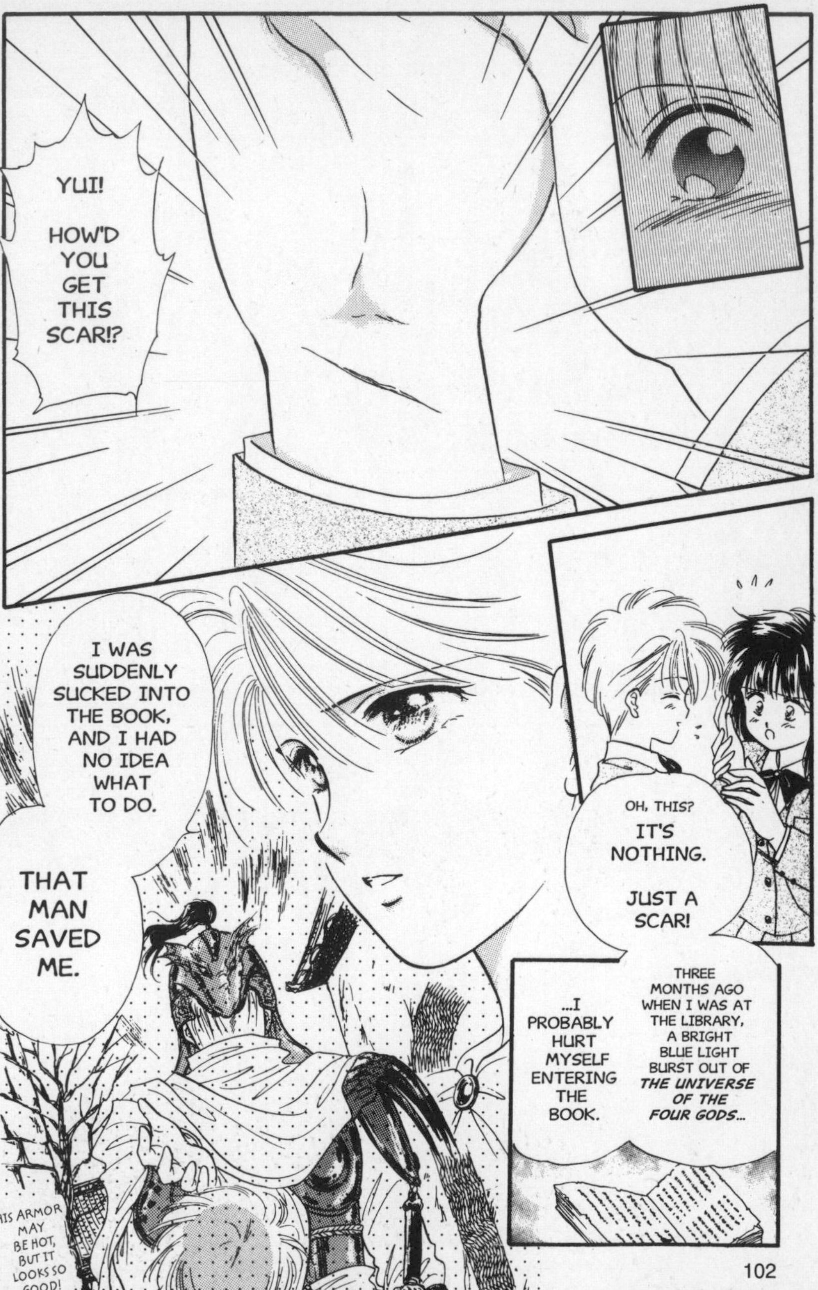
YUI!
HOW'D YOU GET THIS SCAR!?
OH, THIS? IT'S NOTHING. JUST A SCAR!
THREE MONTHS AGO WHEN I WAS AT THE LIBRARY, A BRIGHT BLUE LIGHT BURST OUT OF *THE UNIVERSE OF THE FOUR GODS*...
...I PROBABLY HURT MYSELF ENTERING THE BOOK.
I WAS SUDDENLY SUCKED INTO THE BOOK, AND I HAD NO IDEA WHAT TO DO.
THAT MAN SAVED ME.
HIS ARMOR MAY BE HOT, BUT IT LOOKS SO GOOD!

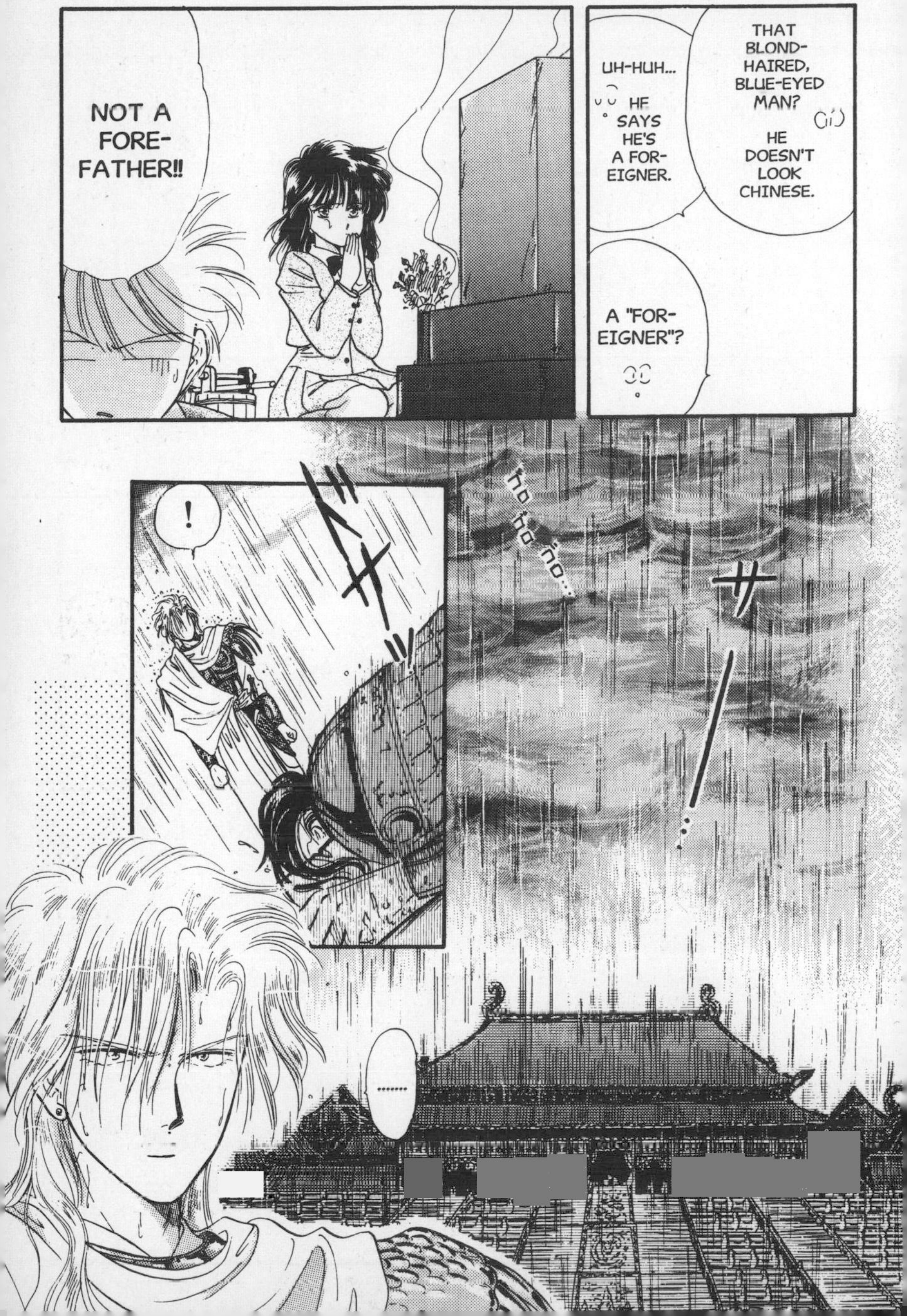
THAT BLOND-HAIRED, BLUE-EYED MAN? HE DOESN'T LOOK CHINESE.
UH-HUH... HE SAYS HE'S A FOR-EIGNER.
A "FOR-EIGNER"?
NOT A FORE-FATHER!!
ho ho ho...
!
......

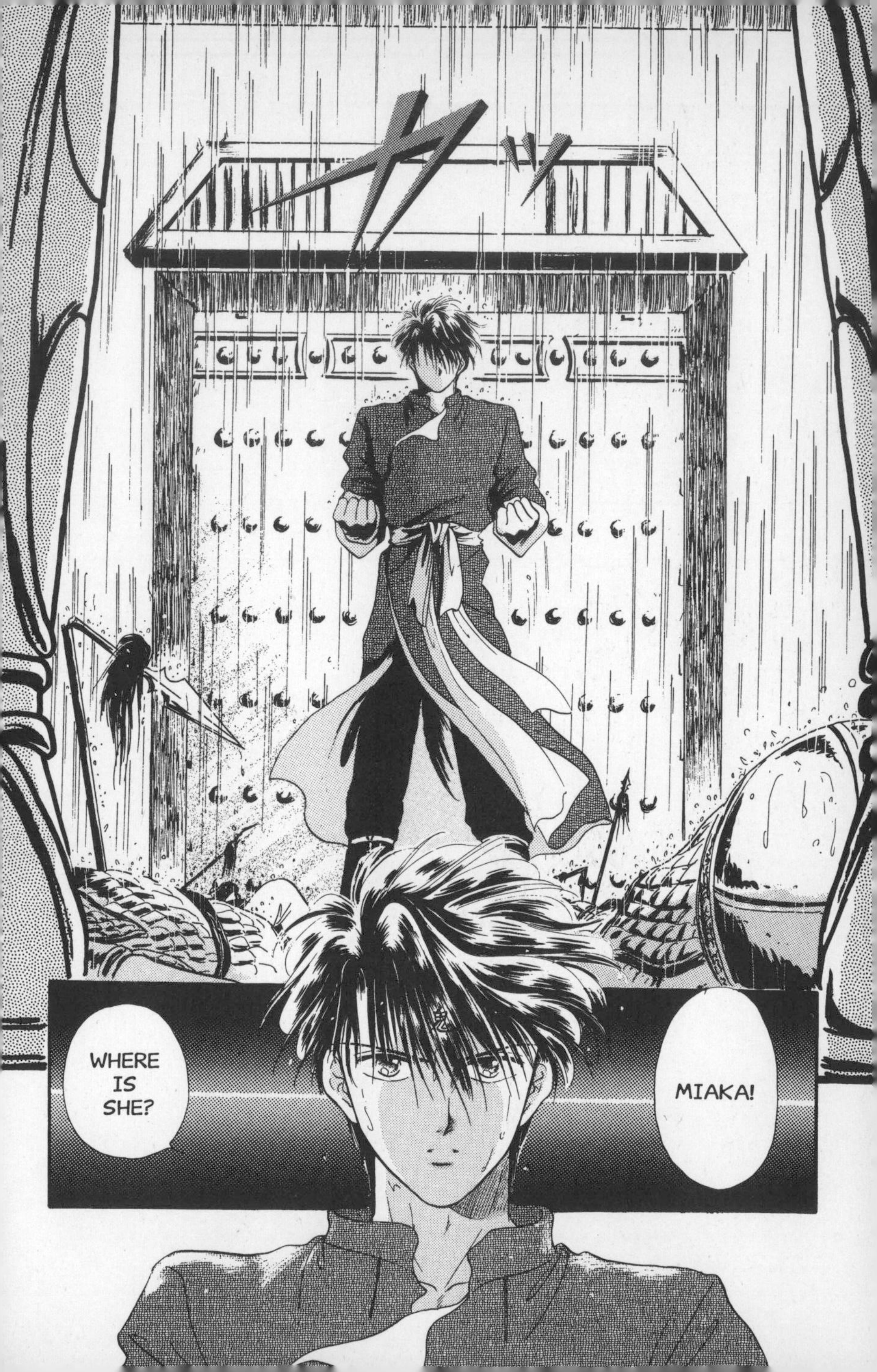
ガッ
MIAKA!
WHERE IS SHE?

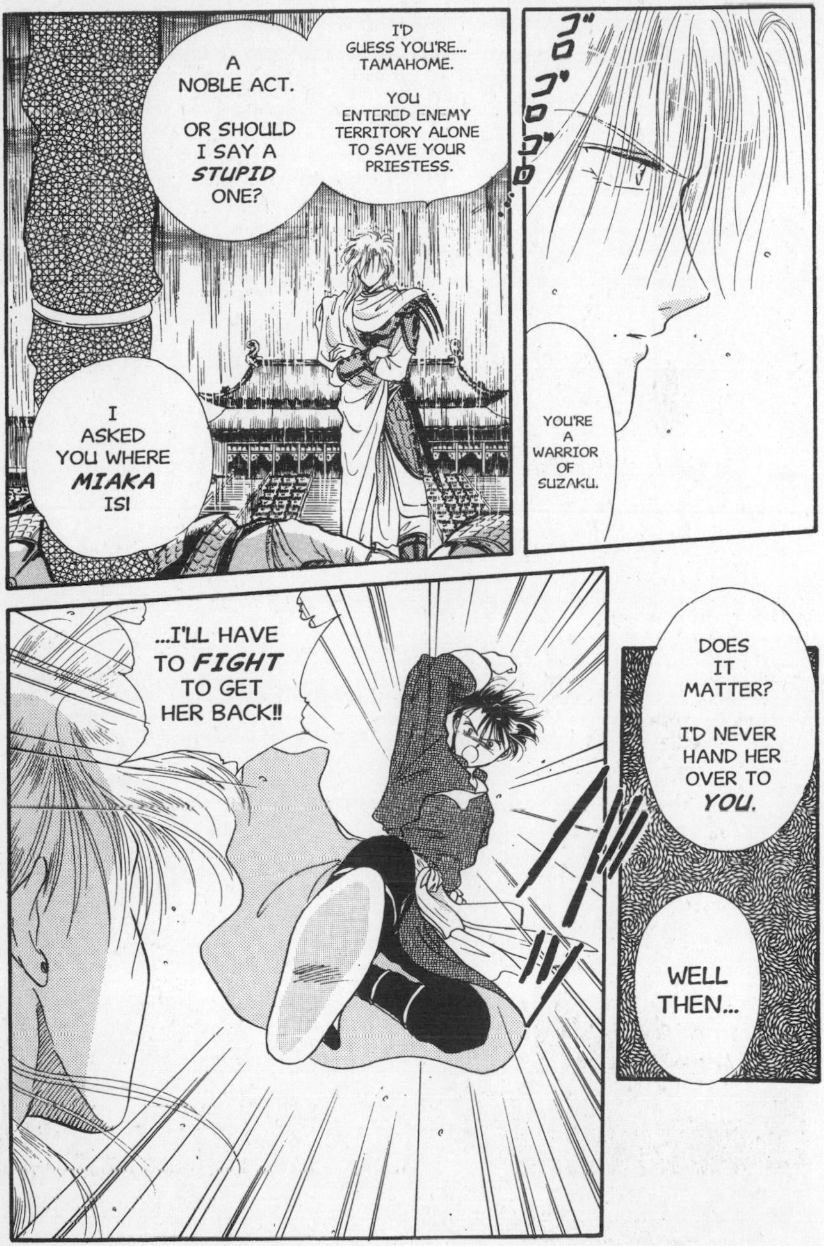
ゴロゴロゴロ
YOU'RE A WARRIOR OF SUZAKU.
I'D GUESS YOU'RE... TAMAHOME.
YOU ENTERED ENEMY TERRITORY ALONE TO SAVE YOUR PRIESTESS.
A NOBLE ACT.
OR SHOULD I SAY A *STUPID* ONE?
I ASKED YOU WHERE *MIAKA* IS!
DOES IT MATTER?
I'D NEVER HAND HER OVER TO *YOU*.
WELL THEN...
...I'LL HAVE TO *FIGHT* TO GET HER BACK!!

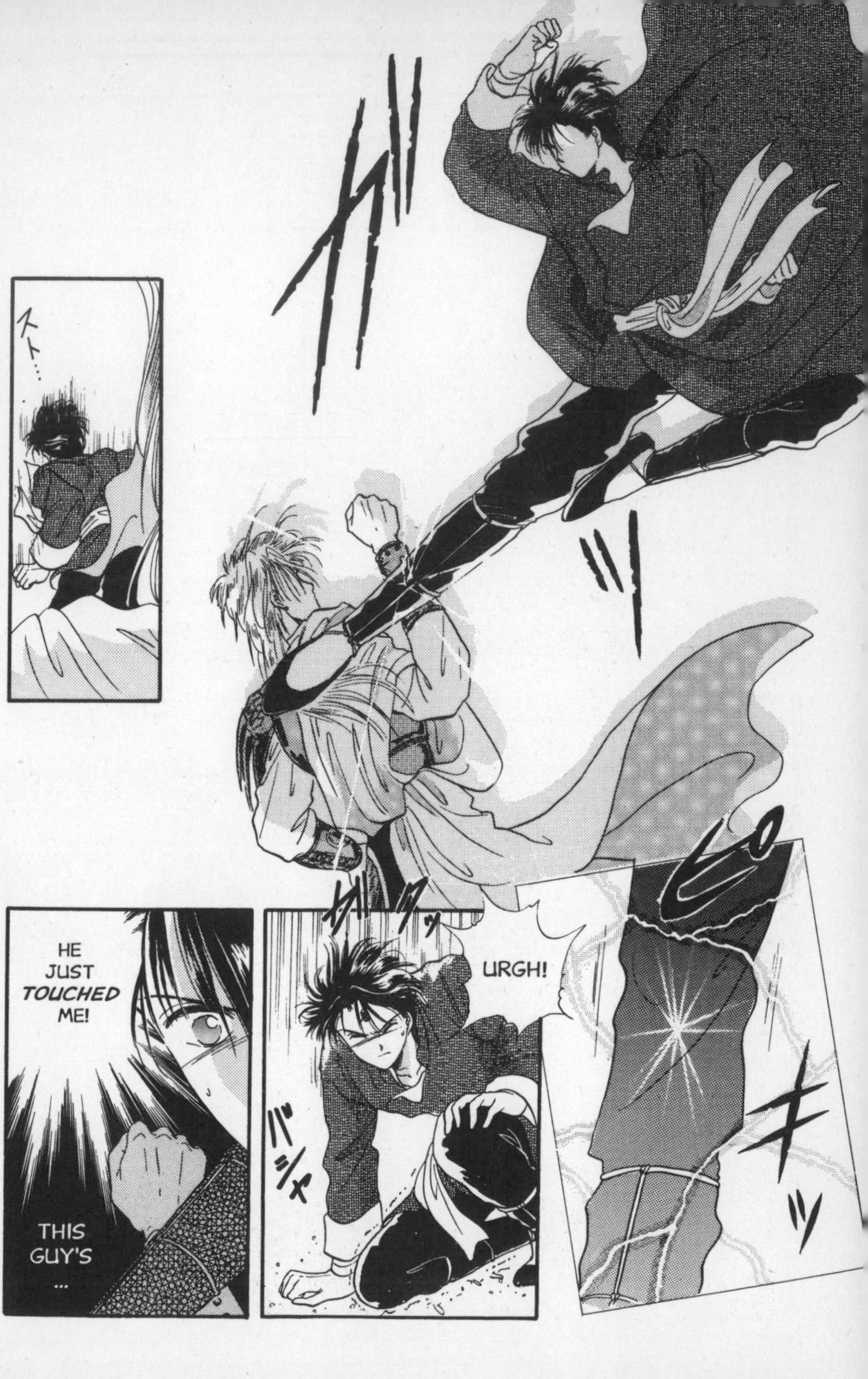
URGH!
HE JUST *TOUCHED* ME!
THIS GUY'S ...

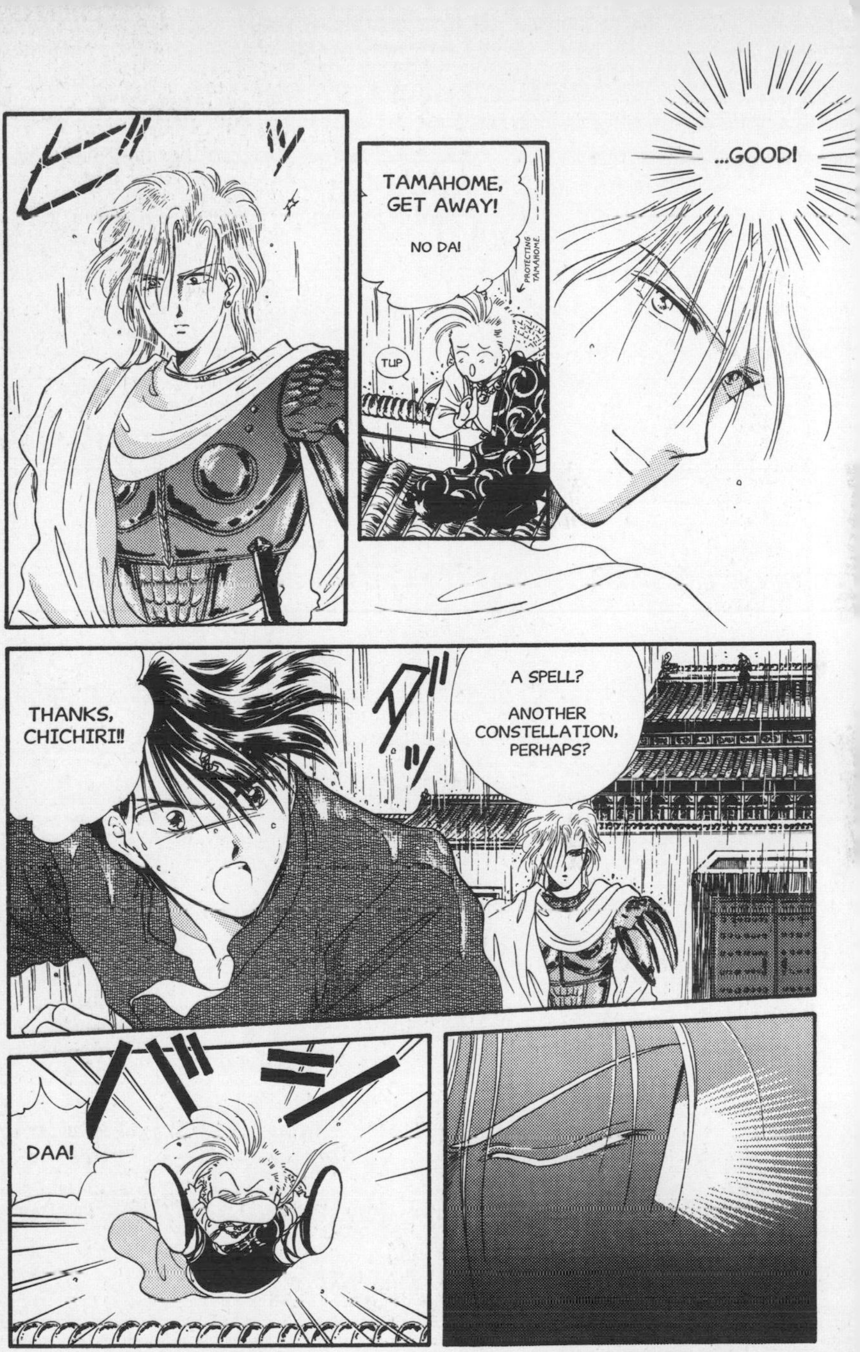
...GOOD!
TAMAHOME, GET AWAY!
NO DA!
PROTECTING TAMAHOME.
TUP
A SPELL?
ANOTHER CONSTELLATION, PERHAPS?
THANKS, CHICHIRI!!
DAA!

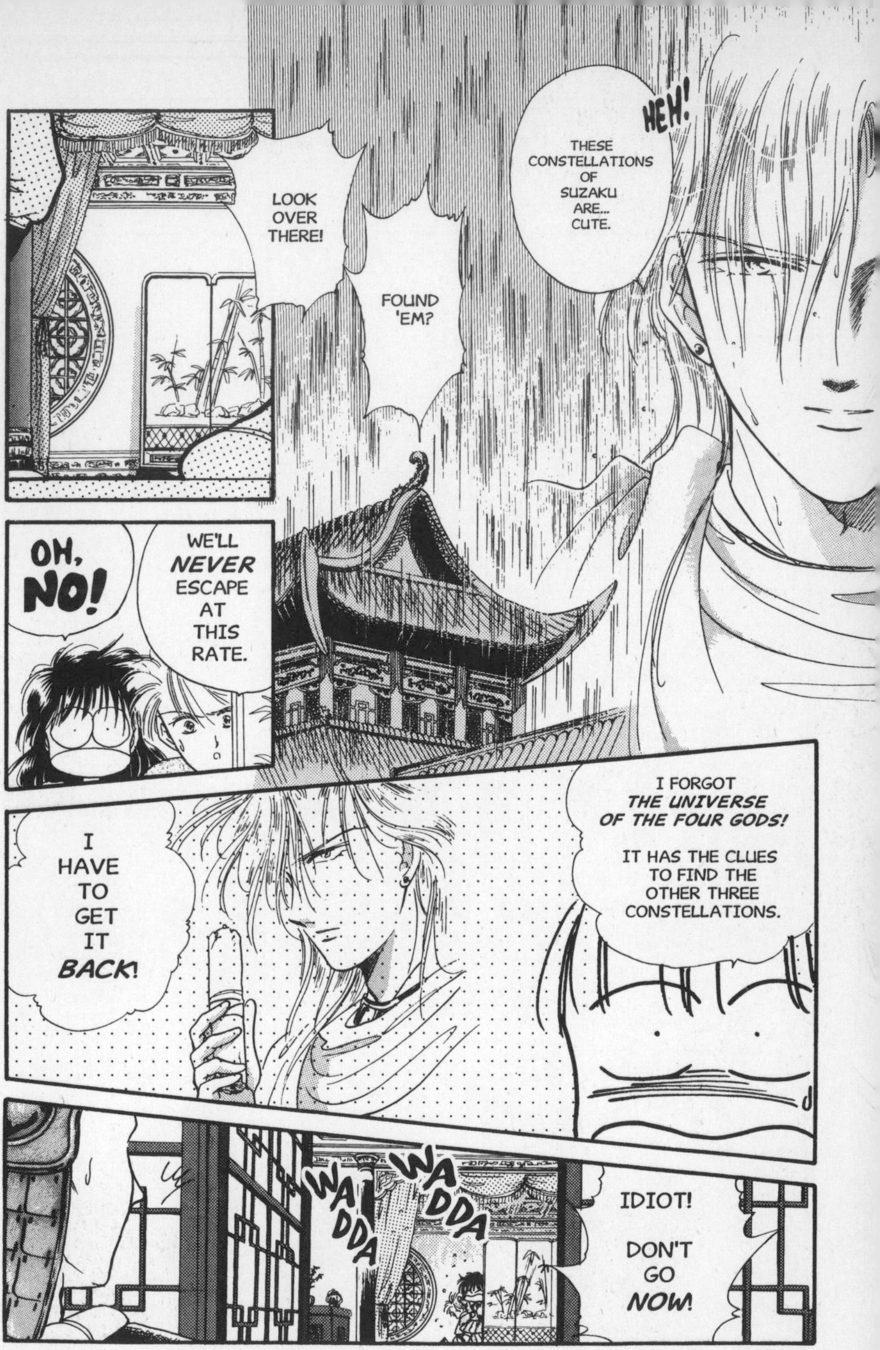
HEH!
THESE CONSTELLATIONS OF SUZAKU ARE... CUTE.
FOUND 'EM?
LOOK OVER THERE!
WE'LL *NEVER* ESCAPE AT THIS RATE.
OH, NO!
I FORGOT *THE UNIVERSE OF THE FOUR GODS!*
IT HAS THE CLUES TO FIND THE OTHER THREE CONSTELLATIONS.
I HAVE TO GET IT *BACK*!
IDIOT!
DON'T GO *NOW*!
WADDA
WADDA

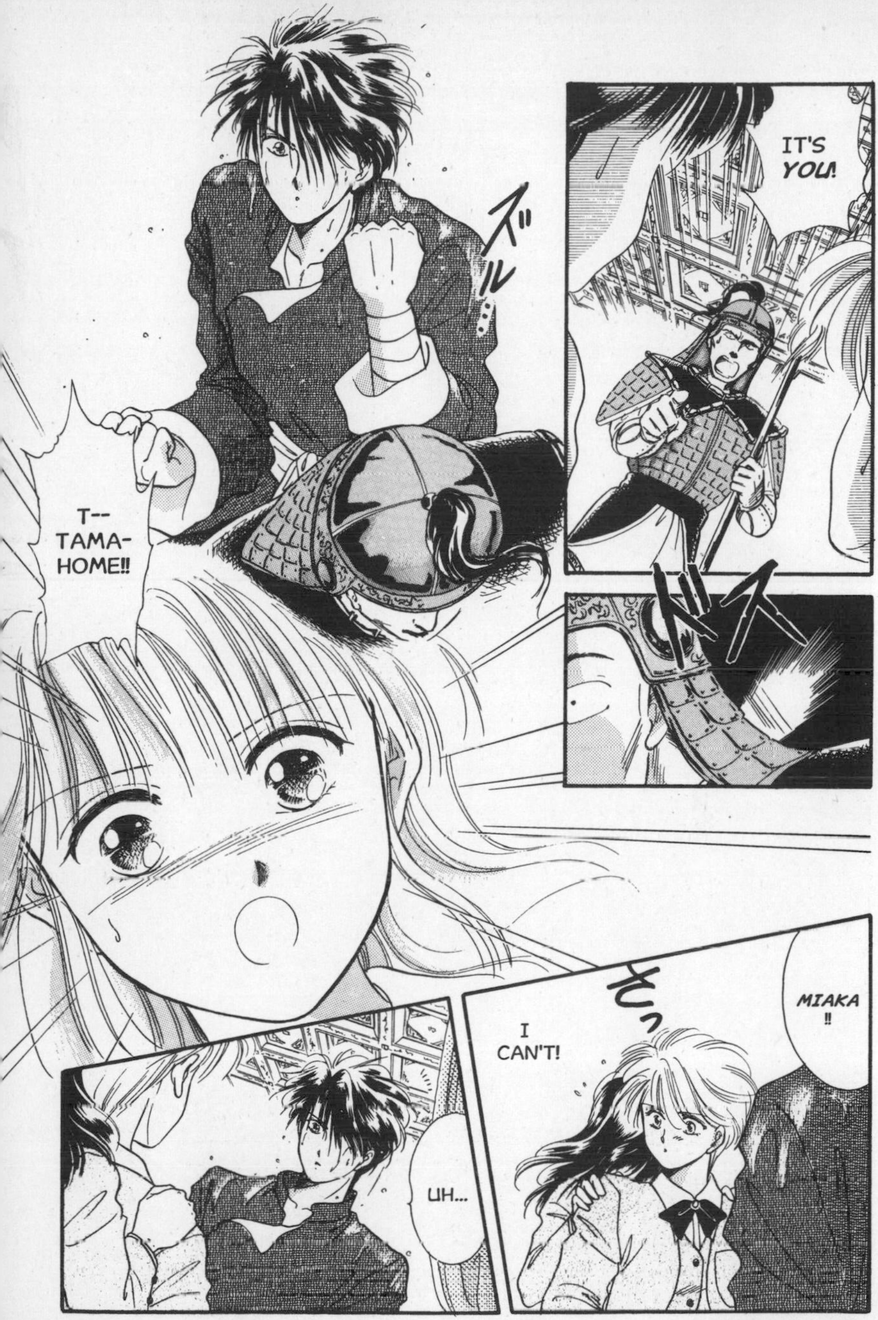
IT'S YOU!
ドス
ズル…
T-- TAMA-HOME!!
MIAKA!!
せっ
I CAN'T!
UH...

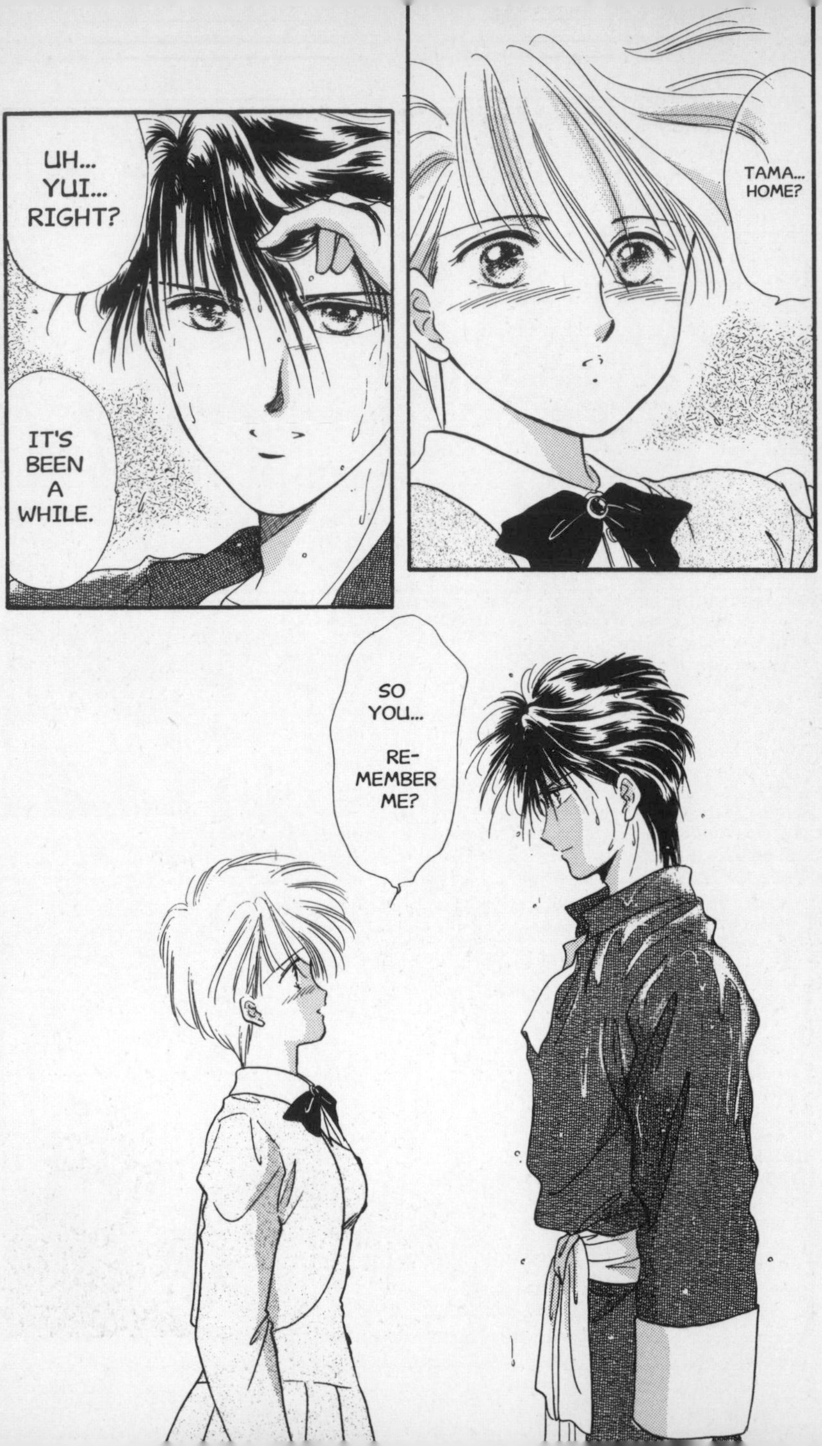
TAMA... HOME?
UH... YUI... RIGHT?
IT'S BEEN A WHILE.
SO YOU... RE-MEMBER ME?

"Where did the title Fushigi Yūgi come from?" I usually don't have trouble coming up with titles, but this one gave me a hard time. I've been planning this story since I was eighteen, but its tentative title, "Suzaku," just didn't seem right, so I had to work really hard for a title that would fit the right image. I looked through a whole bunch of magazines to come up with a good rhyming title, and that's how I came up with "Fushigi Yūgi." I actually think it's a pretty nice title. The kanji for "Yūgi" show up a lot in Hong King films. There's Bruce Lee's "Shibō Yūgi" (The Game of Death), for example. I didn't intend it to mean "frolic," but a nuance more like "game." I guess it would mean "Mysterious Game."*

I was talking about computer games with my assistant M., who insisted that "Fushigi Yūgi" would be a great computer game. We talked about this endlessly. It's not just because we were talking about my story, but because it seemed really fun. Computer games usually begin by introducing the story with drawings, but this one would start with opening the book *The Universe of the Four Gods*. Then a map would come up and you'd see Qu-Dong, Hotohori's palace, Daichi-san, and Tamahome's village. You could follow the plot the same way as the manga, or you could start from any random location and try to find all seven celestial warriors. It'd be an RPG game, so you'd have random enemies appearing, and everybody has different powers and abilities so the way to fight would always change. When you start losing, you could call on Chichiri, who'd suddenly appear and cast a spell. If Tamahome dies (for example), he might be revived at a certain location if he has enough money stored away.

Other ideas: If you go to Qu-Dong immediately without gaining enough experience points, you'd get yourself killed. If Miaka's a player-character, you'd have to have a gauge, not just for power, but for love too. Of course, she'd have to lose a lot of love points when she's away from Tamahome. When she returns to reality, that's the end of the game. Miaka could get advice from her brother. The ideas go on and on.

To be continued...!

*But something like "Miracle Game" just sounds so corny!

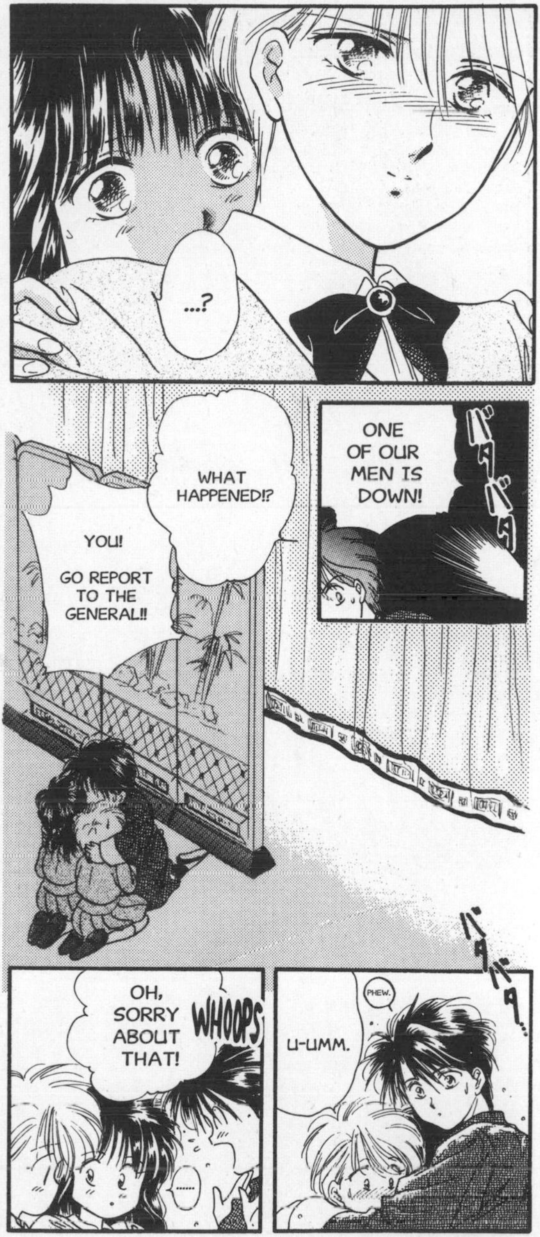
...?
ONE OF OUR MEN IS DOWN!
WHAT HAPPENED!?
YOU!
GO REPORT TO THE GENERAL!!
PHEW.
U-UMM.
OH, SORRY ABOUT THAT!
WHOOPS
......

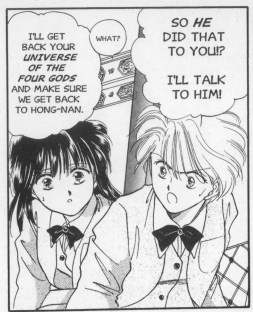

OWW...
W-WHAT'S WRONG!?
IT'S NOTHING. THAT FOREIGN GUY MESSED UP MY LEG A LITTLE!
GOTTA DROWN MY SORROWS!
FOREIGN GUY! NOT A *FORLORN* GUY!
SO *HE* DID THAT TO YOU!? I'LL TALK TO HIM!
WHAT?
I'LL GET BACK YOUR *UNIVERSE OF THE FOUR GODS* AND MAKE SURE WE GET BACK TO HONG-NAN.
DON'T WORRY. HE CAN'T REFUSE ME!
YUI!
...
WHY? WHY DO ALL THIS ON YOUR OWN?

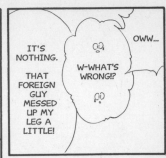

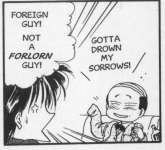

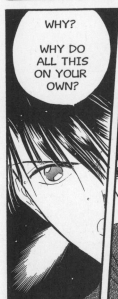

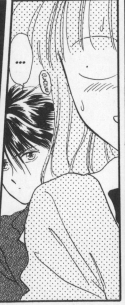

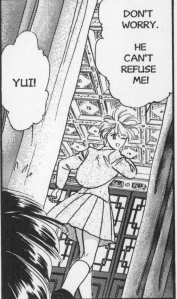

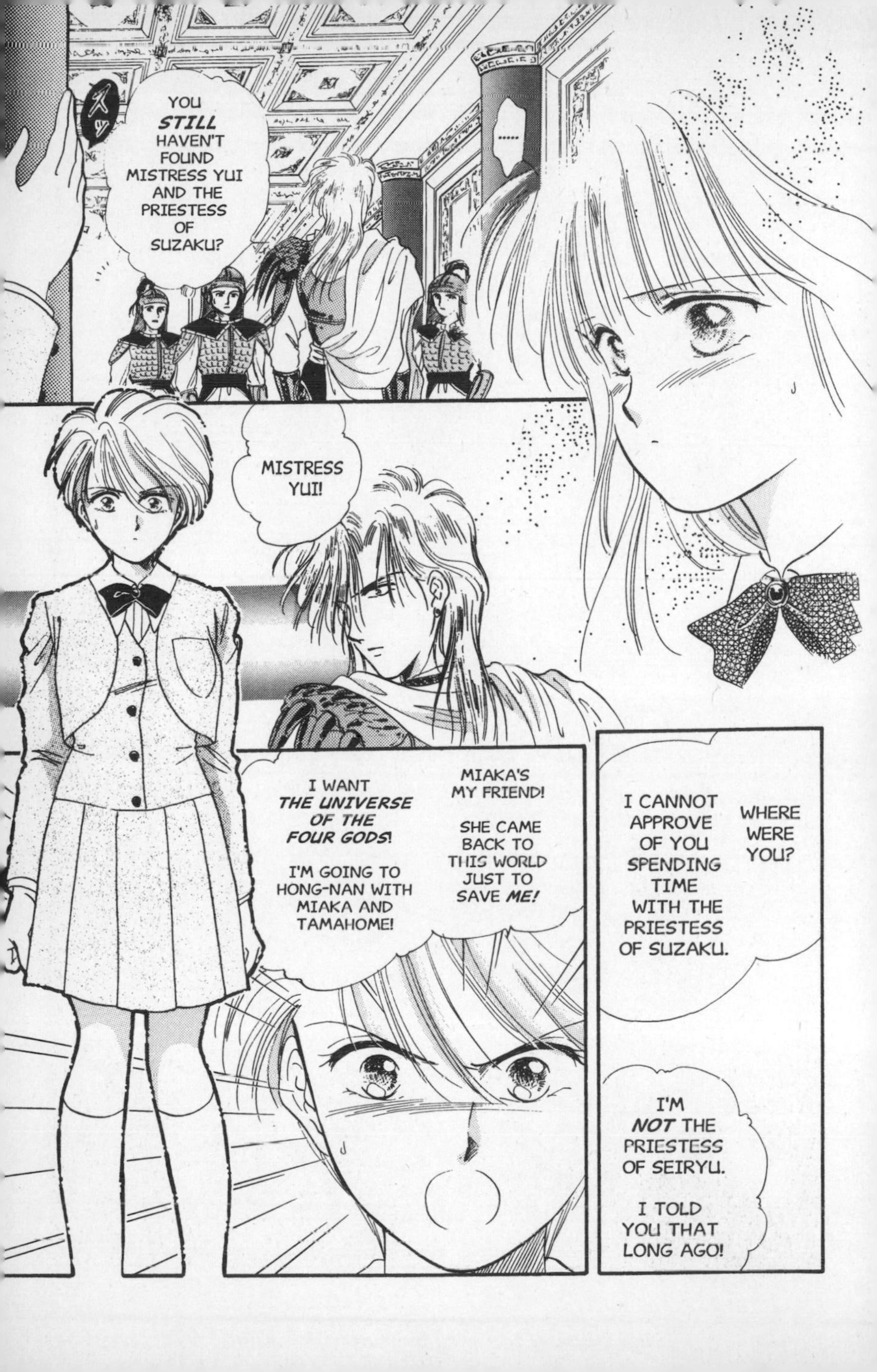
.....
YOU *STILL* HAVEN'T FOUND MISTRESS YUI AND THE PRIESTESS OF SUZAKU?
スッ
MISTRESS YUI!
WHERE WERE YOU?
I CANNOT APPROVE OF YOU SPENDING TIME WITH THE PRIESTESS OF SUZAKU.
I'M *NOT* THE PRIESTESS OF SEIRYU.
I TOLD YOU THAT LONG AGO!
MIAKA'S MY FRIEND!
SHE CAME BACK TO THIS WORLD JUST TO SAVE *ME!*
I WANT *THE UNIVERSE OF THE FOUR GODS*!
I'M GOING TO HONG-NAN WITH MIAKA AND TAMAHOME!

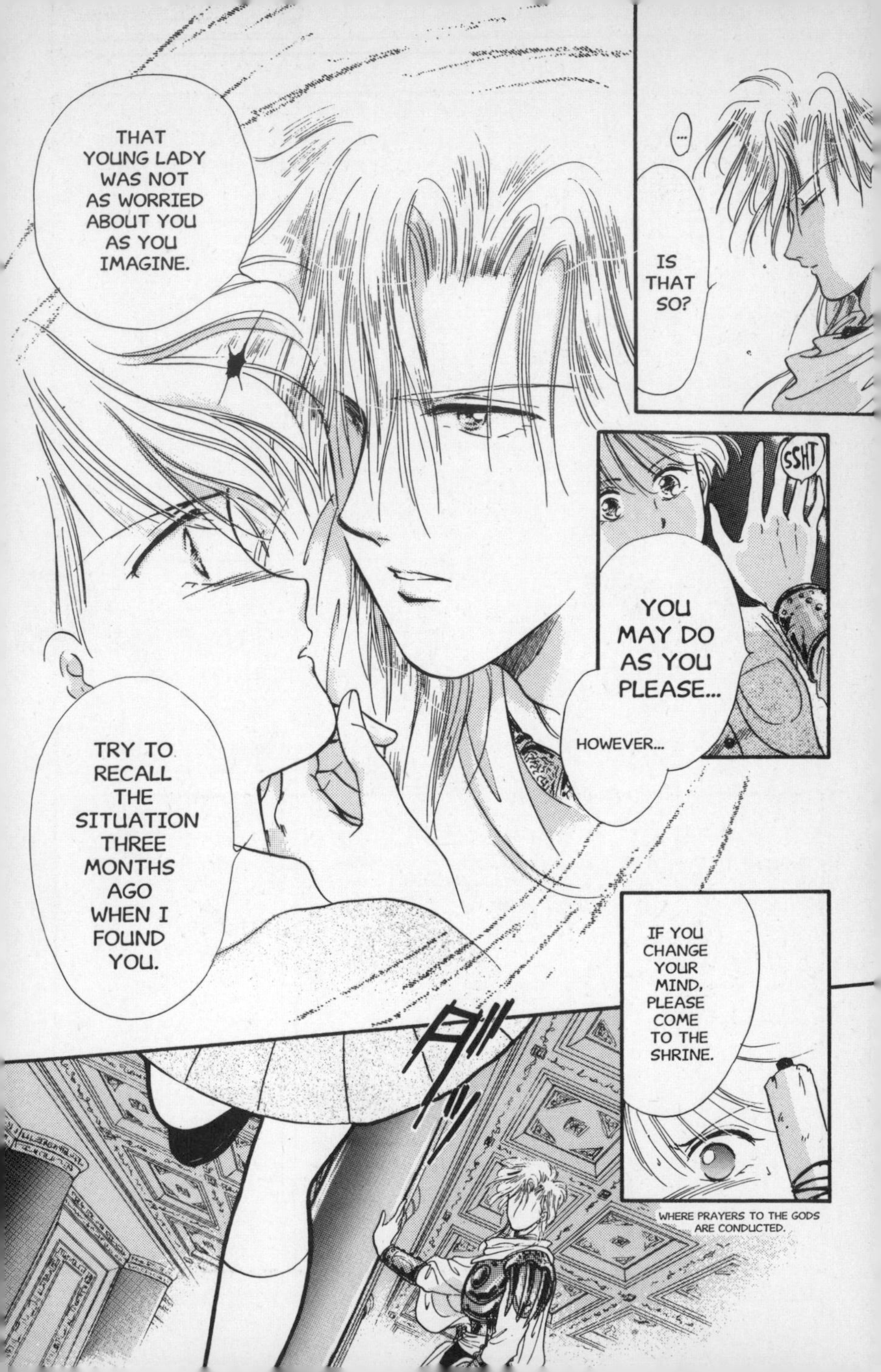
...
IS THAT SO?
SSHT
YOU MAY DO AS YOU PLEASE...
HOWEVER...
THAT YOUNG LADY WAS NOT AS WORRIED ABOUT YOU AS YOU IMAGINE.
TRY TO RECALL THE SITUATION THREE MONTHS AGO WHEN I FOUND YOU.
IF YOU CHANGE YOUR MIND, PLEASE COME TO THE SHRINE.
WHERE PRAYERS TO THE GODS ARE CONDUCTED.
ダッ

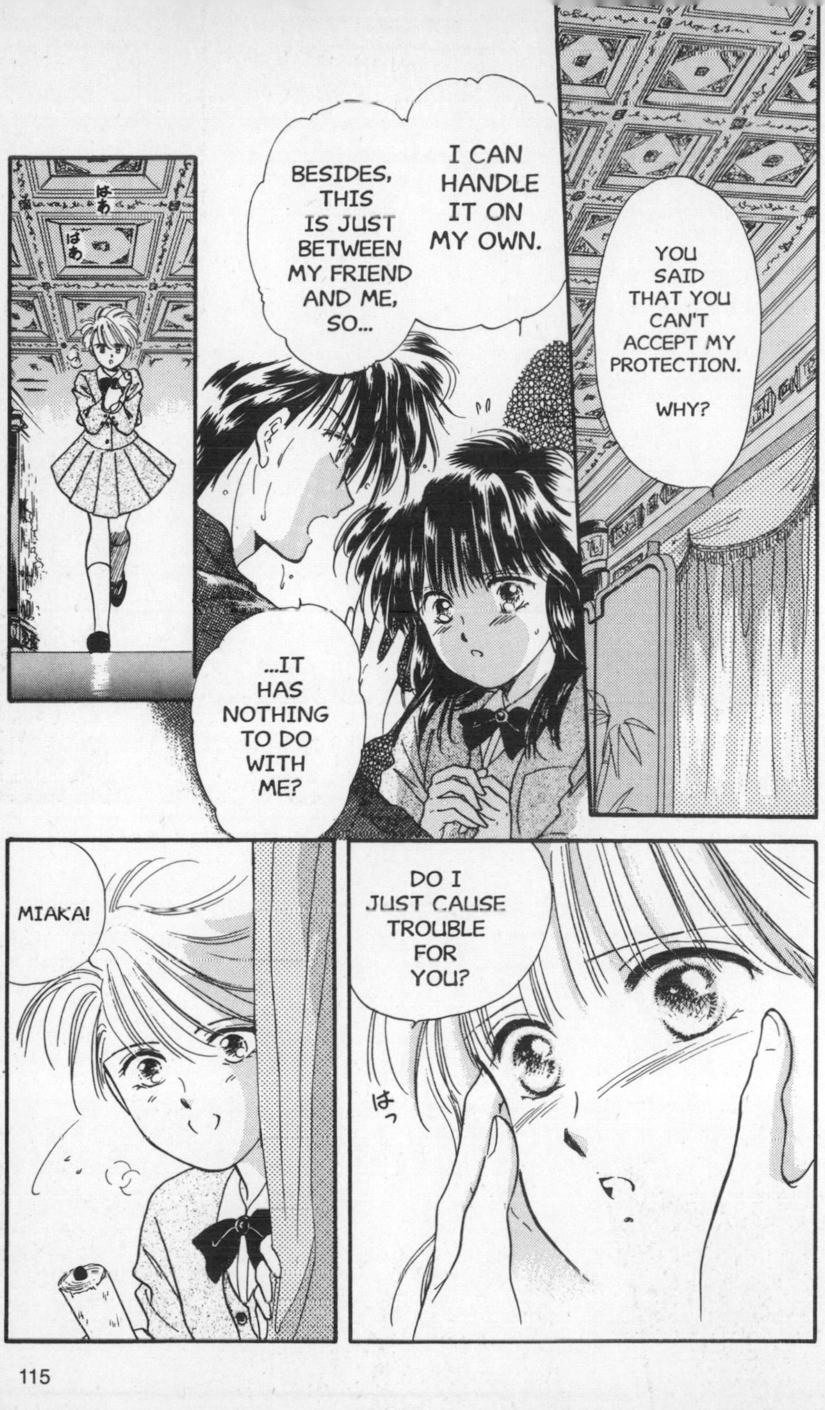
YOU SAID THAT YOU CAN'T ACCEPT MY PROTECTION. WHY?
I CAN HANDLE IT ON MY OWN.
BESIDES, THIS IS JUST BETWEEN MY FRIEND AND ME, SO...
...IT HAS NOTHING TO DO WITH ME?
はあ
はあ
DO I JUST CAUSE TROUBLE FOR YOU?
はっ
MIAKA!

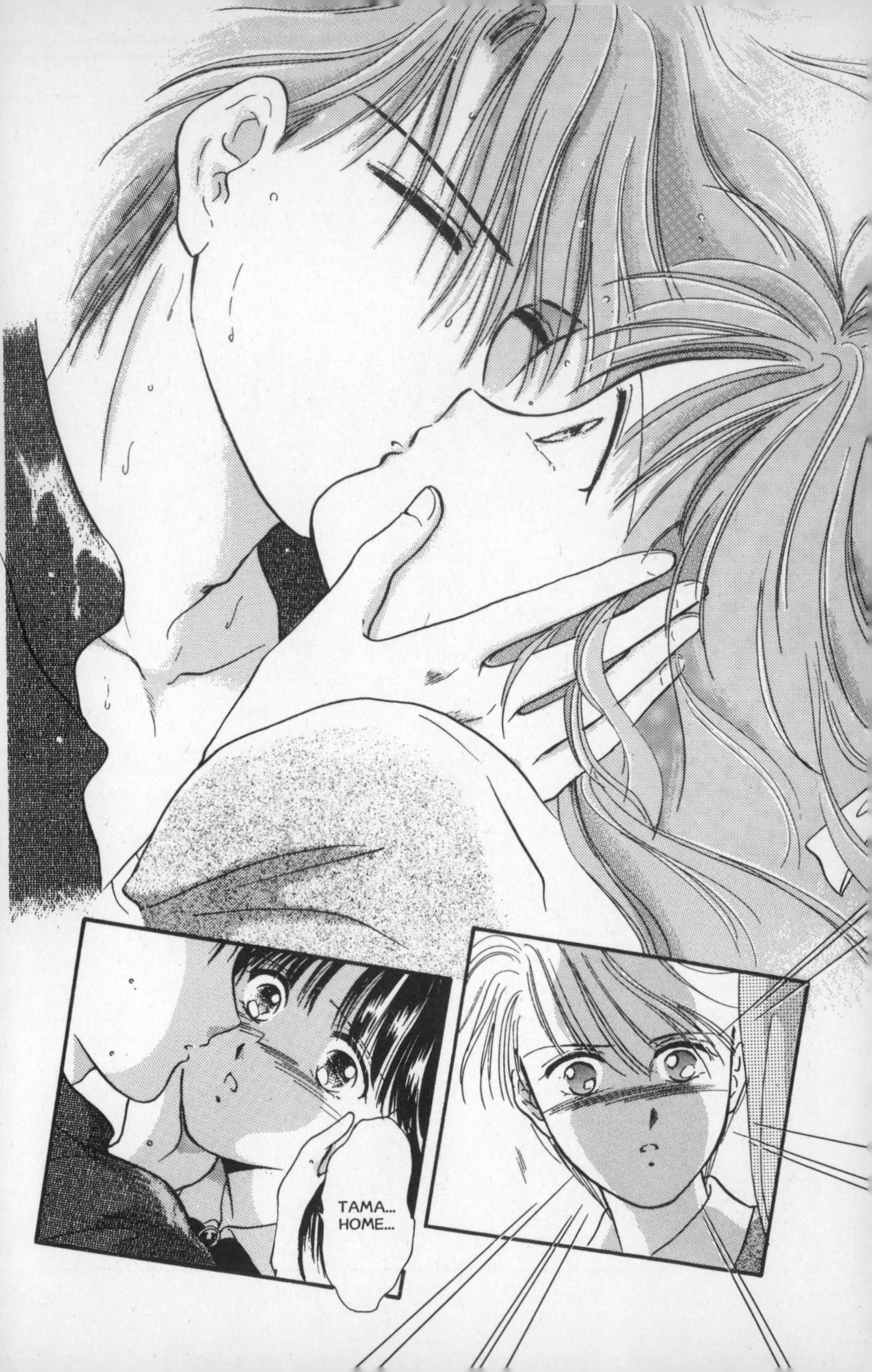
TAMA...
HOME...

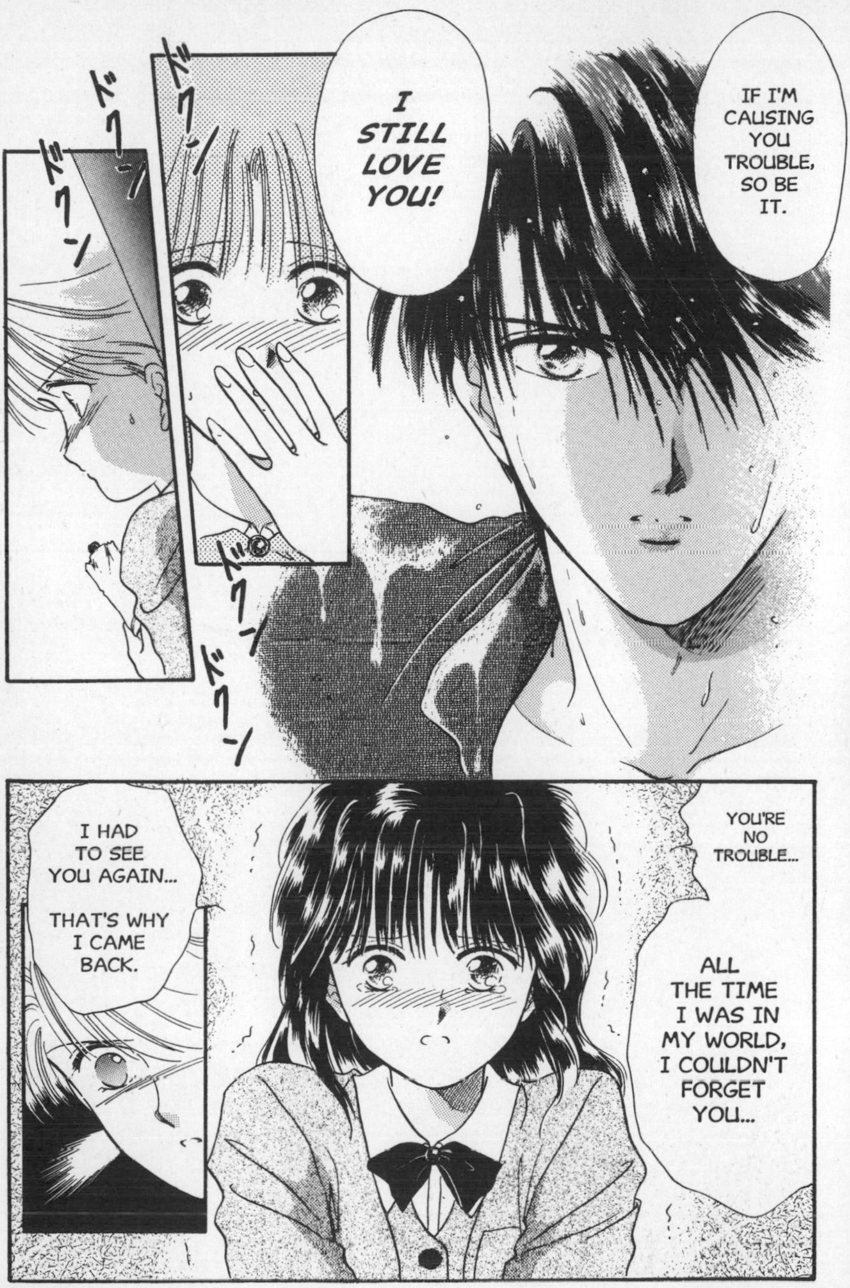
IF I'M CAUSING YOU TROUBLE, SO BE IT.
I STILL LOVE YOU!
ドクン
ドクン
ドクン
ドクン
YOU'RE NO TROUBLE...
ALL THE TIME I WAS IN MY WORLD, I COULDN'T FORGET YOU...
I HAD TO SEE YOU AGAIN...
THAT'S WHY I CAME BACK.

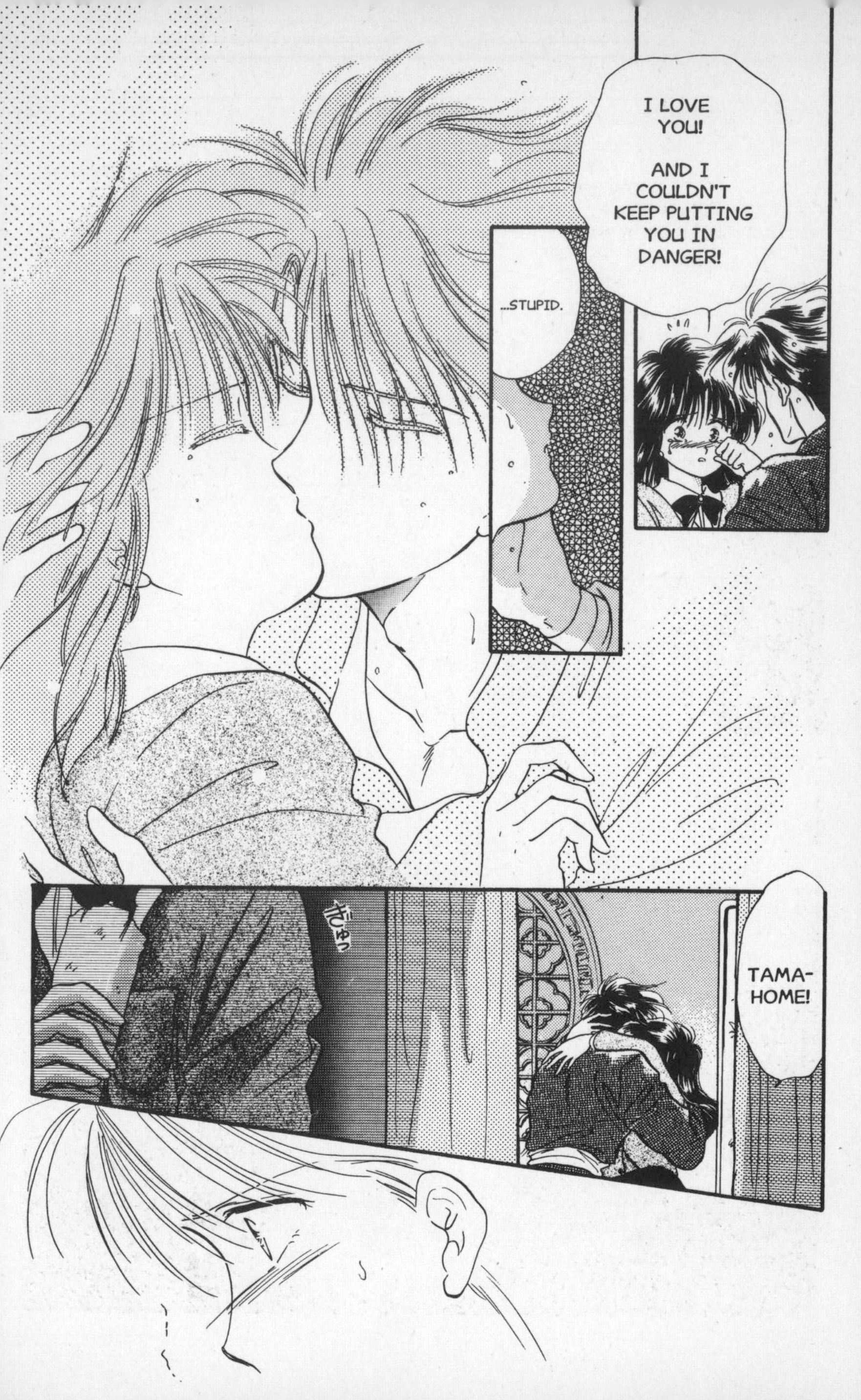
I LOVE YOU!
AND I COULDN'T KEEP PUTTING YOU IN DANGER!
...STUPID.
TAMA-HOME!
ぎゅっ

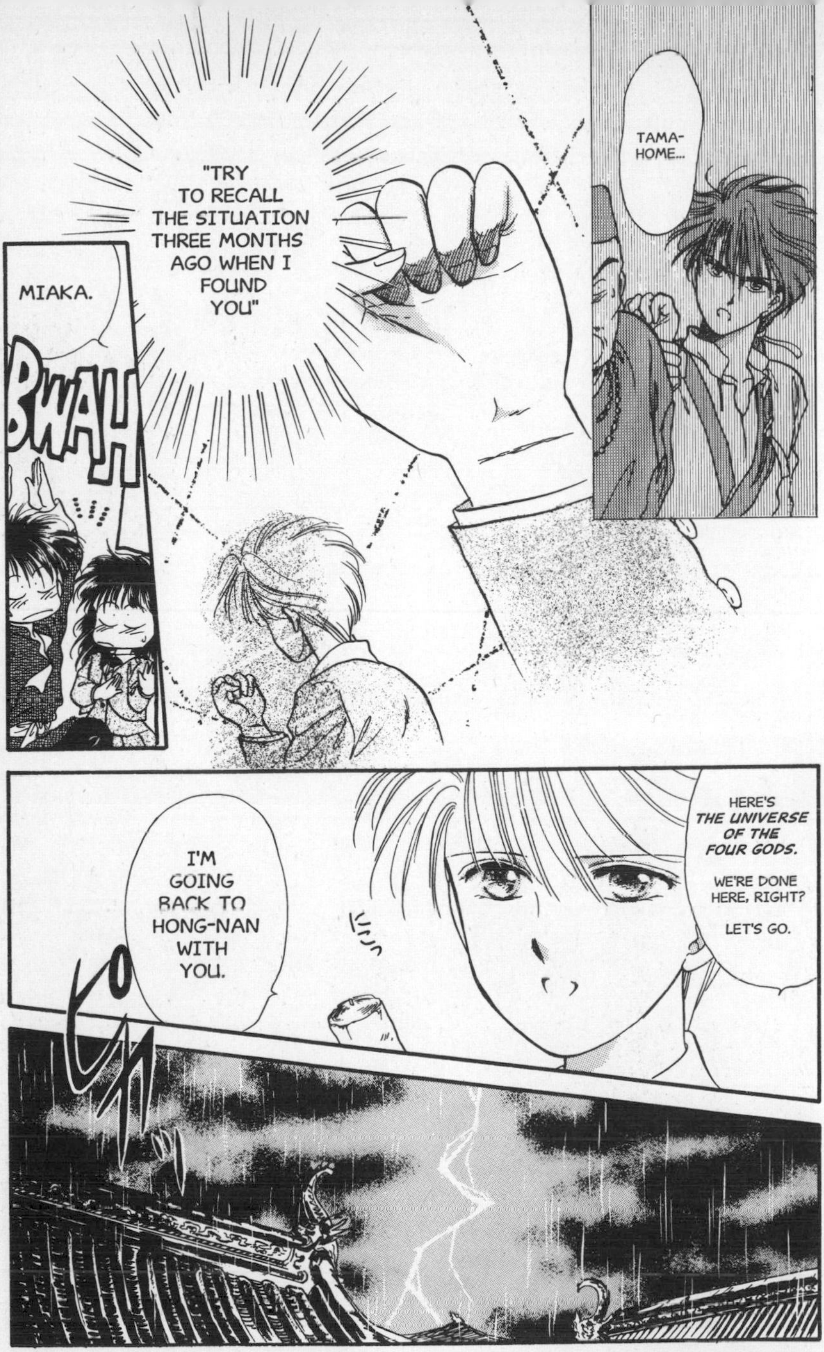
TAMA-HOME...
"TRY TO RECALL THE SITUATION THREE MONTHS AGO WHEN I FOUND YOU"
MIAKA.
BWAH
HERE'S *THE UNIVERSE OF THE FOUR GODS.*
WE'RE DONE HERE, RIGHT?
LET'S GO.
I'M GOING BACK TO HONG-NAN WITH YOU.

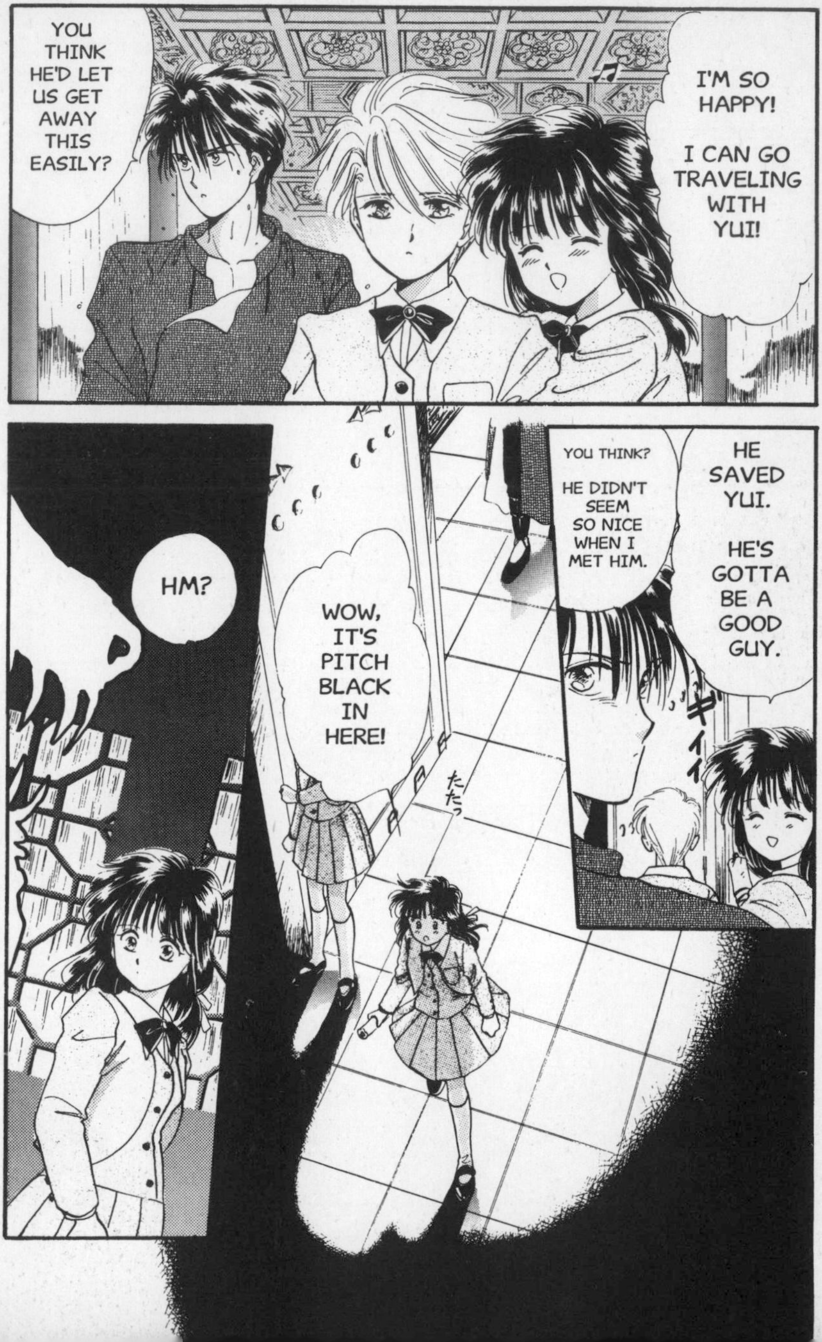
I'M SO HAPPY!
I CAN GO TRAVELING WITH YUI!
YOU THINK HE'D LET US GET AWAY THIS EASILY?
HE SAVED YUI.
HE'S GOTTA BE A GOOD GUY.
YOU THINK?
HE DIDN'T SEEM SO NICE WHEN I MET HIM.
ギイイ
WOW, IT'S PITCH BLACK IN HERE!
たたっ
HM?

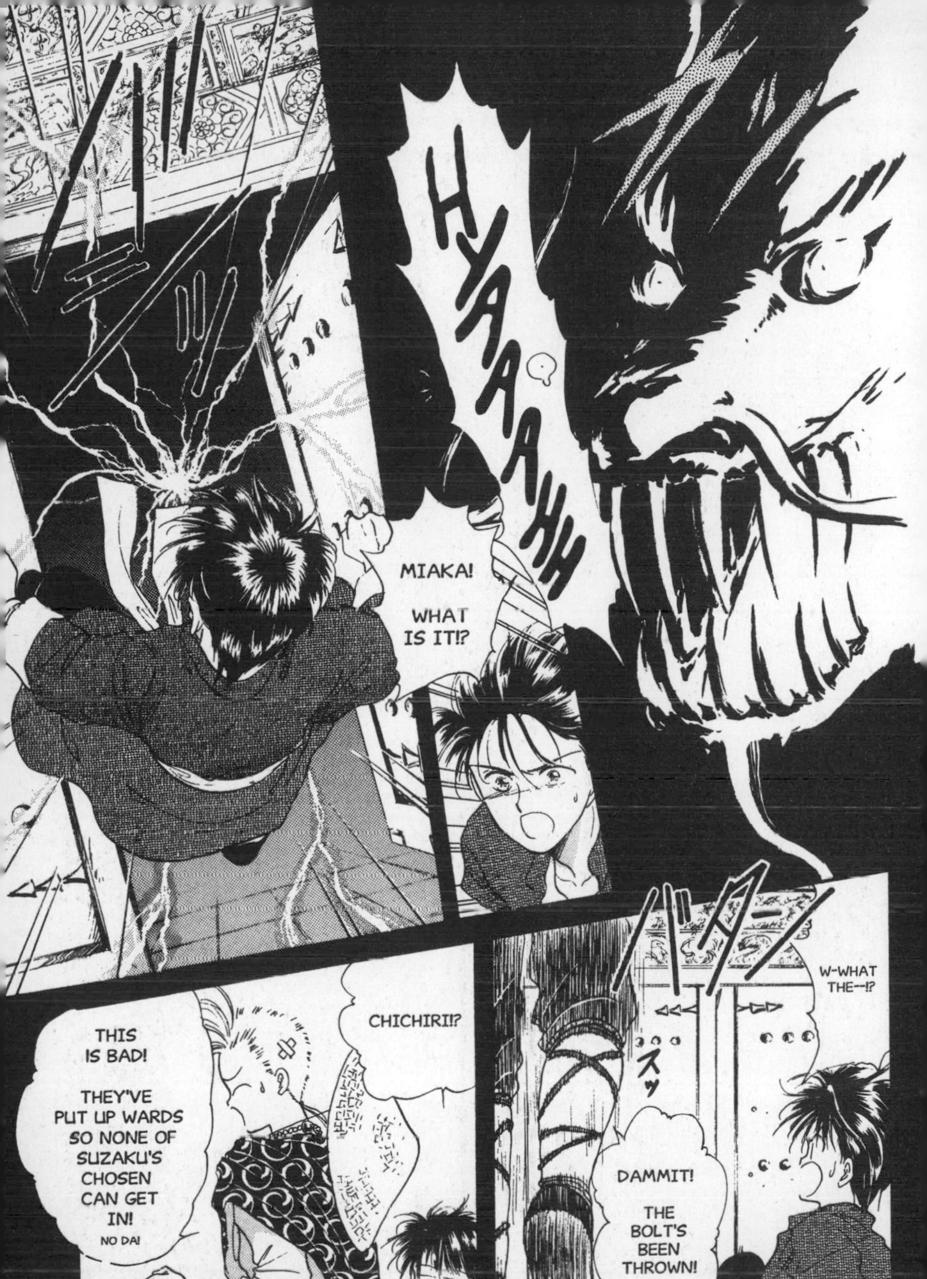

HYAAAHHH
MIAKA!
WHAT IS IT!?
バターン
W-WHAT THE--!?
スッ
DAMMIT!
THE BOLT'S BEEN THROWN!
NO DA!
CHICHIRI!?
THIS IS BAD!
THEY'VE PUT UP WARDS SO NONE OF SUZAKU'S CHOSEN CAN GET IN!
NO DA!

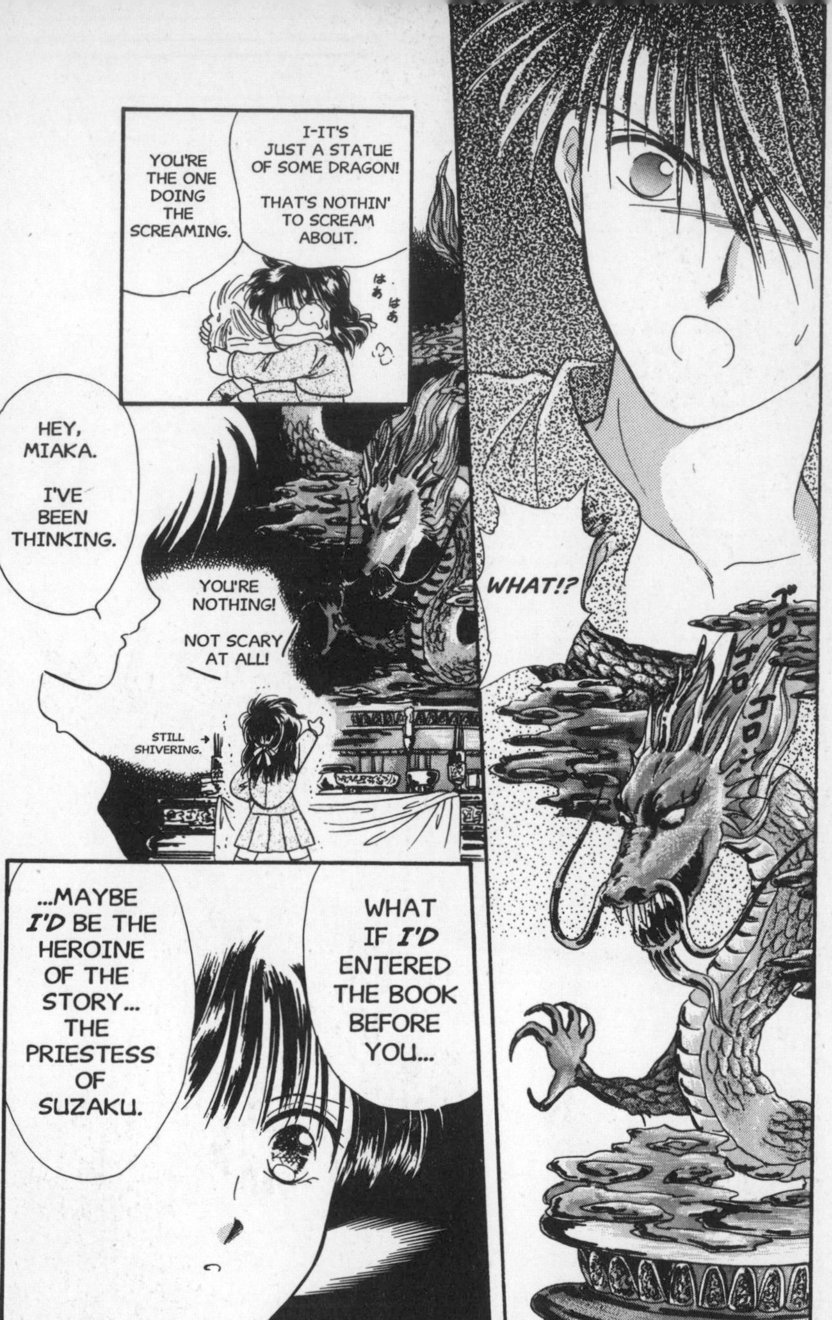
WHAT!?
I-IT'S JUST A STATUE OF SOME DRAGON! THAT'S NOTHIN' TO SCREAM ABOUT.
YOU'RE THE ONE DOING THE SCREAMING.
はぁ はぁ
YOU'RE NOTHING! NOT SCARY AT ALL!
STILL SHIVERING.
HEY, MIAKA. I'VE BEEN THINKING.
WHAT IF *I'D* ENTERED THE BOOK BEFORE YOU...
...MAYBE *I'D* BE THE HEROINE OF THE STORY... THE PRIESTESS OF SUZAKU.

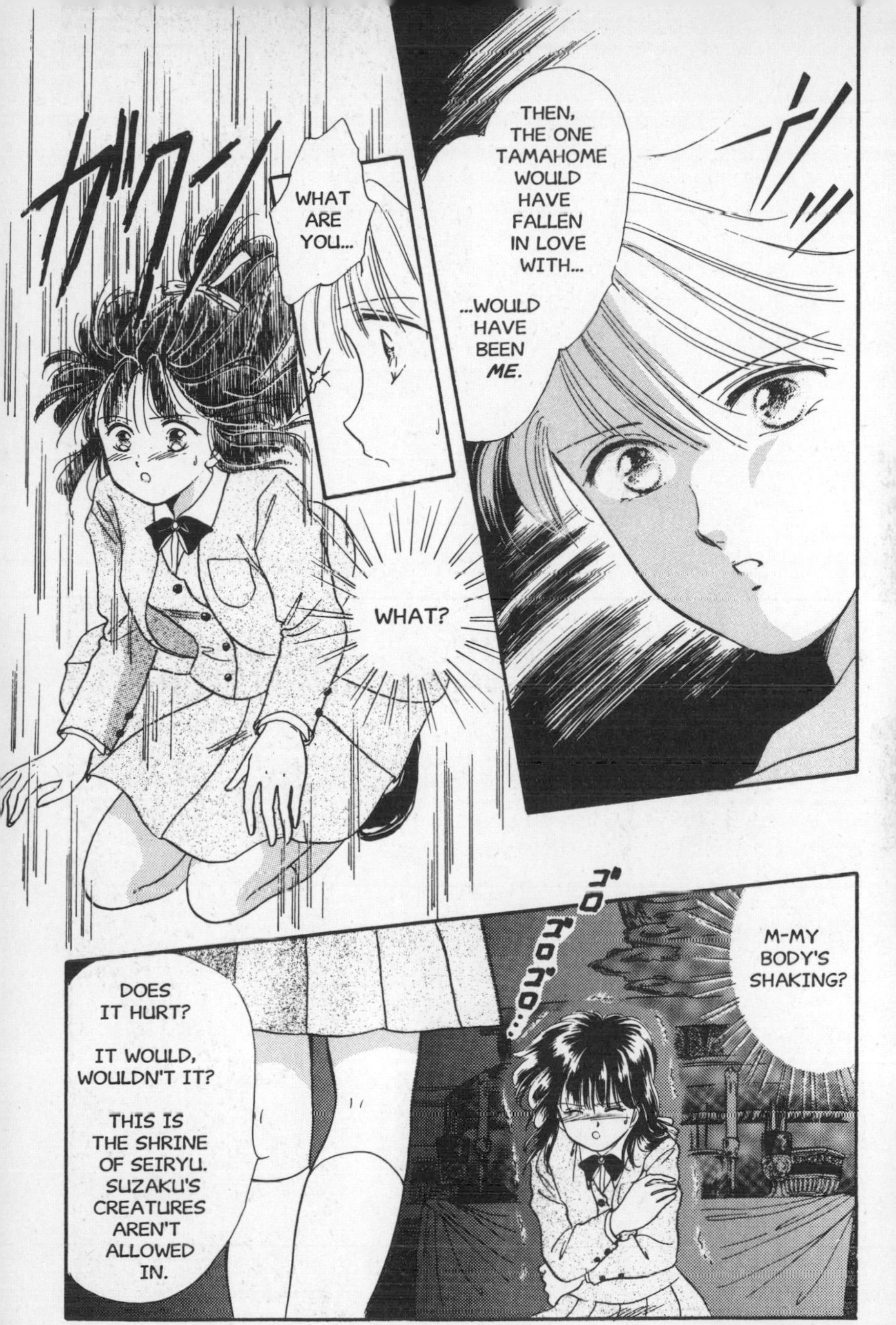
THEN, THE ONE TAMAHOME WOULD HAVE FALLEN IN LOVE WITH...
...WOULD HAVE BEEN *ME*.
WHAT ARE YOU...
WHAT?
M-MY BODY'S SHAKING?
DOES IT HURT?
IT WOULD, WOULDN'T IT?
THIS IS THE SHRINE OF SEIRYU. SUZAKU'S CREATURES AREN'T ALLOWED IN.

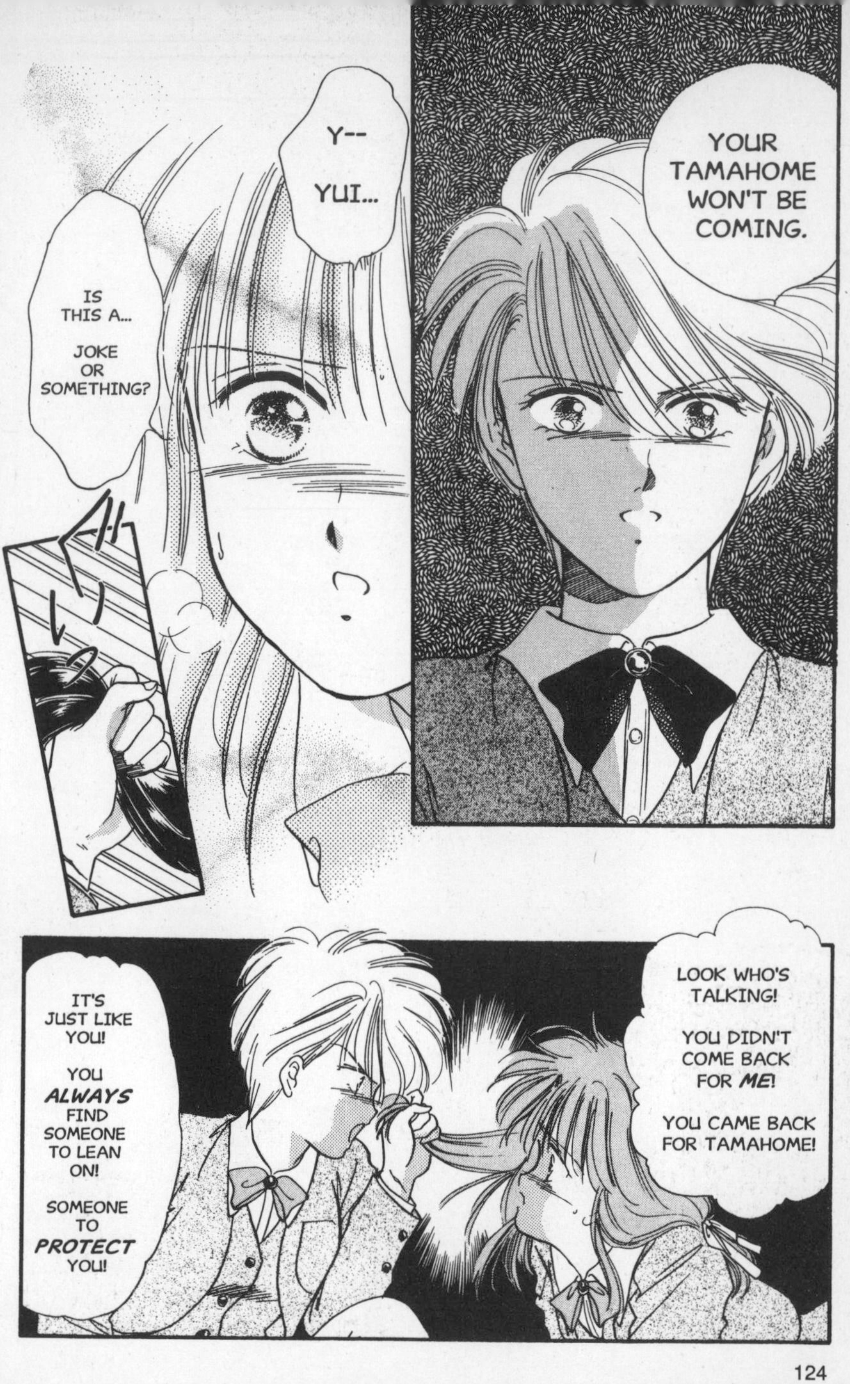
YOUR TAMAHOME WON'T BE COMING.
Y-- YUI...
IS THIS A... JOKE OR SOMETHING?
LOOK WHO'S TALKING! YOU DIDN'T COME BACK FOR *ME*! YOU CAME BACK FOR TAMAHOME!
IT'S JUST LIKE YOU! YOU *ALWAYS* FIND SOMEONE TO LEAN ON! SOMEONE TO *PROTECT* YOU!

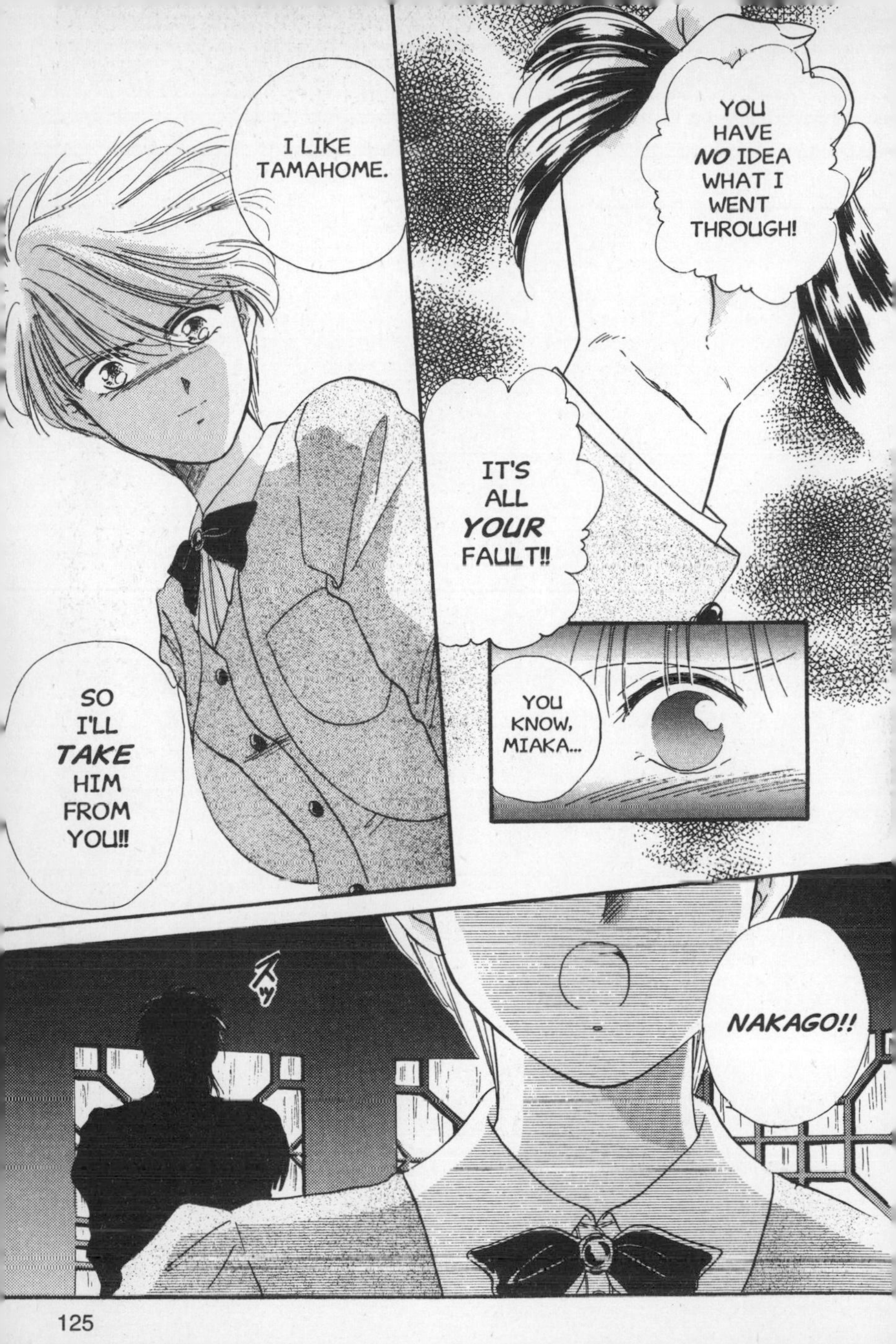
YOU HAVE NO IDEA WHAT I WENT THROUGH!
IT'S ALL YOUR FAULT!!
YOU KNOW, MIAKA...
I LIKE TAMAHOME.
SO I'LL TAKE HIM FROM YOU!!
NAKAGO!!

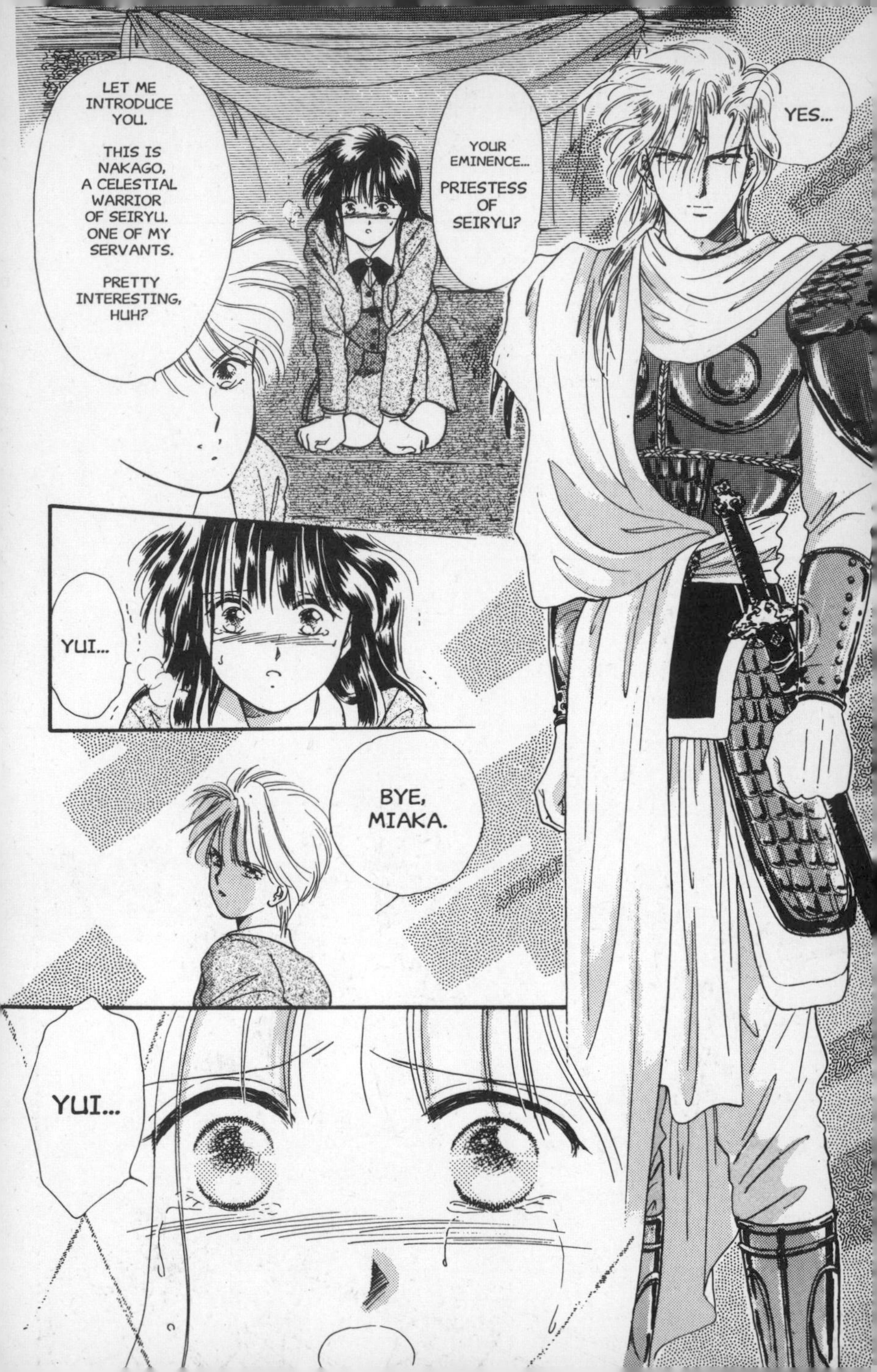
YES...
YOUR EMINENCE... PRIESTESS OF SEIRYU?
LET ME INTRODUCE YOU. THIS IS NAKAGO, A CELESTIAL WARRIOR OF SEIRYU. ONE OF MY SERVANTS. PRETTY INTERESTING, HUH?
YUI...
BYE, MIAKA.
YUI...

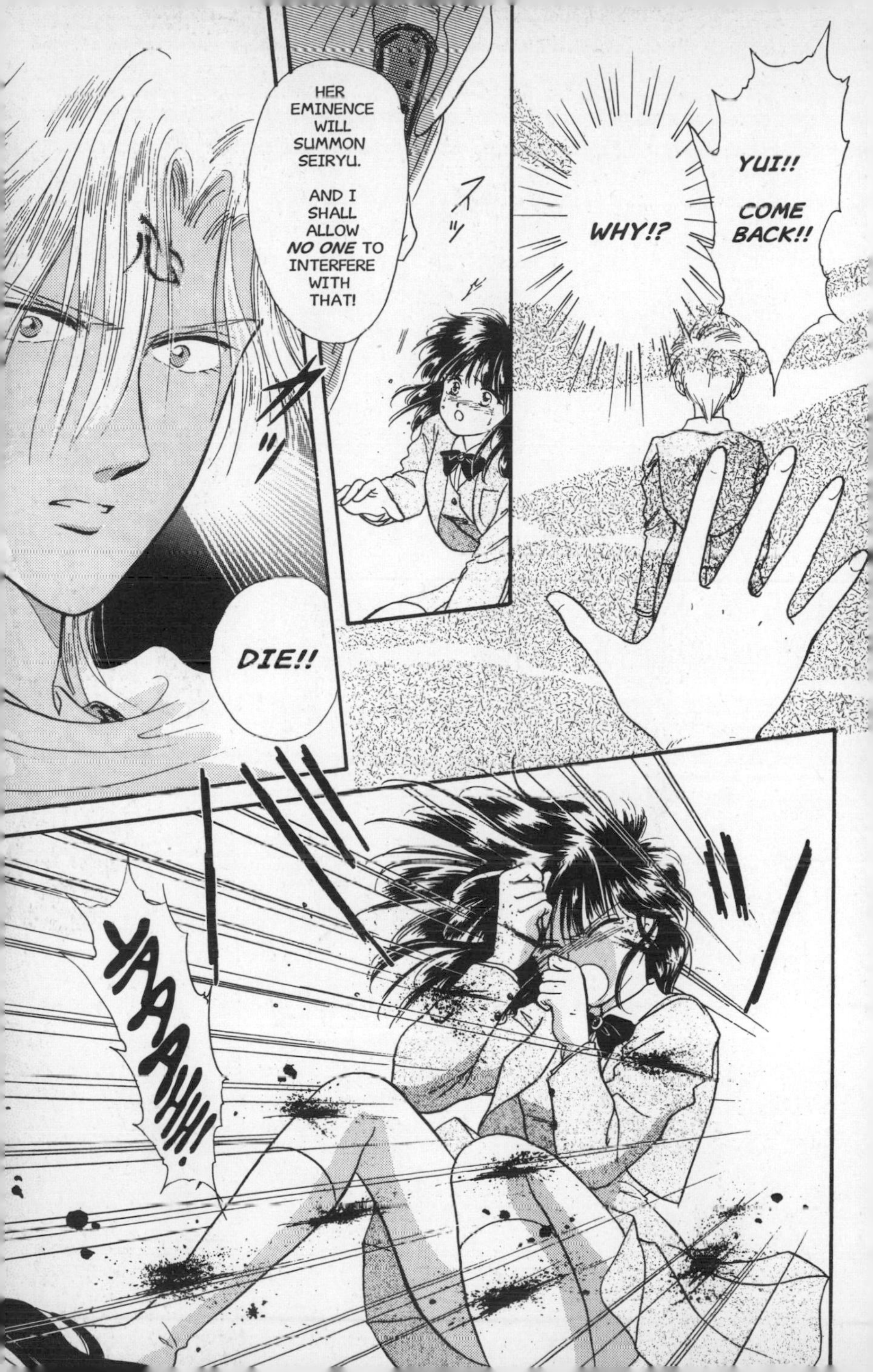
YUI!!
COME BACK!!
WHY!?
HER EMINENCE WILL SUMMON SEIRYU.
AND I SHALL ALLOW *NO ONE* TO INTERFERE WITH THAT!
DIE!!
YAAAHH!!

BACK BY POPULAR DEMAND
PARDON THE PARODY NEWLY RETITLED AS

FUSHIGI AKUGI THE MALICIOUS PLAY ふしぎ悪戯

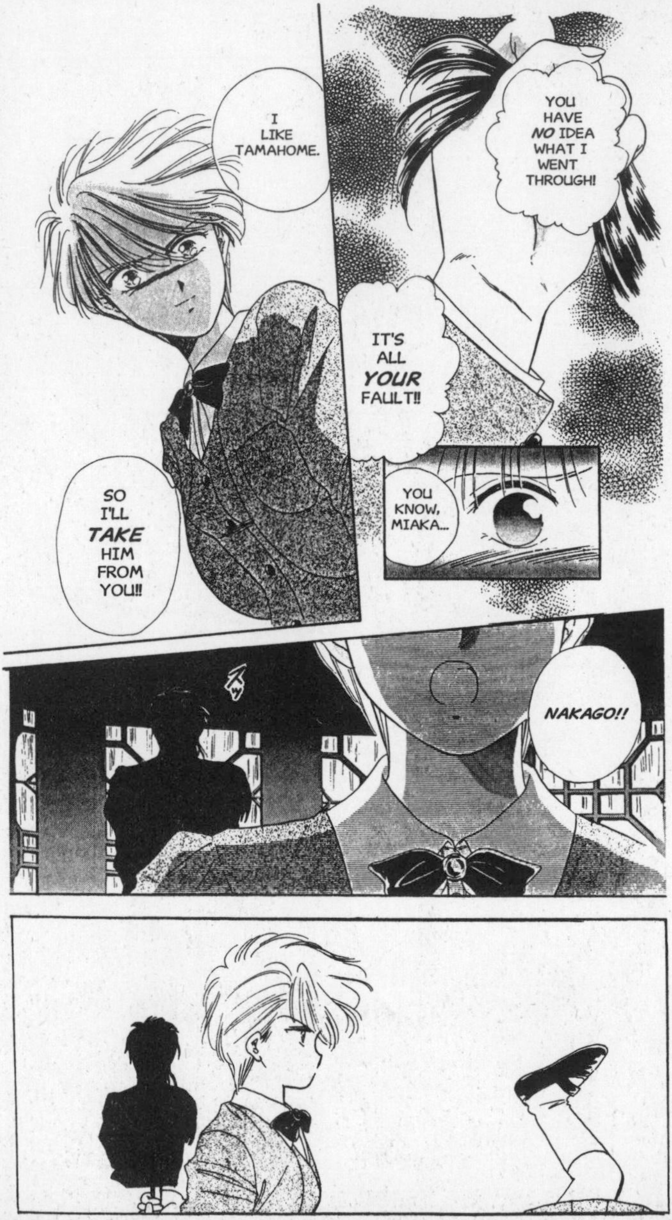
YOU HAVE *NO* IDEA WHAT I WENT THROUGH!
IT'S ALL *YOUR* FAULT!!
YOU KNOW, MIAKA...
I LIKE TAMAHOME.
SO I'LL *TAKE* HIM FROM YOU!!
NAKAGO!!

ANOTHER IDEA ←BY MANGA ARTIST Y.M.

CHAPTER SEVENTEEN
SOULS DRIFTING APART

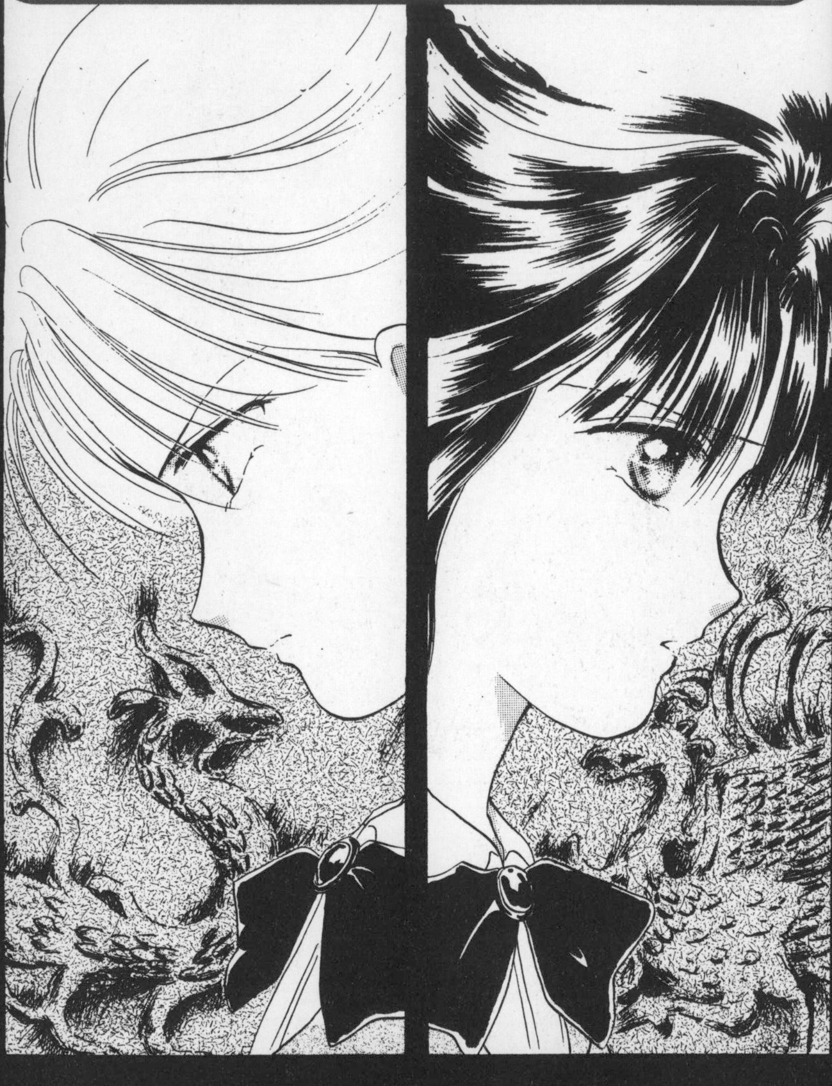

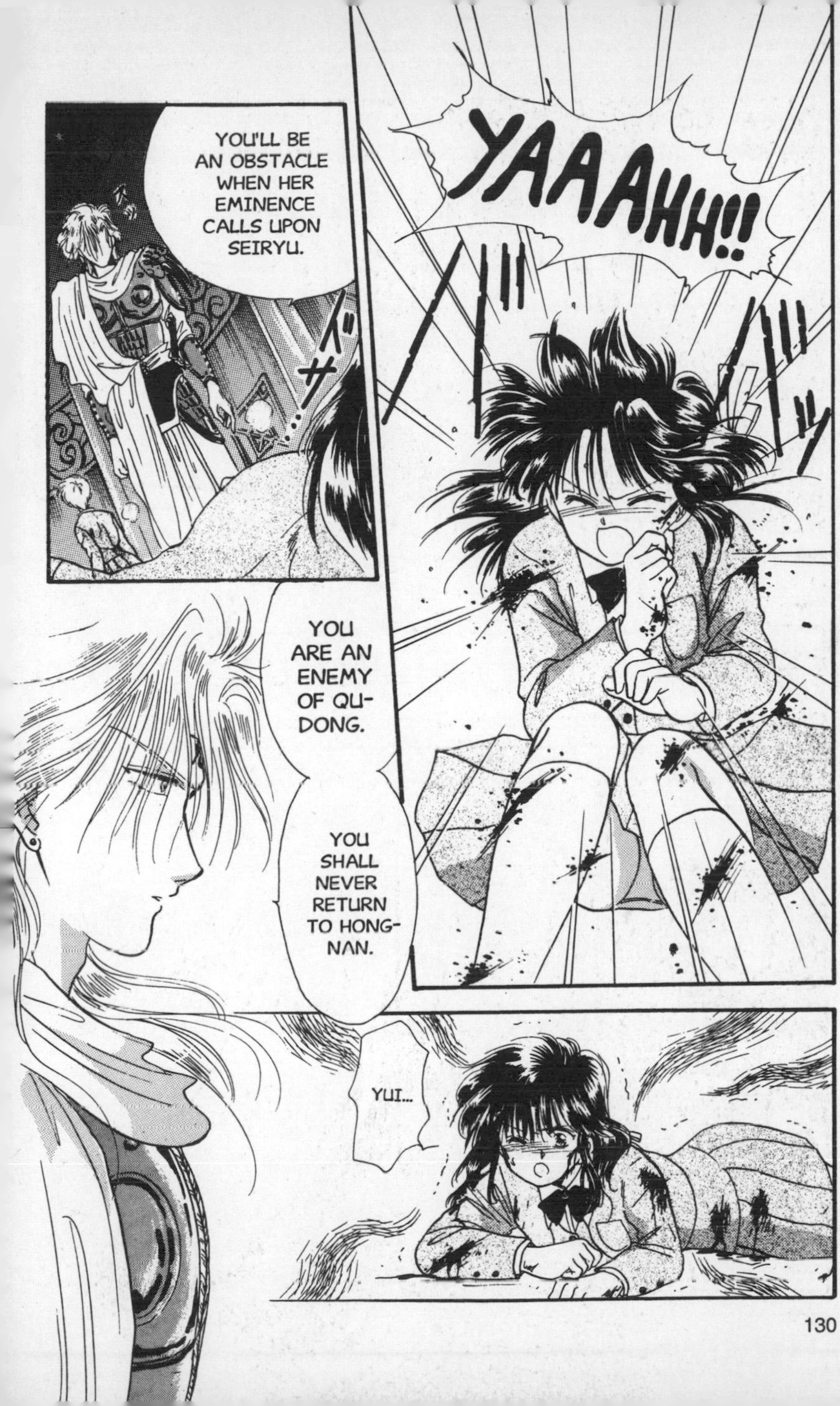
YAAAHH!!
YOU'LL BE AN OBSTACLE WHEN HER EMINENCE CALLS UPON SEIRYU.
YOU ARE AN ENEMY OF QU-DONG.
YOU SHALL NEVER RETURN TO HONG-NAN.
YUI...

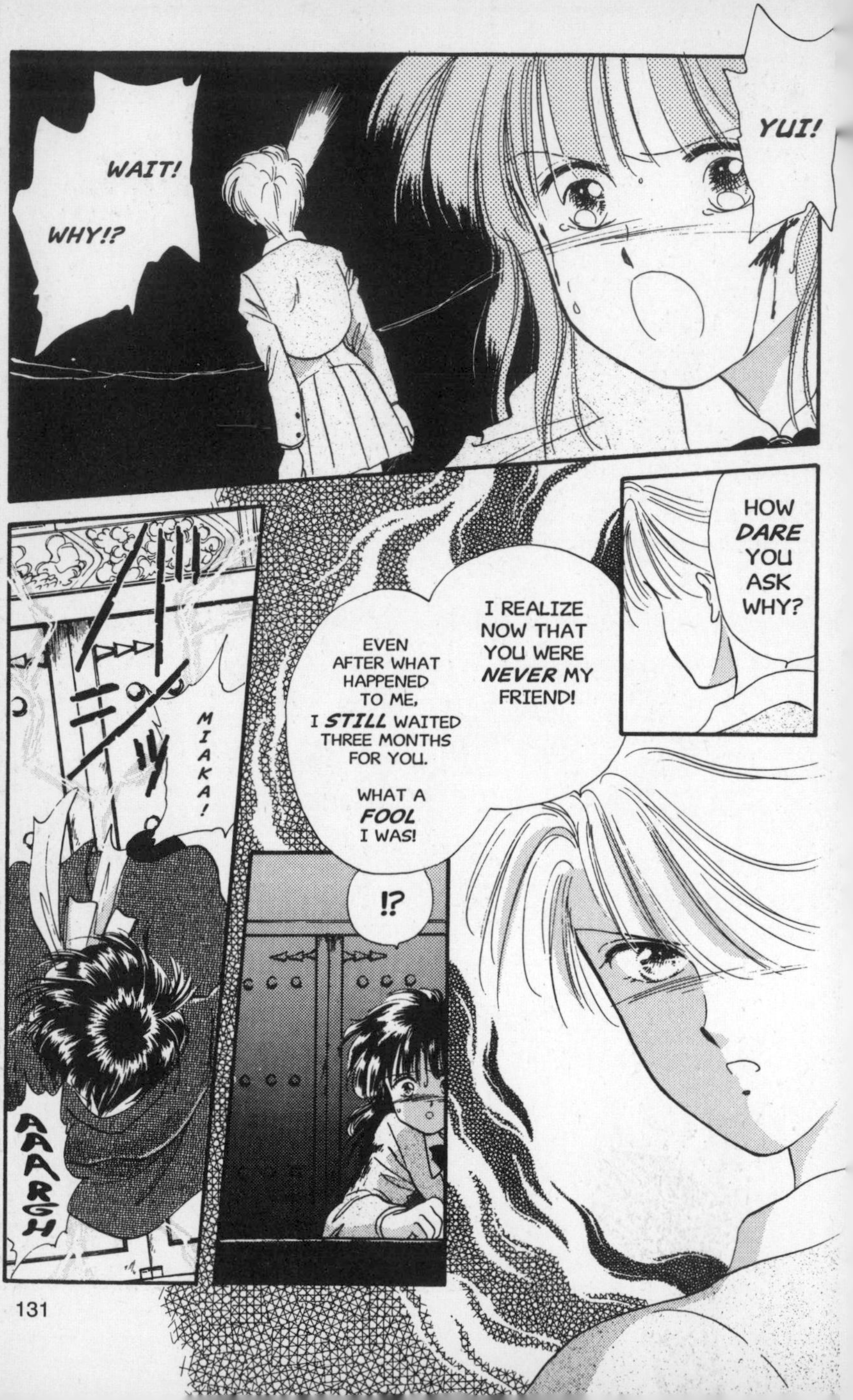
YUI!
WAIT!
WHY!?
HOW DARE YOU ASK WHY?
I REALIZE NOW THAT YOU WERE NEVER MY FRIEND!
EVEN AFTER WHAT HAPPENED TO ME, I STILL WAITED THREE MONTHS FOR YOU.
WHAT A FOOL I WAS!
!?
MIAKA!
AAARGH

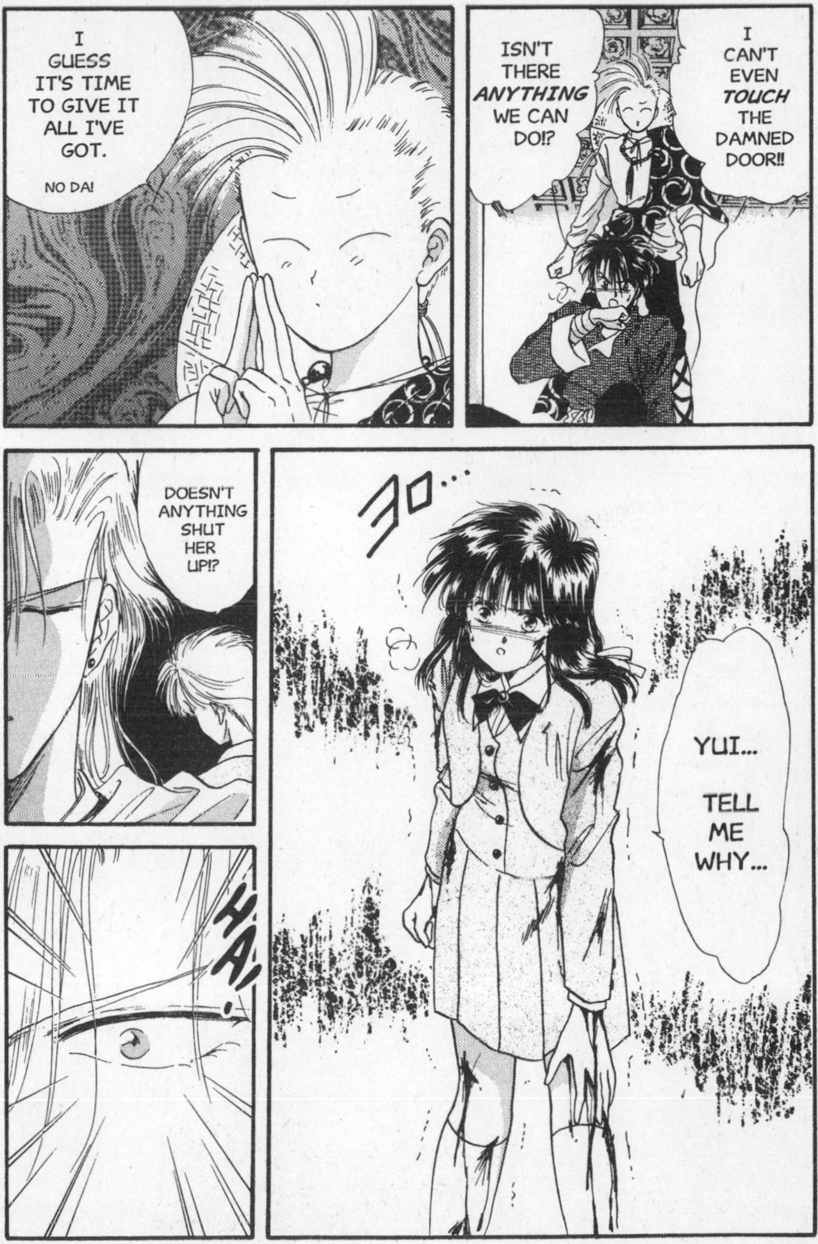
I CAN'T EVEN TOUCH THE DAMNED DOOR!!
ISN'T THERE ANYTHING WE CAN DO!?
I GUESS IT'S TIME TO GIVE IT ALL I'VE GOT.
NO DA!
YUI... TELL ME WHY...
ヨロ...
DOESN'T ANYTHING SHUT HER UP!?
HA!

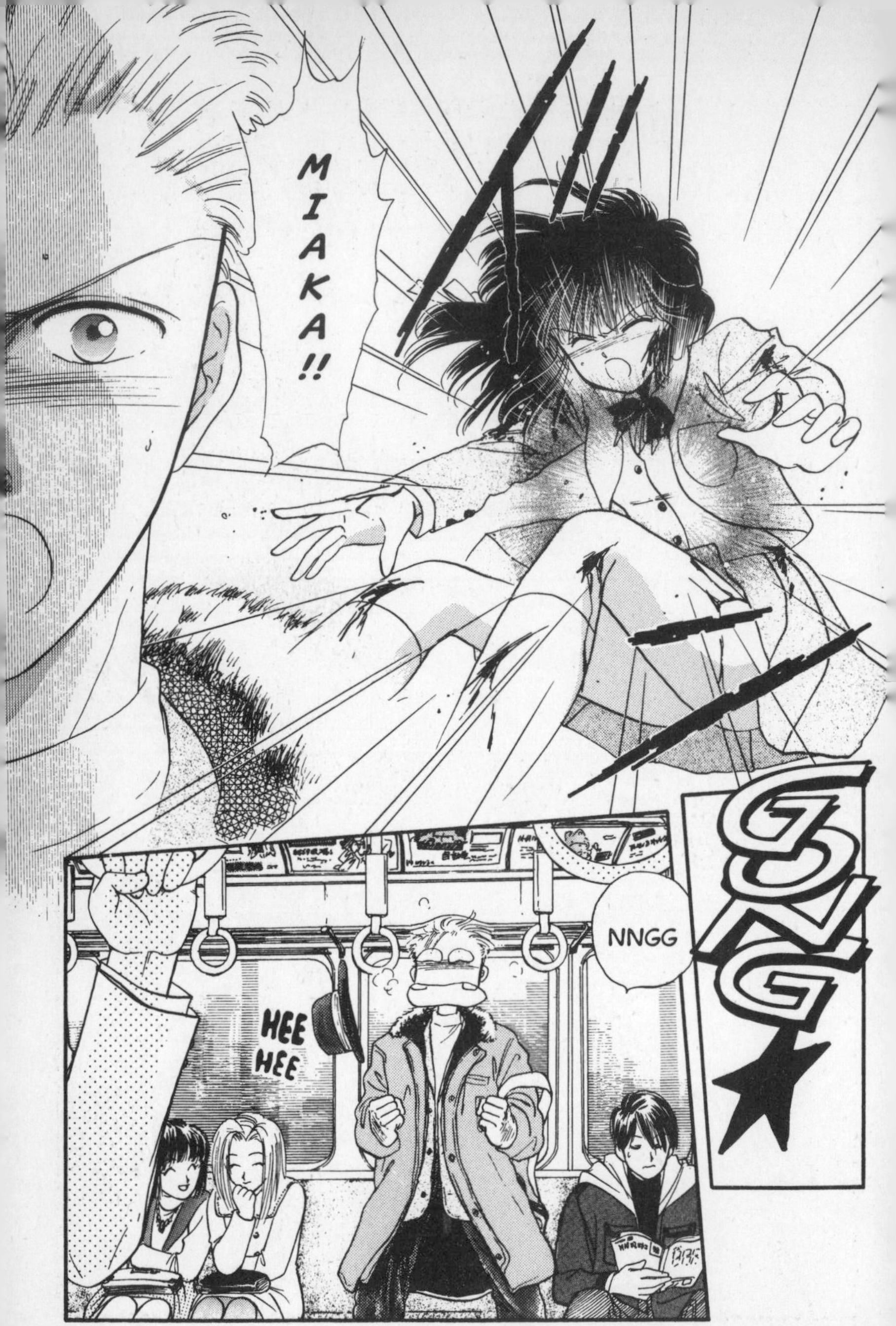
MIAKA!!
GONG
NNGG
HEE HEE

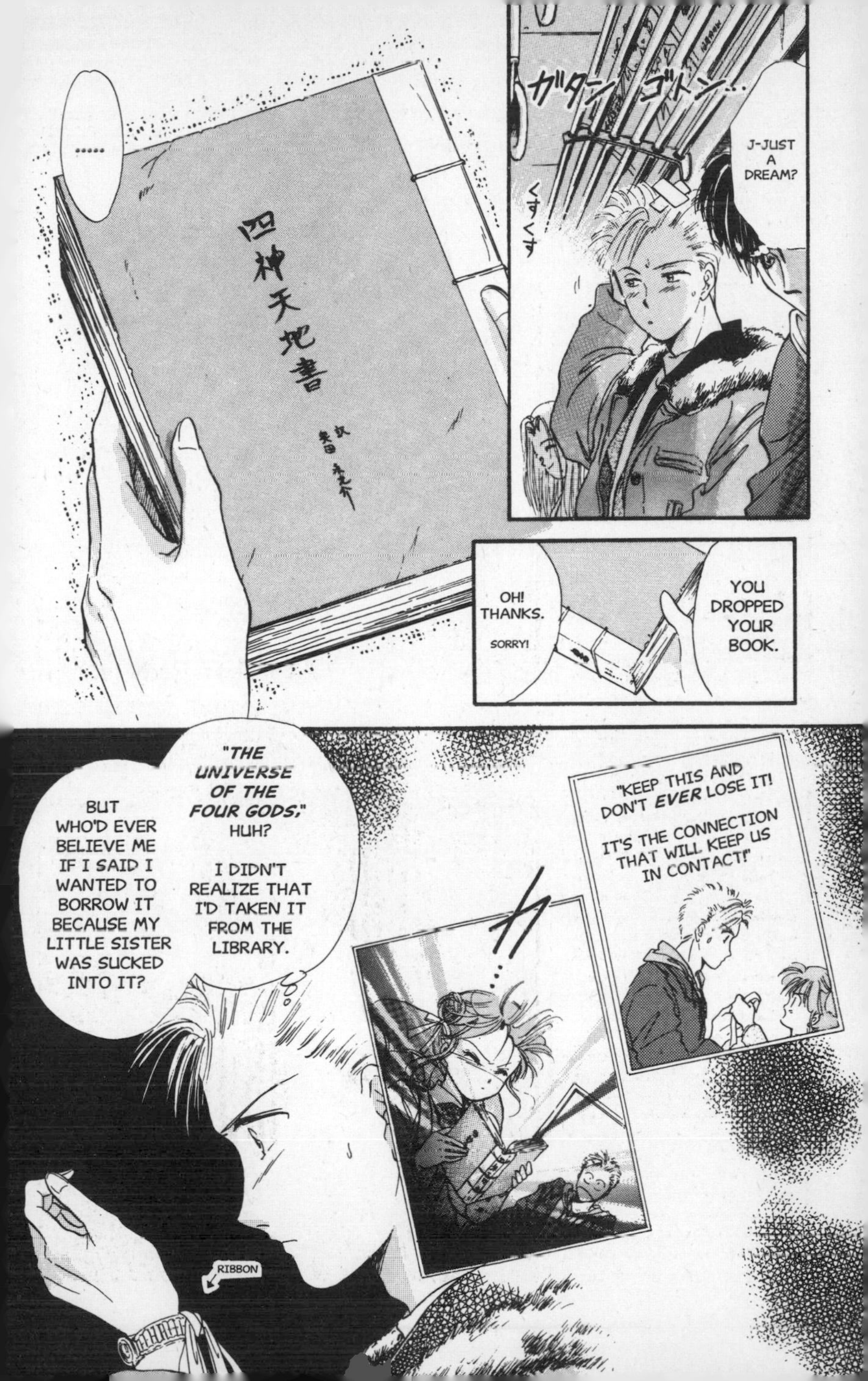
ガタン ゴトン..
J-JUST A DREAM?
くすくす
YOU DROPPED YOUR BOOK.
OH! THANKS.
SORRY!
......
四神天地書
"KEEP THIS AND DON'T *EVER* LOSE IT!
IT'S THE CONNECTION THAT WILL KEEP US IN CONTACT!"
"THE UNIVERSE OF THE FOUR GODS;" HUH?
I DIDN'T REALIZE THAT I'D TAKEN IT FROM THE LIBRARY.
BUT WHO'D EVER BELIEVE ME IF I SAID I WANTED TO BORROW IT BECAUSE MY LITTLE SISTER WAS SUCKED INTO IT?
RIBBON

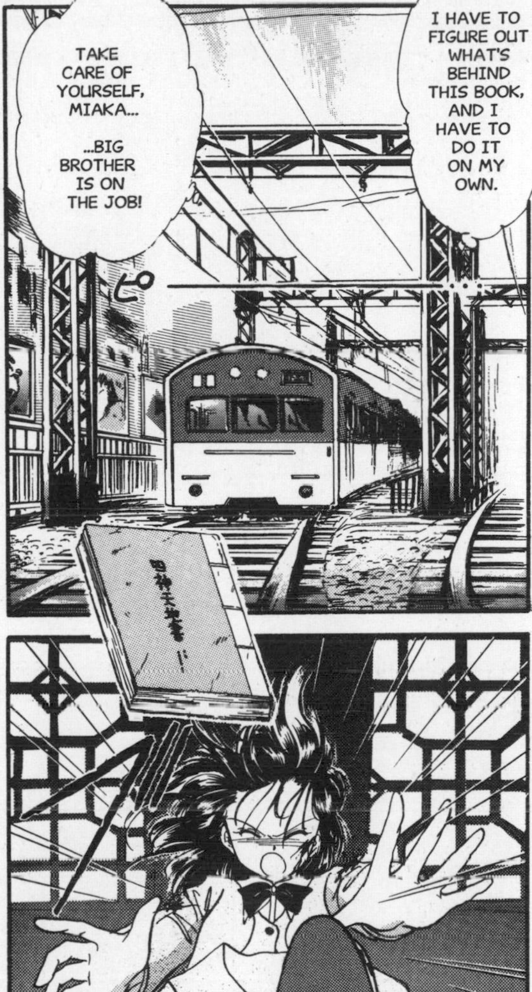
I HAVE TO FIGURE OUT WHAT'S BEHIND THIS BOOK, AND I HAVE TO DO IT ON MY OWN.
TAKE CARE OF YOURSELF, MIAKA...
...BIG BROTHER IS ON THE JOB!
ピ

According to M, the best thing about computer games is the computer graphics. "I look forward to the sequences when you clear each stage." What's to look forward to? Your favorite character stripping! Okay, for women over age 20... If you stroked his ego, Hotohori might be willing to take it all off. But when we realized that most of the players would be guys, our ideas got really out of control. "Fushigi Yūgi Uncensored!" "What if Miaka and Yui were young boys and each of the constellations were different kinds of gorgeous girls!?" "The boys wouldn't be able to resist that!" "Okay, if you finish the entire game the regular way, the special "For Boys" version will appear." Will someone make this game!?

The other thing we thought of was a SD Chichiri doll. When you squeeze it, it says "No da!" I'm sorry for getting so carried away. But these ideas do seem like fun, huh? I'm not serious, of course!

So, now that you've finished chapter 16, it must have been something of a shock. BWA HA HA HA! This was part of my plan all along! I only had the stories through chapter 16 planned at the start, though. Who'da thought this series would have ever gone 15 chapters in the first place!? Now the readers become divided between supporting Miaka or Yui. One thing that made me go "Eh!?" were the letters from readers who wrote in claiming that, "after reading Chapter 16, I don't like Miaka because she's a liar!" Please read from Chapters 12 to 15 again, okay? Miaka lied to Tamahome in order to find Yui. Are you really reading this story closely? I don't mind it if you've always disliked Miaka. Sometimes, people change their minds, and that's interesting in itself. Anyway, I'm taking all your responses into consideration.

By the way, I just remembered, speaking of games, (Sorry, I'm changing the subject all the time.) my game system was disconnected when I moved recently, and I forgot to have it reinstalled!! AARGH! I can't play Final Fantasy! Actually, I don't have any time to play!! Game Boy is more popular at my place anyway. When I'm stuck or need a break, Parodius is good to play. I wish I had time to play more games!!

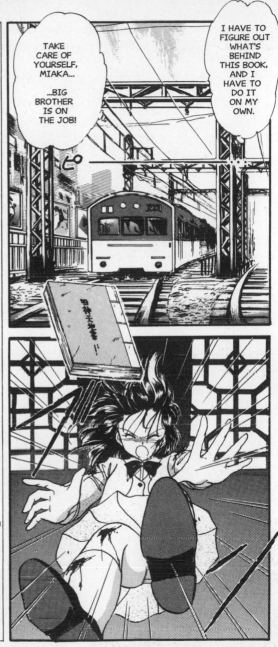

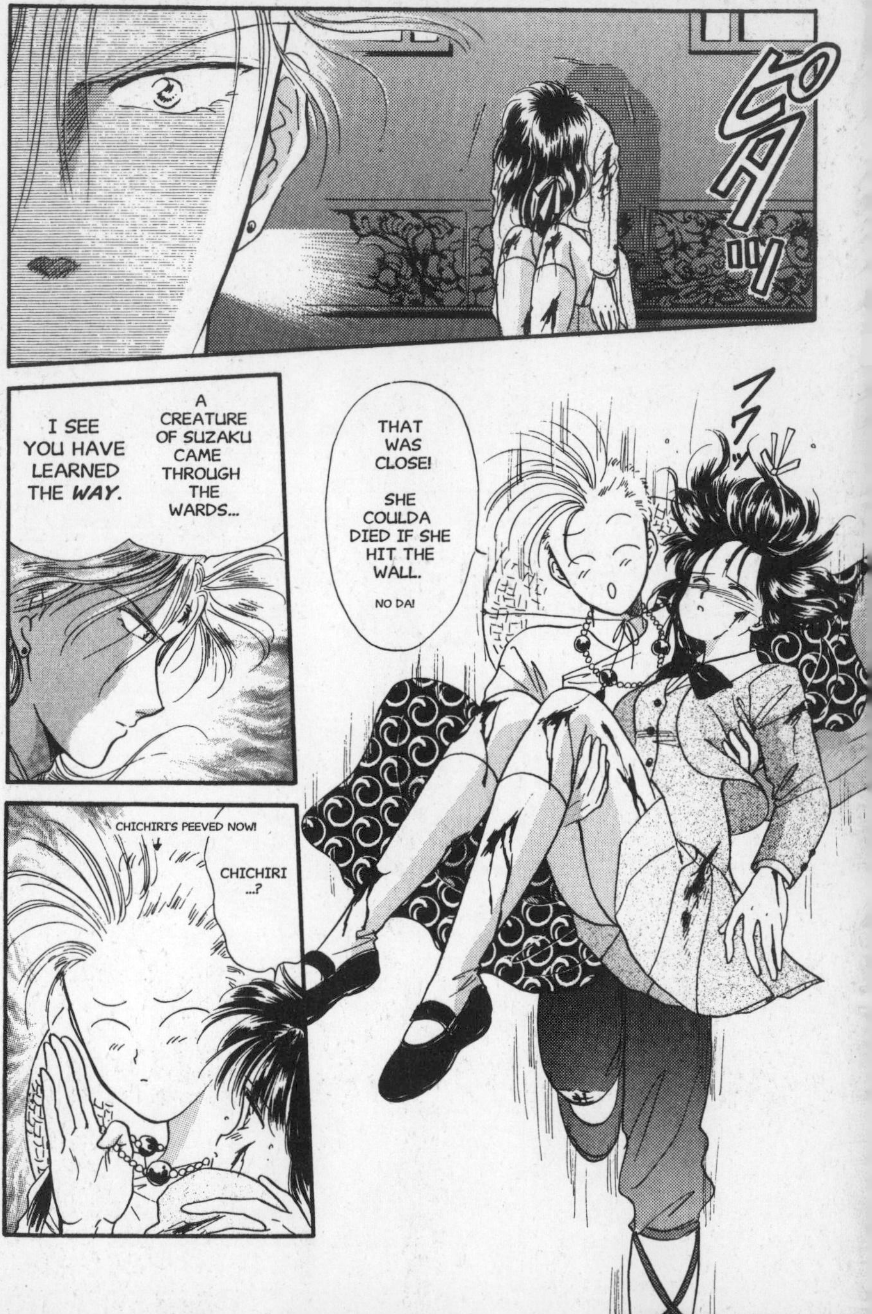
THAT WAS CLOSE!
SHE COULDA DIED IF SHE HIT THE WALL.
NO DA!
A CREATURE OF SUZAKU CAME THROUGH THE WARDS...
I SEE YOU HAVE LEARNED THE *WAY*.
CHICHIRI ...?
CHICHIRI'S PEEVED NOW!

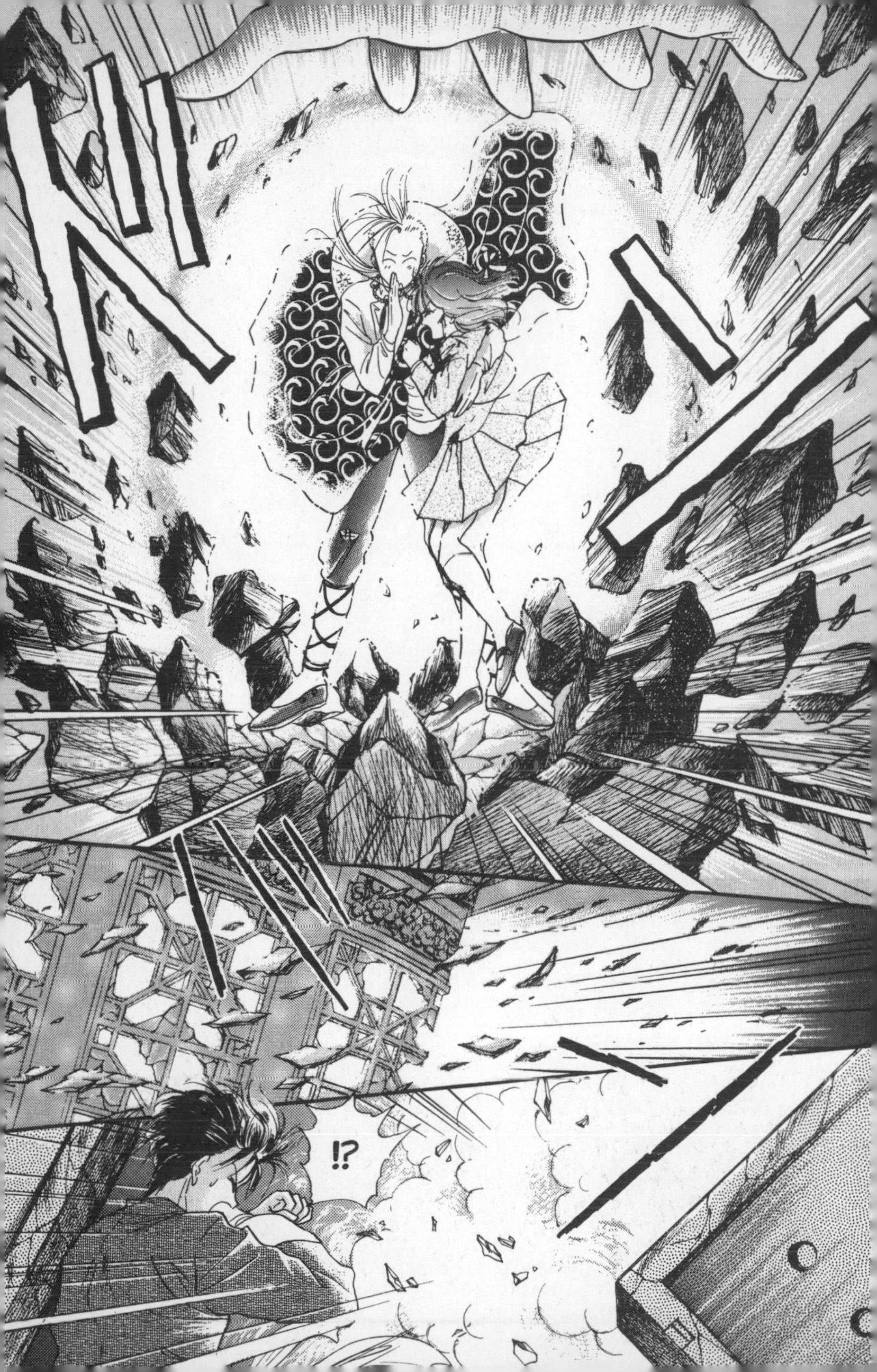
!?

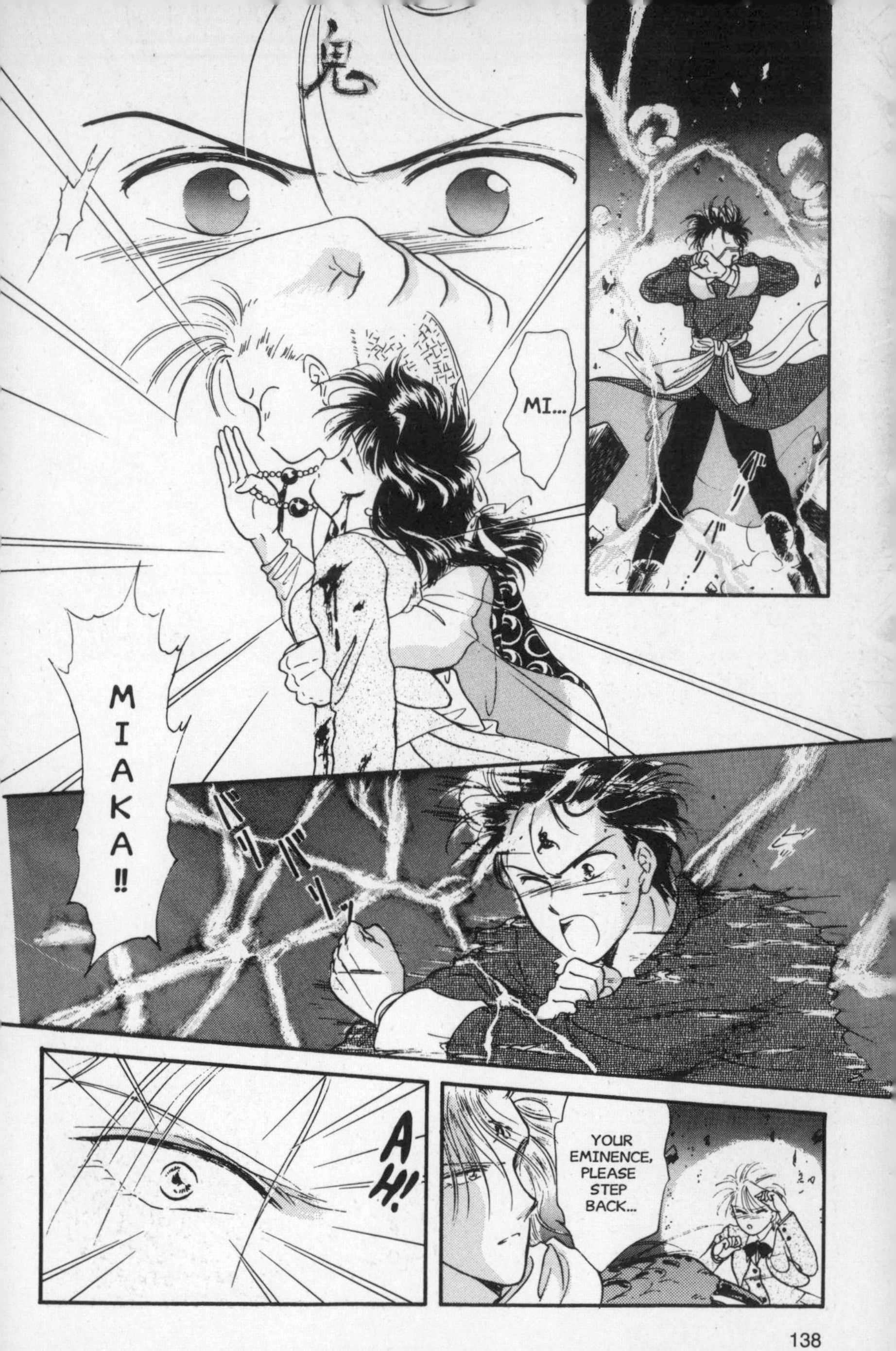
MI...
鬼
MIAKA!!
YOUR EMINENCE, PLEASE STEP BACK...
AH!

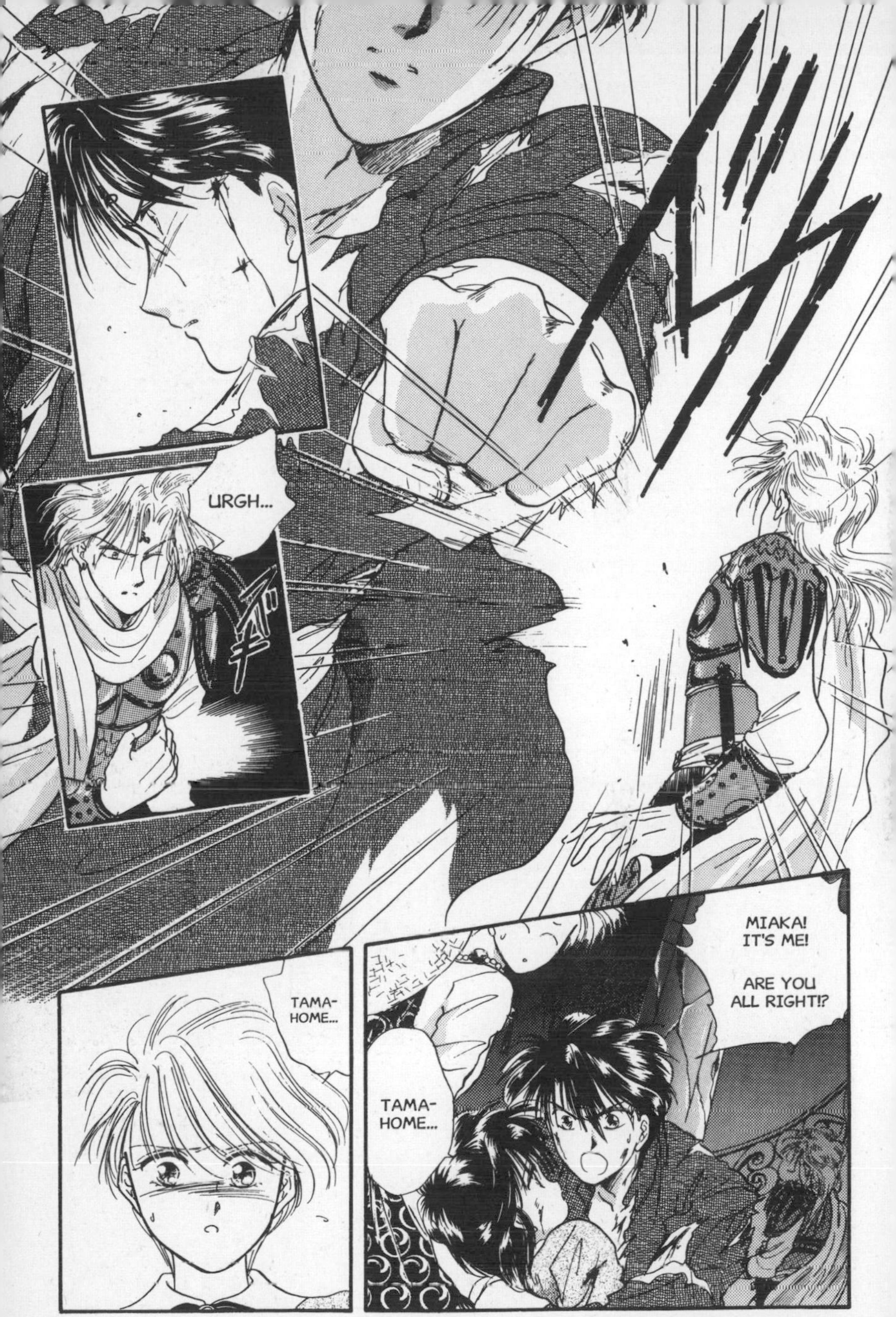
URGH...
MIAKA! IT'S ME!
ARE YOU ALL RIGHT!?
TAMA-HOME...
TAMA-HOME...

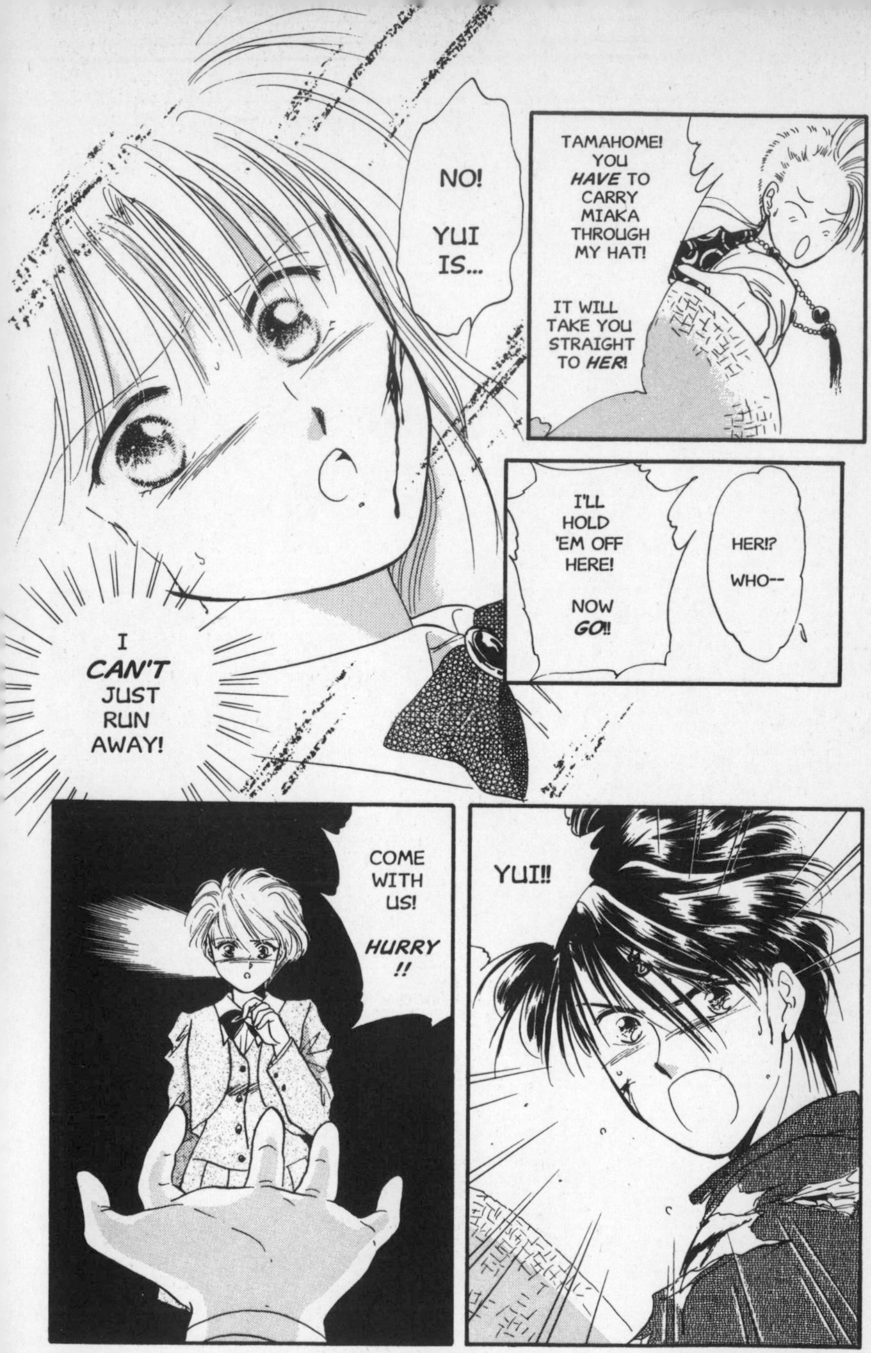
TAMAHOME! YOU *HAVE* TO CARRY MIAKA THROUGH MY HAT!
IT WILL TAKE YOU STRAIGHT TO *HER*!
HER!? WHO--
I'LL HOLD 'EM OFF HERE!
NOW *GO*!!
NO! YUI IS...
I *CAN'T* JUST RUN AWAY!
YUI!!
COME WITH US!
HURRY !!

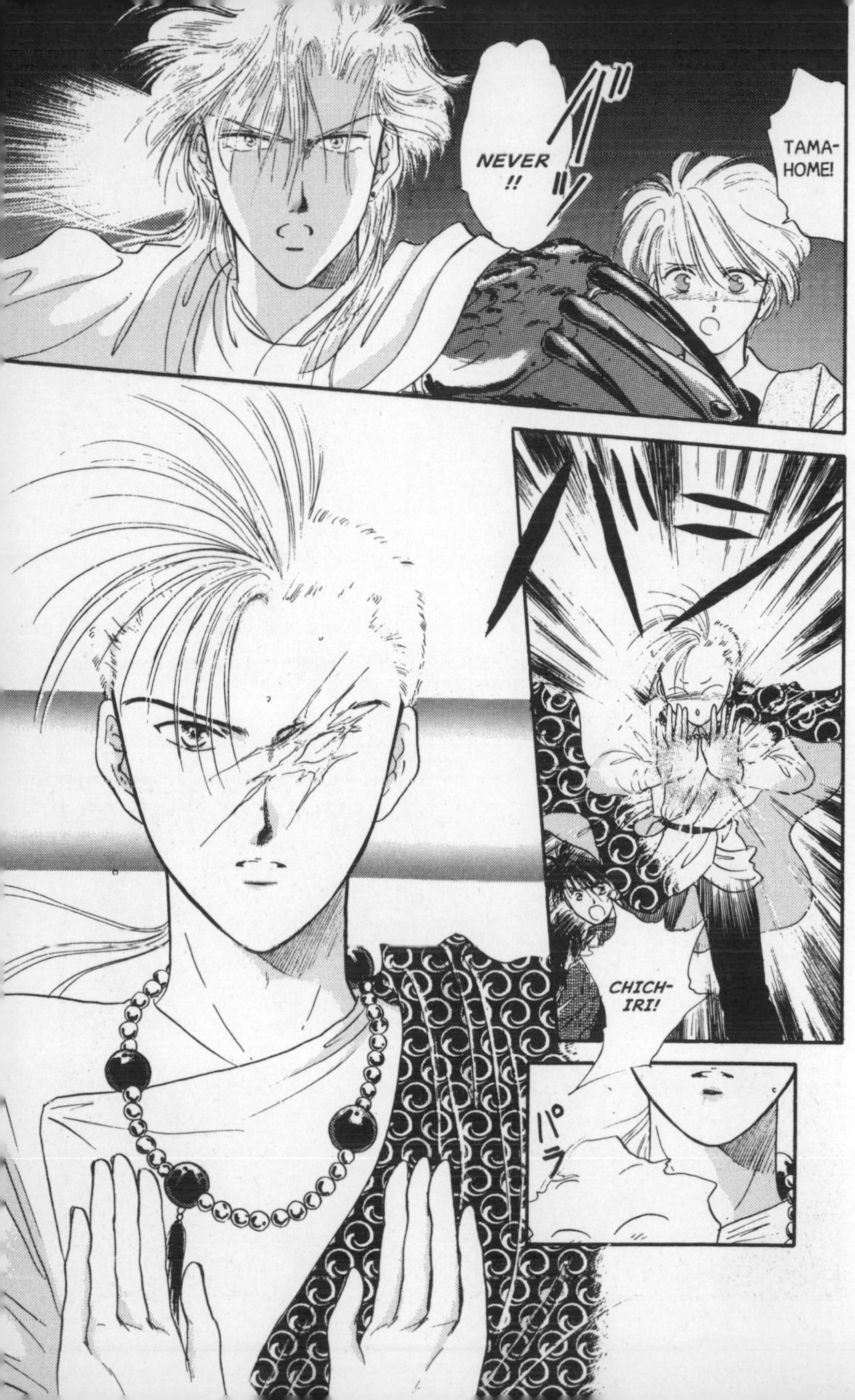
TAMA- HOME!
NEVER !!
CHICH- IRI!
パラ

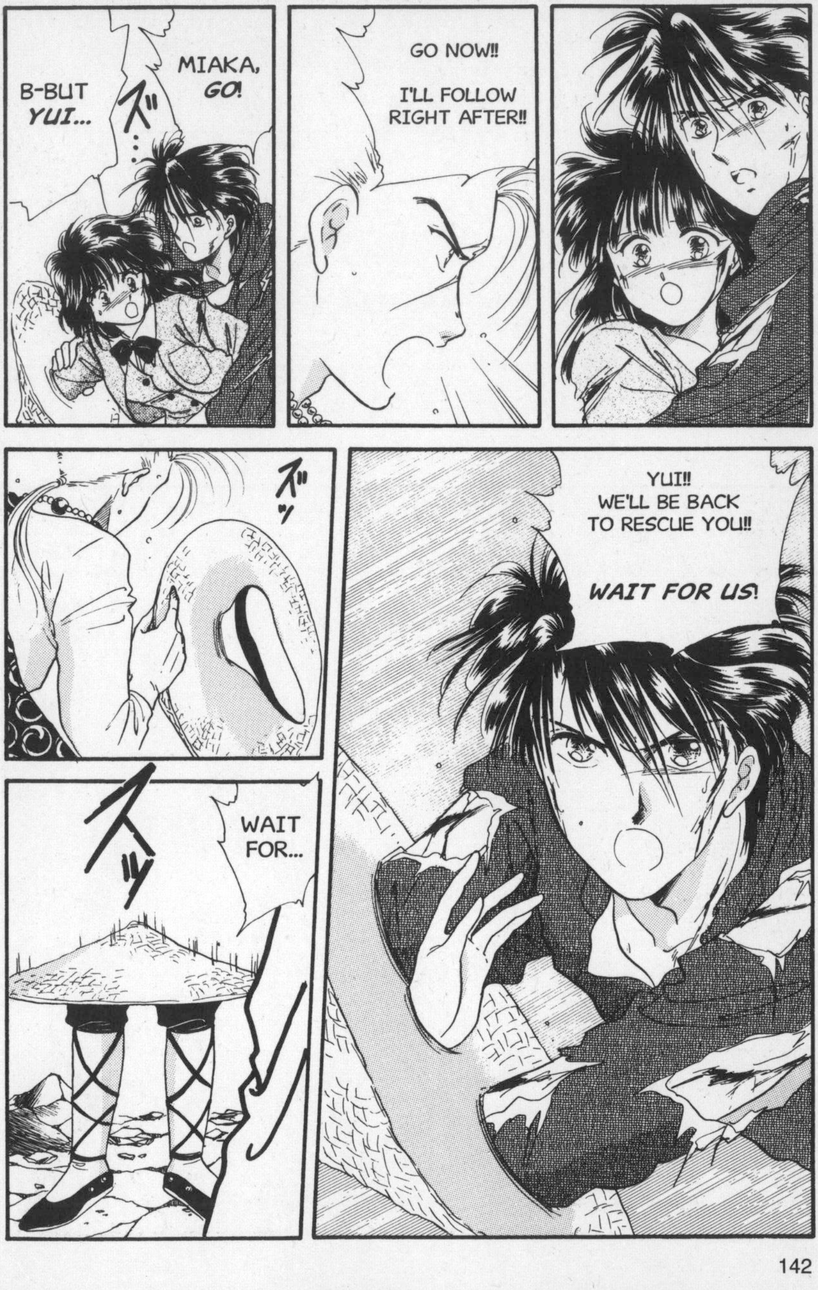
GO NOW!!
I'LL FOLLOW RIGHT AFTER!!
MIAKA, *GO*!
ズ
B-BUT *YUI*...
YUI!! WE'LL BE BACK TO RESCUE YOU!!
WAIT FOR US!
ズッ
WAIT FOR...
スッ

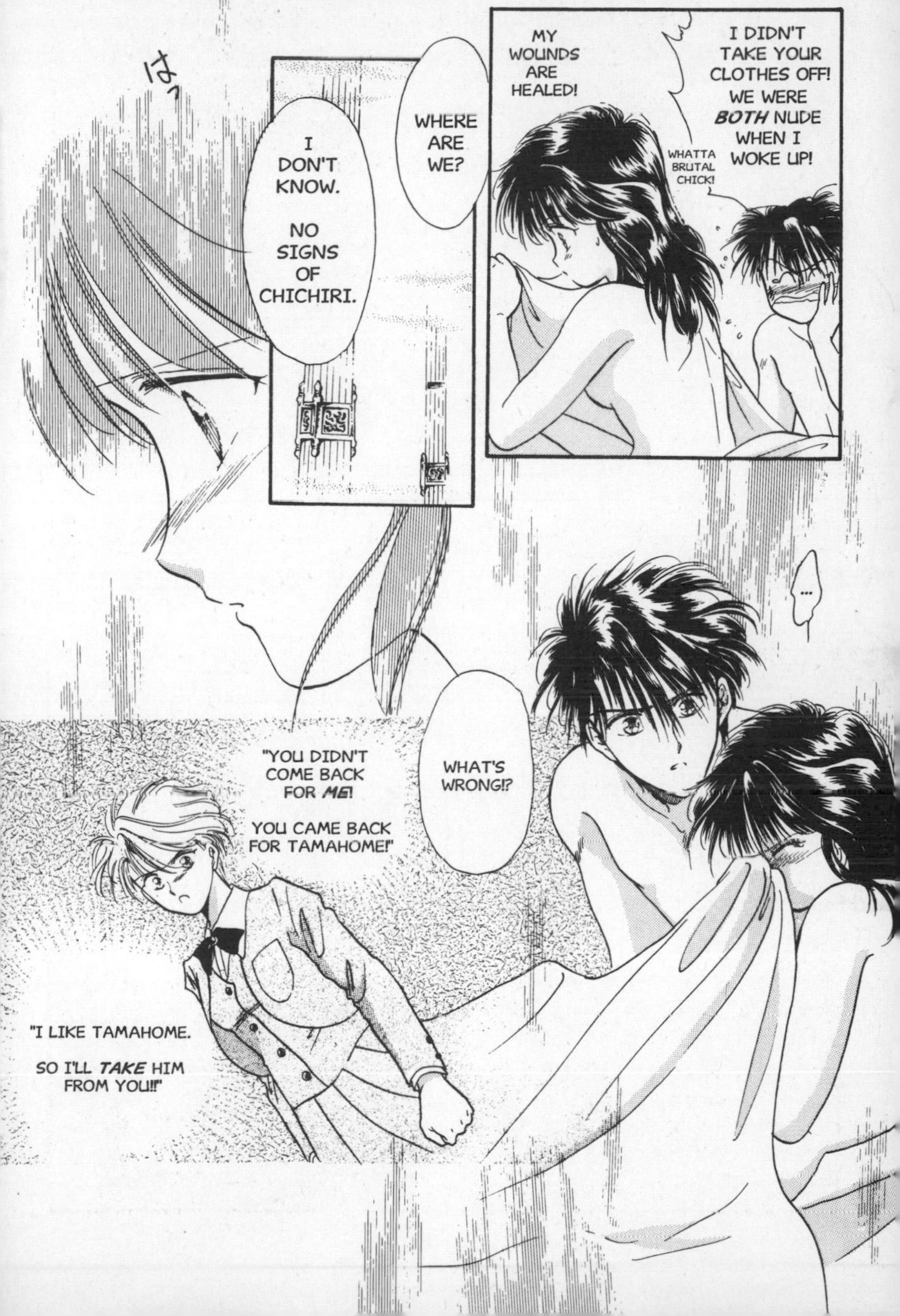
I DIDN'T TAKE YOUR CLOTHES OFF! WE WERE *BOTH* NUDE WHEN I WOKE UP!
MY WOUNDS ARE HEALED!
WHATTA BRUTAL CHICK!
WHERE ARE WE?
I DON'T KNOW.
NO SIGNS OF CHICHIRI.
はっ
...
WHAT'S WRONG!?
"YOU DIDN'T COME BACK FOR *ME*!
YOU CAME BACK FOR TAMAHOME!"
"I LIKE TAMAHOME.
SO I'LL *TAKE* HIM FROM YOU!!"

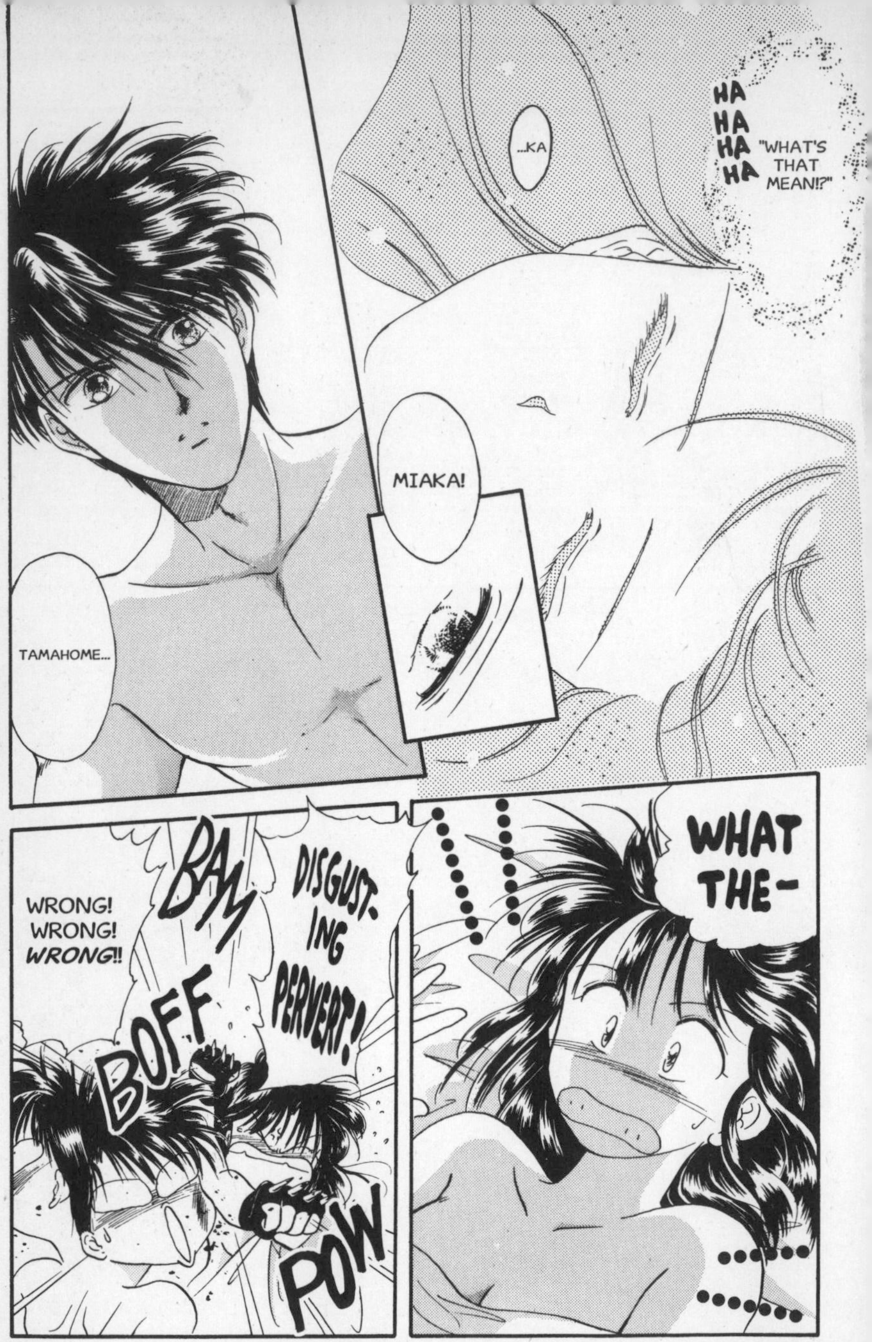

HA HA HA HA "WHAT'S THAT MEAN!?"
...KA
MIAKA!
TAMAHOME...
WHAT THE-
......
......
WRONG! WRONG! WRONG!!
BAM
DISGUST-ING PERVERT!
BOFF
POW

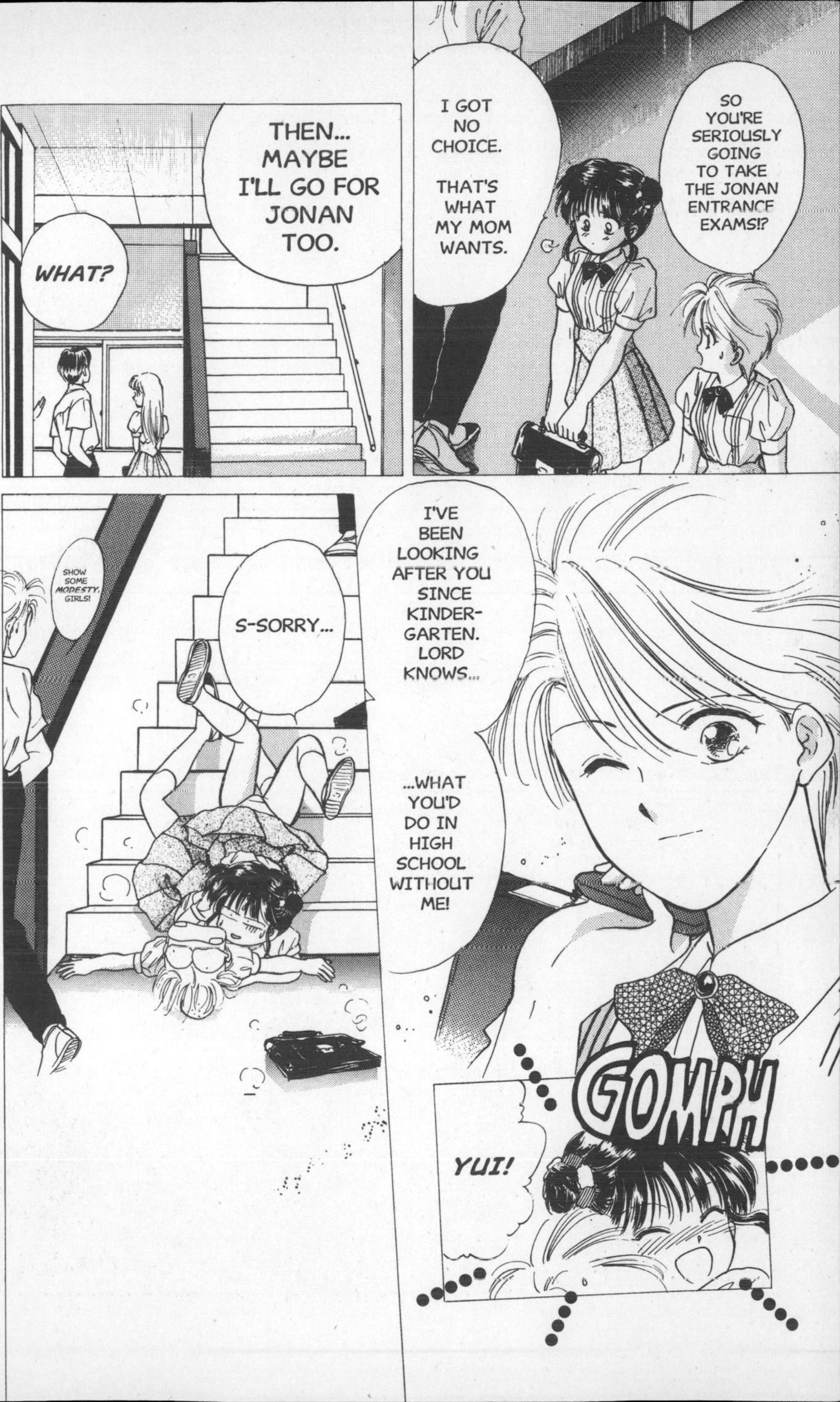
SO YOU'RE SERIOUSLY GOING TO TAKE THE JONAN ENTRANCE EXAMS!?
I GOT NO CHOICE.
THAT'S WHAT MY MOM WANTS.
THEN... MAYBE I'LL GO FOR JONAN TOO.
WHAT?
I'VE BEEN LOOKING AFTER YOU SINCE KINDER-GARTEN. LORD KNOWS...
...WHAT YOU'D DO IN HIGH SCHOOL WITHOUT ME!
GOMPH
YUI!
S-SORRY...
SHOW SOME MODESTY, GIRLS!

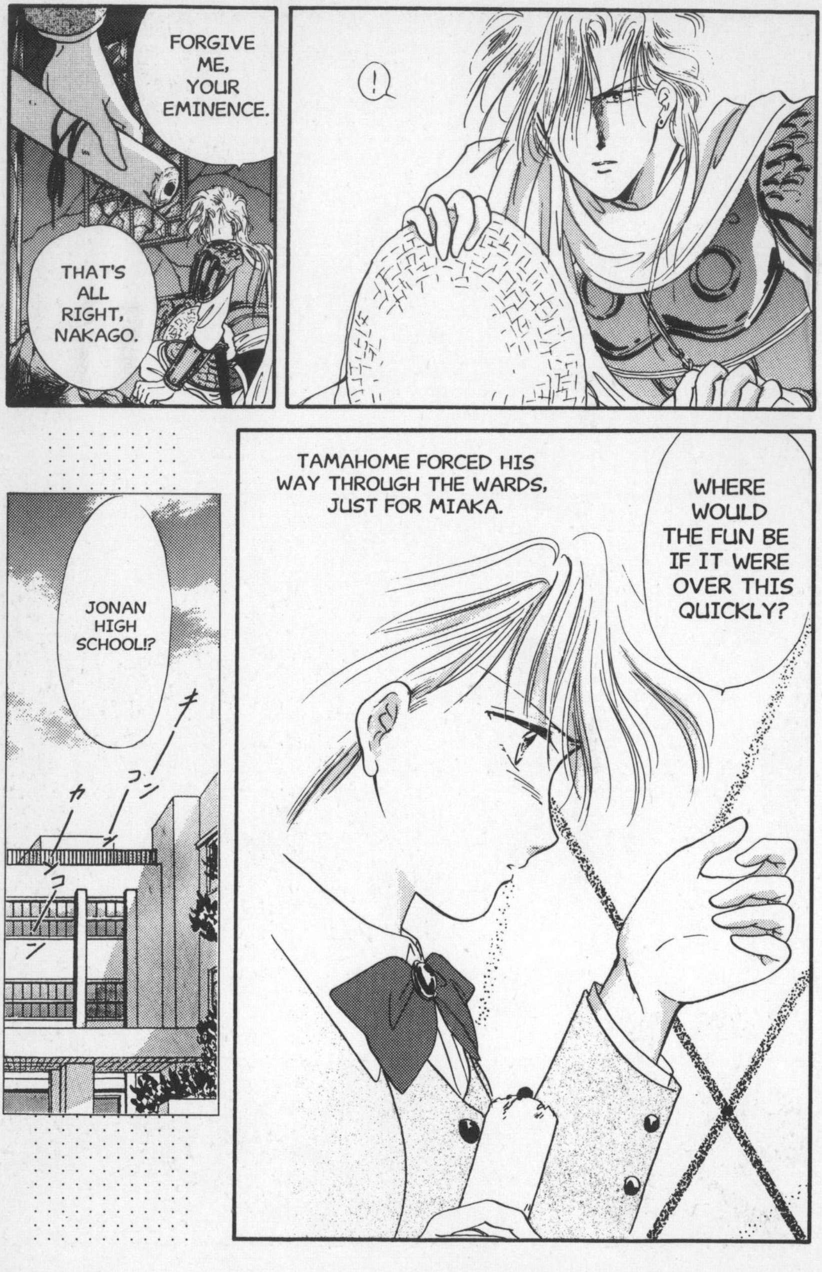
!
FORGIVE ME, YOUR EMINENCE.
THAT'S ALL RIGHT, NAKAGO.
WHERE WOULD THE FUN BE IF IT WERE OVER THIS QUICKLY?
TAMAHOME FORCED HIS WAY THROUGH THE WARDS, JUST FOR MIAKA.
JONAN HIGH SCHOOL!?
キーンコーン
カーンコーン

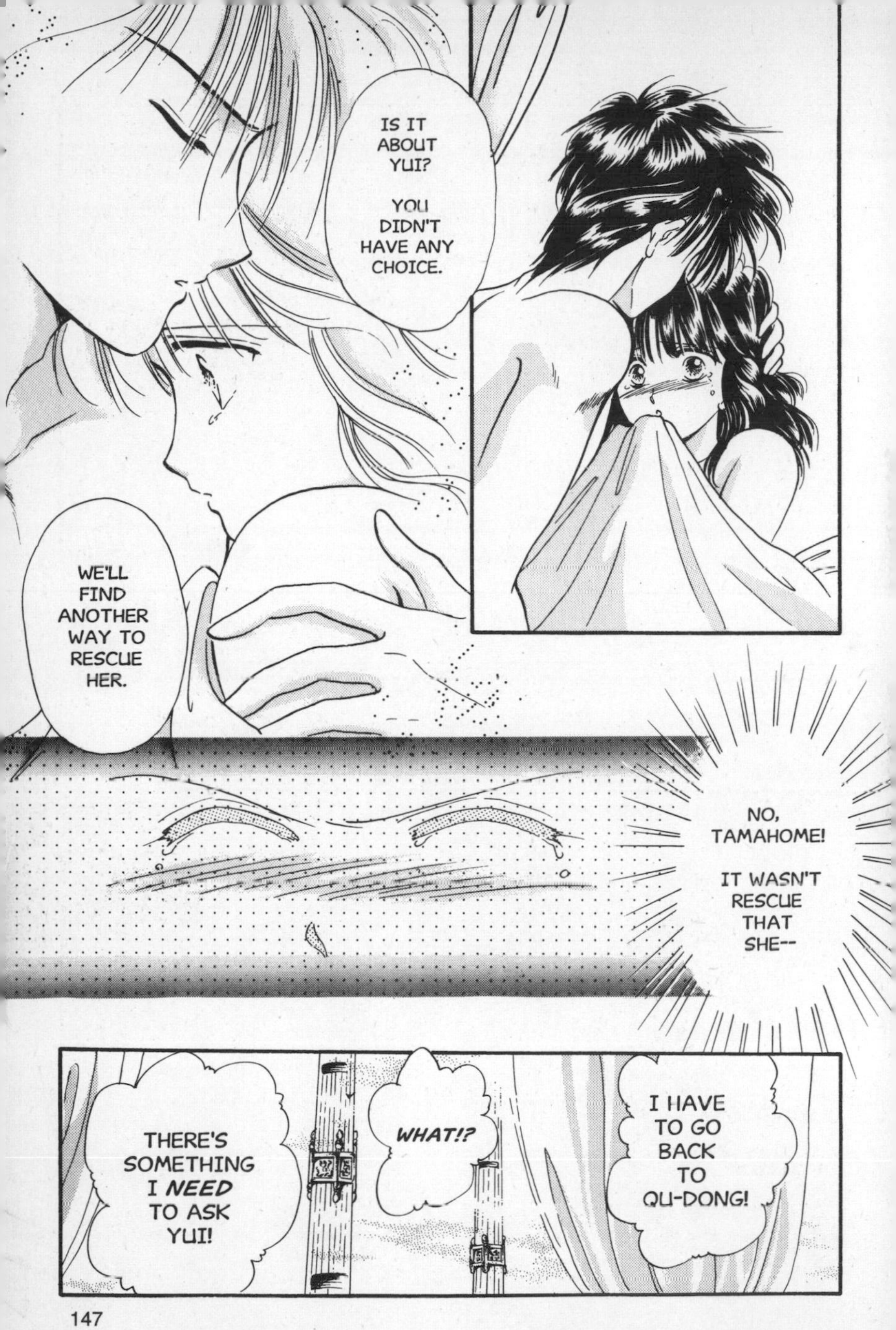
IS IT ABOUT YUI?
YOU DIDN'T HAVE ANY CHOICE.
WE'LL FIND ANOTHER WAY TO RESCUE HER.
NO, TAMAHOME!
IT WASN'T RESCUE THAT SHE--
I HAVE TO GO BACK TO QU-DONG!
WHAT!?
THERE'S SOMETHING I *NEED* TO ASK YUI!

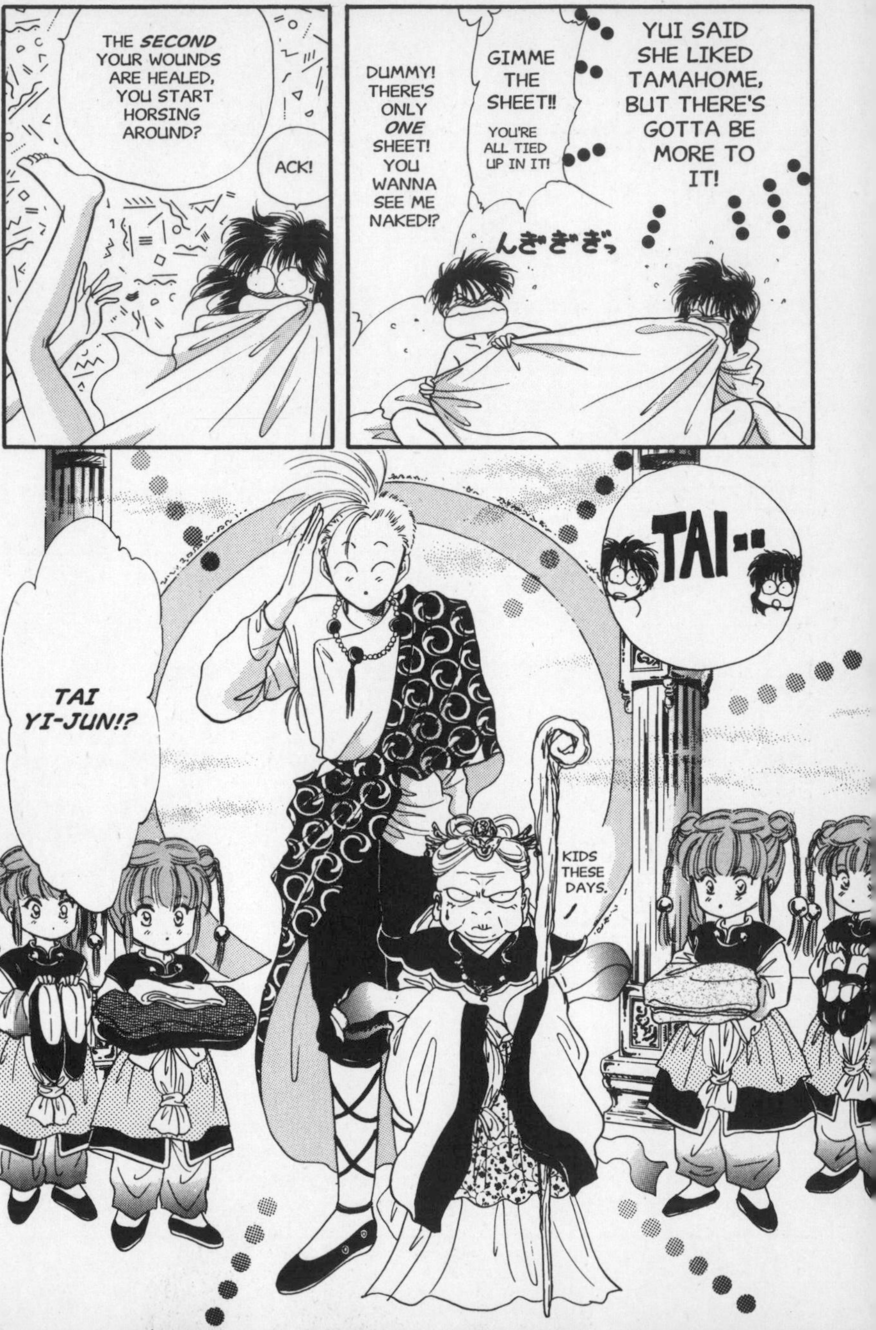
YUI SAID SHE LIKED TAMAHOME, BUT THERE'S GOTTA BE MORE TO IT!
GIMME THE SHEET!!
YOU'RE ALL TIED UP IN IT!
DUMMY! THERE'S ONLY *ONE* SHEET! YOU WANNA SEE ME NAKED!?
んぎぎぎっ
THE *SECOND* YOUR WOUNDS ARE HEALED, YOU START HORSING AROUND?
ACK!
TAI--
TAI YI-JUN!?
KIDS THESE DAYS.

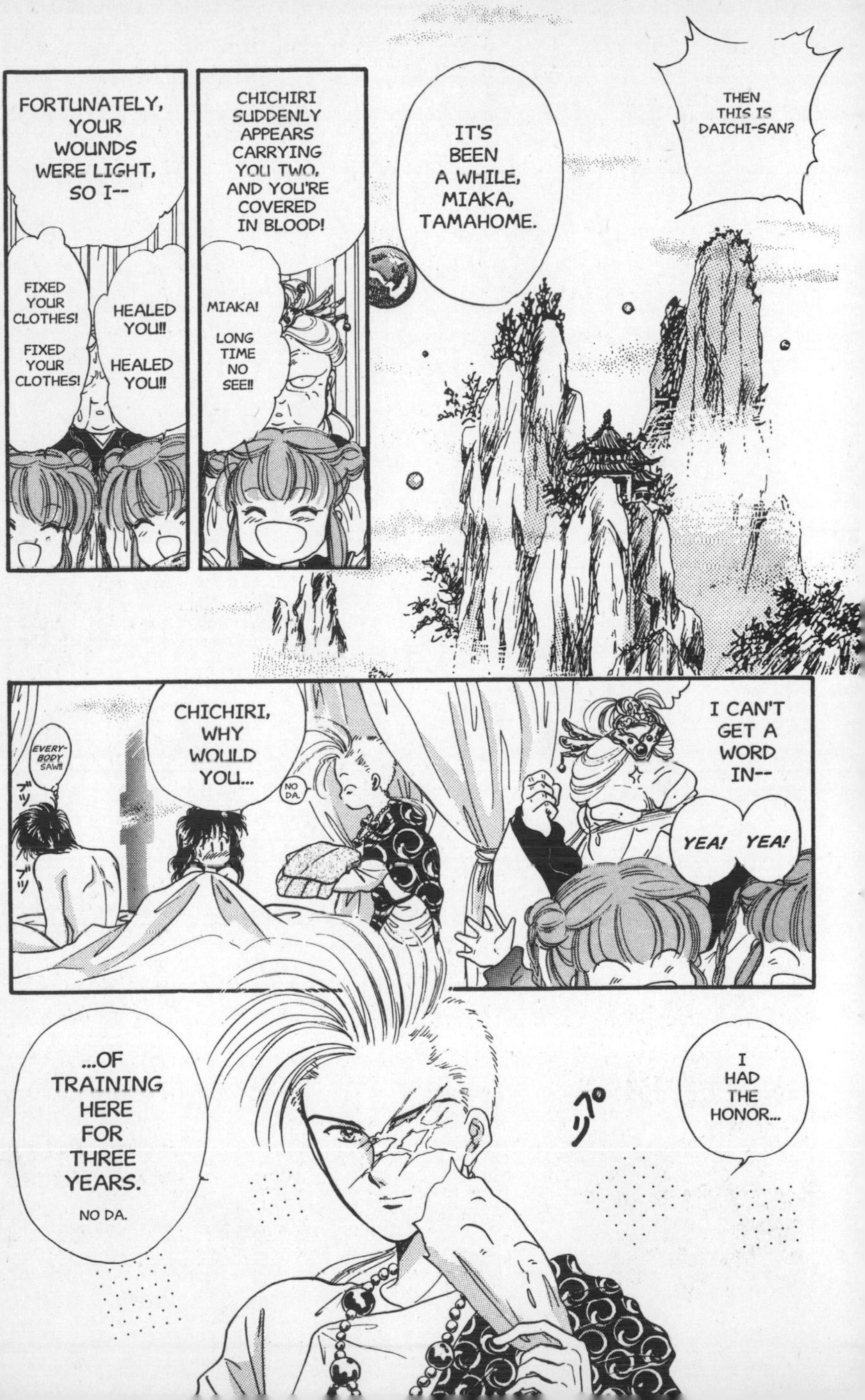
THEN THIS IS DAICHI-SAN?
IT'S BEEN A WHILE, MIAKA, TAMAHOME.
CHICHIRI SUDDENLY APPEARS CARRYING YOU TWO, AND YOU'RE COVERED IN BLOOD!
MIAKA! LONG TIME NO SEE!!
FORTUNATELY, YOUR WOUNDS WERE LIGHT, SO I--
HEALED YOU!! HEALED YOU!!
FIXED YOUR CLOTHES! FIXED YOUR CLOTHES!
I CAN'T GET A WORD IN--
YEA! YEA!
CHICHIRI, WHY WOULD YOU...
NO DA.
EVERY-BODY SAW!!
ブツ ブツ
I HAD THE HONOR...
...OF TRAINING HERE FOR THREE YEARS. NO DA.

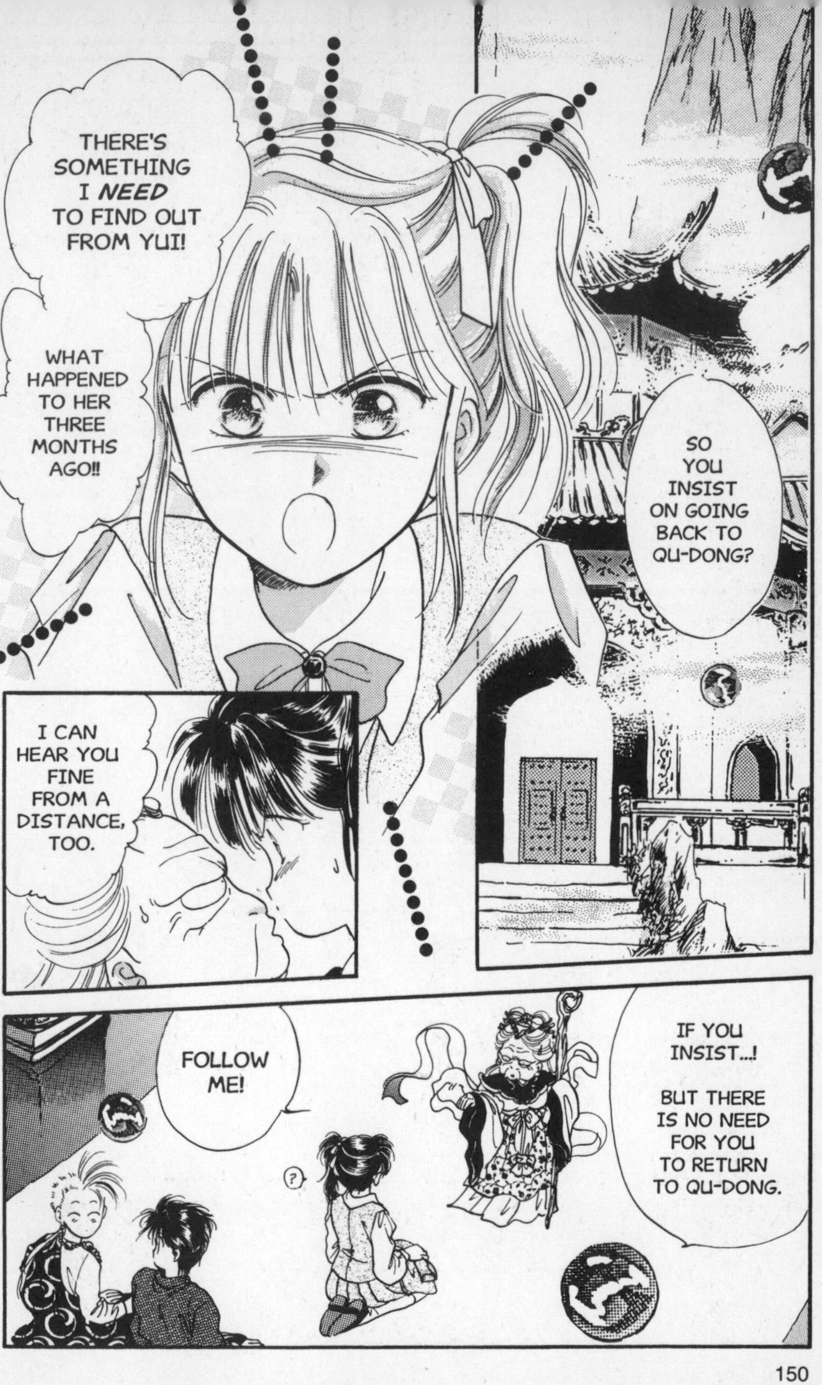
SO YOU INSIST ON GOING BACK TO QU-DONG?
THERE'S SOMETHING I *NEED* TO FIND OUT FROM YUI!
WHAT HAPPENED TO HER THREE MONTHS AGO!!
I CAN HEAR YOU FINE FROM A DISTANCE, TOO.
IF YOU INSIST...!
BUT THERE IS NO NEED FOR YOU TO RETURN TO QU-DONG.
FOLLOW ME!
?

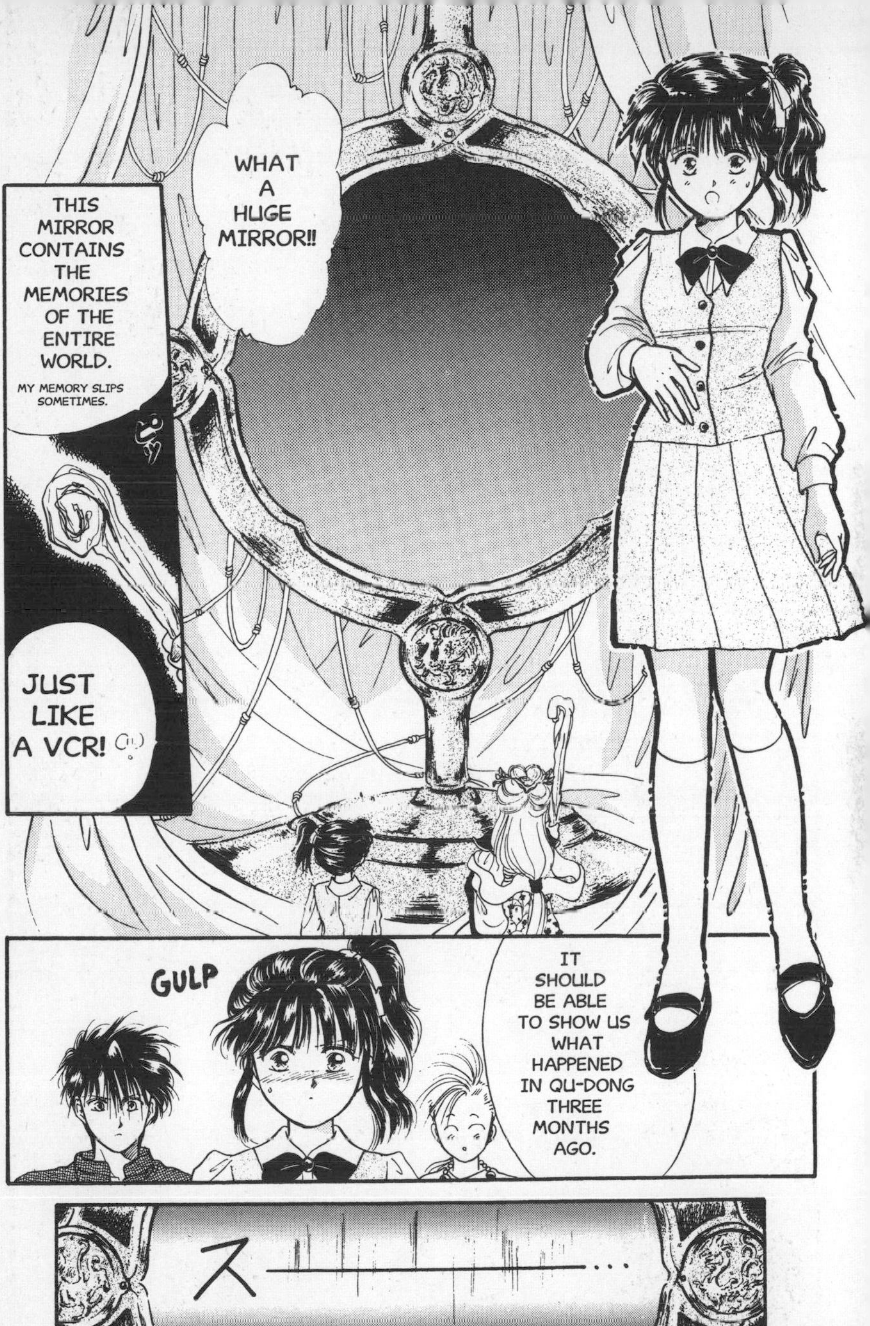
WHAT A HUGE MIRROR!!
THIS MIRROR CONTAINS THE MEMORIES OF THE ENTIRE WORLD.
MY MEMORY SLIPS SOMETIMES.
JUST LIKE A VCR!
IT SHOULD BE ABLE TO SHOW US WHAT HAPPENED IN QU-DONG THREE MONTHS AGO.
GULP
ス————...

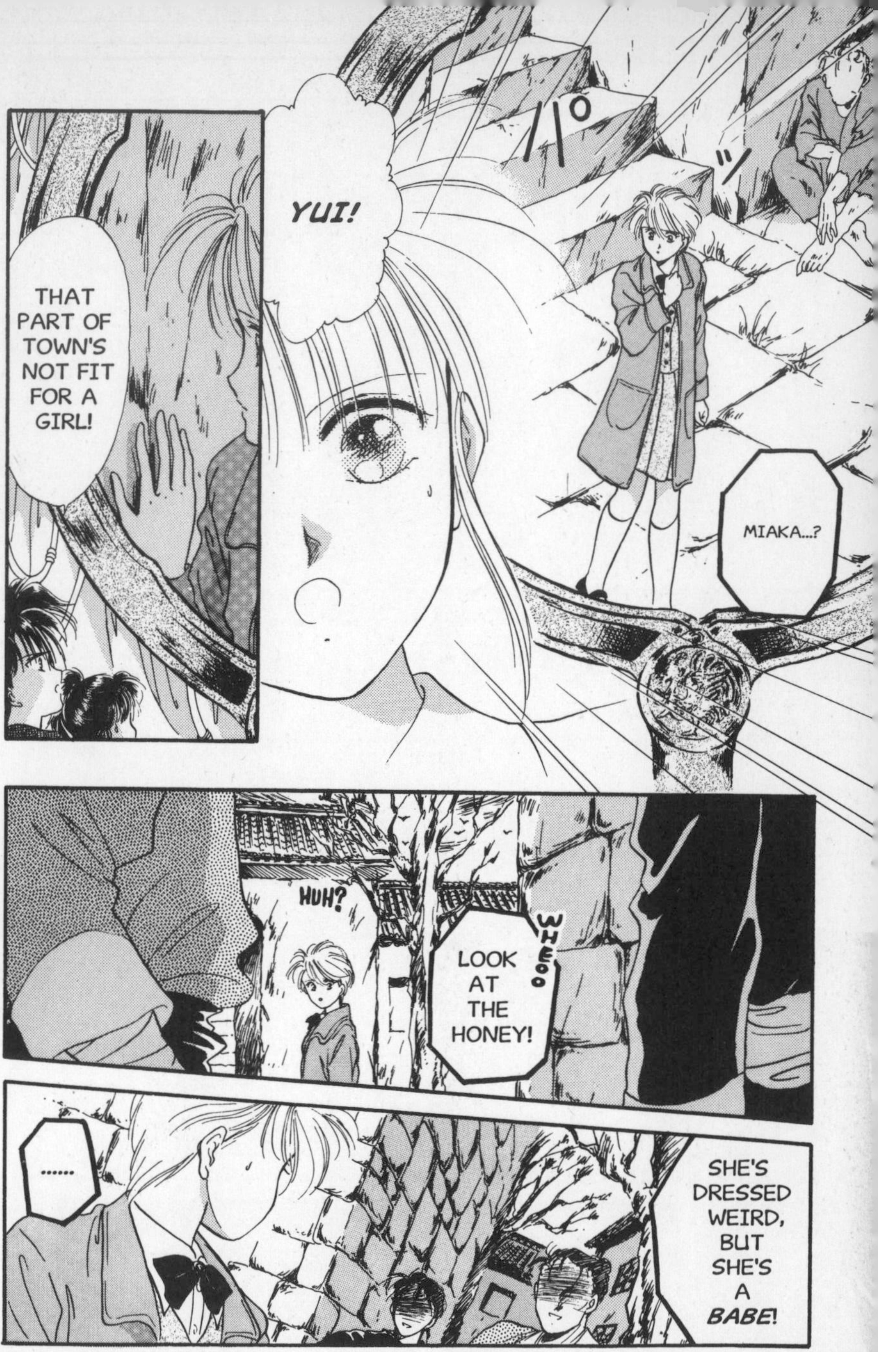
MIAKA...?
YUI!
THAT PART OF TOWN'S NOT FIT FOR A GIRL!
WHEEOO
LOOK AT THE HONEY!
HUH?
SHE'S DRESSED WEIRD, BUT SHE'S A *BABE*!
......

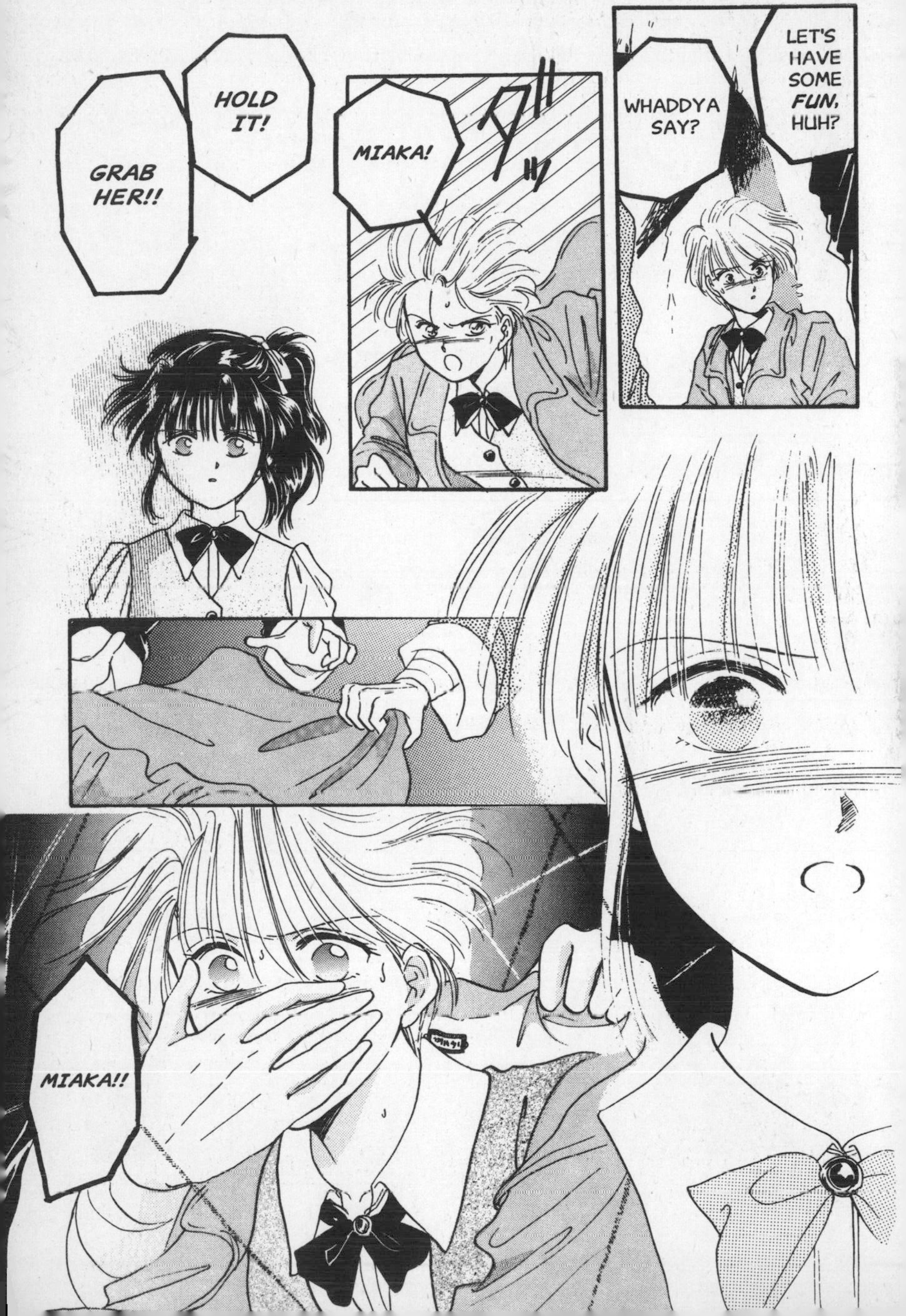
LET'S HAVE SOME FUN, HUH?
WHADDYA SAY?
ダッ
MIAKA!
HOLD IT!
GRAB HER!!
MIAKA!!

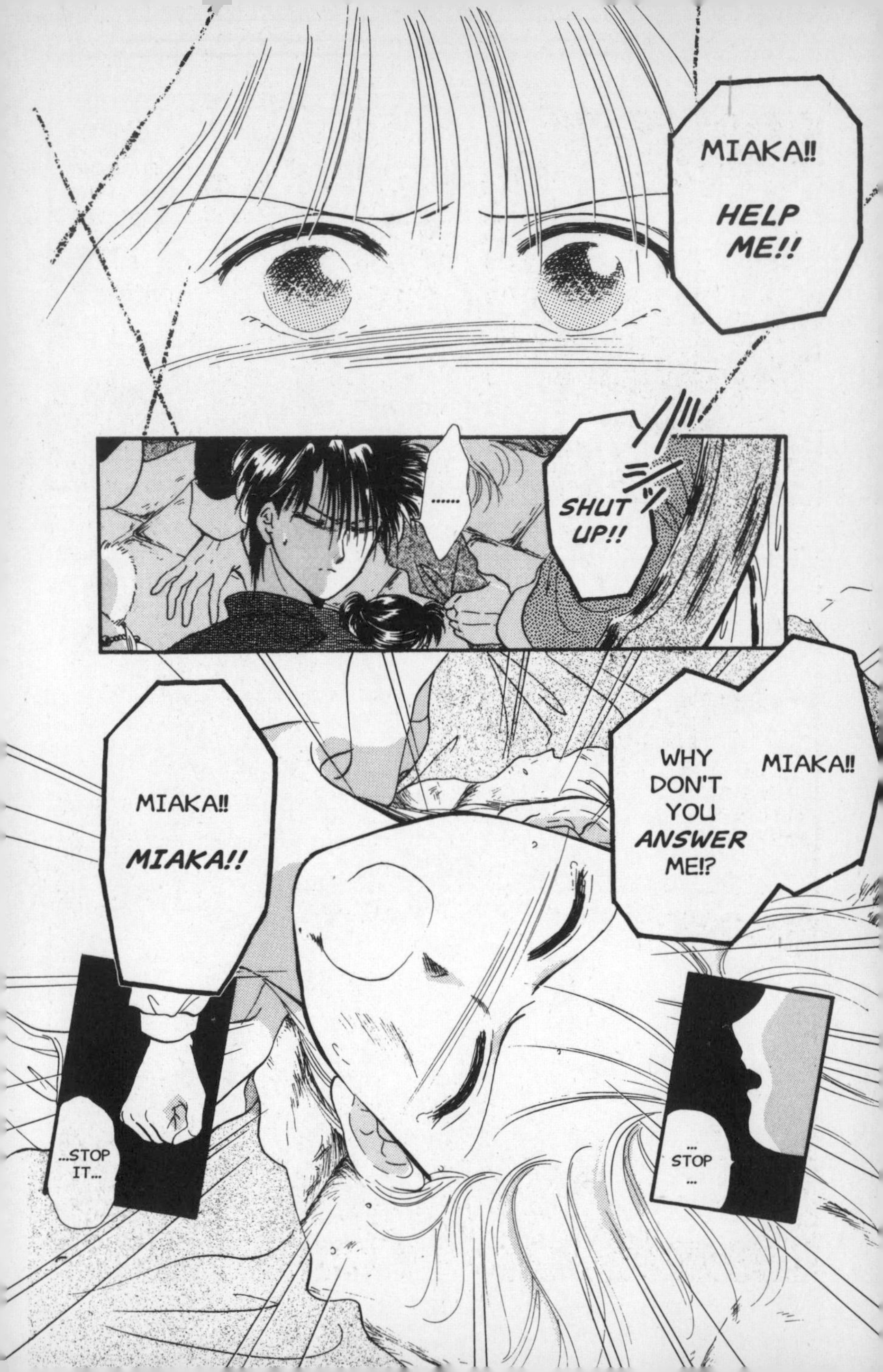
MIAKA!! HELP ME!!
SHUT UP!!
......
MIAKA!! WHY DON'T YOU ANSWER ME!?
MIAKA!! MIAKA!!
...STOP...
...STOP IT...

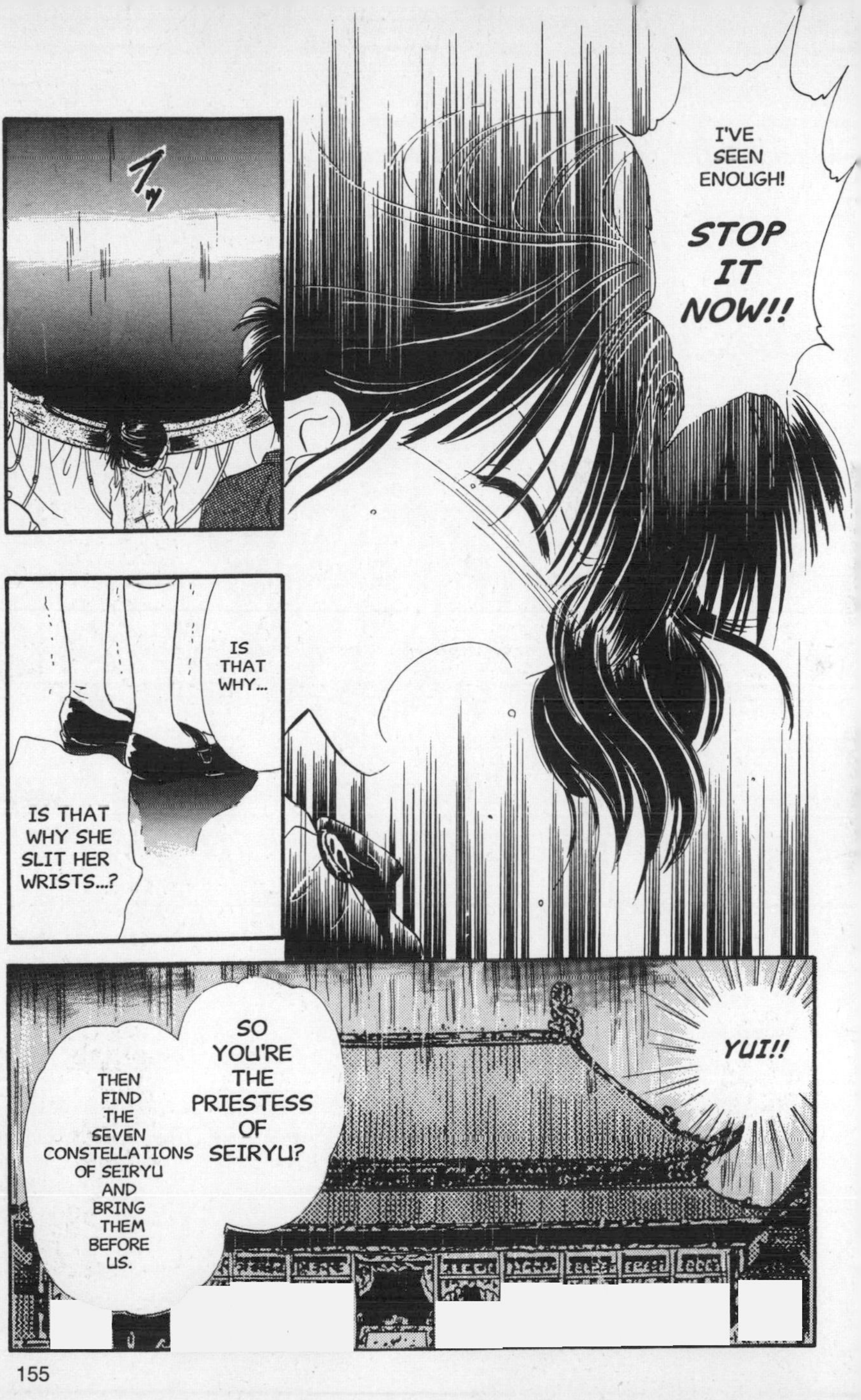
I'VE SEEN ENOUGH!
STOP IT NOW!!
IS THAT WHY...
IS THAT WHY SHE SLIT HER WRISTS...?
YUI!!
SO YOU'RE THE PRIESTESS OF SEIRYU?
THEN FIND THE SEVEN CONSTELLATIONS OF SEIRYU AND BRING THEM BEFORE US.

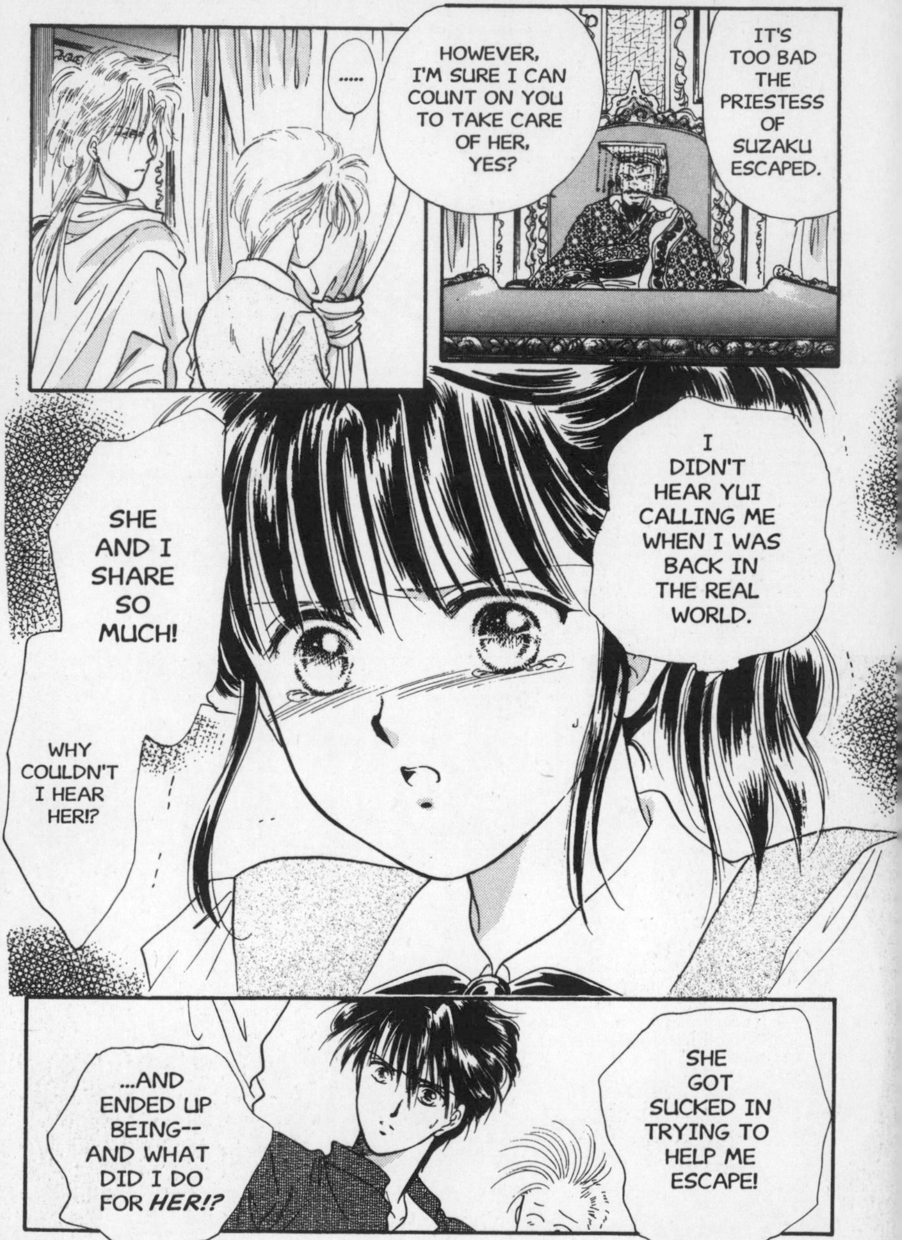
IT'S TOO BAD THE PRIESTESS OF SUZAKU ESCAPED.
HOWEVER, I'M SURE I CAN COUNT ON YOU TO TAKE CARE OF HER, YES?
......
I DIDN'T HEAR YUI CALLING ME WHEN I WAS BACK IN THE REAL WORLD.
SHE AND I SHARE SO MUCH!
WHY COULDN'T I HEAR HER!?
SHE GOT SUCKED IN TRYING TO HELP ME ESCAPE!
...AND ENDED UP BEING-- AND WHAT DID I DO FOR *HER!?*

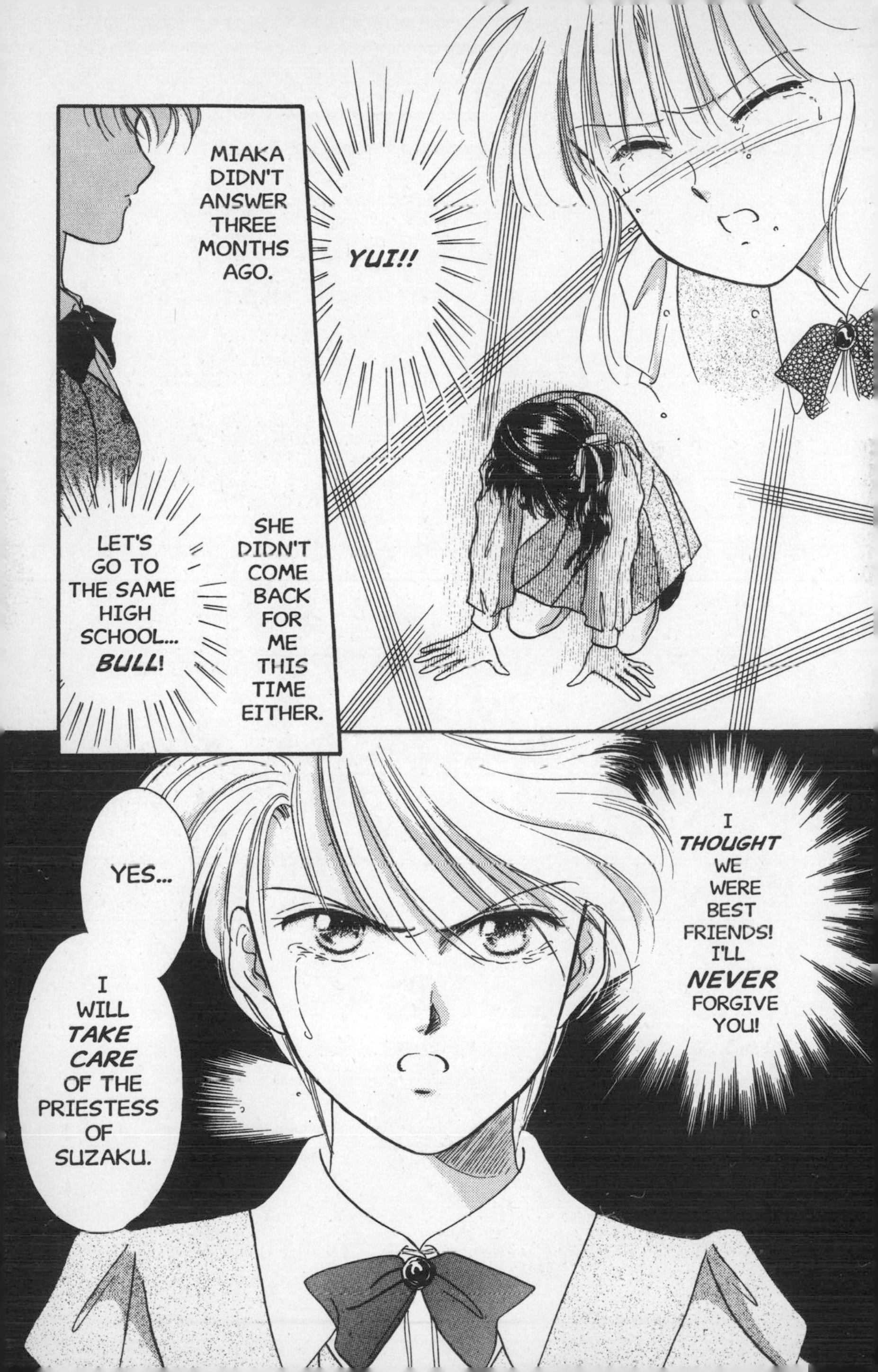
YUI!!
MIAKA DIDN'T ANSWER THREE MONTHS AGO.
SHE DIDN'T COME BACK FOR ME THIS TIME EITHER.
LET'S GO TO THE SAME HIGH SCHOOL... *BULL*!
I *THOUGHT* WE WERE BEST FRIENDS! I'LL *NEVER* FORGIVE YOU!
YES...
I WILL *TAKE CARE* OF THE PRIESTESS OF SUZAKU.

BACK BY POPULAR DEMAND
PARDON THE PARODY NEWLY RETITLED AS

FUSHIGI AKUGI
THE MALICIOUS PLAY

ふしぎ悪戯

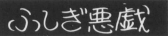

WITH A SLIGHT CHANGE OF WORDING, YOU CAN MAKE THIS INTO SOMETHING YOU'LL FOREVER REGRET!
C'MON, KIDS! TRY THIS AT HOME! (TRY WHAT!?)

......
?
I COULDA SWORN SOMETHING JUST BRUSHED BY ME.
SKR CHA
SKR CHA

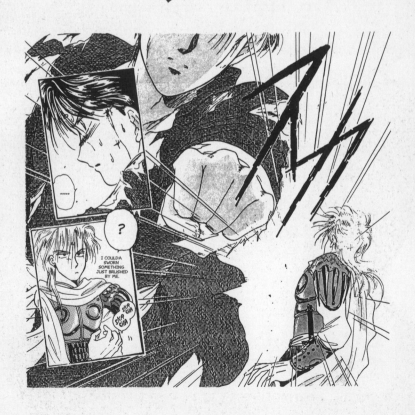

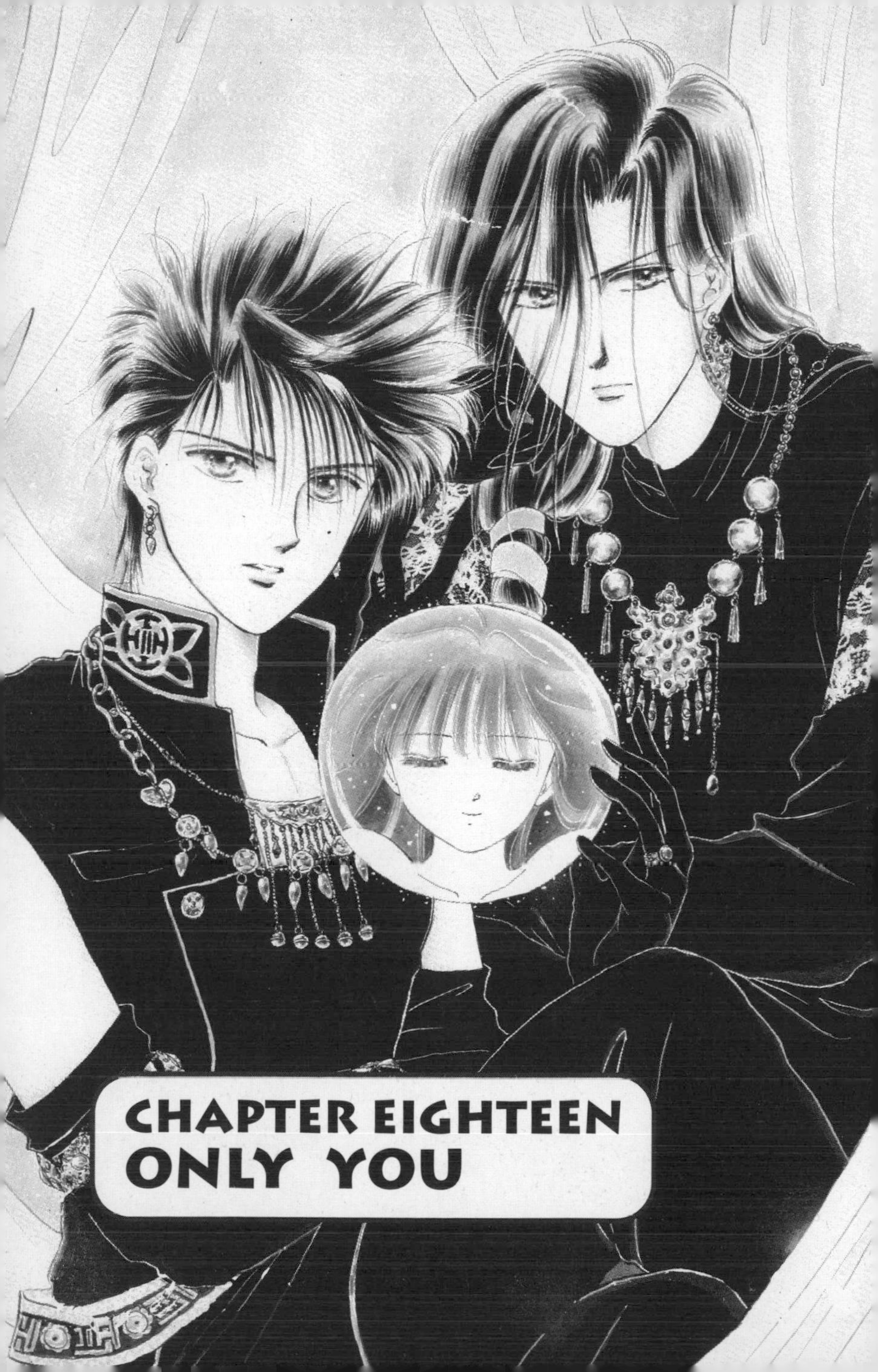
CHAPTER EIGHTEEN
ONLY YOU

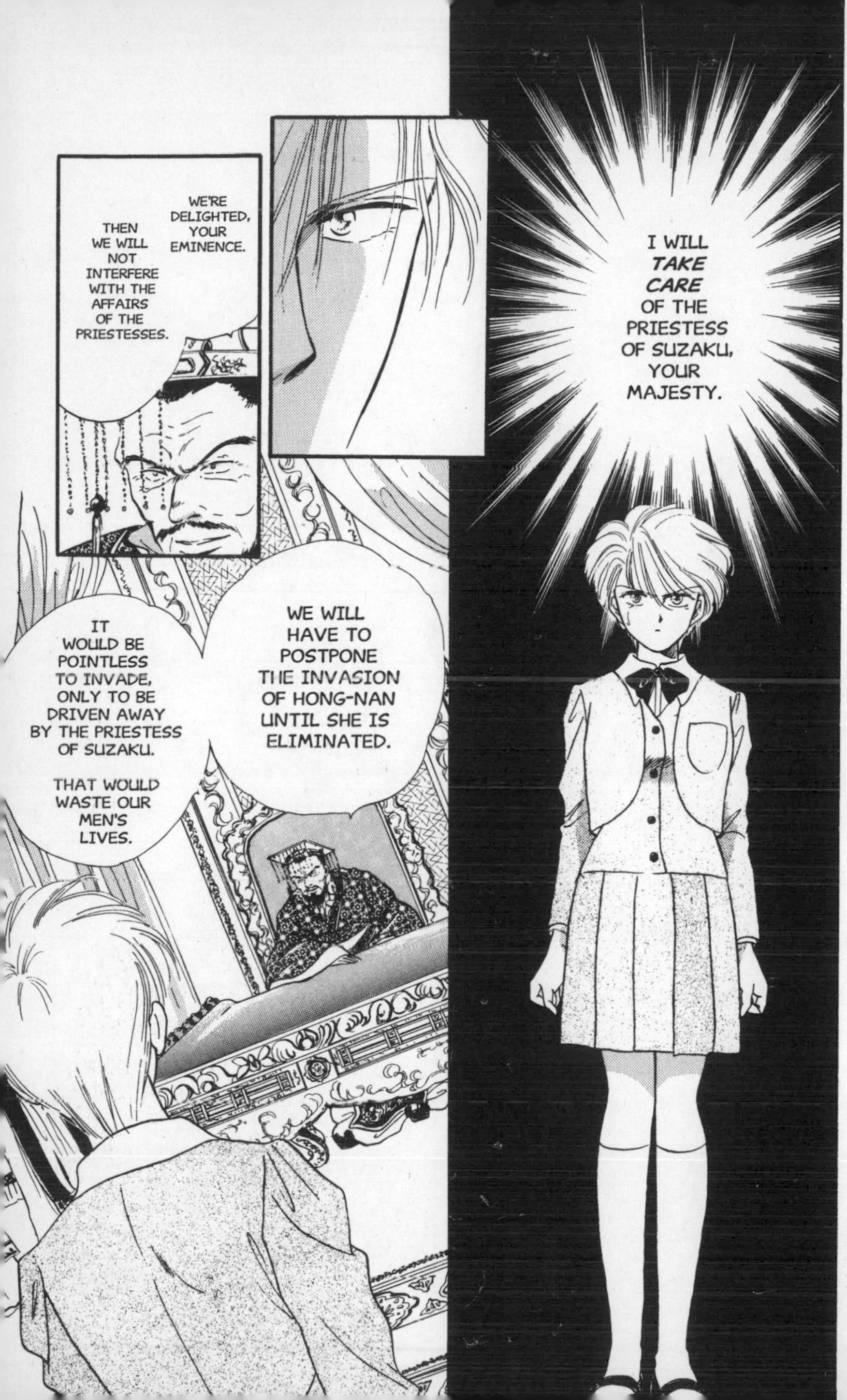
I WILL *TAKE CARE* OF THE PRIESTESS OF SUZAKU, YOUR MAJESTY.
WE'RE DELIGHTED, YOUR EMINENCE.
THEN WE WILL NOT INTERFERE WITH THE AFFAIRS OF THE PRIESTESSES.
WE WILL HAVE TO POSTPONE THE INVASION OF HONG-NAN UNTIL SHE IS ELIMINATED.
IT WOULD BE POINTLESS TO INVADE, ONLY TO BE DRIVEN AWAY BY THE PRIESTESS OF SUZAKU.
THAT WOULD WASTE OUR MEN'S LIVES.

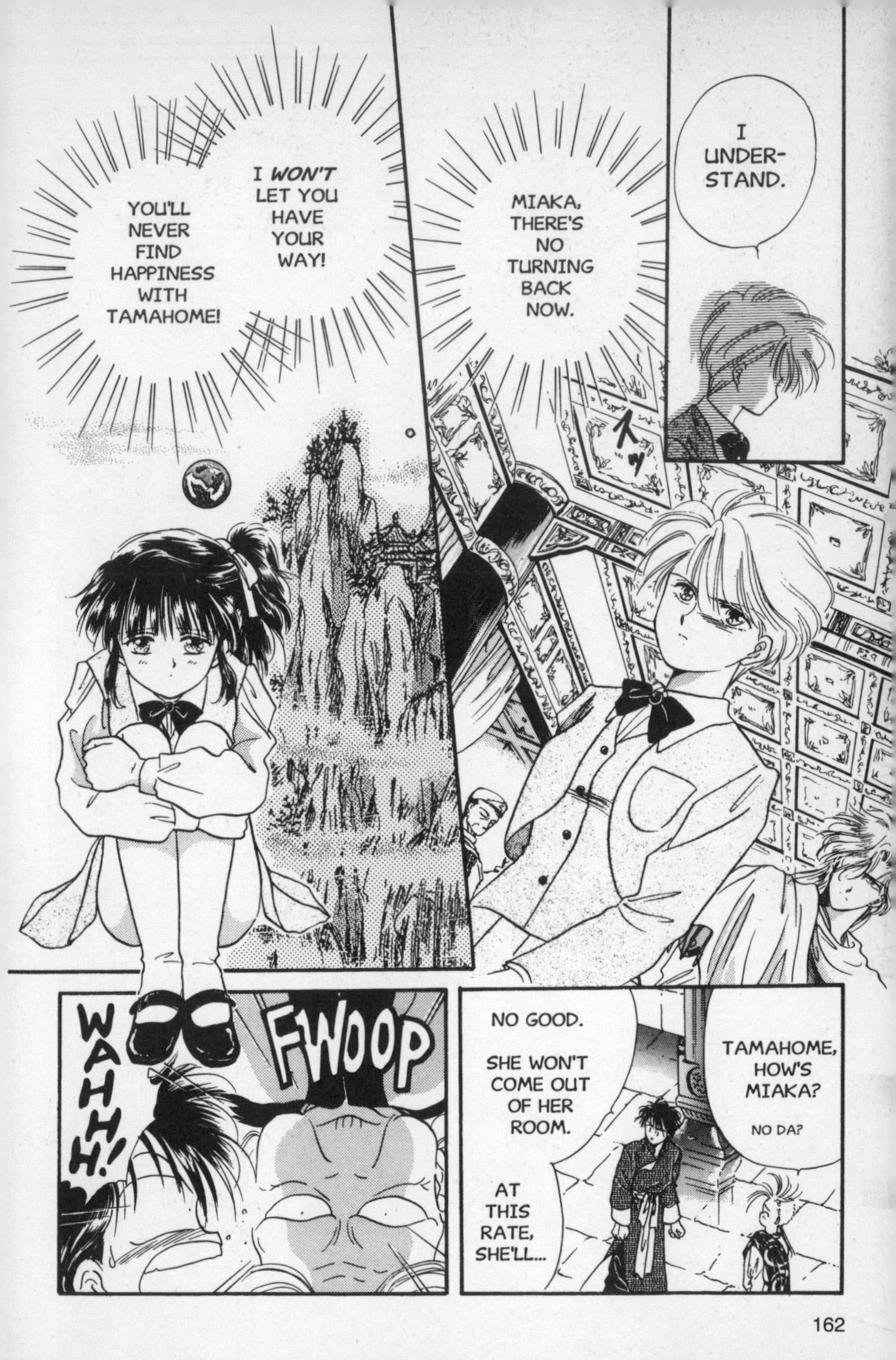
I UNDER-STAND.
MIAKA, THERE'S NO TURNING BACK NOW.
スッ
I *WON'T* LET YOU HAVE YOUR WAY!
YOU'LL NEVER FIND HAPPINESS WITH TAMAHOME!
TAMAHOME, HOW'S MIAKA?
NO DA?
NO GOOD.
SHE WON'T COME OUT OF HER ROOM.
AT THIS RATE, SHE'LL...
FWOOP
WAHHH!

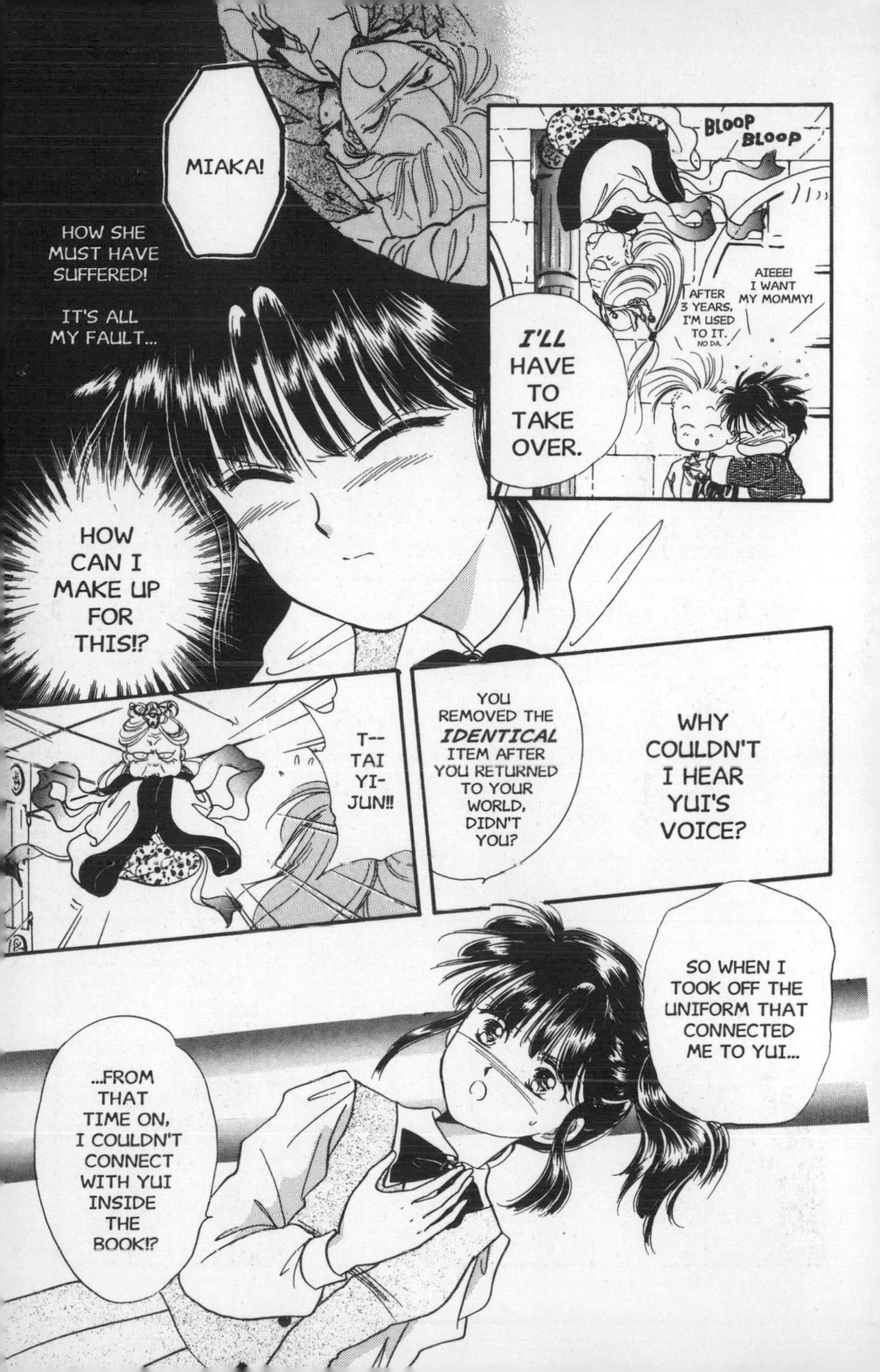
BLOOP BLOOP
I'LL HAVE TO TAKE OVER.
AIEEE! I WANT MY MOMMY!
AFTER 3 YEARS, I'M USED TO IT. NO DA.
MIAKA!
HOW SHE MUST HAVE SUFFERED!
IT'S ALL MY FAULT...
HOW CAN I MAKE UP FOR THIS!?
WHY COULDN'T I HEAR YUI'S VOICE?
YOU REMOVED THE IDENTICAL ITEM AFTER YOU RETURNED TO YOUR WORLD, DIDN'T YOU?
T-- TAI YI-JUN!!
SO WHEN I TOOK OFF THE UNIFORM THAT CONNECTED ME TO YUI...
...FROM THAT TIME ON, I COULDN'T CONNECT WITH YUI INSIDE THE BOOK!?

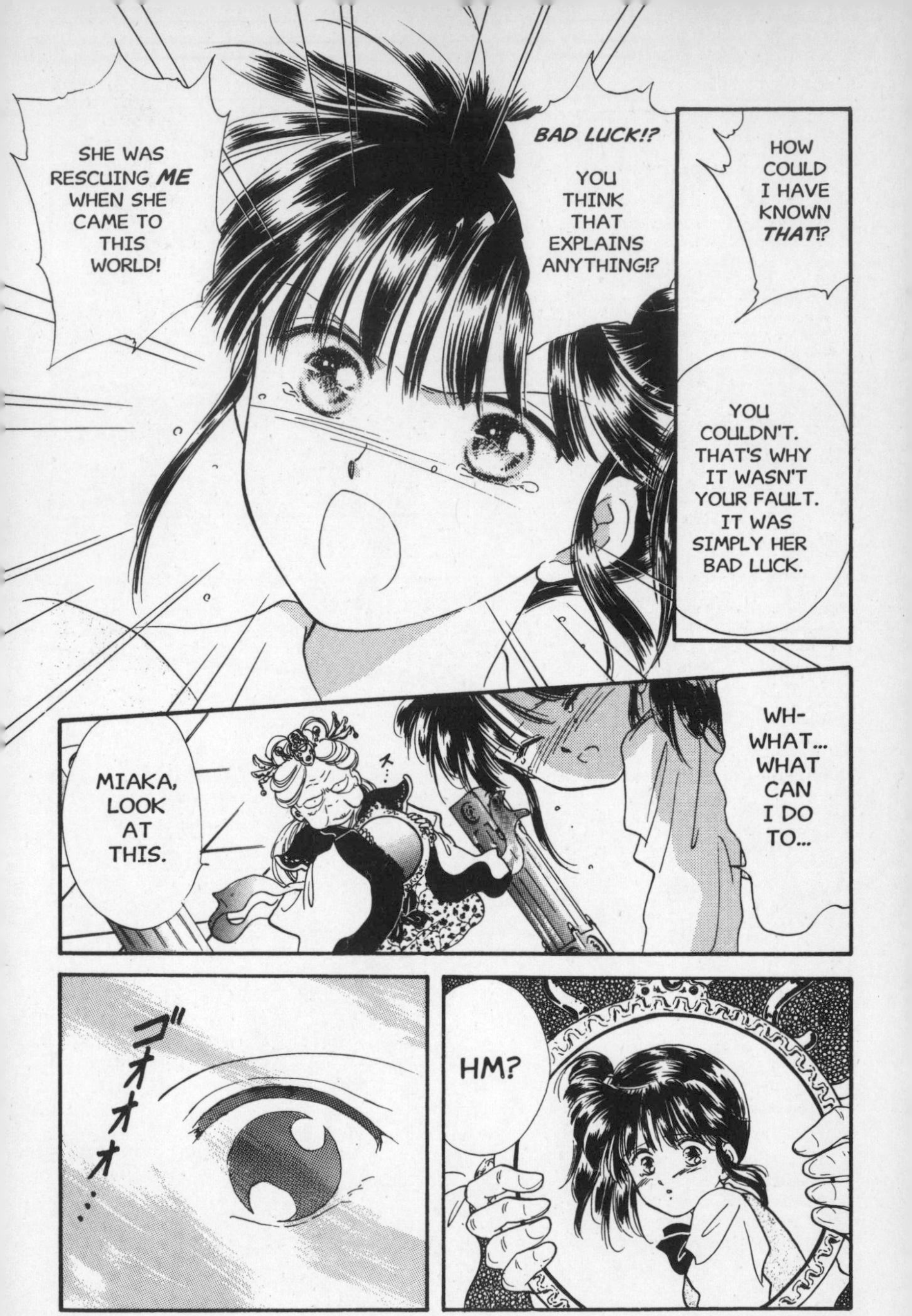
HOW COULD I HAVE KNOWN *THAT*!?
YOU COULDN'T. THAT'S WHY IT WASN'T YOUR FAULT. IT WAS SIMPLY HER BAD LUCK.
BAD LUCK!?
YOU THINK THAT EXPLAINS ANYTHING!?
SHE WAS RESCUING *ME* WHEN SHE CAME TO THIS WORLD!
WH- WHAT... WHAT CAN I DO TO...
ス…
MIAKA, LOOK AT THIS.
HM?
ゴオオオ…

Well, I've been getting responses from you regarding this free chat section. One person wrote in to complain about how I wouldn't give official approval for a project. According to the letter, my failure to give official approval indicated that I was becoming more distant from my readers. But it was my editors' decision. I guess they had problems in the past. I'm not trying to distance myself from my readers! I'm glad to hear that you wouldn't want that, but there's no need to get hung up over getting "official" approval. So don't worry about it, okay? Just because there isn't an official approval doesn't mean that I don't like it. I keep on receiving a lot of fanzines, and I take the time to look through all of them. So go right ahead and make fanzines or dojinshi and send them my way. I thought I'd said that before already. I think it's fine to draw parodies of my work (as long as they're not gross or boring).

Once my story gets published in a magazine, then it becomes part of each reader's imagination, fueled by the way he or she feels about the characters. That's how a work finally becomes complete. I don't know what I'm saying! All I want to say is this book in your hands is your own unique "Fushigi Yūgi." If you see what I mean. Manga is for the reader so... Urgh, I'm getting confused. Those readers who were fans of my work before it merited any "official seal of approval" became the ones that I respect the most. I'm not getting distant! AARGH, I'm getting all jumbled up!

-after a rest-

So fanzines are fine, okay? Oh yeah, I forgot during my rant, I have to apologize for the "Prepubescence Special Edition" not coming out on time. It's not my fault this time! The good news is that a book of illustrations is scheduled to come out next year (I hope). If it doesn't, sorry again! It should be a book of colored illustrations for "Prepubescence" and "Fushigi Yūgi." You want a story, too? Yessir!! I'll do my best.

One last common question: "Do you do illustrations for novels?" I've never had any requests to do one. That's all. This time I answered a lot of questions. Lotta work for those who read through this section.

But who's working hardest here!?

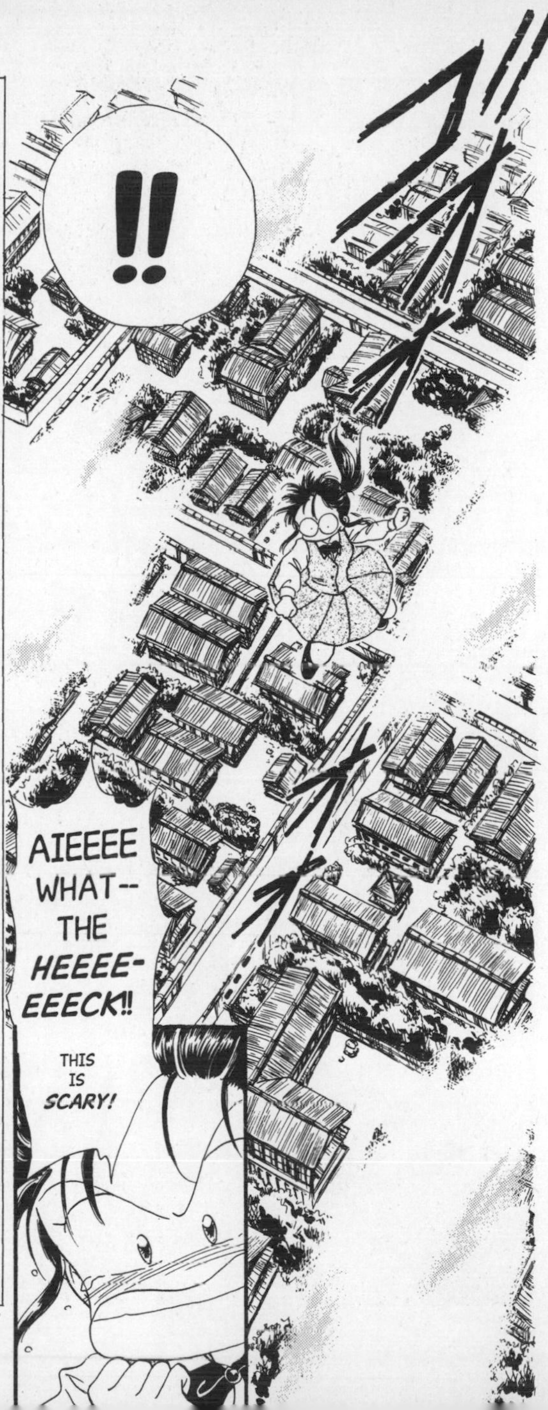
!!
AIEEEE WHAT-- THE HEEEE-EEECK!!
THIS IS SCARY!

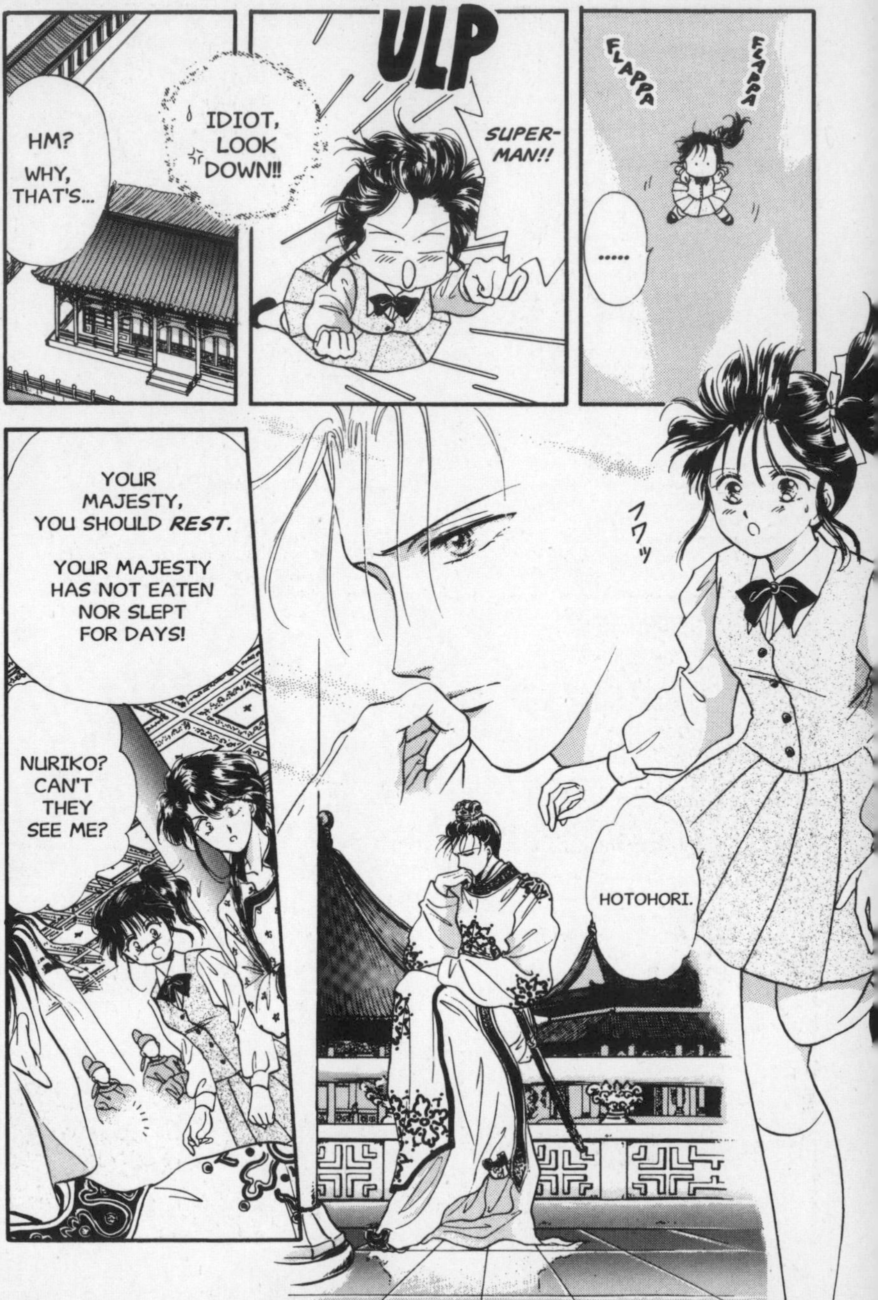
FLAPPA
FLAPPA
......
ULP
SUPER-MAN!!
IDIOT, LOOK DOWN!!
HM? WHY, THAT'S...
フワッ
HOTOHORI.
YOUR MAJESTY, YOU SHOULD *REST*. YOUR MAJESTY HAS NOT EATEN NOR SLEPT FOR DAYS!
NURIKO? CAN'T THEY SEE ME?

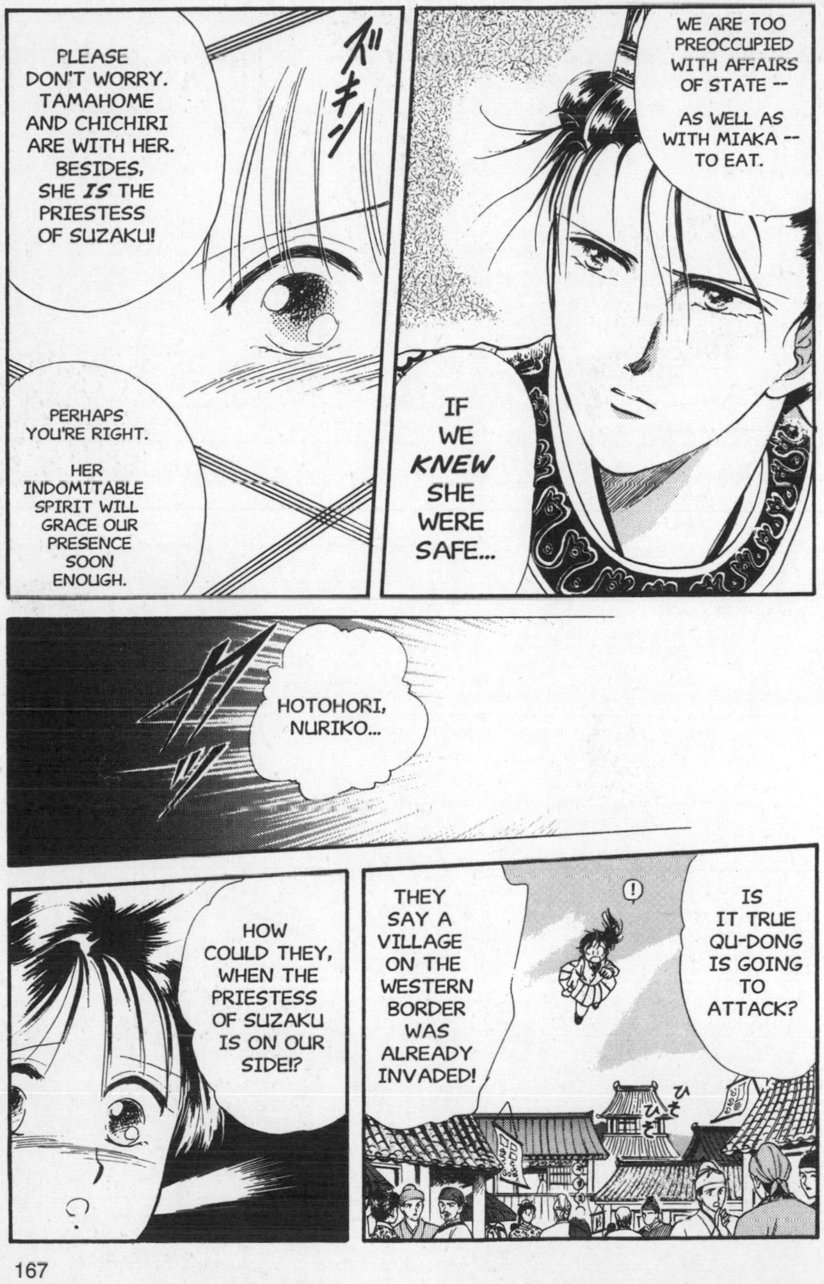
WE ARE TOO PREOCCUPIED WITH AFFAIRS OF STATE --
AS WELL AS WITH MIAKA -- TO EAT.
IF WE *KNEW* SHE WERE SAFE...
ズキン
PLEASE DON'T WORRY. TAMAHOME AND CHICHIRI ARE WITH HER. BESIDES, SHE *IS* THE PRIESTESS OF SUZAKU!
PERHAPS YOU'RE RIGHT.
HER INDOMITABLE SPIRIT WILL GRACE OUR PRESENCE SOON ENOUGH.
HOTOHORI, NURIKO...
IS IT TRUE QU-DONG IS GOING TO ATTACK?
!
ひそひそ
THEY SAY A VILLAGE ON THE WESTERN BORDER WAS ALREADY INVADED!
HOW COULD THEY, WHEN THE PRIESTESS OF SUZAKU IS ON OUR SIDE!?
?

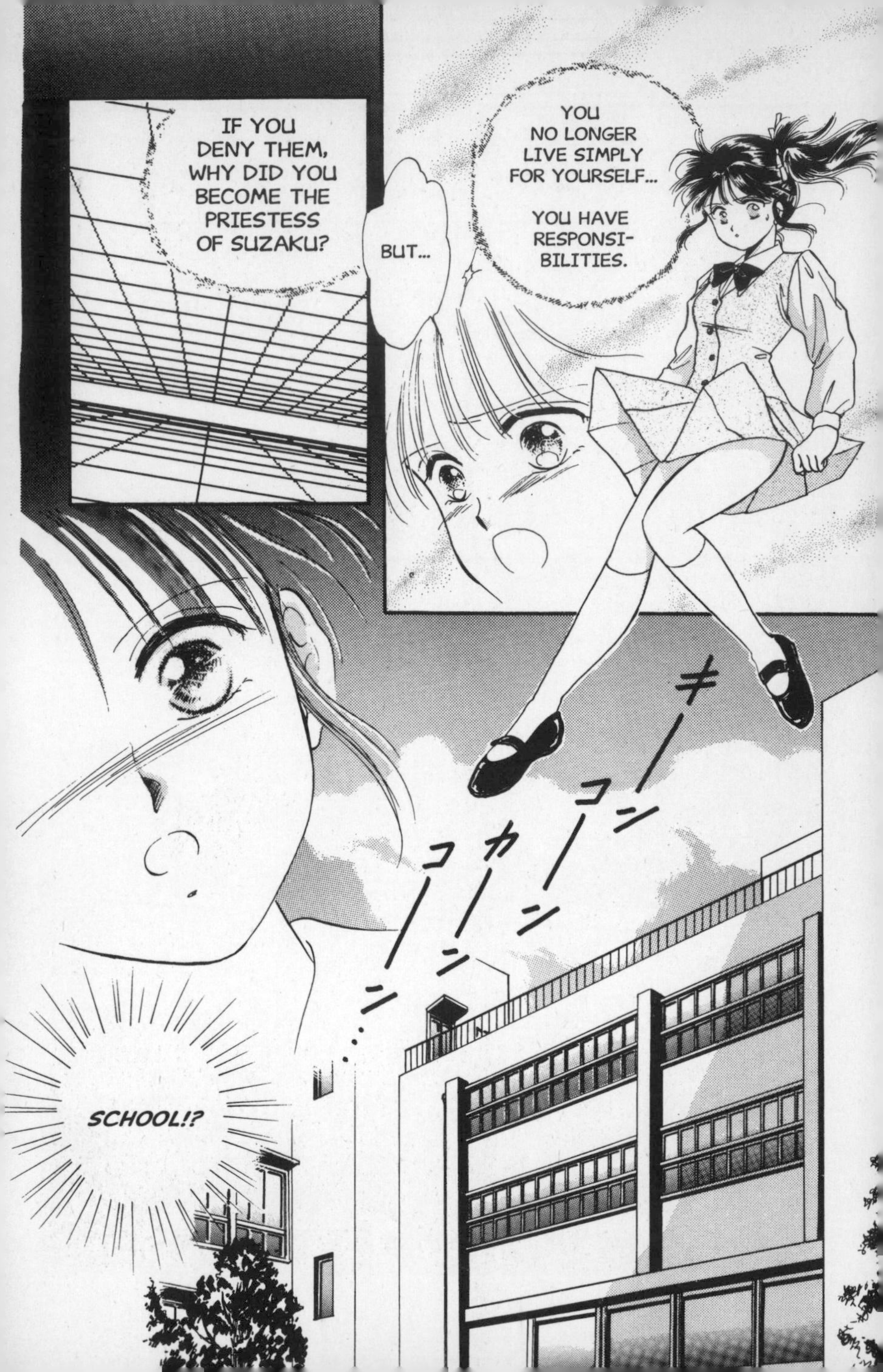
YOU NO LONGER LIVE SIMPLY FOR YOURSELF...
YOU HAVE RESPONSI-BILITIES.
BUT...
IF YOU DENY THEM, WHY DID YOU BECOME THE PRIESTESS OF SUZAKU?
キーンコーン
カーン
コーン…
SCHOOL!?

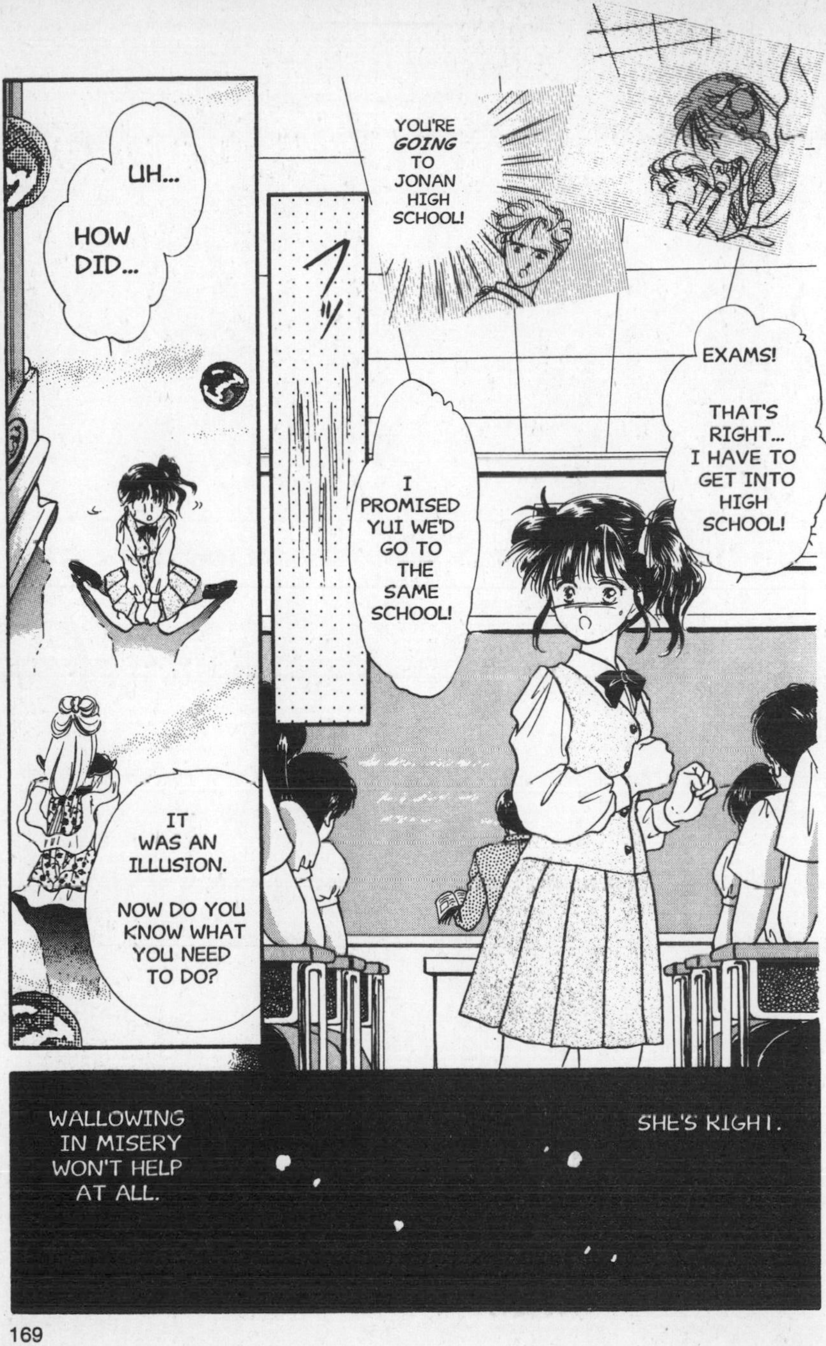
YOU'RE GOING TO JONAN HIGH SCHOOL!
EXAMS! THAT'S RIGHT... I HAVE TO GET INTO HIGH SCHOOL!
I PROMISED YUI WE'D GO TO THE SAME SCHOOL!
UH... HOW DID...
IT WAS AN ILLUSION. NOW DO YOU KNOW WHAT YOU NEED TO DO?
SHE'S RIGHT.
WALLOWING IN MISERY WON'T HELP AT ALL.

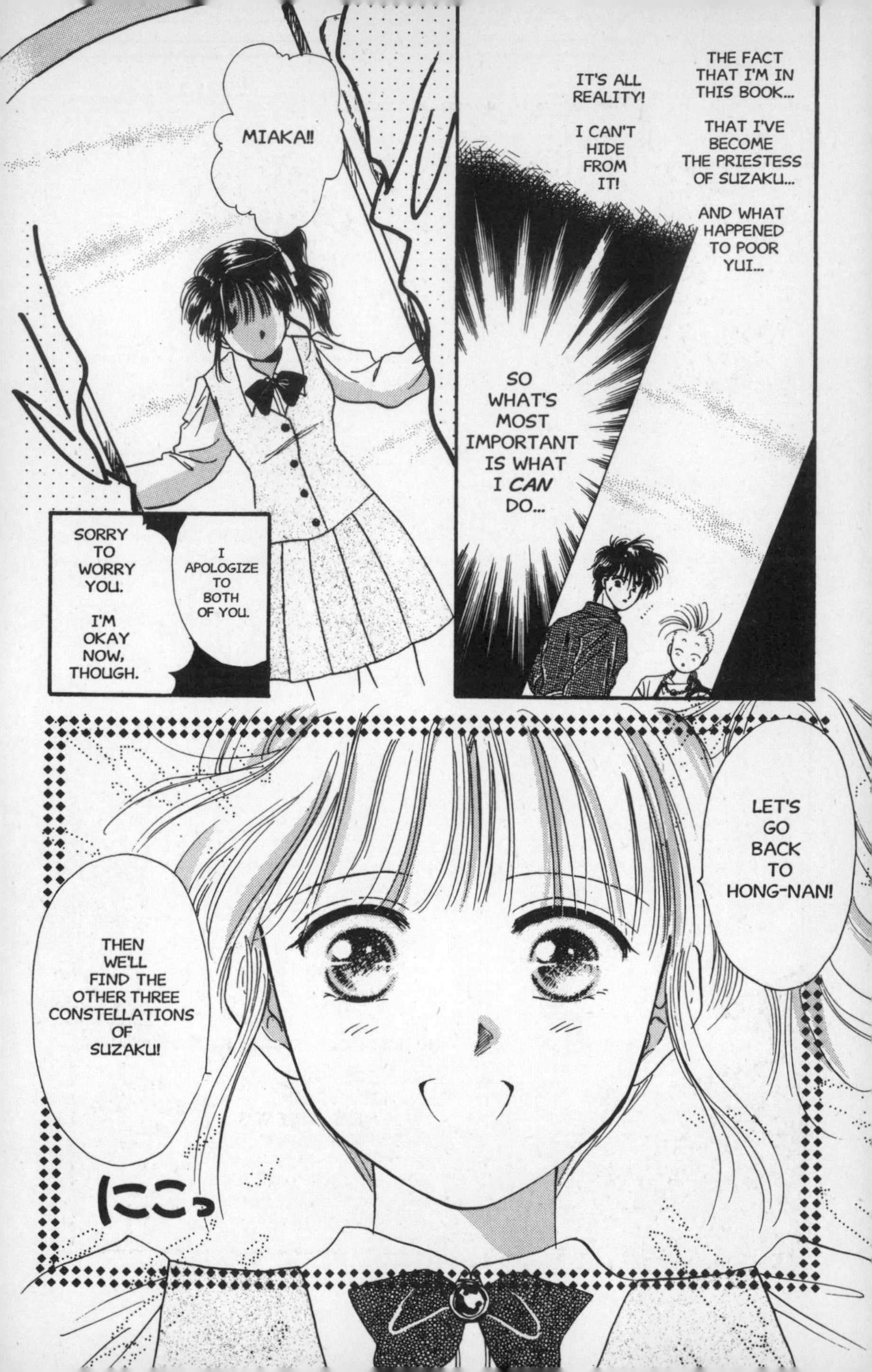
THE FACT THAT I'M IN THIS BOOK...
THAT I'VE BECOME THE PRIESTESS OF SUZAKU...
AND WHAT HAPPENED TO POOR YUI...
IT'S ALL REALITY!
I CAN'T HIDE FROM IT!
SO WHAT'S MOST IMPORTANT IS WHAT I *CAN* DO...
MIAKA!!
I APOLOGIZE TO BOTH OF YOU.
SORRY TO WORRY YOU.
I'M OKAY NOW, THOUGH.
LET'S GO BACK TO HONG-NAN!
THEN WE'LL FIND THE OTHER THREE CONSTELLATIONS OF SUZAKU!
にこっ

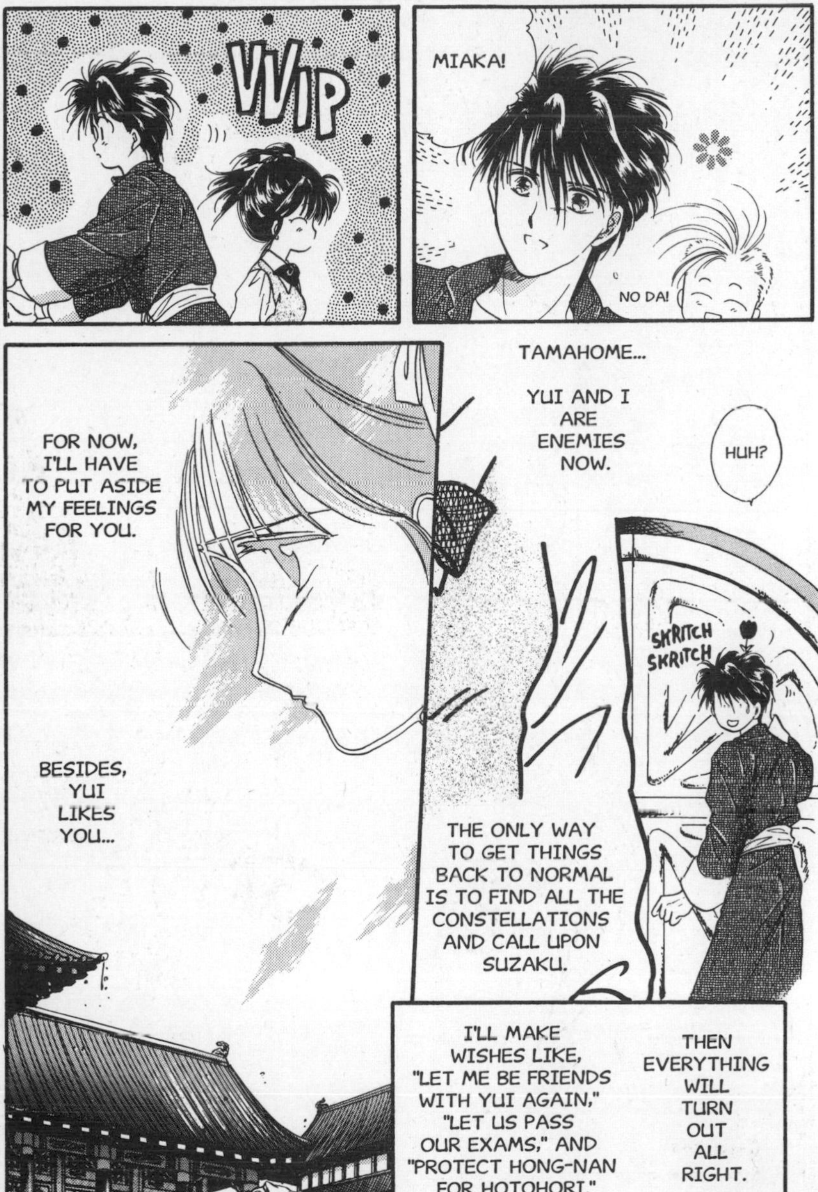
MIAKA!
NO DA!
VVIP
TAMAHOME...
YUI AND I ARE ENEMIES NOW.
HUH?
SKRITCH SKRITCH
THE ONLY WAY TO GET THINGS BACK TO NORMAL IS TO FIND ALL THE CONSTELLATIONS AND CALL UPON SUZAKU.
I'LL MAKE WISHES LIKE, "LET ME BE FRIENDS WITH YUI AGAIN," "LET US PASS OUR EXAMS," AND "PROTECT HONG-NAN FOR HOTOHORI."
THEN EVERYTHING WILL TURN OUT ALL RIGHT.
FOR NOW, I'LL HAVE TO PUT ASIDE MY FEELINGS FOR YOU.
BESIDES, YUI LIKES YOU...

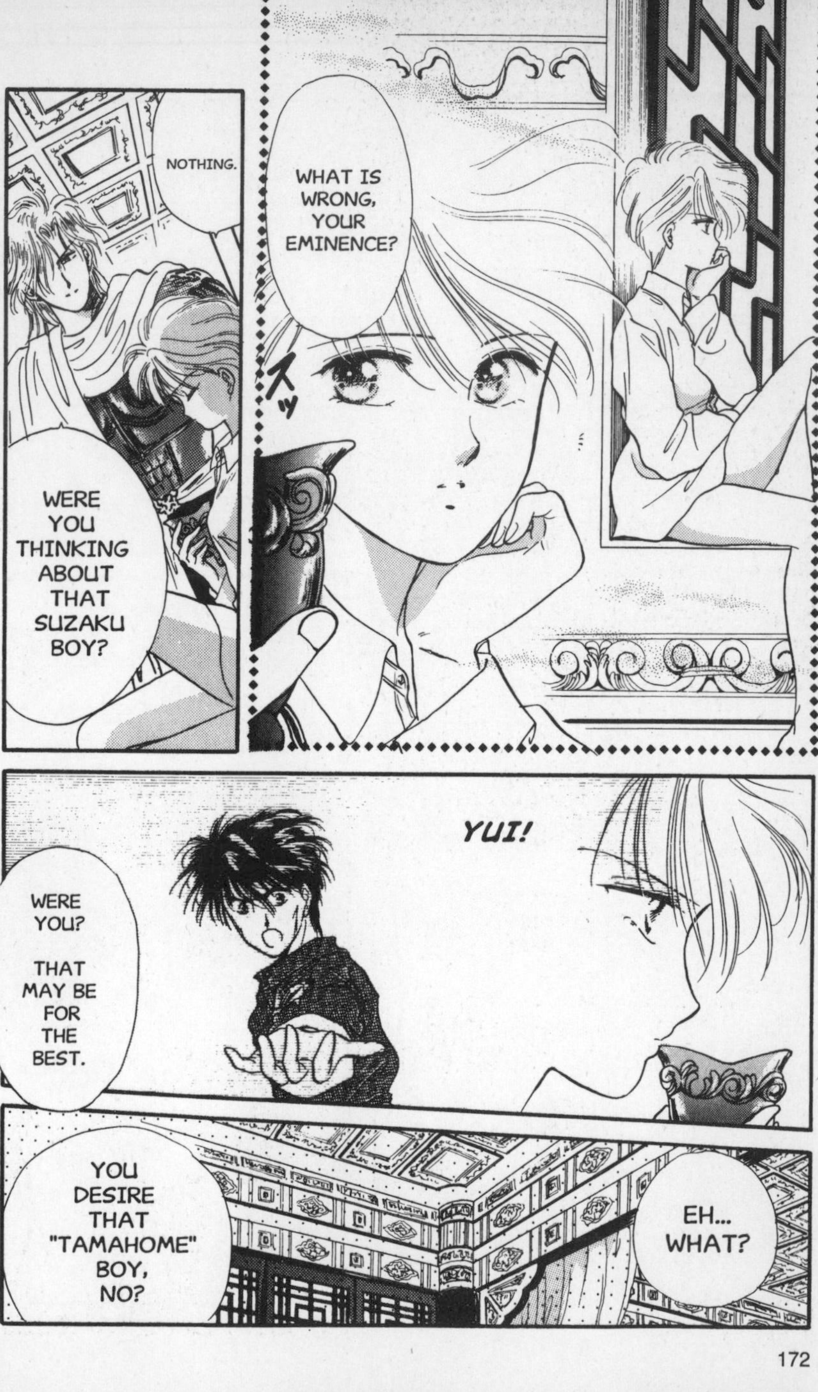
WHAT IS WRONG, YOUR EMINENCE?
スッ
NOTHING.
WERE YOU THINKING ABOUT THAT SUZAKU BOY?
YUI!
WERE YOU? THAT MAY BE FOR THE BEST.
EH... WHAT?
YOU DESIRE THAT "TAMAHOME" BOY, NO?

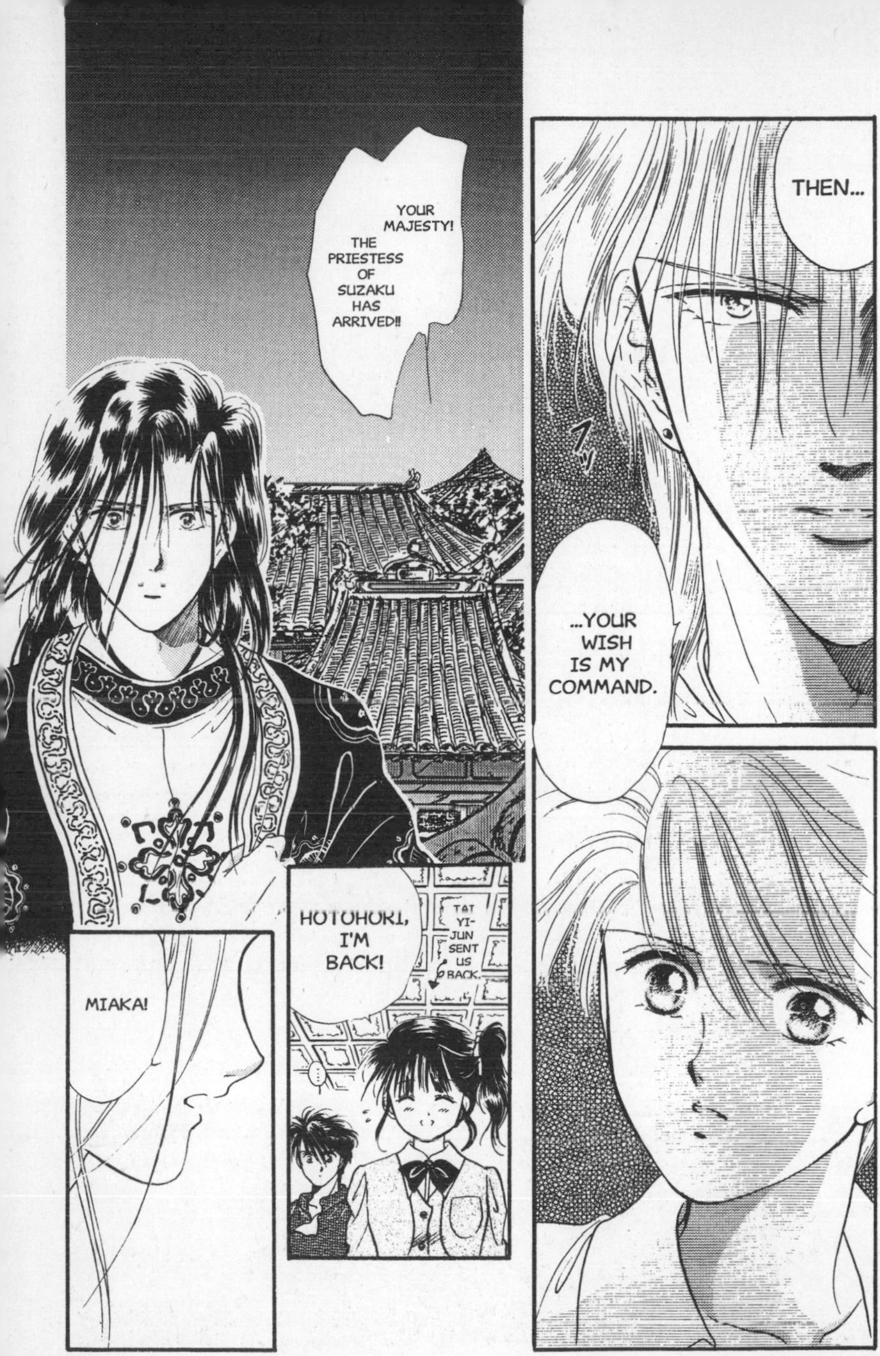
THEN...
...YOUR WISH IS MY COMMAND.
YOUR MAJESTY! THE PRIESTESS OF SUZAKU HAS ARRIVED!!
HOTOHORI, I'M BACK!
TAI YI-JUN SENT US BACK.
...
MIAKA!

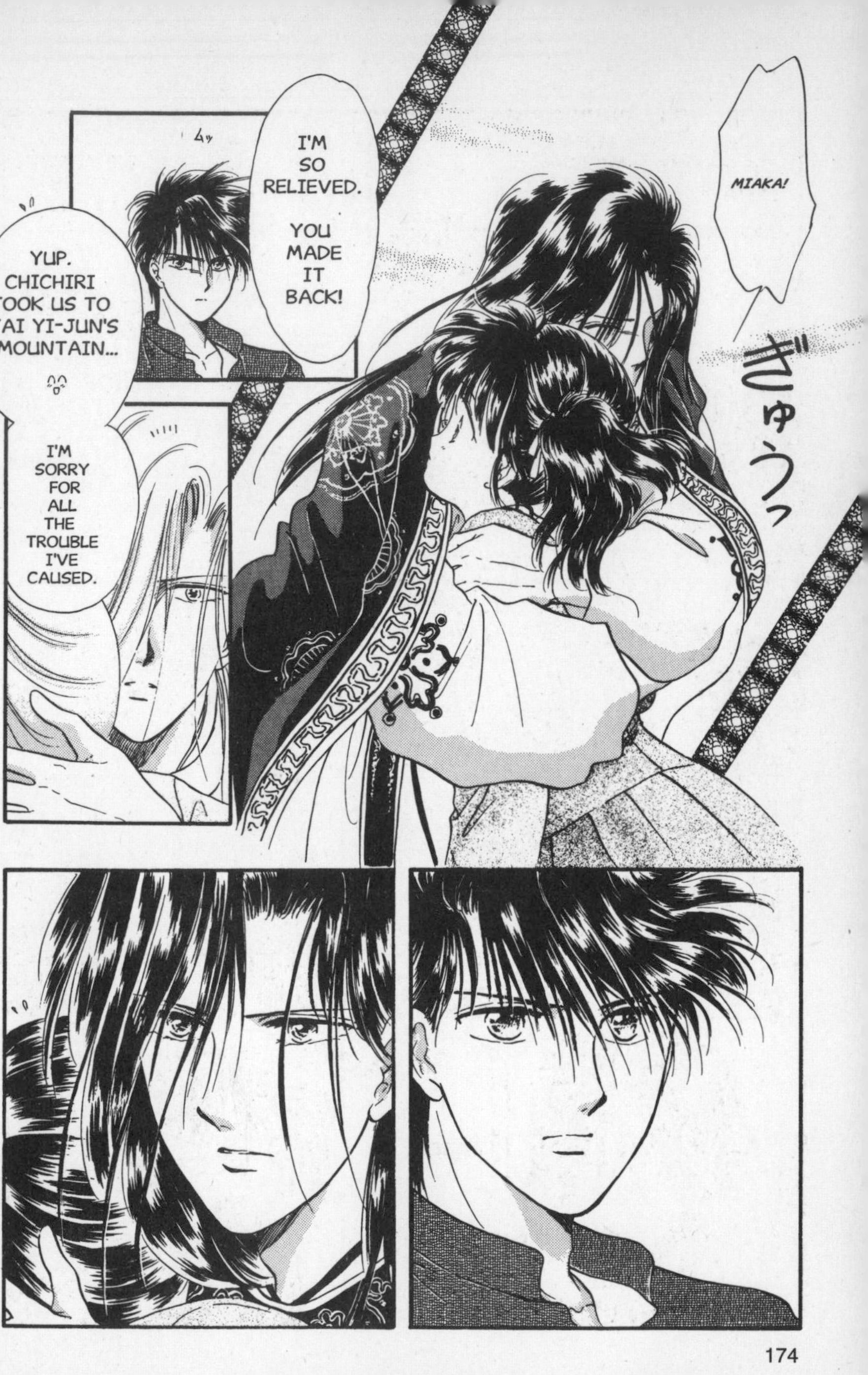
MIAKA!
ぎゅうっ
I'M SO RELIEVED. YOU MADE IT BACK!
ムッ
YUP. CHICHIRI TOOK US TO TAI YI-JUN'S MOUNTAIN...
I'M SORRY FOR ALL THE TROUBLE I'VE CAUSED.

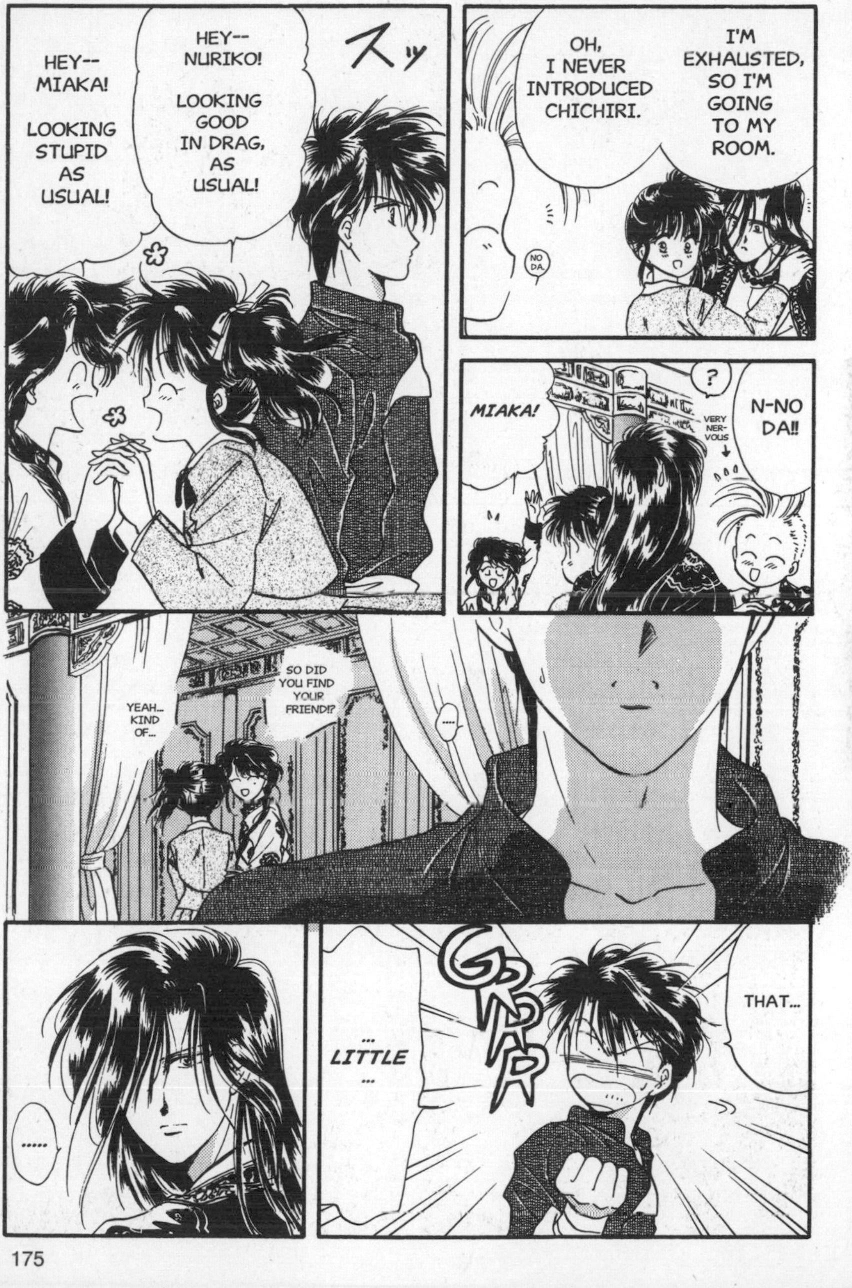
I'M EXHAUSTED, SO I'M GOING TO MY ROOM.
OH, I NEVER INTRODUCED CHICHIRI.
NO DA.
N-NO DA!!
?
VERY NERVOUS
MIAKA!
スッ
HEY-- NURIKO! LOOKING GOOD IN DRAG, AS USUAL!
HEY-- MIAKA! LOOKING STUPID AS USUAL!
.....
SO DID YOU FIND YOUR FRIEND!?
YEAH... KIND OF...
THAT...
GRRR
... LITTLE ...
....
......

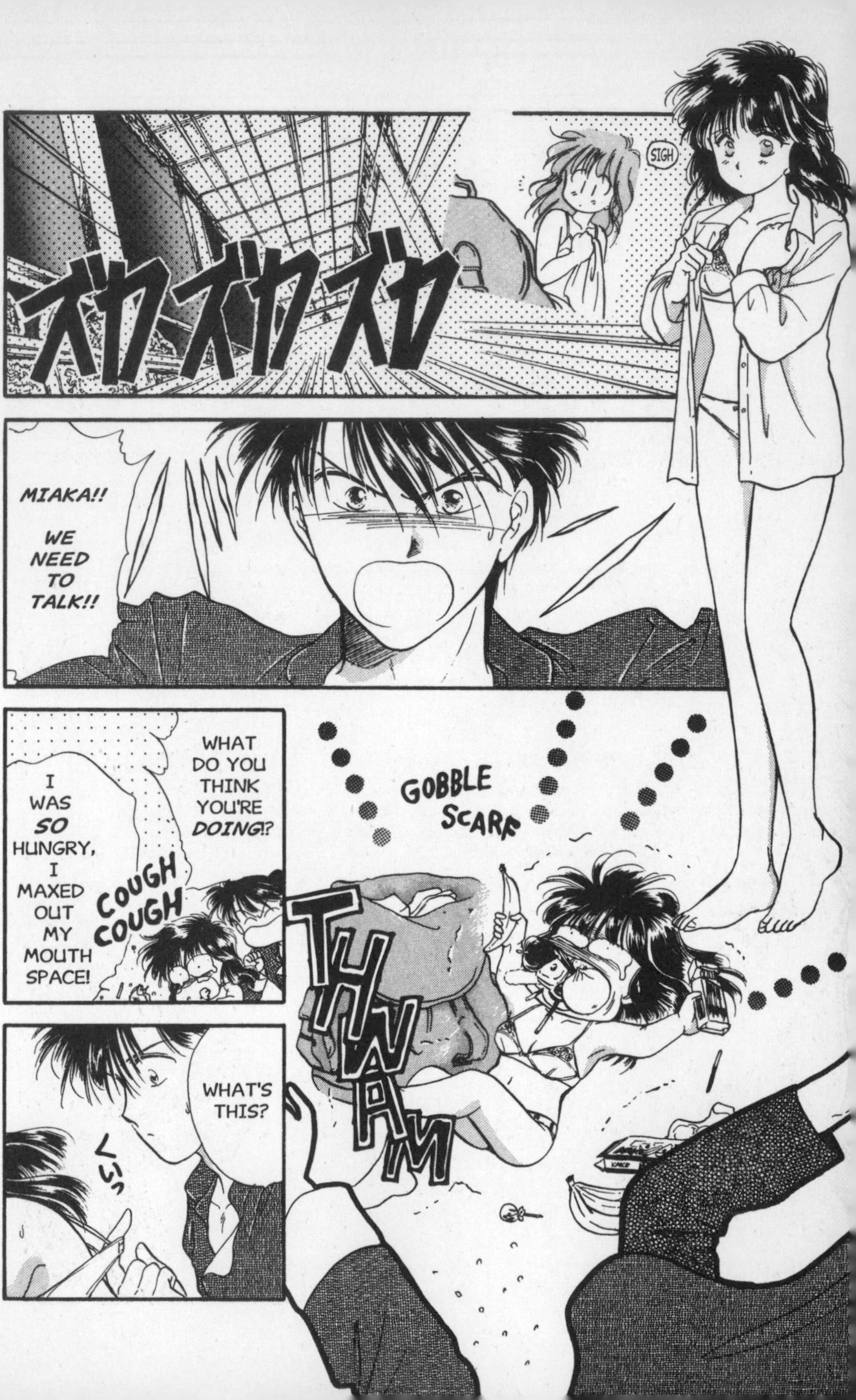
SIGH
ズカズカズカ
MIAKA!!
WE NEED TO TALK!!
GOBBLE
SCARF
THWAM
WHAT DO YOU THINK YOU'RE DOING!?
I WAS SO HUNGRY, I MAXED OUT MY MOUTH SPACE!
COUGH COUGH
WHAT'S THIS?
くいっ

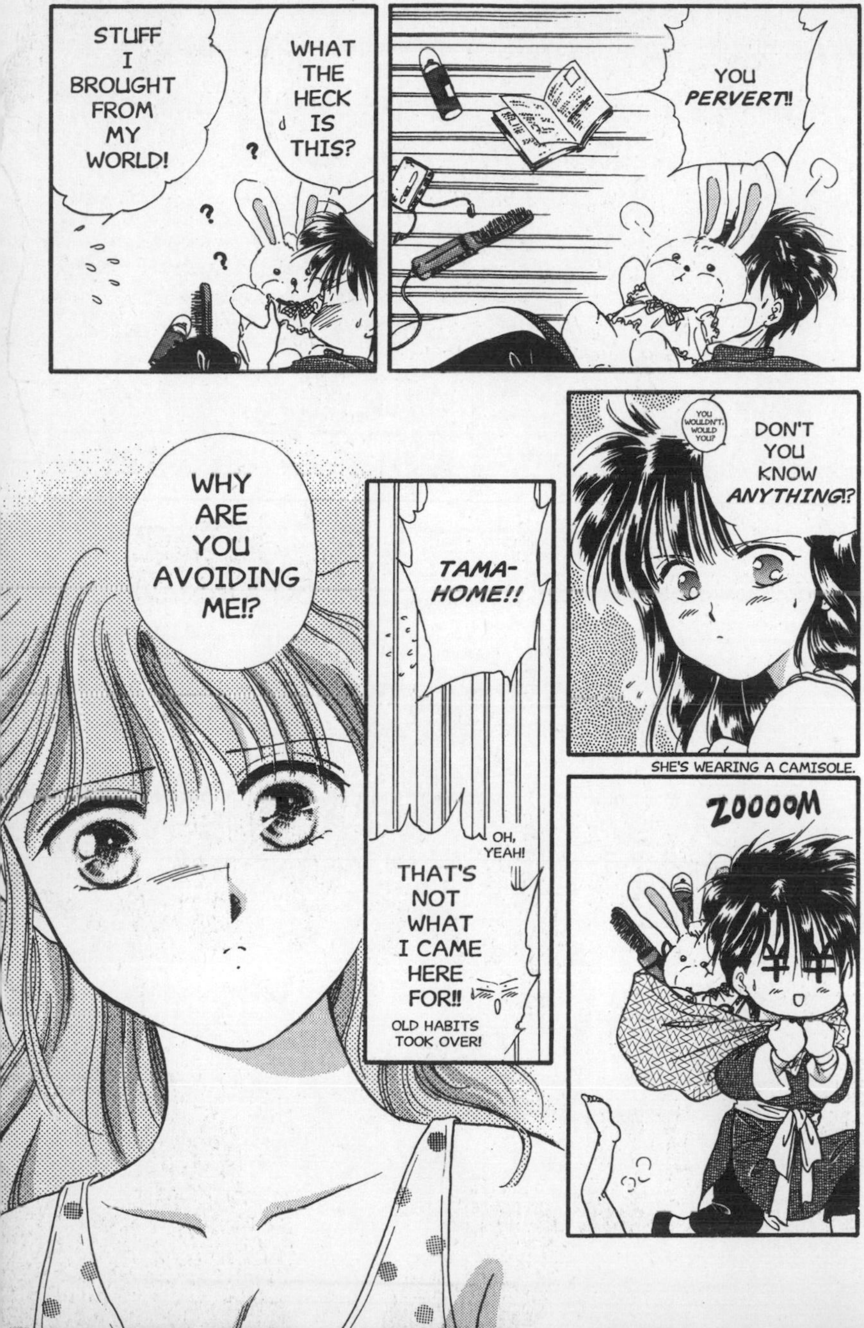
YOU PERVERT!!
WHAT THE HECK IS THIS?
STUFF I BROUGHT FROM MY WORLD!
DON'T YOU KNOW ANYTHING!?
YOU WOULDN'T, WOULD YOU?
SHE'S WEARING A CAMISOLE.
ZOOOOM
TAMA-HOME!!
OH, YEAH!
THAT'S NOT WHAT I CAME HERE FOR!!
OLD HABITS TOOK OVER!
WHY ARE YOU AVOIDING ME!?

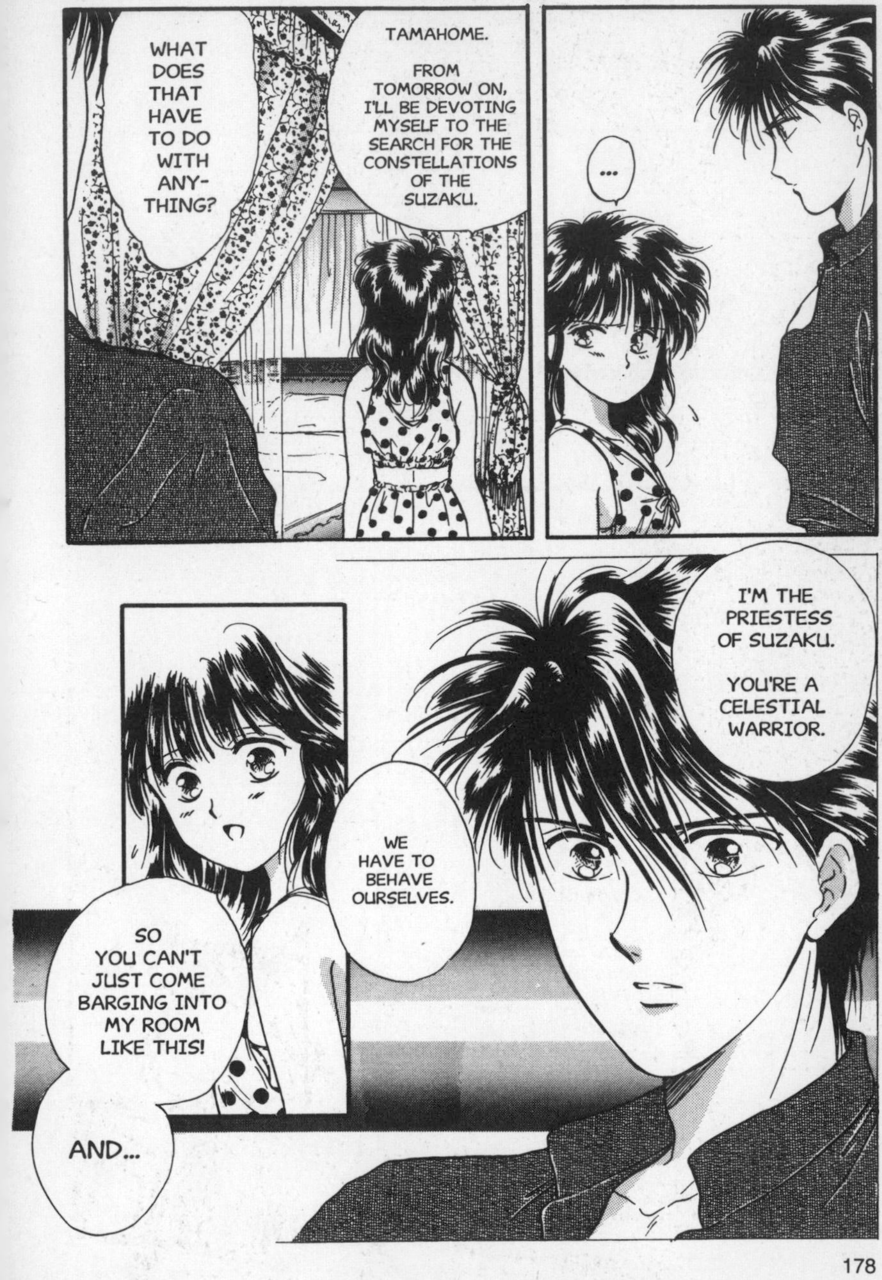
...
TAMAHOME. FROM TOMORROW ON, I'LL BE DEVOTING MYSELF TO THE SEARCH FOR THE CONSTELLATIONS OF THE SUZAKU.
WHAT DOES THAT HAVE TO DO WITH ANY-THING?
I'M THE PRIESTESS OF SUZAKU. YOU'RE A CELESTIAL WARRIOR.
WE HAVE TO BEHAVE OURSELVES.
SO YOU CAN'T JUST COME BARGING INTO MY ROOM LIKE THIS!
AND...

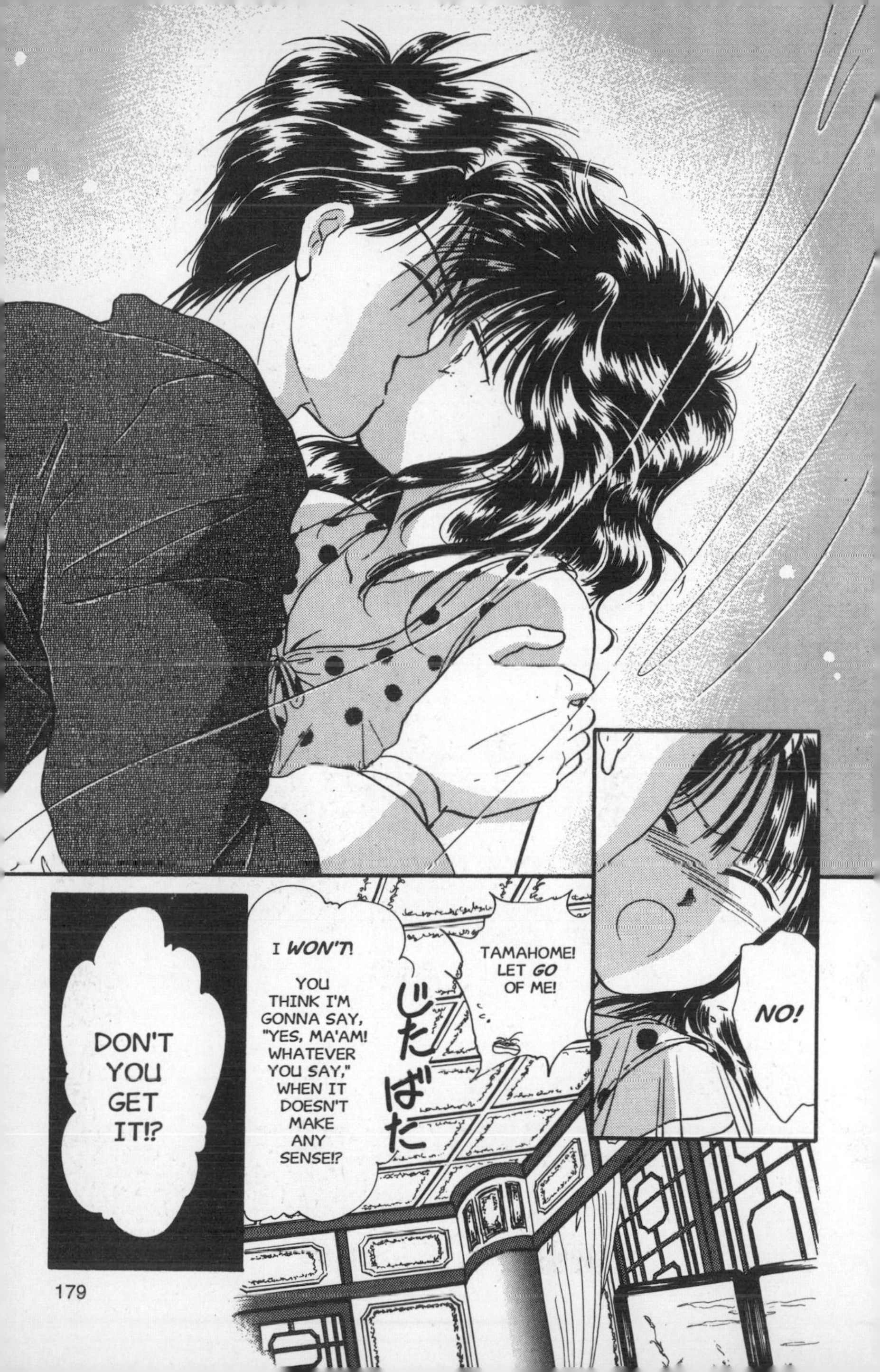
NO!
TAMAHOME! LET GO OF ME!
じたばた
I WON'T! YOU THINK I'M GONNA SAY, "YES, MA'AM! WHATEVER YOU SAY," WHEN IT DOESN'T MAKE ANY SENSE!?
DON'T YOU GET IT!?

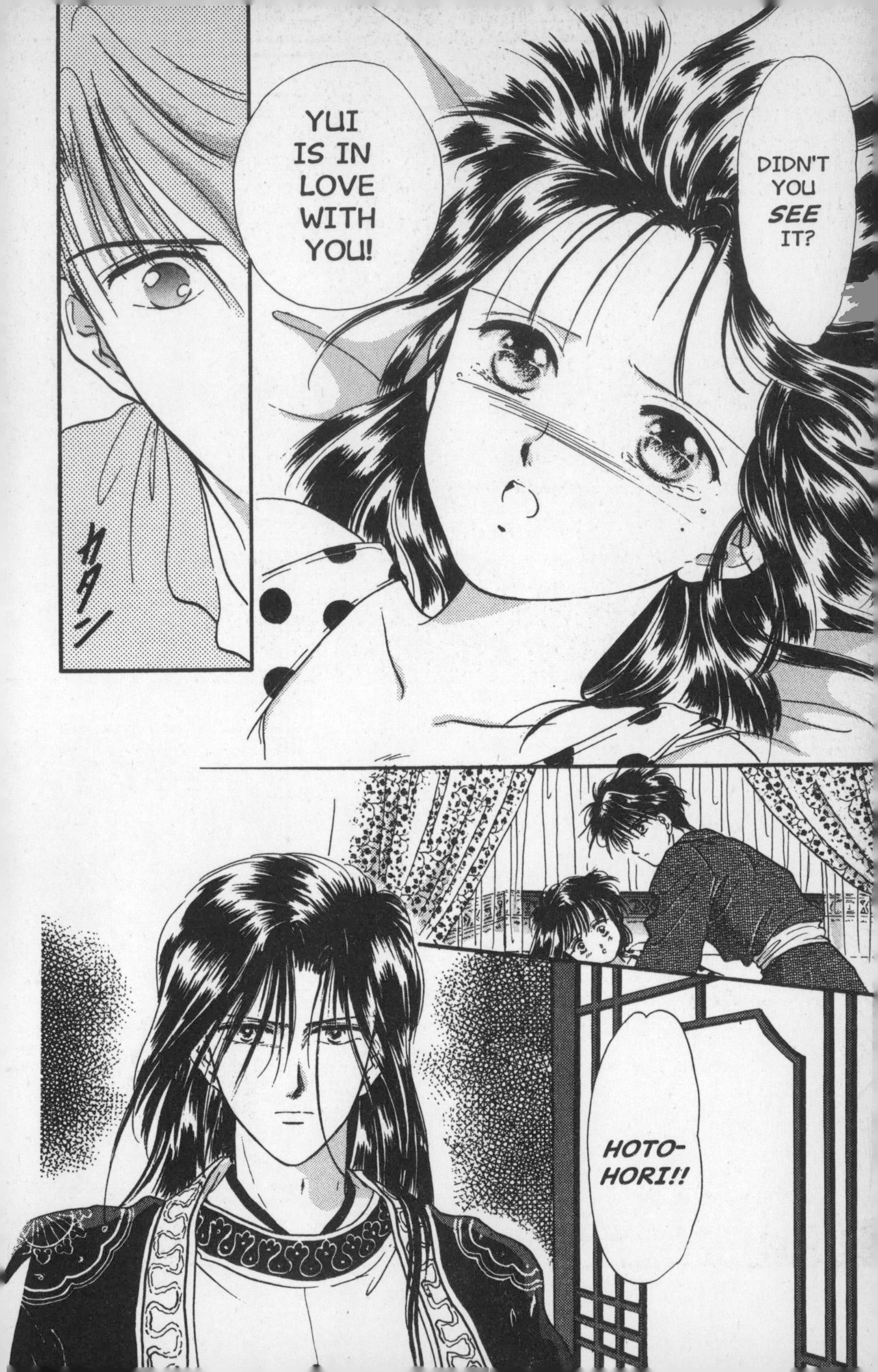
DIDN'T YOU *SEE* IT?
YUI IS IN LOVE WITH YOU!
カタン
HOTO-HORI!!

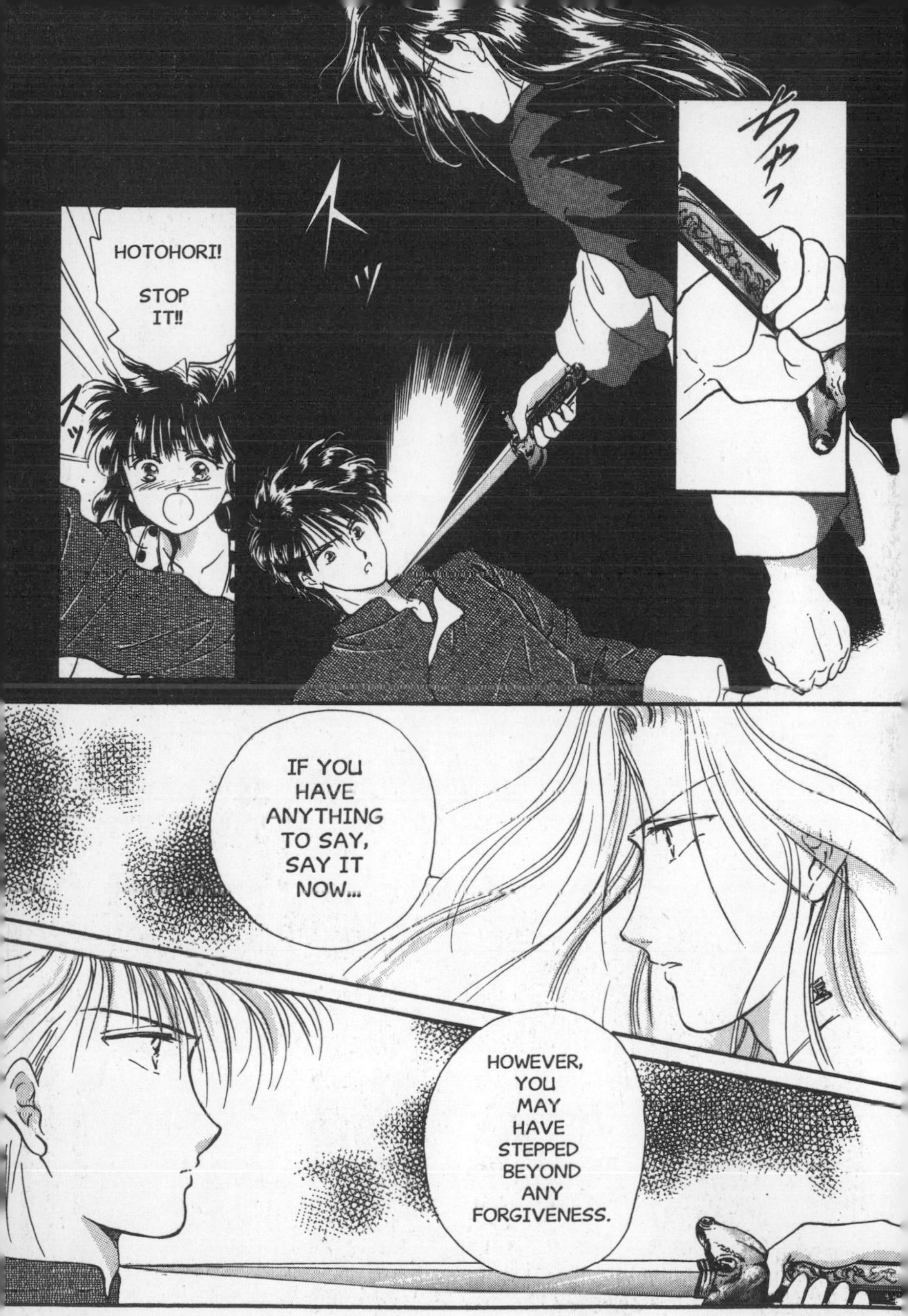
HOTOHORI! STOP IT!!
IF YOU HAVE ANYTHING TO SAY, SAY IT NOW...
HOWEVER, YOU MAY HAVE STEPPED BEYOND ANY FORGIVENESS.

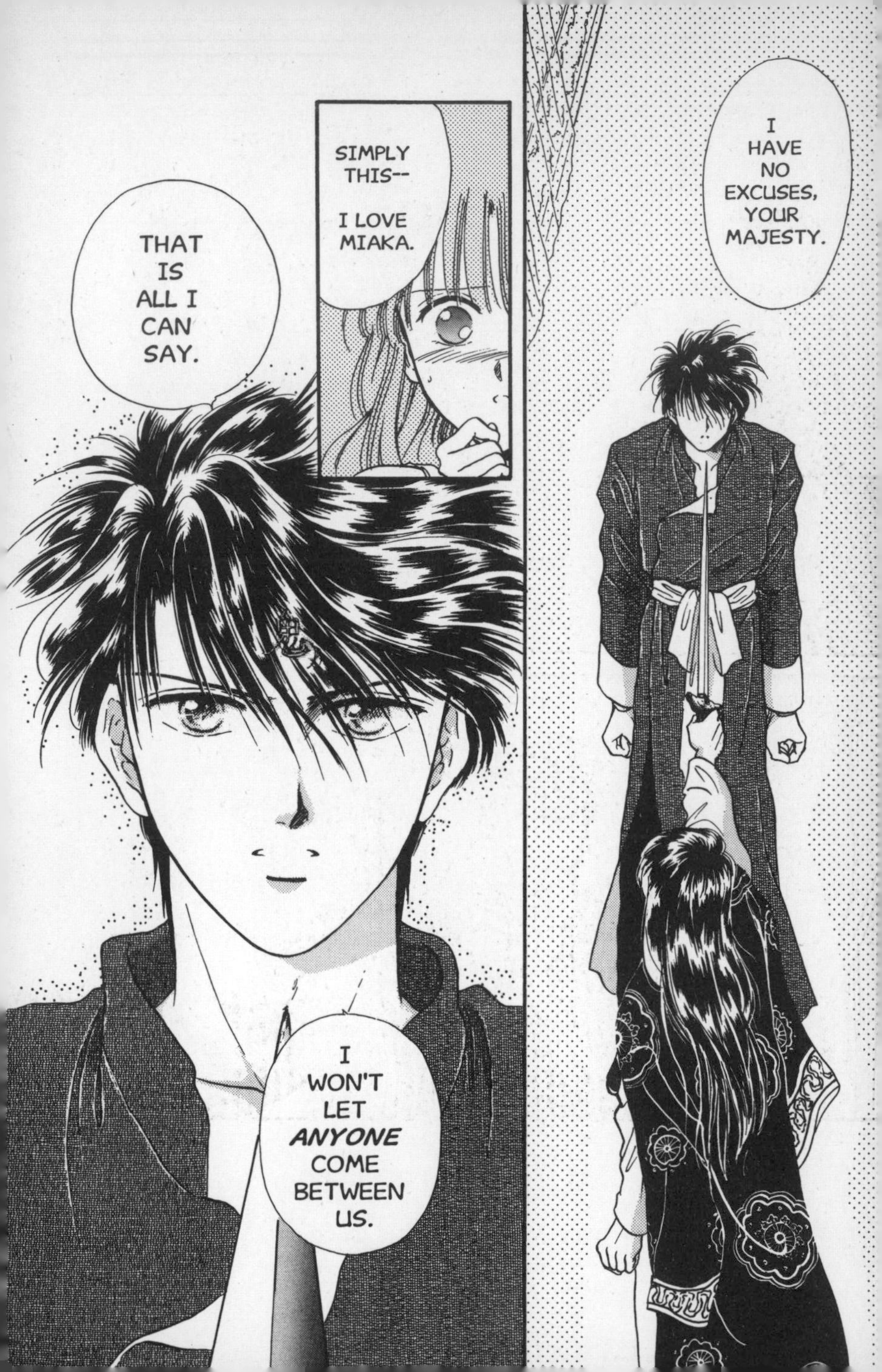
I HAVE NO EXCUSES, YOUR MAJESTY.
SIMPLY THIS--
I LOVE MIAKA.
THAT IS ALL I CAN SAY.
I WON'T LET *ANYONE* COME BETWEEN US.

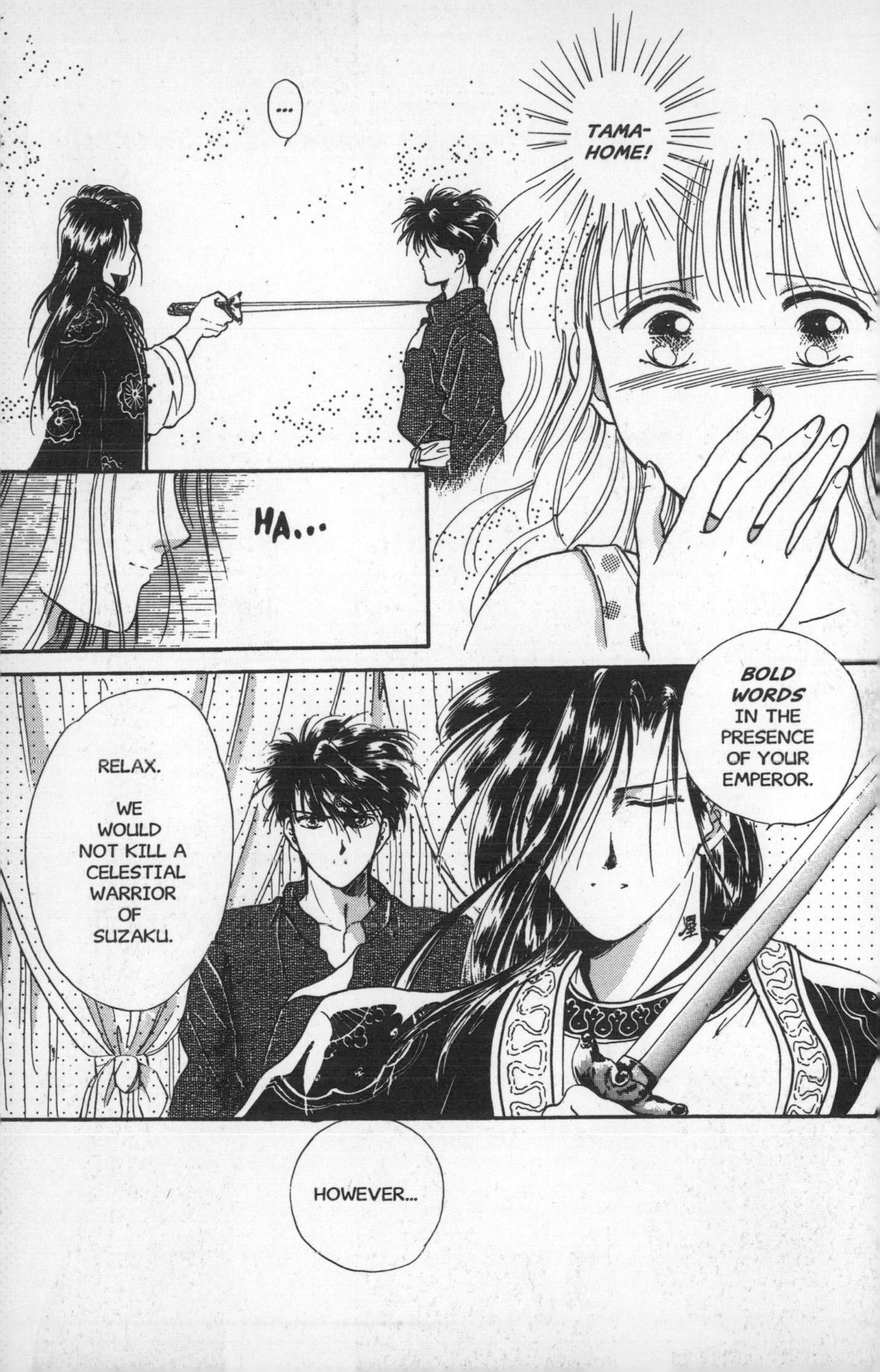
TAMA-HOME!
...
HA...
BOLD WORDS IN THE PRESENCE OF YOUR EMPEROR.
RELAX. WE WOULD NOT KILL A CELESTIAL WARRIOR OF SUZAKU.
HOWEVER...

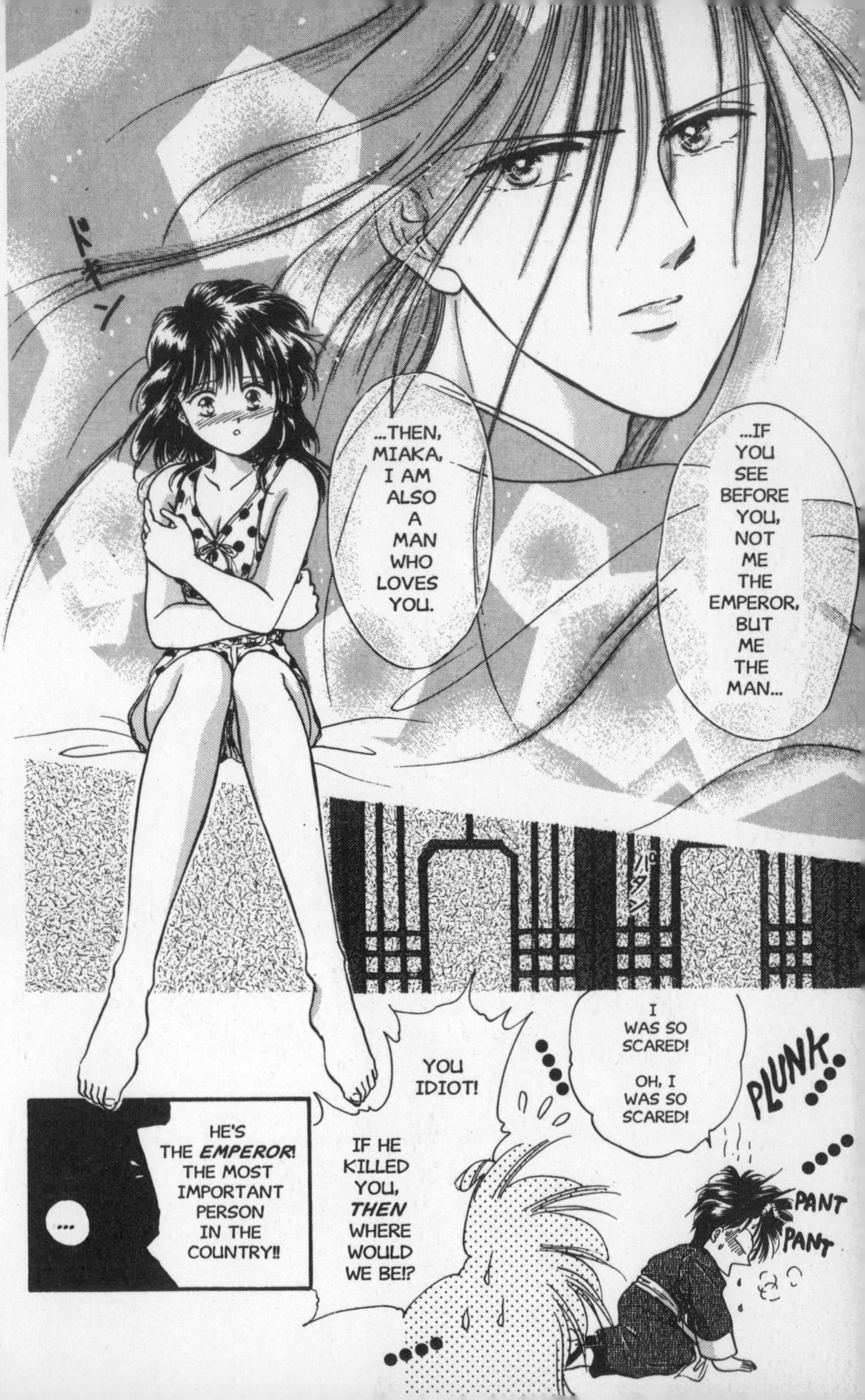

ドキーン
...IF YOU SEE BEFORE YOU, NOT ME THE EMPEROR, BUT ME THE MAN...
...THEN, MIAKA, I AM ALSO A MAN WHO LOVES YOU.
パタン
I WAS SO SCARED! OH, I WAS SO SCARED!
PLUNK
PANT PANT
YOU IDIOT!
IF HE KILLED YOU, *THEN* WHERE WOULD WE BE!?
HE'S THE *EMPEROR*! THE MOST IMPORTANT PERSON IN THE COUNTRY!!
...

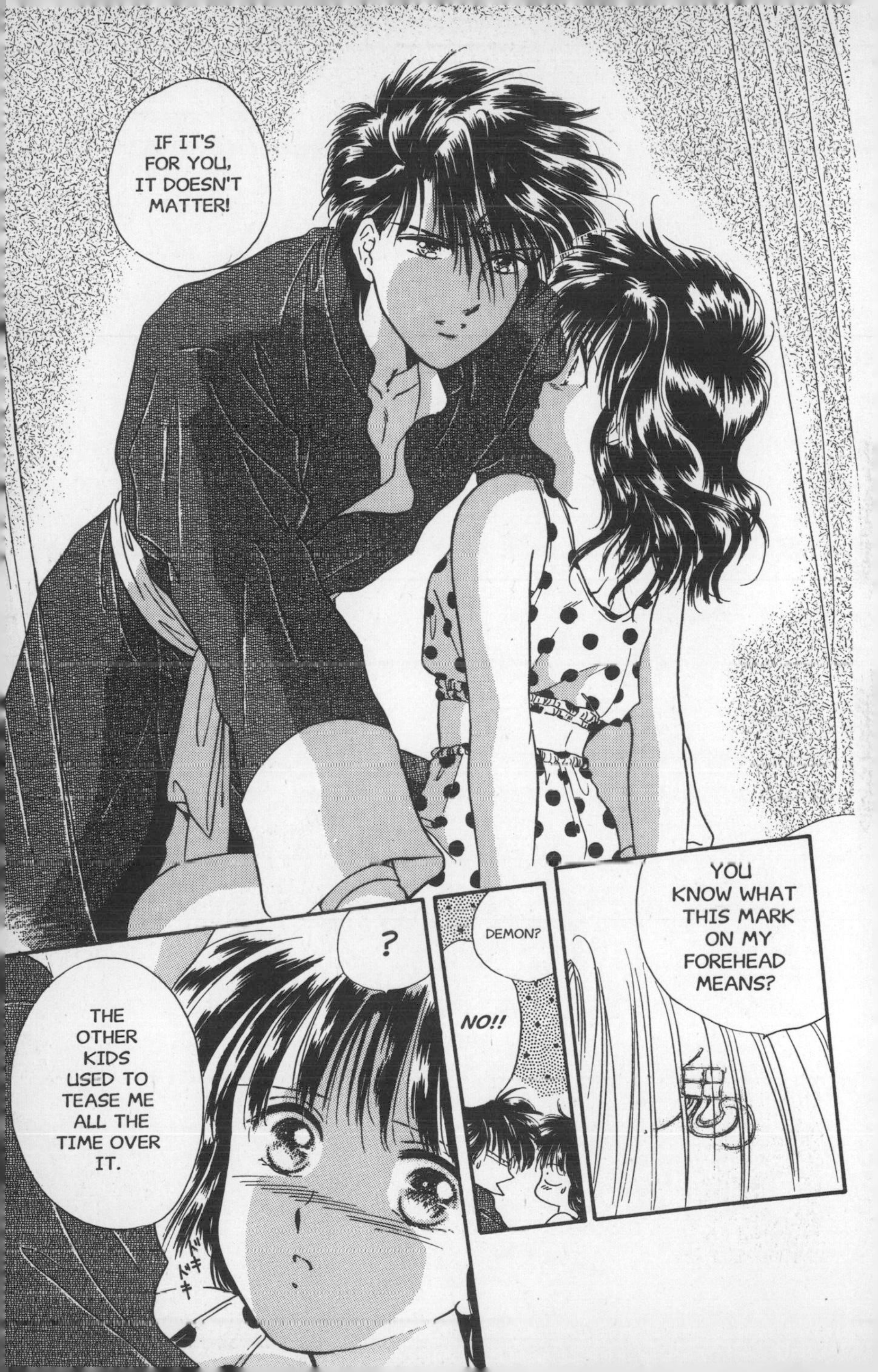
IF IT'S FOR YOU, IT DOESN'T MATTER!
YOU KNOW WHAT THIS MARK ON MY FOREHEAD MEANS?
DEMON?
NO!!
?
THE OTHER KIDS USED TO TEASE ME ALL THE TIME OVER IT.
ドキ ドキ

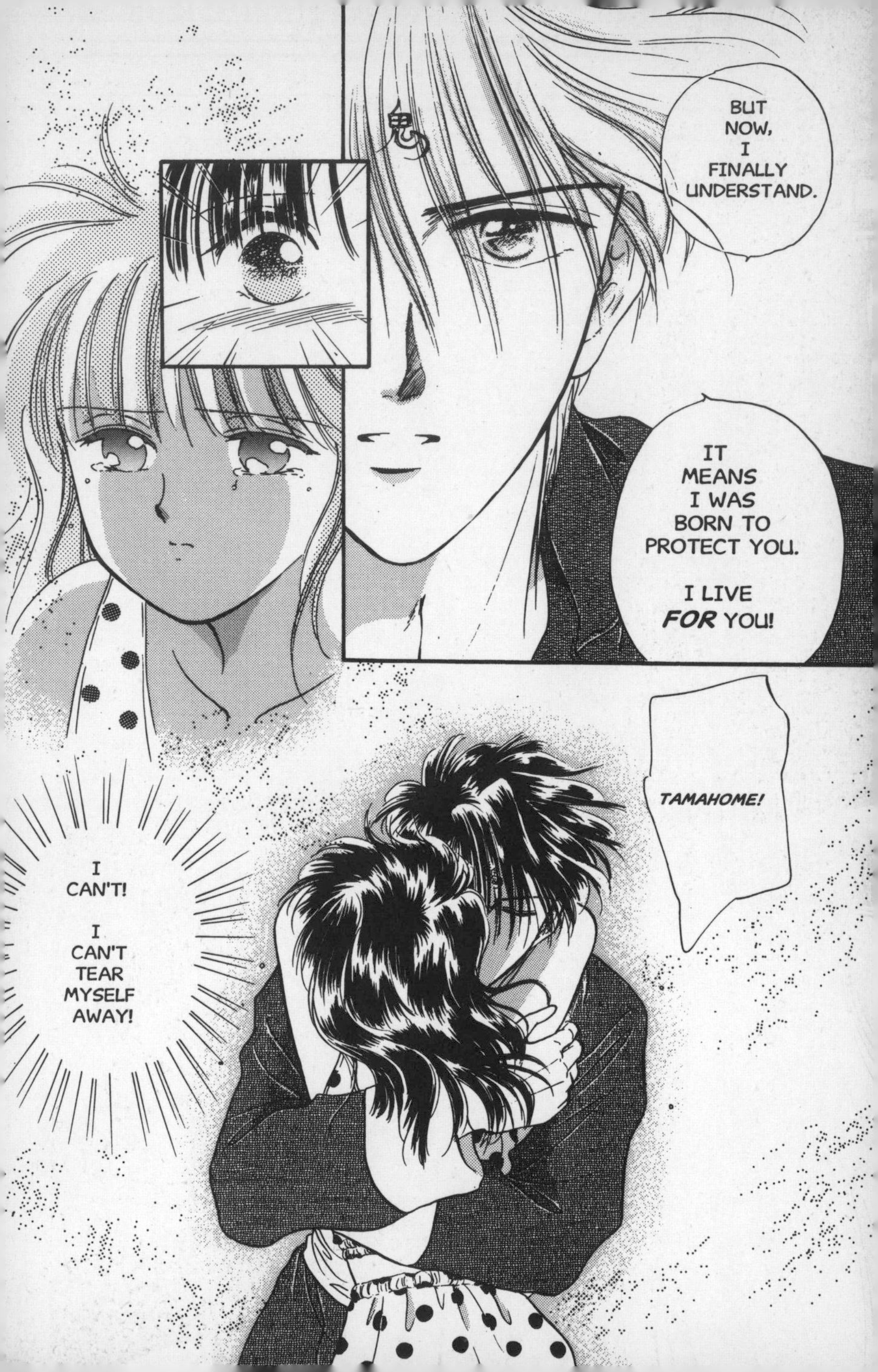
BUT NOW, I FINALLY UNDERSTAND.
IT MEANS I WAS BORN TO PROTECT YOU.
I LIVE ***FOR*** YOU!
TAMAHOME!
I CAN'T!
I CAN'T TEAR MYSELF AWAY!

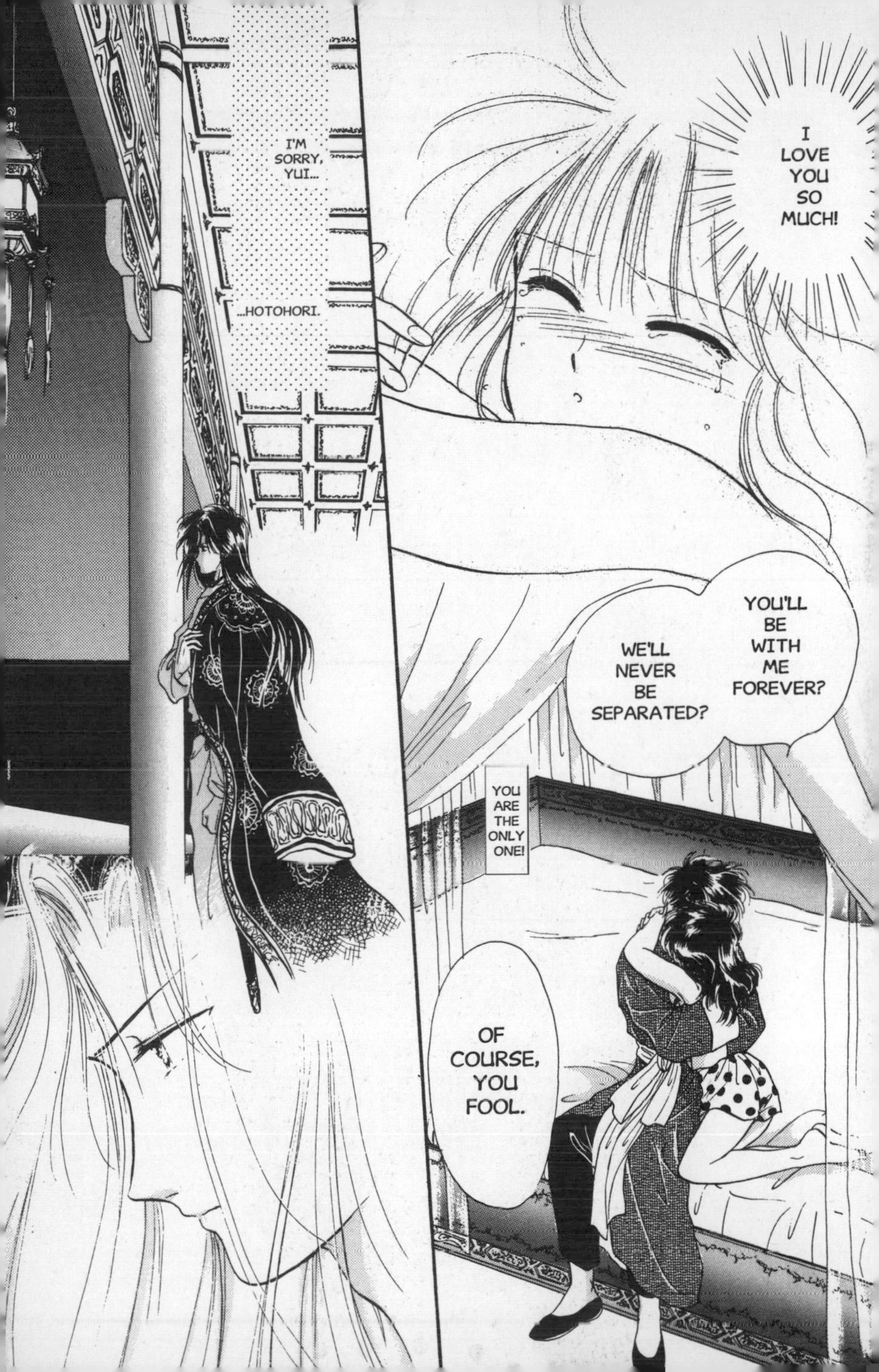
I LOVE YOU SO MUCH!
YOU'LL BE WITH ME FOREVER?
WE'LL NEVER BE SEPARATED?
YOU ARE THE ONLY ONE!
OF COURSE, YOU FOOL.
I'M SORRY, YUI...
...HOTOHORI.

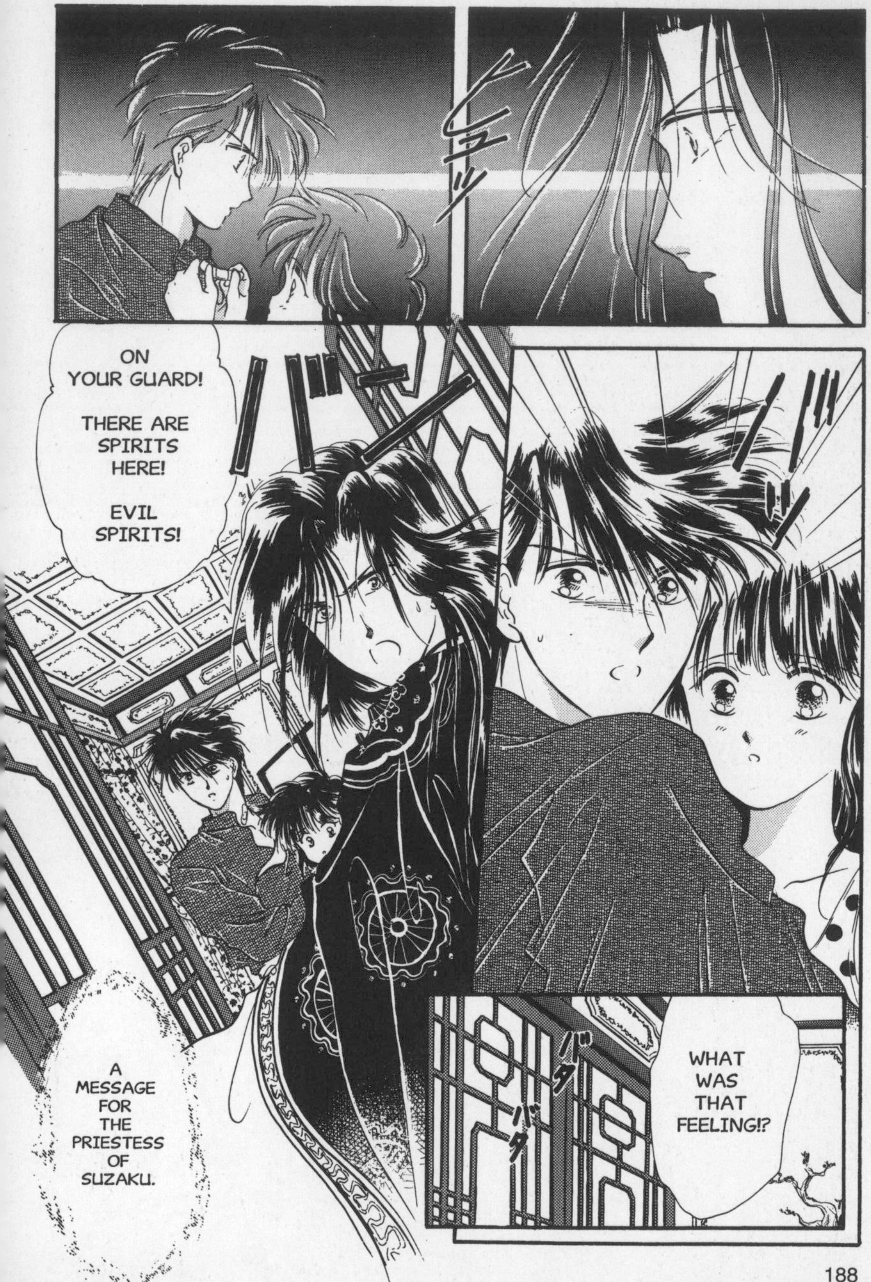
WHAT WAS THAT FEELING!?
ON YOUR GUARD! THERE ARE SPIRITS HERE! EVIL SPIRITS!
A MESSAGE FOR THE PRIESTESS OF SUZAKU.

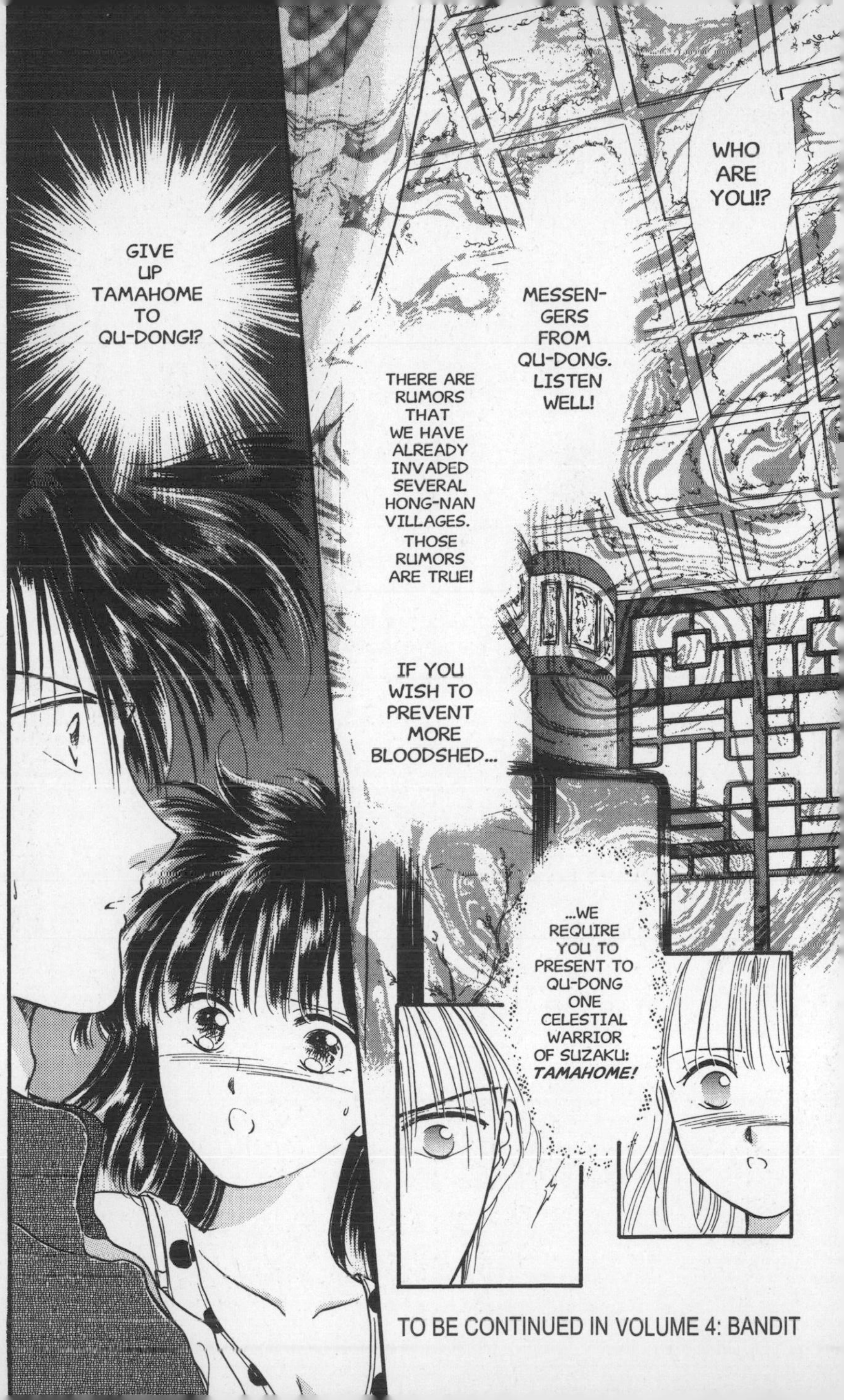
WHO ARE YOU!?
MESSENGERS FROM QU-DONG. LISTEN WELL!
THERE ARE RUMORS THAT WE HAVE ALREADY INVADED SEVERAL HONG-NAN VILLAGES. THOSE RUMORS ARE TRUE!
IF YOU WISH TO PREVENT MORE BLOODSHED...
...WE REQUIRE YOU TO PRESENT TO QU-DONG ONE CELESTIAL WARRIOR OF SUZAKU: *TAMAHOME!*
GIVE UP TAMAHOME TO QU-DONG!?

TO BE CONTINUED IN VOLUME 4: BANDIT

ABOUT THE AUTHOR

Yû Watase was born on March 5 in a town near Osaka, Japan, and she was raised there before moving to Tokyo to follow her dream of creating manga. In the decade since her debut short story, PAJAMA DE OJAMA ("An Intrusion in Pajamas"), she has produced more than 50 compiled volumes of short stories and continuing series. Her latest series, ZETTAI KARESHI ("He'll Be My Boyfriend"), is currently running in the anthology magazine SHÔJO COMIC. Watase's long-running horror/romance story CERES: CELESTIAL LEGEND and her most recent completed series, ALICE 19TH, are now available in North America published by VIZ. She loves science fiction, fantasy and comedy.

The Fushigi Yûgi Guide to Sound Effects

Most of the sound effects in FUSHIGI YÛGI are the way Yû Watase created them, in their original Japanese.

We created this glossary for a page-by-page, panel-by-panel explanation of the action and background noises. By using this guide, you may even learn some Japanese.

The glossary lists page and panel number. For example, page 1, panel 3, would be listed as 1.3.

21.2	FX: Ba (bwah)
23.2	FX: Ka (blush)
25.2	FX: Pasha (splosh)
25.5	FX: Zulu (slip)
26.4	FX: Su (shff)
26.5	FX: Doki (ba-dump)
27.1	FX: Sa (shwa)
27.3	FX: Bun (bwoosh)
27.4	FX: Biku (shudder)
28.1	FX: Ban (bam)
28.3	FX: Zubo (zvoh)
28.4	FX: Bun (bwoosh)
28.5	FX: Pita (stop)
29.1	FX: Bishi (vwap)
29.2	FX: Ba (bwah)
29.3	FX: Don (dwom)
29.4	FX: Su (swish)
30.1	FX: Ba (vwip)
30.2	FX: Don (thwakam)
31.1	FX: Su (shwa)
31.2	FX: Su (shwosh)
31.3	FX: Ba (grasp)
31.3	FX: Pata pata (paft paft)
32.2	FX: Shan (ching)
32.4	FX: Kapo (fwip)
33.2	FX: Da (dash)

CHAPTER FOURTEEN:
LET ME PROTECT YOU

37.3	FX: Dan (bam)

CHAPTER THIRTEEN:
THE INVISIBLE ENEMY

6.1	FX: Zaza (zshaa)
6.2	FX: Zu (zwoosh)
6.3	FX: Za (zsh)
6.4	FX: Zawa (rustle)
7.2	FX: Ba (yank)
8.1	FX: Kapo (kwop)
8.2	FX: Su (swoosh)
8.3	FX: Pata (pft)
9.1	FX: Za (zsh)
9.4	FX: Gaku gaku (tremble tremble)
9.5	FX: Gyu (squeeze)
11.1	FX: Ban (bam)
12.2	FX: Chun chichi (chirp chirp)
12.3	FX: Butsu butsu (mumble mumble)
12.4	FX: Gata (gatunk)
12.5	FX: Katan (katunk)
13.1	FX: Bululu (neeeigh)
13.2	FX: Jiii (staaare)
13.3	FX: Suuuu (zzzz)
14.1	FX: Koso (sneak)
15.1	FX: Doki (ba-dump)
15.3	FX: Ehehe (hee hee)
15.3	FX: Ka (clomp)
15.4	FX: Galan (glonk)
16.2	FX: Dokin (ba-dump)
17.3	FX: Jala (clink)
19.3	FX: Gyu (squeeze)

64.5-6 FX: Gala gala gala (clop clop clop)
64.6 FX: Tosa (twft)

65.3 FX: Gala gala gala (clop clop clop)

CHAPTER FIFTEEN: CAPTIVE WOMEN

68.3 FX: Gyulululu (grrrrowwl)

69.2 FX: Gatan (gonk)

70.2 FX: Da (dash)

71.2 FX: Niko (grin)

74.1 FX: Chichichi (chirp chirp)

77.1 FX: Ka (clop)

78.2 FX: Ka ka (clop clop)

79.1 FX: Golo golo golo (rumble rumble rumble)
79.3 FX: Hala (hwaf)
79.4 FX: Hiso hiso hiso (whisper whisper whisper)

80.2 FX: Gashi (grab)
80.3 FX: Boka (bonk)
80.3 FX: Su (shw)
80.5 FX: Bi (freeze)

81.1 FX: Ka (clop)
81.2 FX: Biku (jolt)
81.3 FX: Ka (clop)

82.3 FX: Fu (fwash)

83.1 FX: Suto (shatunk)
83.2 FX: Doki (ba-dump)

86.1 FX: Dooon dooon dooon (dooong dooong dooong)

87.4 FX: Kapo (kwoft)
87.5 FX: Sala (shf)

89.1 FX: Zawa (gasp)
89.5 FX: Su (fht)

90.1 FX: Fula (wobble)

39.2 FX: Byu (vwip)
39.3 FX: Shulu (shwwrrsh)

40.5 FX: Su (sshh)
40.6 FX: Shan (clang)

41.1 FX: Su (shwa)
41.2 FX: Bala bala (crumble crumble)

42.1 FX: Shu (fwoosh)
42.2 FX: Ba (vwah)
42.3 FX: Bi (rip)

43.1 FX: Gyu (clutch)
43.2 FX: Boki beki (crack snap)
43.6 FX: Dosu (thunk)

46.4 FX: Niko (grin)

48.1 FX: Washi washi ("That's me. Me.")

53.3 FX: Da (dash)
53.4 FX: Su (shwa)

54.4 FX: Ka ka (caw caw)
54.5 FX: Za (zash)

55.4 FX/: Ga (roooaaar)

56.1 FX: Ba (bwosh)
56.2 FX: Gaku gaku (tremble tremble)
FX: Gululu (grrrrrr)
56.4 FX: Gyu (grip)

57.1 FX: Ba (pounce)
57.2 FX: Byu (vwish)
57.3 FX: Ga (gack)

58.1 FX: Ga (roar)
58.3 FX: Dogo (thwack)
58.4 FX: Do (thud)

60.4 FX: Dokin dokin dokin (ba-dump ba-dump ba-dump)

61.1 FX: Gyu (squeeze)

62.3 FX: Zulu (slip)

64.2 FX: Yoro (wobble)
64.4 FX: Gala gala gala (clop clop clop)
64.5 FX: Tata (dash)

117.2-.3 FX: Dokun dokun dokun dokun dokun
(ba-dump ba-dump ba-dump
ba-dump ba-dump)

118.4   FX: Gyu (clench)

119.4   FX: Niko (grin)
119.5   FX: Pika (flash)

120.2   FX: Giii (creeeeak)
120.3   FX: Tata (scamper)

121.1   FX: Ka (flash)
121.2   FX: Bashi (bzatt)
121.3   FX: Batan (bam)
121.4   FX: Su (shwa)

122.1   FX: Golo golo golo (rumble rumble rumble)

122.2   FX: Ha ha (gasp wheeze)

123.1   FX: Ka (flash)
123.3   FX: Gakun (gakunk)
123.4   FX: Golo golo golo (rumble rumble rumble)

124.3   FX: Gui (yank)

125.4   FX: Su (shwa)

127.2   FX: Su (shwa)
127.3   FX: Ka (krah)
127.4   FX: Ba (vwish)

128.5   FX: Su (shwa)

CHAPTER SEVENTEEN:
SOULS DRIFTING APART

130.1   FX: Baba (bwatch)
130.2   FX: Dosa (thud)
130.2   FX: Su (step)

131.5   FX: Bashi (bzap)

132.1   FX: Ha ha (huff huff)
132.3   FX: Yoro (wobble)

133.1   FX: Don (vwamk)

134.1   FX: Gatan goton (glonk gatunk)
134.5   FX: Ka (flash)

92.3   FX: Dosa (thud)

93.1   FX: Polo polo (weep weep)

94.3   FX: Zawa zawa (chatter chatter)

CHAPTER SIXTEEN:
THE PRIESTESS OF SEIRYU

99.3   FX: Za (zash)

100.1   FX: Bata bata (stomp stomp)
100.4   FX: Don (shove)

101.2   FX: Da (dash)
101.3   FX: Bata bata (dart dash)
101.4   FX: Ha ha ha (gasp pant)

103.3   FX: Saaaa (fshhhh)
103.3   FX: Golo golo golo (rumble rumble rumble)
103.4   FX: Dosa (thud)

104.1   FX: Ka (flash)

105.1   FX: Golo golo golo (rumble rumble rumble)
105.4   FX: Ba (bwah)

106.1   FX: Ga (gonk)
106.2   FX: Suto (shtk)
106.3   FX: Piki (pwik)
106.4   FX: Gata (falter)
106.4   FX: Basha (splosh)

107.3   FX: BI (vwlp)
107.4   FX: Da (dash)
107.6   FX: Bashi (vwap)

109.2   FX: Dosu (donk)
109.3   FX: Zulu (topple)
109.4   FX: Sa (swish)

111.2   FX: Bata bata (stomp stomp)
111.4   FX: Bata bata (stomp stomp)

113.1   FX: Su (shwa)

114.5   FX: Da (dash)

115.3   FX: Ha ha (huff huff)
115.4   FX: Ha (gasp)

164.3   FX: Su (swsh)
164.5   FX: Gooooo (gwooooh)

165.1   FX: Gooooo (gwooooh)

166.5   FX: Fuwa (float)

167.2   FX: Zukin (zing)
167.3   FX: Ka (flash)
167.4   FX: Hiso hiso (whisper whisper)

168.3   FX: Kiiin kooon kaan koon
             (diiing doong diiing doong)

169.3   FX: Fu (fwosh)

170.5   FX: Niko (smile)

172.2   FX: Su (shw)

173.1   FX: Fu (fha)

174.1   FX: Gyuu (embrace)
174.2   FX: Mu (grr)

175.3   FX: Su (swish)

176.2   FX: Zuka zuka zuka (stomp stomp stomp)
176.3   FX: Ban (bam)

179.3   FX: Jita bata (struggle struggle)

180.2   FX: Katan (katunk)

181.1   FX: Cha (chlik)
181.2   FX: Su (swish)

184.2   FX: Dokin (ba-dump)
184.3   FX: Patan (pft)

185.4   FX: Doki doki (ba-dump ba-dump)

188.1-2 FX: Hyu (hwoosh)
188.3   FX: Ba (bwah)
188.4   FX: Bata bata (dash dash)
188.5   FX: Ban (bam)

135.1   FX: Piiii (bweeeeep)
135.2   FX: Bun (bam)

136.1   FX: Pita (freeze)
136.2   FX: Fuwa (float)

137.1   FX: Don (daboom)
137.2   FX: Ban (bam)

138.1   FX: Bali bali (crackle bzzzap)
138.3   FX: Bali bali (crackle bzzzap)

139.1   FX: Doka (punch)
139.3   FX: Zuki (zing)

141.1   FX: Ba (bwah)
141.2   FX: Bashi (bwam)
141.3   FX: Pala (fwip)

142.3   FX: Zu (zwip)
142.5   FX: Zu (zwop)
142.6   FX: Su (swish)

143.4   FX: Kiin koon kaan koon
             (diiing doong diing doong)

146.3   FX: Ha (gasp)

149.4   FX: Butsu butsu (mumble grumble)
149.5   FX: Peli (rip)

151.2   FX: Pi (point)
151.4   FX: Suuu (shwaaa)

152.1   FX: Pa (flash)
152.3   FX: boso (mutter)

153.1   FX: Ha (gasp)
153.2   FX: Da (dash)

154.2   FX: Bashi (slap)

155.2   FX: Fu (fwosh)

158.1   FX: Suka (skoosh)

CHAPTER EIGHTEEN:
ONLY YOU

162.2   FX: Su (stride)

EDITOR'S RECOMMENDATIONS

Did you like *FUSHIGI YÛGI*?
Here's what VIZ recommends you try next:

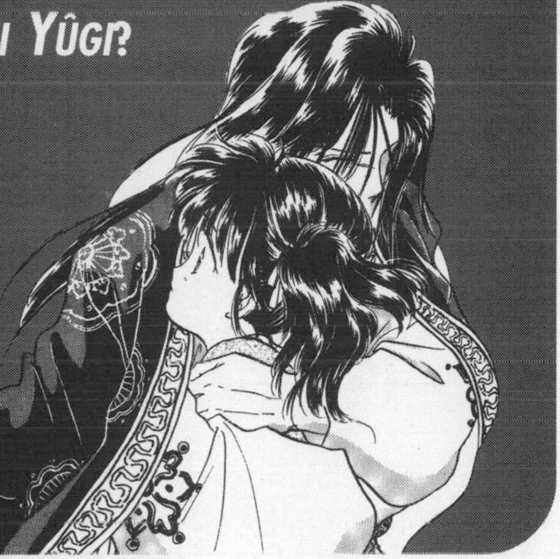

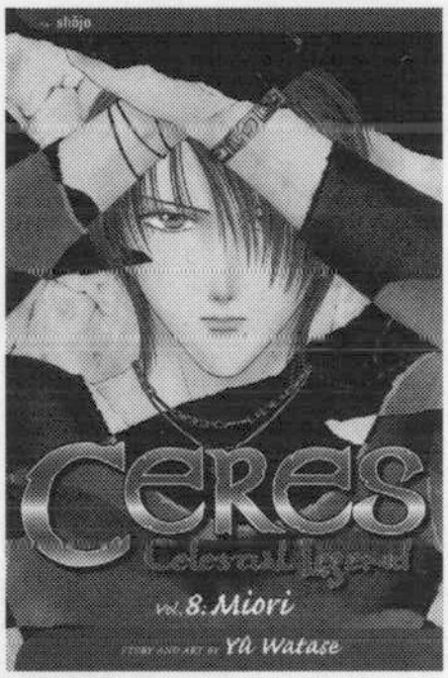

shôjo
CERES
Celestial Legend
vol. 8: Miori
Yû Watase

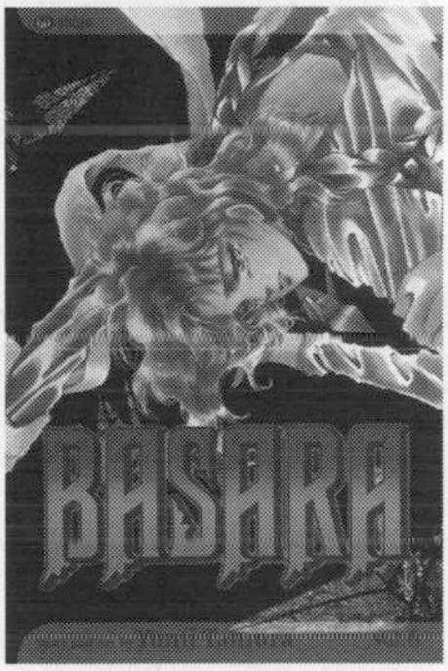

BASARA

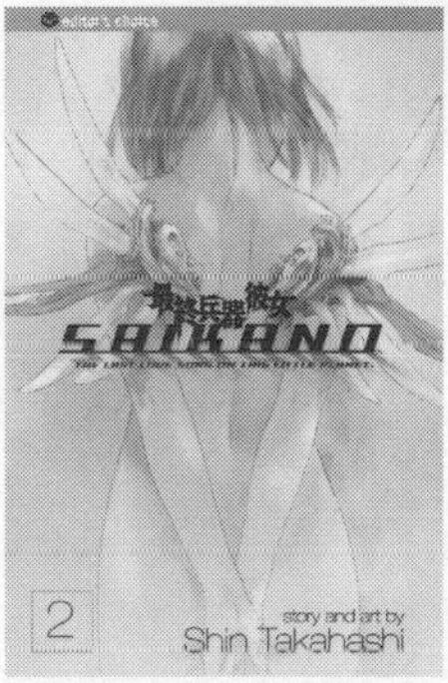

SAIKANO
2
story and art by
Shin Takahashi

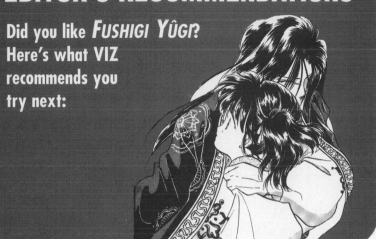

CERES: CELESTIAL LEGEND is an engaging story of love, betrayal and revenge by FUSHIGI YÛGI's creator Yû Watase. Aya's world is turned upside when her family tries to kill her on her sixteenth birthday because of her family's deep, dark secret.

BASARA is another great heroic shôjo adventure by shôjo-manga mainstay Yumi Tamura. Set in the distant future, a young girl has to take her dead twin brother's place as the "Boy of Destiny," even though "destiny" has already proved itself untrustworthy.

SAIKANO is a compelling love story. A few days after they start dating, Shuji discovers his girlfriend Chise has a secret–she's been secretly engineered by the military to transform into a powerful weapon. Chise is becoming increasingly powerful as the Ultimate Weapon, and is torn between her life as a fighting machine and living as an ordinary teenager.

From the creator of **Ceres** and **Fushigi Yûgi**

Alice 19th™

©2001 Yuu Watase/Shogakukan, Inc.

Actions Aren't Always Louder Than Words

Alice Seno has always kept her feelings to herself. But an encounter with a magical rabbit shows her how much power words can hold when she accidentally sends her sister to a world of darkness! Can Alice work with her crush (and sister's boyfriend!) and become a master of Lotis Words in time to save her sister?

The latest from Yû Watase — start your graphic novel collection today!

ONLY $9.95 A VOLUME

story and art by **Yû Watase**

shôjo

www.viz.com

shôjo

AT THE HEART OF THE MATTER

- Alice 19th
- Angel Sanctuary
- Banana Fish
- Basara
- B.B. Explosion
- Boys Over Flowers *
- Ceres, Celestial Legend *
- Fushigi Yûgi
- Hana-Kimi
- Hot Gimmick
- Imadoki
- Please Save My Earth *
- Red River
- Revolutionary Girl Utena
- Sensual Phrase
- Wedding Peach
- X/1999

Start Your Shôjo Graphic Novel Collection Today!

STARTING @ $9.95!

Also available on DVD from VIZ

© 2000 YUU WATASE/SHOGAKUKAN, INC.

www.viz.com

Heaven Is About to Become Hell On Earth

CERES
Celestial Legend

The fate of a legend is redefined in this exciting conclusion to the anime series! From the creator of Fushigi Yûgi and based on the best-selling manga—now available from VIZ!

- Exclusive sleeve illustration from creator Yû Watase
- Features never before seen Yû Watase interview
- Collector's Edition, Volume 1: Reincarnation and Collector's Edition, Volume 2: Ascension — now available

Each volume includes 12 Episodes, 2-Discs $49.98!

Special Offer!

Buy Ceres Collector's Edition and get one of two FREE* limited edition display boxes!

* By mail. Must send proof-of-purchase and original store receipt, with shipping and handling.
©Yuu Watase / Shogakukan • Bandai Visual • Studio Pierrot. All rights reserved.

shôjo

www.viz.com

How many anime and/or manga titles have you purchased in the last year? How many were VIZ titles? (please check one from each column)

ANIME
- ☐ None
- ☐ 1-4
- ☐ 5-10
- ☐ 11+

MANGA
- ☐ None
- ☐ 1-4
- ☐ 5-10
- ☐ 11+

VIZ
- ☐ None
- ☐ 1-4
- ☐ 5-10
- ☐ 11+

I find the pricing of VIZ products to be: (please check one)

☐ Cheap   ☐ Reasonable   ☐ Expensive

What genre of manga and anime would you like to see from VIZ? (please check two)

☐ Adventure   ☐ Comic Strip   ☐ Science Fiction   ☐ Fighting

☐ Horror   ☐ Romance   ☐ Fantasy   ☐ Sports

What do you think of VIZ's new look?

☐ Love It   ☐ It's OK   ☐ Hate It   ☐ Didn't Notice   ☐ No Opinion

Which do you prefer? (please check one)

☐ Reading right-to-left

☐ Reading left-to-right

Which do you prefer? (please check one)

☐ Sound effects in English

☐ Sound effects in Japanese with English captions

☐ Sound effects in Japanese only with a glossary at the back

THANK YOU! Please send the completed form to:

NJW Research
42 Catharine St.
Poughkeepsie, NY 12601

All information provided will be used for internal purposes only. We promise not to sell or otherwise divulge your information.

NO PURCHASE NECESSARY. Requests not in compliance with all terms of this form will not be acknowledged or returned. All submissions are subject to verification and become the property of VIZ, LLC. Fraudulent submission, including use of multiple addresses or P.O. boxes to obtain additional VIZ information or offers may result In prosecution. VIZ reserves the right to withdraw or modify any terms of this form. Void where prohibited, taxed, or restricted by law. VIZ will not be liable for lost, misdirected, mutilated, illegible, incomplete or postage-due mail. © 2003 VIZ, LLC. All Rights Reserved. VIZ, LLC, property titles, characters, names and plots therein under license to VIZ, LLC. All Rights Reserved.

COMPLETE OUR SURVEY AND LET US KNOW WHAT YOU THINK!

☐ Please do NOT send me information about VIZ products, news and events, special offers, or other information.

☐ Please do NOT send me information from VIZ's trusted business partners.

Name: _____

Address: _____

City: _____ **State:** _____ **Zip:** _____

E-mail: _____

☐ Male ☐ Female **Date of Birth** (mm/dd/yyyy): ___/___/_____ (Under 13? Parental consent required)

What race/ethnicity do you consider yourself? (please check one)

☐ Asian/Pacific Islander ☐ Black/African American ☐ Hispanic/Latino

☐ Native American/Alaskan Native ☐ White/Caucasian ☐ Other: _____

What VIZ product did you purchase? (check all that apply and indicate title purchased)

☐ DVD/VHS _____

☐ Graphic Novel _____

☐ Magazines _____

☐ Merchandise _____

Reason for purchase: (check all that apply)

☐ Special offer ☐ Favorite title ☐ Gift

☐ Recommendation ☐ Other _____

Where did you make your purchase? (please check one)

☐ Comic store ☐ Bookstore ☐ Mass/Grocery Store

☐ Newsstand ☐ Video/Video Game Store ☐ Other: _____

☐ Online (site: _____)

What other VIZ properties have you purchased/own? _____

_____